MULTICULTURAL PERSPECTIVES

Senior Consultants

ARTHUR N. APPLEBEE
State University of New York at Albany

JUDITH A. LANGER
State University of New York at Albany

Authors

DAVID W. FOOTE

MARGARET GRAUFF FORST

MARY HYNES-BERRY

JULIE WEST JOHNSON

BASIA C. MILLER

BRENDA PIERCE PERKINS

McDougal, Littell & Company
Evanston, Illinois
New York • Dallas • Sacramento • Columbia, SC

Copyright © 1993 by McDougal, Littell & Company
Box 1667, Evanston, Illinois 60204

All rights reserved.
Printed in the United States of America.

ISBN 0-8123-7640-4 (softcover)
ISBN 0-8123-7097-X (hardbound)

9 10 - QPF - 00 99 98

Acknowledgments

Margaret Walker Alexander "Lineage" from *For My People* by Margaret Walker. Copyright 1942 by Yale University Press. Reprinted by permission of the author.

Aunt Lute Books "The Youngest Doll" by Rosario Ferré from *Reclaiming Medusa: Short Stories by Contemporary Puerto Rican Women*, edited and translated by Diana Vélez. Copyright © 1988 by Diana Vélez. Reprinted by permission of Aunt Lute Books.

Toni Cade Bambara "My Delicate Heart Condition" by Toni Cade Bambara. Copyright © 1965 by Toni Cade Bambara. Reprinted by permission of the author.

Beacon Press "Autobiographical Notes" from *Notes of a Native Son* by James Baldwin. Copyright 1955 by James Baldwin. Reprinted by permission of Beacon Press.

Robert Bly "Ode to the Watermelon" by Pablo Neruda, from *Neruda and Vallejo: Selected Poems*. Chosen and translated by Robert Bly. Copyright © 1971 by Beacon Press, Boston. Copyright © 1971 by Robert Bly, reprinted with his permission.

Gwendolyn Brooks "Kitchenette Building," "One wants a Teller in a time like this," "Speech to the Young," and "Horses Graze" from *Blacks* by Gwendolyn Brooks. Copyright © 1987 by Gwendolyn Brooks. Publisher, The David Company, Chicago. Reprinted by permission of the author.

Diana Chang "Rhythms" by Diana Chang from *The Painted Bride Quarterly 2*, No. 1, Winter 1975. Copyright © 1975 by Diana Chang. "Saying Yes" by Diana Chang. Reprinted by permission of the author.

Eugenia Collier "Sweet Potato Pie" by Eugenia Collier. Copyright 1972 by Johnson Publishing Company, Inc. Reprinted by permission of Eugenia Collier and *Black World Magazine*. "Marigolds" by Eugenia Collier. Copyright © 1969 by Johnson Publishing Company, Inc. Reprinted by permission of Johnson Publishing Company and the author.

Confluence Press "The Secret Lion" from *The Iguana Killer: Twelve Stories of the Heart* by Alberto Alvaro Ríos. Copyright © 1984 by Alberto Alvaro Ríos. Reprinted by permission of Confluence Press at Lewis-Clark State College, Lewiston, Idaho.

Joan Daves "I Have a Dream" by Martin Luther King, Jr. Copyright © 1963 by Martin Luther King, Jr. Reprinted by permission of Joan Daves.

Dial Books for Young Readers Excerpt from *To Be a Slave* by Julius Lester. Text copyright © 1968 by Julius Lester. Reprinted by permission of the publisher, Dial Books for Young Readers.

Doubleday "A Visit to Grandmother" from *Dancers on the Shore* by William Melvin Kelley. Copyright © 1962 by Fawcett Publications. Excerpt from *When Heaven and Earth Changed Places* by Le Ly Hayslip. Copyright © 1989 by Le Ly Hayslip and Charles Jay Wurts. Used by permission of Doubleday, a division of Bantam, Doubleday, Dell Publishing Group.

Mari Evans "If There Be Sorrow" from *I Am A Black Woman* by Mari Evans. Published by William Morrow & Company, 1970. Reprinted by permission of the author.

Farrar, Straus and Giroux, Inc. "What I Have Been Doing Lately" from *At the Bottom of the River* by Jamaica Kincaid. Copyright © 1978, 1979, 1981, 1982, 1983 by Jamaica Kincaid. Reprinted by permission of Farrar, Straus and Giroux, Inc.

(Continued on page 439)

Authors & Consultants

SENIOR CONSULTANTS

The senior consultants guided all conceptual development for the *Responding to Literature* series. They participated actively in shaping tables of contents and prototype materials for all major components and features, and they reviewed completed units to assure consistency with current research and the philosophy of the series.

Arthur N. Applebee, Professor of Education, State University of New York at Albany; Director, Center for the Learning and Teaching of Literature

Judith A. Langer, Professor of Education, State University of New York at Albany; Co-Director, Center for the Learning and Teaching of Literature

AUTHORS

The authors of this text wrote lessons for the literary selections.

David W. Foote, Evanston Township High School, Evanston, Illinois

Margaret Grauff Forst, Lake Forest High School, Lake Forest, Illinois

Mary Hynes-Berry, Writer and Educator, Chicago, Illinois

Julie West Johnson, New Trier Township High School, Winnetka, Illinois

Basia C. Miller, Tutor on the Faculty at St. John's College, Santa Fe, New Mexico

Brenda Pierce Perkins, Lake Forest High School, Lake Forest, Illinois

ACADEMIC CONSULTANTS

The academic consultants worked with the senior consultants to establish the theoretical framework for the *Responding to Literature* series and the pedagogical design of the lessons. The consultants reviewed prototype lessons for the student book and Teacher's Guide, read selected units to assure philosophical consistency, and suggested writing assignments.

Susan Hynds, Director of English Education, Syracuse University, Syracuse, New York

James Marshall, Professor of English and Education, University of Iowa, Iowa City

Robert E. Probst, Professor of English Education, Georgia State University, Atlanta

William Sweigart, Assistant Professor of English, Indiana University Southeast, New Albany; formerly, Research Associate, Center for the Study of Writing, University of California at Berkeley

LITERARY CONSULTANTS

The literary consultants commented on selections and made suggestions for additional material.

Carlos J. Cumpián, Editor and Researcher, Hispanic Literature, Chicago, Illinois

Edris Makward, Professor, African Studies Program, University of Wisconsin, Madison

Peter Jaffe-Notier, Instructor of World Literature, Lyons Township High School, La Grange, Illinois

Carrie E. Reed, Pre-doctoral Teaching Associate I in Chinese, Department of Asian Language and Literature, University of Washington, Seattle

Michael W. Smith, Department of Curriculum and Instruction, University of Wisconsin, Madison

CONSULTANT-REVIEWERS

The consultant-reviewers evaluated the lesson design and reviewed selections for the purpose of assessing effectiveness and appropriateness for students and teachers.

Elizabeth Anderson, English Department Chairman, Olathe South High School, Olathe, Kansas

Joanne Bergman, English Department Chairman, Countryside High School, Clearwater, Florida

Michael F. Bernauer, Language Arts Instructor, Forest Lake Senior High School, Forest Lake, Minnesota

Nancy J. Boersma, Coordinator of English, White Plains Public Schools, White Plains, New York

Jennifer C. Boyd, Instructor of English, Nampa High School, Nampa, Idaho

Joanne Schenck Brower, Curriculum Specialist, Guilford County School System, Greensboro, North Carolina

Helen Brown, Educational Consultant, Baton Rouge, Louisiana

Clifton Browning, Department Head, English, Jefferson Davis High School, Montgomery, Alabama

Marilyn K. Buehler, Arizona State Teacher of the Year 1989, English Instructor, North High School, Phoenix, Arizona

Patrick Cates, Chairman, English Department, Lubbock High School, Lubbock, Texas

Charles R. Chew, Director, Division of Communications Arts and Social Science Instruction, New York State Department of Education, Albany, New York

Willie Mae Crews, English Program Specialist, Birmingham Board of Education, Birmingham, Alabama

Bonnie M. Davis, Staff Development Teacher, Mehlville School District, St. Louis, Missouri

Harriet C. Fether, Language Arts Chairperson, Miami Senior High School, Miami, Florida

Contents

Unit 3   AFFIRMING IDENTITY

Unit 6 EXAMINING LIFE EXPERIENCES   306

Celebrating Heritage

*"I heard my people singing — in the glow
of parlor coalstone and on summer porches sweet with
lilac air, from choir loft and Sunday morning pews
— and my soul was filled with their harmonies."*

PAUL ROBESON

Celebrating Heritage

In 1782 Jean de Crèvecoeur posed the question "What then is the American?" He provided his own answer: "Here individuals of all nations are melted into a new race." For nearly two centuries, Crèvecoeur's view of the United States as a melting pot in which minorities gradually lose their cultural differences prevailed. In recent decades, however, another view has emerged: American society is now compared to a rainbow, a collage, a chorus, or a quilt. These comparisons suggest a society strengthened and enriched by the unique heritages of groups that retain their cultural identities.

In the 1960's and 1970's, a minority arts movement developed out of the civil rights movement. "Black is beautiful" became a popular slogan as African-American artists and entertainers explored the richness of black culture. The number of African-American writers publishing in the United States increased dramatically and included for the first time a significant number of African-American women. Beginning in the 1970's, increasing numbers of Hispanic, Asian-American, and Native-American writers joined African Americans in giving voice to their cultural experiences.

The writers represented in this unit convey respect and appreciation for the values and traditions of their cultures. Américo Paredes celebrates a Mexican-American hero in his story "The Legend of Gregorio Cortez." Le Ly Hayslip expresses the values of the Vietnamese people in the excerpt from her autobiography *When Heaven and Earth Changed Places*. Alice Walker portrays the culture of Southern blacks with warmth and respect in her short story "Everyday Use." Teresa Palomo Acosta, Gloria Oden, and Simon Ortiz offer tender poetic tributes to parents whose qualities of mind and heart are treasured legacies.

As you read the selections that follow, notice the ways in which each writer celebrates the priceless gift of heritage. Consider also the contributions made to American society by the vibrant cultures portrayed in the selections.

$\mathcal{L}$iterary Vocabulary

INTRODUCED IN THIS SECTION

Aphorism.   An aphorism is a brief statement that expresses a general observation about life in a clever or pointed way. An example of an aphorism is the statement "Language is the only homeland," quoted by Paule Marshall in "From the Poets in the Kitchen."

Cultural Hero.   A cultural hero is a larger-than-life figure who reflects the values of a people. This kind of hero evolves from communal tales told orally or sung to musical accompaniment, passed down from one generation to the next.

Figurative Language: Extended Metaphor.   Figurative language is language that communicates ideas beyond the literal meanings of the words. One of the most common figures of speech is a metaphor. A metaphor makes a comparison between two things that are actually unlike yet have something in common. In an extended metaphor, two things are compared at length and in various ways. For example, in the poem "Mother to Son" the line "Life for me ain't been no crystal stair" introduces a comparison between the speaker's life and a flight of stairs. Throughout the poem the speaker uses phrases such as "boards torn up," "places with no carpets on the floor," "reachin' landin's," and "turnin' corners" to develop the comparison.

Foil.   A foil is a character who provides a striking contrast to another character. For example, in a story or play a writer might present two roommates: one, incorrigibly sloppy; the other, a stickler for neatness.

Sound Devices.   Poets use the sound devices of **alliteration, consonance,** and **assonance** to impart a musical quality to their poems, to create mood, to reinforce meaning, to emphasize words, and to unify lines or stanzas. Alliteration is the repetition of consonant sounds at the beginnings of words, as in the phrase "silver skate," in which the *s* sound is repeated. Consonance is the repetition of consonant sounds within and at the ends of words, as in the phrase "lurking in the dark," in which the *r* and the *k* sounds are repeated. Assonance is the repetition of a vowel sound within words, as in the phrase "my life and my bride," in which the *i* sound is repeated.

Theme.   Theme is a central idea or message in a work of literature. Theme should not be confused with subject, or what the work is about. Rather, theme is a perception about life or humanity that a writer expresses about a subject.

The Legend of Gregorio Cortez

AMÉRICO PAREDES

A biography of Paredes appears on page 428.

Approaching the Story

The following story is a prose retelling of a *corrido,* a fast-paced ballad that derives from the Mexican oral tradition. Corridos were first sung in Mexico in the mid-nineteenth century and soon spread to the border regions of South Texas, where Mexican culture exerted a strong influence. A corrido generally involves a cultural conflict. For example, the background of "The Legend of Gregorio Cortez" is the struggle between Mexicans and Anglos in Texas around the turn of the century. This corrido, which mixes fact with fiction, is based on the life of a real person.

Connecting Writing and Reading

Whom do you regard as a hero? Your hero could be a character from movies, television, or books, or an individual from your family, school, or neighborhood. In your journal identify your hero and copy the following list of qualities:

_____ honest

_____ loyal

_____ kind

_____ physically strong

_____ cunning

_____ intelligent

_____ respectful

_____ skilled

On a scale of 1 to 5, with 1 being lowest and 5 being highest, rate your hero on each quality. You may add qualities to the list if you want. Then as you read, compare your hero with Gregorio Cortez.

*T*HEY STILL SING of him—in the cantinas[1] and the country stores, in the ranches when men gather at night to talk in the cool dark, sitting in a circle, smoking and listening to the old songs and the tales of other days. Then the *guitarreros*[2] sing of the border raids and the skirmishes, of the men who lived by the phrase, "I will break before I bend."

They sing with deadly serious faces, throwing out the words of the song like a challenge, tearing savagely with their stiff, callused fingers at the strings of the guitars.

And that is how, in the dark quiet of the ranches, in the lighted noise of the saloons, they sing of Gregorio Cortez.

After the song is sung there is a lull. Then the old men, who have lived long and seen almost everything, tell their stories. And when they tell about Gregorio Cortez, the telling goes like this:

HOW GREGORIO CORTEZ CAME TO BE IN THE COUNTY OF EL CARMEN

That was good singing, and a good song; give the man a drink. Not like these pachucos[3] nowadays, mumbling damn-foolishness into a microphone; it is not done that way. Men should sing with their heads thrown back, with their mouths wide open and their eyes shut. Fill your lungs, so they can hear you at the pasture's farther end. And when you sing, sing songs like *El Corrido de Gregorio Cortez*. There's a song that makes the hackles rise. You can almost see him there—Gregorio Cortez, with his pistol in his hand.

He was a man, a Border man. What did he look like? Well, that is hard to tell. Some say he was short and some say he was tall; some say he was Indian brown and some say he was blond like a newborn cockroach. But I'd say he was not too dark and not too fair, not too thin and not too fat, not too short and not too tall: and he looked just a little bit like me. But does it matter so much what he looked like? He was a man, very much of a man; and he was a Border man. Some say he was born in Matamoros; some say Reynosa; some say Hidalgo county on the other side. And I guess others will say other things. But Matamoros, or Reynosa, or Hidalgo, it's all the same Border; and short or tall, dark or fair, it's the man that counts. And that's what he was, a man.

Not a gunman, no, not a bravo. He never came out of a cantina wanting to drink up the sea at one gulp. Not that kind of man, if you can call that kind a man. No, that wasn't Gregorio Cortez at all. He was a peaceful man, a hard-working man like you and me.

He could shoot. Forty-four and thirty-thirty, they were the same to him. He could put five bullets into a piece of board and not make but one hole, and quicker than you could draw a good deep breath. Yes, he could shoot. But he could also work.

He was a vaquero,[4] and a better one there has not ever been from Laredo to the mouth. He could talk to horses, and they would understand. They would follow him around, like dogs, and no man knew a good horse better then Gregorio Cortez. As for cattle, he could set up school for your best caporal.[5] And if an animal was lost, and nobody could pick up a trail, they would send for Gregorio Cortez. He could always find a trail. There was no better tracker in all the Border country, nor a man who could hide his tracks better if he wanted to. That was Gregorio Cortez, the best vaquero and range man that there ever was.

But that is not all. You farmers, do you think that Gregorio Cortez did not know your business too? You could have told him nothing

---

1. **cantinas** (kan tē′ nəs): saloons or barrooms.
2. *guitarreros* (gi tä re′ rôs) *Spanish:* guitar players.
3. **pachucos** (pə chōō′ kōz): buddies or pals.
4. **vaquero** (vä ker′ ō): a cowboy.
5. **caporal** (kap′ ə ral′): the boss of a ranch.

about cotton or beans or corn. He knew it all. He could look into the sky of a morning and smell it, sniff it the way a dog sniffs, and tell you what kind of weather there was going to be. And he would take a piece of dirt in his hands and rub it back and forth between his fingers—to see if the land had reached its point—and you would say he was looking into it. And perhaps he was, for Gregorio Cortez was the seventh son of a seventh son.[6]

You piddling modern farmers, vain of yourselves when you make a bale! You should have seen the crops raised by Gregorio Cortez. And when harvesting came, he was in there with the rest. Was it shucking corn? All you could see was the shucks fly and the pile grow, until you didn't know there was a man behind the pile. But he was even better at cotton-picking time. He would bend down and never raise his head till he came out the other end, and he would be halfway through another row before the next man was through with his. And don't think the row he went through wasn't clean. No flags, no streamers, nothing left behind, nothing but clean, empty burrs where he had passed. It was the same when clearing land. There were men who went ahead of him, cutting fast along their strip in the early morning, but by noontime the man ahead was always Gregorio Cortez, working at his own pace, talking little and not singing very much, and never acting up.

For Gregorio Cortez was not of your noisy, hell-raising type. That was not his way. He always spoke low, and he was always polite, whoever he was speaking to. And when he spoke to men older than himself he took off his hat and held it over his heart. A man who never raised his voice to parent or elder brother, and never disobeyed. That was Gregorio Cortez, and that was the way men were in this country along the river. That was the way they were before these modern times came, and God went away.

He should have stayed on the Border; he should not have gone up above, into the North. But it was going to be that way, and that was the way it was. Each man has a certain lot in life, and no other thing but that will be his share. People were always coming down from places in the North, from Dallas and San Antonio and Corpus and Foro West. And they would say, "Gregorio Cortez, why don't you go north? There is much money to be made. Stop eating beans and tortillas and that rubbery jerked beef. One of these days you're going to pull out one of your eyes, pull and pull with your teeth on that stuff and it suddenly lets go. It's a wonder all you Border people are not one-eyed. Come up above with us, where you can eat white bread and ham."

But Gregorio Cortez would only smile, because he was a peaceful man and did not take offense. He did not like white bread and ham; it makes people flatulent and dull. And he liked it where he was. So he always said, "I like this country. I will stay here."

But Gregorio Cortez had a brother, a younger brother named Román. Now Román was just like the young men of today, loud-mouthed and discontented. He was never happy where he was, and to make it worse he loved a joke more than any other thing. He would think nothing of playing a joke on a person twice his age. He had no respect for anyone, and that is why he ended like he did. But that is yet to tell.

Román talked to Gregorio and begged him that they should move away from the river and go up above, where there was much money to be made. And he talked and begged so, that finally Gregorio Cortez said he would go with

6. **seventh son of a seventh son:** according to the folklore of several cultures, the seventh son of a seventh son is always lucky and specially gifted, sometimes with occult powers.

his brother Román, and they saddled their horses and rode north.

Well, they did not grow rich, though things went well with them because they were good workers. Sometimes they picked cotton, sometimes they were vaqueros, and sometimes they cleared land for the Germans. Finally they came to a place called El Carmen, and there they settled down and farmed. And that was how Gregorio Cortez came to be in the county of El Carmen, where the tragedy took place.

ROMÁN'S HORSE TRADE AND WHAT CAME OF IT

Román owned two horses, two beautiful sorrels[7] that were just alike, the same color, the same markings, and the same size. You could not have told them apart, except that one of them was lame. There was an American who owned a little sorrel mare. This man was dying to get Román's sorrel—the good one—and every time they met he would offer to swap the mare for the horse. But Román did not think much of the mare. He did not like it when the American kept trying to make him trade.

"I wonder what this Gringo[8] thinks," Román said to himself. "He takes me for a fool. But I'm going to make him such a trade that he will remember me forever."

And Román laughed a big-mouthed laugh. He thought it would be a fine joke, besides being a good trade. There were mornings when the American went to town in his buggy along a narrow road. So Román saddled the lame sorrel, led him a little way along the road, and stopped under a big mesquite[9] that bordered on the fence. He fixed it so the spavined[10] side was against the mesquite. Román waited a little while, and soon he heard the buggy coming along the road. Then he got in the saddle and began picking mesquites off the tree and eating them. When the American came around the bend, there was Román on his sorrel horse. The American stopped his buggy beside Román and looked at the horse

with much admiration. It was a fine animal, exactly like the other one, but the American could not see the spavined leg.

"Changed your mind?" the American said.

Román stopped chewing on a mesquite and said, "Changed my mind about what?"

"About trading that horse for my mare."

"You're dead set on trading your mare for this horse of mine?" Román said.

"You know I am," the American said. "Are you ready to come around?"

"I'm in a trading mood," said Román. "With just a little arguing you might convince me to trade this horse for that worthless mare of yours. But I don't know: you might go back on the deal later on."

"I never go back on my word," the American said. "What do you think I am, a Mexican?"

"We'll see, we'll see," said Román. "How much are you willing to give in hand?"

"Enough to give you the first square meal you've had in your life," the American said.

Román just laughed, and it was all he could do to keep from guffawing. He knew who was getting the best of things.

So they made the deal, with Román still sitting on his spavined horse under the tree, chewing on mesquites.

"Where's the mare?" Román said.

"She's in my yard," said the American, "hung to a tree. You go get her and leave the horse there for me because I'm in a hurry to get to town."

That was how Román had figured it, so he

---

7. **sorrels:** horses of a light reddish brown.

8. **gringo** (griŋ' gō): a negative term for a foreigner, especially an American, used throughout Latin America.

9. **mesquite** (mes kēt'): a thorny, shrublike tree.

10. **spavined** (spav' ind): afflicted with spavin, a disease in which a horse's hind leg joint becomes enlarged, resulting in lameness.

said, "All right, I'll do it, but when I finish with these mesquites."

"Be sure you do, then," the American said.

"Sure, sure," said Román. "No hurry about it, is there?"

"All right," the American said, "take your time." And he drove off leaving Román still sitting on his horse under the mesquite, and as he drove off the American said, "Now isn't that just like a Mexican. He takes his time."

Román waited until the American was gone, and then he stopped eating mesquites. He got off and led the horse down the road to the American's yard and left him there in place of the little sorrel mare. On the way home Román almost fell off his saddle a couple of times, just laughing and laughing to think of the sort of face the American would pull when he came home that night.

The next morning, when Gregorio Cortez got up he said to his brother Román, "Something is going to happen today."

"Why do you say that?" asked Román.

"I don't know," said Gregorio Cortez. "I just know that something is going to happen today. I feel it. Last night my wife began to sigh for no reason at all. She kept sighing and sighing half the night, and she didn't know why. Her heart was telling her something, and I know some unlucky thing will happen to us today."

But Román just laughed, and Gregorio went inside the house to shave. Román followed him into the house and stood at the door while Gregorio shaved. It was a door made in two sections; the upper part was open and Román was leaning on the lower part, like a man leaning out of a window or over a fence. Román began to tell Gregorio about the horse trade he had made the day before, and he laughed pretty loud about it, because he thought it was a good joke. Gregorio Cortez just shaved, and he didn't say anything.

When what should pull in at the gate but a buggy, and the American got down, and the Major Sheriff of the county of El Carmen got down too. They came into the yard and up to where Román was leaning over the door, looking out.

The American had a very serious face. "I came for the mare you stole yesterday morning," he said.

Román laughed a big-mouthed laugh. "What did I tell you, Gregorio?" he said. "This Gringo . . . has backed down on me." . . .

Just as the word "Gringo" . . . came out of Román's mouth, the sheriff whipped out his pistol and shot Román. He shot Román as he stood there with his head thrown back, laughing at his joke. The sheriff shot him in the face, right in the open mouth, and Román fell away from the door, at the Major Sheriff's feet.

And then Gregorio Cortez stood at the door, where his brother had stood, with his pistol in his hand. Now he and the Major Sheriff met, each one pistol in hand, as men should meet when they fight for what is right. For it is a pretty thing to see, when two men stand up for their right, with their pistols in their hands, front to front and without fear. And so it was, for the Major Sheriff also was a man.

Yes, the Major Sheriff was a man; he was a gamecock[11] that had won in many pits, but in Gregorio Cortez he met a cockerel[12] that pecked his comb. The Major Sheriff shot first, and he missed; and Gregorio Cortez shot next, and he didn't miss. Three times did they shoot, three times did the Major Sheriff miss, and three times did Gregorio Cortez shoot the sheriff of El Carmen. The Major Sheriff fell dead at the feet of Gregorio Cortez, and it was in this way that Gregorio Cortez killed the first sheriff of many that he was to kill.

When the Major Sheriff fell, Gregorio Cortez looked up, and the other American said, "Don't kill me; I am unarmed."

---

11. **gamecock:** a rooster trained for fighting.
12. **cockerel:** a young rooster.

"I will not kill you," said Gregorio Cortez. "But you'd better go away."

So the American went away. He ran into the brush and kept on running until he came to town and told all the other sheriffs that the Major Sheriff was dead.

Meanwhile, Gregorio Cortez knew that he too must go away. He was not afraid of the law; he knew the law, and he knew that he had the right. But if he stayed, the Rangers would come, and the Rangers have no regard for law. You know what kind of men they are. When the Governor of the State wants a new Ranger, he asks his sheriffs, "Bring all the criminals to me." And from the murderers he chooses the Ranger, because no one can be a Ranger who has not killed a man. So Gregorio Cortez knew that the best thing for him was to go away, and his first thought was of the Border, where he had been born. But first he must take care of his brother, so he put Román in the buggy and drove into town, where his mother lived.

Now there was a lot of excitement in town. All the Americans were saddling up and loading rifles and pistols, because they were going out to kill Cortez. When all of a sudden, what should come rolling into town but the buggy, driven by Gregorio Cortez. They met him on the edge of town, armed to the teeth, on horseback and afoot, and he on the buggy, holding the reins lightly in his hands. Román was in the back, shot in the mouth. He could neither speak nor move, but just lay there like one who is dead.

They asked him, "Who are you?"

And he said to them, "I am Gregorio Cortez."

They all looked at him and were afraid of him, because they were only twenty or twenty-five, and they knew that they were not enough. So they stepped aside and let him pass and stood talking among themselves what would be the best thing to do. But Gregorio Cortez just drove ahead, slowly, without seeming to care about the men he left behind. He came to his mother's house, and there he took down his brother and carried him in the house. He stayed there until dawn, and during the night groups of armed men would go by the house and say, "He's in there. He's in there." But none of them ever went in.

At dawn Gregorio Cortez came out of his mother's house. There were armed men outside, but they made no move against him. They just watched as he went down the street, his hands resting on his belt. He went along as if he was taking a walk, and they stood there watching until he reached the brush and he jumped into it and disappeared. And then they started shooting at him with rifles, now that he was out of pistol range.

"I must get me a rifle," said Gregorio Cortez, "a rifle and a horse."

They gathered in a big bunch and started after him in the brush. But they could not catch Gregorio Cortez. No man was ever as good as him in hiding his own tracks, and he soon had them going around in circles, while he doubled back and headed for home to get himself a rifle and a horse.

HOW GREGORIO CORTEZ RODE THE LITTLE SORREL MARE ALL OF FIVE HUNDRED MILES

He went in and got his thirty-thirty, and then he looked around for the best horse he had. It is a long way from El Carmen to the Border, all of five hundred miles. The first thing he saw in the corral was the little sorrel mare. Gregorio Cortez took a good look at her, and he knew she was no ordinary mare.

"You're worth a dozen horses," said Gregorio Cortez, and he saddled the little mare.

But by then the whole wasp's nest was beginning to buzz. The President of the United States offered a thousand dollars for him, and many men went out to get Gregorio Cortez. The Major Sheriffs of the counties and all their sheriffs were out. There were Rangers from the counties, armed to the teeth, and the King Ranch Rangers from the Capital, the meanest of them all, all armed and looking for Cortez. Every road was blocked and every bridge guarded. There were trackers out with those dogs they call hounds, that can follow a track better than the best tracker. They had railroad cars loaded with guns and ammunition and with men, moving up and down trying to head him off. The women and children stayed in the houses, behind locked doors, such was the fear they all had of Gregorio Cortez. Every town from the Capital to the Border was watching out for him. The brush and the fields were full of men, trying to pick up his trail. And Gregorio Cortez rode out for the Border, through brush and fields and barbed wire fences, on his little sorrel mare.

He rode and rode until he came to a great broad plain, and he started to ride across. But just as he did, one of the sheriffs saw him. The sheriff saw him, but he hid behind a bush, because he was afraid to take him on alone. So he called the other sheriffs together and all the Rangers he could find, and they went off after Gregorio Cortez just as he came out upon the plain.

Gregorio Cortez looked back and saw them coming. There were three hundred of them.

"We'll run them a little race," said Gregorio Cortez.

Away went the mare, as if she had been shot from a gun, and behind her came the sheriffs and the Rangers, all shooting and riding hard. And so they rode across the plain, until one by one their horses foundered and fell to the ground and died. But still the little mare ran on, as fresh as a lettuce leaf, and pretty soon she was running all alone.

"They'll never catch me like that," said Gregorio Cortez, "not even with those dogs called hounds."

Another big bunch of sheriffs rode up, and they chased him to the edge of the plain, and into the brush went Cortez, with the trackers after him, but they did not chase him long. One moment there was a trail to follow, and next moment there was none. And the dogs called hounds sat down and howled, and the men scratched their heads and went about in circles looking for the trail. And Gregorio Cortez went on, leaving no trail, so that people thought he was riding through the air.

There were armed men everywhere, and he could not stop to eat or drink, because wherever he tried to stop armed men were there before him. So he had to ride on and on. Now they saw him, now they lost him, and so the chase went on. Many more horses foundered, but the mare still ran, and Gregorio Cortez rode on and on, pursued by hundreds and fighting hundreds every place he went.

"So many mounted Rangers," said Gregorio Cortez, "to catch just one Mexican."

It was from the big bunches that he ran. Now and again he would run into little ones of ten or a dozen men, and they were so scared of him that they would let him pass. Then, when he was out of range they would shoot at him, and he would shoot back at them once or twice, so they could go back and say, "We met up with Gregorio Cortez, and we traded shots with him." But from the big ones he had to run. And it was the little sorrel mare that took him safe away, over the open spaces and into the brush, and once in the brush, they might as well have been following a star.

So it went for a day, and when night fell Cortez arrived at a place named Los Fresnos and called at a Mexican house. When the man of the house came out, Cortez told him, "I am Gregorio Cortez."

That was all he had to say. He was given to eat and drink, and the man of the house offered Gregorio Cortez his own horse and his rifle and his saddle. But Cortez would not take them. He thanked the man, but he would not give up his little sorrel mare. Cortez was sitting there, drinking a cup of coffee, when the Major Sheriff of Los Fresnos came up with his three hundred men. All the other people ran out of the house and hid, and no one was left in the house, only Gregorio Cortez, with his pistol in his hand.

Then the Major Sheriff called out, in a weepy voice, as the corrido says. He sounded as if he wanted to cry, but it was all done to deceive Gregorio Cortez.

"Cortez," the Major Sheriff said, "hand over your weapons. I did not come to kill you. I am your friend."

"If you come as my friend," said Gregorio Cortez, "why did you bring three hundred men? Why have you made me a corral?"[13]

The Major Sheriff knew that he had been caught in a lie, and the fighting began. He killed the Major Sheriff and the second sheriff under him, and he killed many sheriffs more. Some of the sheriffs got weak in the knees, and many ran away.

"Don't go away," said Gregorio Cortez. "I am the man you are looking for. I am Gregorio Cortez."

They were more than three hundred, but he jumped their corral, and he rode away again, and those three hundred did not chase him any more.

He rode on and on, until he came to a river called the San Antonio. It is not much of a river, but the banks are steep and high, and he could not find a ford. So he rode to a ranch house nearby, where they were holding a *baile*[14] because the youngest child of the house had been baptized that day, and he asked the man of the house about a ford.

"There are only two fords," the man said. "One is seven miles upstream and the other is seven miles down."

"I will take another look at the river," said Gregorio Cortez. He left the baile and rode slowly to the river. It was steep, and far below he could see the water flowing; he could barely see it because it was so dark. He stood there thinking, trying to figure out a way, when he heard the music at the baile stop.

He knew the Rangers were at the baile now. So he leaned over in his saddle and whispered in the mare's ear. He talked to her, and she understood. She came to the edge of the bank, with soft little steps, because she was afraid. But Gregorio Cortez kept talking to her and talking to her, and finally she jumped. She jumped far out and into the dark water below, she and Gregorio Cortez.

The other bank was not so high, but it was just as steep. Gregorio Cortez took out his reata, and he lassoed a stump high on the bank. He climbed up the rope and got a stick, and with the stick he worked on the bank as fast as he could, for he could hear the racket of the dogs. The ground was soft, and he knocked off part of the top, until he made something like a slope. Then he pulled and talked until the mare struggled up the bank to where he was. After that they rested up a bit and waited for the Rangers. Up they came with their dogs, to the spot where the mare had jumped. When they came up to the river's edge, Cortez fired a shot in the air and yelled at them, "I am Gregorio Cortez!"

Then he rode away, leaving them standing there on the other side, because none of them was brave enough to do what Cortez had done.

He rode on and on, and sometimes they chased him and sometimes he stood and fought. And every time he fought he would kill them a Ranger or two. They chased him across the Arroyo del Cíbolo and into the oak grove, and there they made him a corral. Then they sent the dogs away and sat down to wait, for they wanted to catch him asleep. Gregorio Cortez thought for a little while what he

13. **corral** (kə ral′): an enclosure that resembles a pen for confining animals.
14. *baile* (bäj′ lā) *Spanish:* a dance.

should do. Then he made his mare lie down on the ground, so she would not be hurt. After that Gregorio Cortez began talking to himself and answering himself in different voices, as if he had many men. This made the Rangers say to one another, "There is a whole army of men with Gregorio Cortez." So they broke up their corral and went away, because they did not think there were enough of them to fight Gregorio Cortez and all the men he had. And Gregorio Cortez rode away, laughing to himself.

He kept riding on and on, by day and by night, and if he slept the mare stood guard and she would wake him up when she heard a noise. He had no food or cigarettes, and his ammunition was running low. He was going along a narrow trail with a high barbed wire fence on one side and a nopal thicket on the other, and right before he hit a turn he heard horses ahead. The first man that came around the turn ran into Gregorio Cortez, with his pistol in his hand. There was a whole line of others behind the first, all armed with rifles, but they had to put the rifles away. Then Gregorio Cortez knocked over a tall nopal plant with his stirrup and made just enough room for his mare to back into while the Rangers filed by. He stopped the last one and took away his tobacco, matches, and ammunition. And then he rode away.

He rode on to La Grulla, and he was very thirsty, because he had not had water in a long time, and the mare was thirsty too. Near La Grulla there was a dam where the vaqueros watered their stock. But when Gregorio Cortez got there, he saw twenty armed men resting under the trees that grew close to the water. Gregorio Cortez stopped and thought what he could do. Then he went back into the brush and began rounding up cattle, for this was cattle country and steers were everywhere. Pretty soon he had two hundred head, and he drove them to water and while the cattle drank he

and the mare drank too. After he had finished, some of the Rangers that were resting under the trees came over and helped him get the herd together again, and Gregorio Cortez rode off with the herd, laughing to himself.

He rode on and on, and by now he knew that the Río Grande was near. He rode till he came to Cotulla, and there he was chased again. The little mare was tired, and now she began to limp. She had cut her leg and it was swelling up. Gregorio Cortez rode her into a thicket, and the Rangers made him a corral. But once in the brush, Gregorio Cortez led the mare to a coma tree and tied her there. He unsaddled her and hung the saddle to the tree, and he patted her and talked to her for a long while. Then he slipped out of the thicket, and the Rangers didn't see him because they were waiting for him to ride out. They waited for three days and finally they crept in and found only the mare and the saddle.

HOW EL TECO SOLD GREGORIO CORTEZ FOR A MORRAL[15] FULL OF SILVER DOLLARS

Gregorio Cortez was gone. While all the armed men were guarding the thicket where the mare was tied, he walked into Cotulla itself. He walked into town and mixed with the Mexicans there. He sat on the station platform and listened to other men while they talked of all the things that Gregorio Cortez had done. Then he went to a store and bought himself new clothes and walked out of the town. He went to the river and took a bath and then swam across, because the bridge was guarded. That sort of man was Gregorio Cortez. They don't make them like him any more.

He had only three cartridges left, one for one pistol and two for the other, and he had left his rifle with the mare. But he was very near the Río Grande, and he expected to cross it soon. Still he needed ammunition, so he

---

15. *morral* (mô räl′) *Spanish:* a large bag or pouch.

walked into El Sauz and tried to buy some, but they did not sell cartridges in that town. Then he thought of trying some of the houses, and chose one in which there was a pretty girl at the door because he knew it would be easier if he talked to a girl. There was not a woman that did not like Gregorio Cortez.

The girl was alone, and she invited him into the house. When he asked for ammunition, she told him she had none.

"My father has taken it all," she said. "He is out looking for a man named Gregorio Cortez."

Gregorio Cortez was embarrassed because he could see that the girl knew who he was. But she did not let on and neither did he. He stayed at the house for a while, and when he left she told him how to get to the Río Grande by the quickest way.

Now all the people along the river knew that Gregorio Cortez was on the Border, and that he would soon cross, but no one told the sheriffs what they knew. And Gregorio Cortez walked on, in his new clothes, with his pistols in a *morral,* looking like an ordinary man, but the people he met knew that he was Gregorio Cortez. And he began to talk to people along the way.

Soon he met a man who told him, "You'll be on the other side of the river tonight, Gregorio Cortez."

"I think I will," he said.

"You'll be all right then," said the man.

"I guess so," said Gregorio Cortez.

"But your brother won't," the man said. "He died in the jail last night."

"He was badly wounded," said Gregorio Cortez. "It was his lot to die, but I have avenged his death."

"They beat him before he died," the man said. "The Rangers came to the jail and beat him to make him talk."

This was the first news that Gregorio Cortez had heard, and it made him thoughtful.

He walked on, and he met another man who said, "Your mother is in the jail, Gregorio Cortez."

"Why?" said Gregorio Cortez. "Why should the sheriffs do that to her?"

"Because she is your mother," the man said. "That's why. Your wife is there too, and so are your little sons."

Gregorio Cortez thought this over, and he walked on. Pretty soon he met another man who said, "Gregorio Cortez, your own people are suffering, and all because of you."

"Why should my people suffer?" said Cortez. "What have I done to them?"

"You have killed many sheriffs, Gregorio Cortez," said the man. "The Rangers cannot catch you, so they take it out on other people like you. Every man that's given you a glass of water has been beaten and thrown in jail. Every man who has fed you has been hanged from a tree branch, up and down, up and down, to make him tell where you went, and some have died rather than tell. Lots of people have been shot and beaten because they were your people. But you will be safe, Gregorio Cortez; you will cross the river tonight."

"I did not know these things," said Gregorio Cortez.

And he decided to turn back, and to give himself up to the Governor of the State so that his own people would not suffer because of him.

He turned and walked back until he came to a place called Goliad, where he met eleven Mexicans, and among them there was one that called himself his friend. This man was a vaquero named El Teco, but Judas should have been his name. Gregorio Cortez was thirsty, and he came up to the eleven Mexicans to ask for water, and when El Teco saw Gregorio Cortez he thought how good it would be if he could get the thousand-dollar reward. So he walked up to Cortez and shook his hand and told the others, "Get some water for my friend Gregorio Cortez."

Then El Teco asked Gregorio Cortez to let him see the pistols he had, and that he would get him some ammunition. Gregorio Cortez smiled, because he knew. But he handed over the guns to El Teco, and El Teco looked at them and put them in his own morral. Then El Teco called the sheriffs to come and get Gregorio Cortez.

When Gregorio Cortez saw what El Teco had done, he smiled again and said to him, "Teco, a man can only be what God made him. May you enjoy your reward."

But El Teco did not enjoy the reward, though the sheriffs gave him the money, one thousand dollars in silver, more than a morral could hold. He did not enjoy it because he could not spend it anywhere. If he went to buy a taco at the marketplace, the taco vendor would tell him that tacos were worth two thousand dollars gold that day. People cursed him in the streets and wished that he would be killed or die. So El Teco became very much afraid. He buried the money and never spent it, and he never knew peace until he died.

How Gregorio Cortez Went to Prison, But Not for Killing the Sheriffs

When the sheriffs came to arrest Gregorio Cortez, he spoke to them and said, "I am not your prisoner yet. I will be the prisoner only of the Governor of the State. I was going to the Capital to give myself up, and that is where I'll go."

The sheriffs saw that he was in the right, so they went with him all the way to the Capital, and Cortez surrendered himself to the Governor of the State.

Then they put Cortez in jail, and all the Americans were glad, because they no longer were afraid. They got together, and they tried to lynch him. Three times they tried, but they could not lynch Gregorio Cortez.

And pretty soon all the people began to see that Gregorio Cortez was in the right, and they did not want to lynch him anymore. They brought him gifts to the jail, and one day one of the judges came and shook the hand of Gregorio Cortez and said to him, "I would have done the same."

But Gregorio Cortez had many enemies, for he had killed many men, and they wanted to see him hanged. So they brought him to trial for killing the Major Sheriff of the county of El Carmen. The lawyer that was against him got up and told the judges that Cortez should die, because he had killed a man. Then Gregorio Cortez got up, and he spoke to them.

"Self-defense is allowed to any man," said Gregorio Cortez. "It is in your own law, and by your own law do I defend myself. I killed the sheriff, and I am not sorry, for he killed my brother. He spilled my brother's blood, which was also my blood. And he tried to kill me too. I killed the Major Sheriff defending my right."

And Gregorio Cortez talked for a long time to the judges, telling them about their own law. When he finished, even the lawyer who was against him at the start was now for him. And all the judges came down from their benches and shook hands with Gregorio Cortez.

The judges said, "We cannot kill this man."

They took Gregorio Cortez all over the State, from town to town, and in each town he was tried before the court for the killing of a man. But in every court it was the same. Gregorio Cortez spoke to the judges, and he told them about the law, and he proved that he had the right. And each time the judges said, "This man was defending his right. Tell the sheriffs to set him free."

And so it was that Gregorio Cortez was not found guilty of any wrong because of the sheriffs he had killed. And he killed many of them, there is no room for doubt. No man has killed more sheriffs than did Gregorio Cortez, and he always fought alone. For that is the way the real men fight, always on their own. There are young men around here today, who think that they are brave. Dangerous men they call themselves, and it takes five or six of them to jump a fellow and slash him in the arm. Or they hide in the brush and fill him full of buckshot as he goes by. They are not men. But that was not the way with Gregorio Cortez, for he was a real man.

Now the enemies of Gregorio Cortez got together and said to each other, "What are we going to do? This man is going free after killing so many of our friends. Shall we kill him ourselves? But we would have to catch him asleep, or shoot him in the back, because if we meet him face to face there will be few of us left."

Then one of them thought of the little sorrel mare, and there they had a plan to get Gregorio Cortez. They brought him back to court, and the lawyer who was against him asked, "Gregorio Cortez, do you recognize this mare?"

"I do," said Gregorio Cortez. "And a better little mare there never was."

The lawyer asked him, "Have you ridden this mare?"

And Gregorio Cortez answered, "She carried me all the way from El Carmen to the Border, a distance of five hundred miles."

Then the lawyer asked him, "Is this mare yours?"

And Gregorio Cortez saw that they had him, but there was nothing he could do, because he was an honest man and he felt that he must tell the truth. He said no, the mare did not belong to him.

Then the judges asked Gregorio Cortez, "Is this true, Gregorio Cortez? Did you take this mare that did not belong to you?"

And Gregorio Cortez had to say that the thing was true.

So they sentenced Gregorio Cortez, but not for killing the sheriffs, as some fools will tell you even now, when they ought to know bet-

ter. No, not for killing the sheriffs but for stealing the little sorrel mare. The judge sentenced him to ninety-nine years and a day. And the enemies of Gregorio Cortez were happy then, because they thought Cortez would be in prison for the rest of his life.

HOW PRESIDENT LINCOLN'S DAUGHTER FREED GREGORIO CORTEZ, AND HOW HE WAS POISONED AND DIED

But Gregorio Cortez did not stay in prison long. Inside of a year he was free and this is the way it came about. Every year at Christmastime, a pretty girl can come to the Governor of the State and ask him to give her a prisoner as a Christmas present. And the Governor then has to set the prisoner free and give him to the girl. So it happened to Cortez. One day President Lincoln's daughter visited the prison, and she saw Gregorio Cortez. As soon as she saw him she went up and spoke to him.

"I am in love with you, Gregorio Cortez," President Lincoln's daughter said, "and if you promise to marry me, I will go to the Governor next Christmas and tell him to give you to me."

Gregorio Cortez looked at President Lincoln's daughter, and he saw how beautiful she was. It made him thoughtful, and he did not know what to say.

"I have many rich farms," President Lincoln's daughter said. "They are all my own. Marry me and we will farm together."

Gregorio Cortez thought about that. He could see himself already like a German, sitting on the gallery, full of ham and beer, and belching and breaking wind while a half-dozen little blond cockroaches played in the yard. And he was tempted. But then he said to himself, "I can't marry a Gringo girl. We would not make a matching pair."

So he decided that President Lincoln's daughter was not the woman for him, and he told her, "I thank you very much, but I cannot marry you at all."

But President Lincoln's daughter would not take his no. She went to the Governor and said, "I would like to have a prisoner for Christmas."

And the Governor looked at her and saw she was a pretty girl, so he said, "Your wish is granted. What prisoner do you want?"

And President Lincoln's daughter said, "I want Gregorio Cortez."

The Governor thought for a little while and then he said, "That's a man you cannot have. He's the best prisoner I got."

But President Lincoln's daughter shook her head and said, "Don't forget that you gave your word."

"So I did," the Governor said, "and I cannot go back on it."

And that was how Gregorio Cortez got out of prison, where he had been sentenced to ninety-nine years and a day, not for killing the sheriffs, as some fools will tell you, but for stealing the little sorrel mare. Gregorio Cortez kept his word, and he did not marry President Lincoln's daughter, and when at last she lost her hopes, she went away to the North.

Still, the enemies of Gregorio Cortez did not give up. When they heard that he was getting out of prison they were scared and angry, and they started thinking of ways to get revenge. They got a lot of money together and gave it to a man who worked in the prison, and this man gave Cortez a slow poison just before Gregorio Cortez got out of jail.

And that was how he came to die, within a year from the day he got out of jail. As soon as he came out and his friends saw him, they said to each other, "This man is sick. This man will not last the year."

And so it was. He did not last the year. He died of the slow poison they gave him just before he was let out, because his enemies did not want to see him free.

And that was how Gregorio Cortez came to die. He's buried in Laredo some place, or maybe it's Brownsville, or Matamoros, or somewhere up above. To tell the truth, I don't know. I don't know the place where he is buried any more than the place where he was born. But he was born and lived and died, that I do know. And a lot of Rangers could also tell you that.

So does the corrido; it tells about Gregorio Cortez and who he was. They started singing the corrido soon after he went to jail, and there was a time when it was forbidden in all the United States, by order of the President himself. Men sometimes got killed or lost their jobs because they sang *El Corrido de Gregorio Cortez*. But everybody sang it just the same, because it spoke about things that were true.

Now it is all right to sing *El Corrido de Gregorio Cortez*, but not everybody knows it any more. And they don't sing it as it used to be sung. These new singers change all the old songs a lot. But even so, people still remember Gregorio Cortez. And when a good singer sings the song—good and loud and clear—you can feel your neck feathers rise, and you can see him standing there, with his pistol in his hand.

Thinking About the Story

sharing impressions

1. Did you enjoy this retelling of the corrido? Record your opinion in your journal.

constructing interpretations

2. Do you think Gregorio Cortez's death is appropriate for the kind of man he was? Explain your answer.

3. Which events in this story seem realistic, and which strike you as exaggerated?

4. How does Gregorio Cortez compare with the hero you identified in your prereading journal entry?

> **Think about**
> - the occupations in which he excels
> - his skills as a fighter
> - how he handles his legal battles
> - the family values that guide his conduct
> - the definition of manhood he exemplifies

A CREATIVE RESPONSE

5. How might this story be different if Gregorio Cortez had not lived by the heroic code "I will break before I bend"?

A CRITICAL RESPONSE

6. The corrido diverges considerably from the facts of Cortez's life and times. Cortez killed only two sheriffs: the sheriff who had killed his brother and another sheriff during a gun battle with a posse. Cortez eluded several posses, some with as many as three hundred men, but was finally captured—exhausted, out of ammunition, and on foot—near the border town of Laredo. After a three-year legal battle, Cortez was finally acquitted for killing the first sheriff but sentenced to life for killing the second. Abraham Lincoln did not have a daughter and Cortez spent about thirteen years in prison before being pardoned by the governor of Texas in 1913. He died three years later of unknown causes at the age of forty-one. Consider the specific ways that the corrido alters the facts of Gregorio Cortez's life, and explain why you think those changes were made.

7. Which qualities demonstrated by Cortez are still considered admirable in a hero today? Explain your answer.

Analyzing the Writer's Craft

CULTURAL HERO

Recall some of the qualities you explored when you compared Gregorio Cortez with your personal hero in question 4.

Building a Literary Vocabulary. A cultural hero is a larger-than-life figure who reflects the values of a people. This kind of hero is not the creation of a solitary writer. Rather, the hero evolves from communal tales told orally or sung to musical accompaniment, passed down from one generation to the next. The role of the cultural hero is to provide a noble image that will inspire and guide the actions of all who share that culture. The hero's story is al-ways one of glory, both personally and for the culture represented. The qualities of Gregorio Cortez celebrated in the corrido were ideals for Mexicans of the Southwestern United States in the early years of the twentieth century.

Application: Analyzing a Cultural Hero. Working with a small group, make a chart with two columns, similar to the following. In the first column list five of Cortez's acts or decisions recounted in the corrido. In the second column, identify the cultural values represented in these acts or decisions. Share your conclusions with other groups.

Cortez	Values he represents

Connecting Reading and Writing

1. Based on details about Gregorio Cortez in the corrido, write his **obituary** for the local newspaper.

Option: Write a **eulogy** about Cortez that might be given at his funeral.

2. Imagine that a student who exhibits Gregorio Cortez's heroic qualities has enrolled at your school. Create a **comic strip** depicting his experiences during the first week.

Option: Write **diary entries** in which you describe your impressions of him during the first week of school.

3. If you were casting parts for a film, what actor would you select to play Gregorio Cortez? Explain your choice in a **proposal** to the producer of the film.

Option: Write a **press release** to explain your casting decision.

4. Write a **narrative poem** celebrating the personal hero you identified in your prereading journal entry.

Option: Compose a **rap song** about your personal hero.

Guitarreros

Américo Paredes

Black against twisted black
The old mesquite
Rears up against the stars
Branch bridle hanging,
While the bull comes down from the mountain
Driven along by your fingers,
Twenty nimble stallions prancing up and down
   the *redil*[1] of the guitars.
One leaning on the trunk, one facing—
Now the song:
Not cleanly flanked, not pacing,
But in a stubborn yielding that unshapes
And shapes itself again,
Hard-mouthed, zigzagged, thrusting,
Thrown, not sung,
One to the other.
The old man listens in his cloud
Of white tobacco smoke.
"It was so," he says,
"In the old days it was so."

1. redil (re dēl'): *Spanish:* sheepfold.

from When Heaven and Earth Changed Places

LE LY HAYSLIP

A biography of Hayslip appears on page 424.

Approaching the Selection

Vietnam is a country with a long history of war. In the third century B.C., Vietnam was conquered by the Chinese under the Han dynasty. The Vietnamese maintained their resistance to Chinese rule for over twelve hundred years. During the late nineteenth and early twentieth centuries, the French attempted to colonize Vietnam but were finally defeated by Ho Chi Minh and his communist organization, the Viet Minh. After World War II, the country was divided into communist North Vietnam and noncommunist South Vietnam. Republican forces in South Vietnam, supported by Americans, fought against the Viet Cong, communist rebels who were backed by the North Vietnamese government. It is at this point in time that the selection takes place.

In this excerpt from her autobiography, Le Ly Hayslip (lā lē hā′ slip) shares childhood memories of her father and reveals the impact of war on Vietnamese families. Bay Ly (bī lē) is the writer's childhood nickname, *Bay* meaning "six." She was the youngest of six children.

Connecting Writing and Reading

Get together with another student and brainstorm associations with the word *Vietnam.* In your journal create a cluster diagram that shows these associations. As you read, note whether the selection confirms or contradicts your impressions of Vietnam.

AFTER MY BROTHER Bon went North, I began to pay more attention to my father.

He was built solidly—big-boned—for a Vietnamese man, which meant he probably had well-fed, noble ancestors. People said he had the body of a natural-born warrior. He was a year younger and an inch shorter than my mother, but just as good-looking. His face was round, like a Khmer or Thai,[1] and his complexion was brown as soy from working all his life in the sun. He was very easygoing about everything and seldom in a hurry. Seldom, too, did he say no to a request—from his children or his neighbors. Although he took everything in stride, he was a hard and diligent worker. Even on holidays, he was always mending things or tending to our house and animals. He would not wait to be asked for help if he saw someone in trouble. Similarly, he always said what he thought, although he knew, like most honest men, when to keep silent. Because of his honesty, his empathy, and his openness to people, he understood life deeply. Perhaps that is why he was so easygoing. Only a half-trained mechanic thinks everything needs fixing.

He loved to smoke cigars and grew a little tobacco in our yard. My mother always wanted him to sell it, but there was hardly ever enough to take to market. I think for her it was the principle of the thing: smoking cigars was like burning money. Naturally, she had a song for such gentle vices—her own habit of chewing betel nuts included:

> Get rid of your tobacco,
> And you will get a water buffalo.
> Give away your betel,
> And you will get more paddy land.

Despite her own good advice, she never abstained from chewing betel, nor my father from smoking cigars. They were rare luxuries that life and the war allowed them.

My father also liked rice wine, which we made, and enjoyed an occasional beer, which he purchased when there was nothing else we needed. After he'd had a few sips, he would tell jokes and happy stories and the village kids would flock around. Because I was his youngest daughter, I was entitled to listen from his knee—the place of honor. Sometimes he would sing funny songs about whoever threatened the village and we would feel better. For example, when the French or Moroccan soldiers were near, he would sing:

> There are many kinds of vegetables,
> Why do you like spinach?
> There are many kinds of wealth,
> Why do you use Minh money?
> There are many kinds of people,
> Why do you love terrorists?

We laughed because these were all the things the French told us about the Viet Minh fighters, whom we favored in the war. Years later, when the Viet Cong were near, he would sing:

> There are many kinds of vegetables,
> Why do you like spinach?
> There are many kinds of money,
> Why do you use Yankee dollars?
> There are many kinds of people,
> Why do you disobey your ancestors?

This was funny because the words were taken from the speeches the North Vietnamese cadres delivered to shame us for

---

1. Khmer or Thai (kə mer′, tī): one of the native races of Cambodia; natives of Thailand.

helping the Republic. He used to have a song for when the Viet Minh were near too, which asked in the same way, "Why do you use francs?" and "Why do you love French traitors?" Because he sang these songs with a comical voice, my mother never appreciated them. She couldn't see the absurdity of our situation as clearly as we children. To her, war and real life were different. To us, they were all the same.

Even as a parent, my father was more lenient than our mother, and we sometimes ran to him for help when she was angry. Most of the time it didn't work, and he would lovingly rub our heads as we were dragged off to be spanked. The village saying went: "A naughty child learns more from a whipping stick than a sweet stick." We children were never quite sure about that but agreed the whipping stick was an eloquent teacher. When he absolutely had to punish us himself, he didn't waste time. Wordlessly, he would find a long, supple bamboo stick and let us have it behind our thighs. It stung, but he could have whipped us harder. I think seeing the pain in his face hurt more than receiving his half-hearted blows. Because of that, we seldom did anything to merit a father's spanking—the highest penalty in our family. Violence in any form offended him. For this reason, I think, he grew old before his time.

One of the few times my father ever touched my mother in a way not consistent with love was during one of the yearly floods, when people came to our village for safety from the lower ground. We sheltered many in our house, which was nothing more than a two-room hut with woven mats for a floor. I came home one day in winter rain to see refugees and Republican soldiers milling around outside. They did not know I lived there, so I had to elbow my way inside. It was nearly supper time, and I knew my mother would be fixing as much food as we could spare.

In the part of the house we used as our kitchen, I discovered my mother crying. She and my father had gotten into an argument outside a few minutes before. He had assured the refugees he would find something to eat for everyone, and she insisted there would not be enough for her children if everyone was fed. He repeated his order to her, this time loud enough for all to hear. Naturally, he thought this would end the argument. She persisted in contradicting him, so he had slapped her.

This show of male power—we called it *do danh vo*[2]—was usual behavior for Vietnamese husbands but unusual for my father. My mother could be as strict as she wished with his children, and he would seldom interfere. Now, I discovered there were limits even to his great patience. I saw the glowing red mark on her cheek and asked if she was crying because it hurt. She said no. She said she was crying because her action had caused my father to lose face in front of strangers. She promised that if I ever did what she had done to a husband, I would have both cheeks glowing: one from his blow and one from hers.

Once, when I was the only child at home, my mother went to Da Nang[3] to visit Uncle Nhu, and my father had to take care of me. I woke up from my nap in the empty house and cried for my mother. My father came in from the yard and reassured me, but I was still cranky and continued crying. Finally, he gave me a rice cookie to shut me up. Needless to say, this was a tactic my mother never used.

The next afternoon I woke up, and although I was not feeling cranky, I thought a rice cookie might be nice. I cried a fake cry, and my father came running in.

"What's this?" he asked, making a worried face. "Little Bay Ly doesn't want a cookie?"

I was confused again.

---

2. *do danh vo* (dỗ zäny vổ).
3. **Da Nang** (dä naŋ): seaport in central Vietnam.

"Look under your pillow," he said with a smile.

I twisted around and saw that, while I was sleeping, he had placed a rice cookie under my pillow. We both laughed, and he picked me up like a sack of rice and carried me outside while I gobbled the cookie.

In the yard, he plunked me down under a tree and told me some stories. After that, he got some scraps of wood and showed me how to make things: a doorstop for my mother and a toy duck for me. This was unheard of—a father doing these things with a child that was not a son! Where my mother would instruct me on cooking and cleaning and tell stories about brides, my father showed me the mystery of hammers and explained the customs of our people.

His knowledge of the Vietnamese went back to the Chinese Wars in ancient times. I learned how one of my distant ancestors, a woman named Phung Thi Chinh,[4] led Vietnamese fighters against the Han. In one battle, even though she was pregnant and surrounded by Chinese, she delivered the baby, tied it to her back, and cut her way to safety wielding a sword in each hand. I was amazed at this warrior's bravery and impressed that I was her descendant. Even more, I was amazed and impressed by my father's pride in her accomplishments (she was, after all, a humble female) and his belief that I was worthy of her example. *"Con phai theo got chan co ta"*[5] ("follow in her footsteps"), he said. Only later would I learn what he truly meant.

Never again did I cry after my nap. Phung Thi women were too strong for that. Besides, I was my father's daughter, and we had many things to do together.

On the eve of my mother's return, my father cooked a feast of roast duck. When we sat down to eat it, I felt guilty and my feelings showed on my face. He asked why I acted so sad.

"You've killed one of mother's ducks," I said. "One of the fat kind she sells at the market.

She says the money buys gold, which she saves for her daughters' weddings. Without gold for a dowry—*con o gia*[6]—I will be an old maid!"

My father looked suitably concerned, then brightened and said, "Well, Bay Ly, if you can't get married, you will just have to live at home forever with me!"

I clapped my hands at the happy prospect.

My father cut into the rich, juicy bird and said, "Even so, we won't tell your mother about the duck, okay?"

I giggled and swore myself to secrecy.

The next day, I took some water out to him in the fields. My mother was due home any time, and I used every opportunity to step outside and watch for her. My father stopped working, drank gratefully, then took my hand and led me to the top of a nearby hill. It had a good view of the village and the land beyond it, almost to the ocean. I thought he was going to show me my mother coming back, but he had something else in mind.

He said, "Bay Ly, you see all this here? This is the Vietnam we have been talking about. You understand that a country is more than a lot of dirt, rivers, and forests, don't you?"

I said, "Yes, I understand." After all, we had learned in school that one's country is as sacred as a father's grave.

"Good. You know, some of these lands are battlefields where your brothers and cousins are fighting. They may never come back. Even your sisters have all left home in search of a better life. You are the only one left in my house. If the enemy comes back, you must be both a daughter and a son. I told you how the Chinese used to rule our land. People in this village had to risk their lives diving in the ocean just to find pearls for the Chinese emperor's gown. They had to risk tigers and

---

4. **Phung Thi Chinh** (fơɔŋ ti chịny).
5. *Con phai theo got chan co ta* (kôn fĭ teô′ gô chän kô tä).
6. *con o gia* (kôn u yä).

snakes in the jungle just to find herbs for his table. Their payment for this hardship was a bowl of rice and another day of life. That is why Le Loi,[7] Gia Long,[8] the Trung Sisters, and Phung Thi Chinh fought so hard to expel the Chinese. When the French came, it was the same old story. Your mother and I were taken to Da Nang to build a runway for their airplanes. We labored from sunup to sundown and well after dark. If we stopped to rest or have a smoke, a Moroccan would come up and whip our behinds. Our reward was a bowl of rice and another day of life. Freedom is never a gift, Bay Ly. It must be won and won again. Do you understand?"

I said that I did.

"Good." He moved his finger from the patchwork of brown dikes, silver water, and rippling stalks to our house at the edge of the village. "This land here belongs to me. Do you know how I got it?"

I thought a moment, trying to remember my mother's stories, then said honestly, "I can't remember."

He squeezed me lovingly. "I got it from your mother."

"What? That can't be true!" I said. Everyone in the family knew my mother was poor and my father's family was wealthy. Her parents were dead, and she had to work like a slave for her mother-in-law to prove herself worthy. Such women don't have land to give away!

"It's true." My father's smile widened. "When I was a young man, my parents needed someone to look after their lands. They had to be very careful about whom they chose as wives for their three sons. In the village, your mother had a reputation as the hardest worker of all. She raised herself and her brothers without parents. At the same time, I noticed a beautiful woman working in the fields. When my mother said she was going to talk to the matchmaker about this hard-working village girl she'd heard about, my heart sank. I was too

attracted to this mysterious tall woman I had seen in the rice paddies. You can imagine my surprise when I found out the girl my mother heard about and the woman I admired were the same.

"Well, we were married and my mother tested your mother severely. She not only had to cook and clean and know everything about children, but she had to be able to manage several farms and know when and how to take the extra produce to the market. Of course, she was testing her other daughters-in-law as well. When my parents died, they divided their several farms among their sons, but you know what? They gave your mother and me the biggest share because they knew we would take care of it best. That's why I say the land came from her, because it did."

I suddenly missed my mother very much and looked down the road to the south, hoping to see her. My father noticed my sad expression.

"Hey." He poked me in the ribs. "Are you getting hungry for lunch?"

"No. I want to learn how to take care of the farm. What happens if the soldiers come back? What did you and Mother do when the soldiers came?"

My father squatted on the dusty hilltop and wiped the sweat from his forehead. "The first thing I did was to tell myself that it was my duty to survive—to take care of my family and my farm. That is a tricky job in wartime. It's as hard as being a soldier. The Moroccans were very savage. One day the rumor passed that they were coming to destroy the village. You may remember the night I sent you and your brothers and sisters away with your mother to Da Nang."

"You didn't go with us!" My voice still held the horror of the night I thought I had lost my father.

---

7. **Le Loi** (lā lō′ ē).
8. **Gia Long** (zä lôŋ).

"Right! I stayed near the village—right on this hill—to keep an eye on the enemy and on our house. If they really wanted to destroy the village, I would save some of our things so that we could start over. Sure enough, that was their plan.

"The real problem was to keep things safe and avoid being captured. Their patrols were everywhere. Sometimes I went so deep in the forest that I worried about getting lost, but all I had to do was follow the smoke from the burning huts and I could find my way back.

"Once, I was trapped between two patrols that had camped on both sides of a river. I had to wait in the water for two days before one of them moved on. When I got out, my skin was shriveled like an old melon's. I was so cold I could hardly move. From the waist down, my body was black with leeches. But it was worth all the pain. When your mother came back, we still had some furniture and tools to cultivate the earth. Many people lost everything. Yes, we were very lucky."

My father put his arms around me. "My brother Huong[9]—your uncle Huong—had three sons and four daughters. Of his four daughters, only one is still alive. Of his three sons, two went north to Hanoi[10] and one went south to Saigon.[11] Huong's house is very empty. My other brother, your uncle Luc, had only two sons. One went north to Hanoi, the other was killed in the fields. His daughter is deaf and dumb. No wonder he has taken to drink, eh? Who does he have to sing in his house and tend his shrine when he is gone? My sister Lien had three daughters and four sons. Three of the four sons went to Hanoi and the fourth went to Saigon to find his fortune. The girls all tend their in-laws and mourn slain husbands. Who will care for Lien when she is too feeble to care for herself? Finally, my baby sister Nhien lost her husband to French bombers. Of her two sons, one went to Hanoi and the other joined the Republic, then defected, then was murdered in his house. Nobody knows which side killed him. It doesn't really matter."

My father drew me out to arm's length and looked me squarely in the eye. "Now, Bay Ly, do you understand what your job is?"

I squared my shoulders and put on a soldier's face. "My job is to avenge my family. To protect my farm by killing the enemy. I must become a woman warrior like Phung Thi Chinh!"

My father laughed and pulled me close. "No, little peach blossom. Your job is to stay alive—to keep an eye on things and keep the village safe. To find a husband and have babies and tell the story of what you've seen to your children and anyone else who'll listen. Most of all, it is to live in peace and tend the shrine of our ancestors. Do these things well, Bay Ly, and you will be worth more than any soldier who ever took up a sword."

---

9. **Huong** (hoo ôŋ′).
10. **Hanoi** (hä noi′): capital of North Vietnam (1954–1976), now capital of the unified country of Vietnam.
11. **Saigon** (sī′ gän′): capital of South Vietnam (1954–1976), now called Ho Chi Minh City.

Mother, 1960

Father, 1960

Le Ly Hayslip, 1990

Sister Lan, 1960

Brother Sau Ban, 1960

Father, 1960

Le Ly's
Family Photos

Thinking About the Selection

A PERSONAL RESPONSE

sharing impressions

1. What is your impression of Bay Ly's father? Describe your response to him in your journal.

constructing interpretations

2. How well does Bay Ly's family seem to maintain its unity in a time of war?

Think about
- the relationships among Bay Ly, her father, and her mother
- the story Bay Ly is told about her ancestor Phung Thi Chinh
- the father's actions when the Moroccan soldiers return
- the fates of Bay Ly's brothers, sisters, uncles, and aunts

3. Compare what you have learned about Vietnam from this selection with the associations you recorded on your prereading diagram. Add to the diagram any new associations with the word *Vietnam*.

4. Bay Ly's father tells her that her job is not to fight but to stay alive and raise a family. Reflect on why he might believe this. What do you think of this advice?

A CREATIVE RESPONSE

5. If Bay Ly had not been the youngest daughter and the only child left at home, how do you think her relationship with her father might have been different?

A CRITICAL RESPONSE

6. What makes you aware of the writer's attitude toward her father?

7. What does this selection reveal to you about the values of the Vietnamese people? Give examples to support your conclusions.

8. Both Bay Ly's father and Gregorio Cortez faced life-or-death challenges. Which of the two do you think showed greater courage? Explain your answer.

Analyzing the Writer's Craft

THEME

Which ideas from this selection do you think are worth remembering?

Building a Literary Vocabulary. Theme is a central idea or message in a work of literature. Theme should not be confused with subject, or what the work is about. Rather, theme is a perception about life or humanity that a writer expresses in relation to a subject. Most works communicate several themes, one of which usually predominates. In this autobiography the writer shares many insights about life. One theme of this excerpt is that in wartime the most important task

for an individual is to survive. This theme is stated directly. Often, however, themes are expressed indirectly and become clear only after careful reading and thinking about a work.

Application: Identifying Themes. Reread this selection, copying statements that communicate themes directly. Then think about the piece and write down other messages expressed indirectly. Working as a whole class, make a list of the themes on the board and choose the three you believe are most important.

Connecting Reading and Writing

1. Write a **nomination** giving reasons why the writer's father should receive a parenting award.

Option: In a **guest column** for *Parents* magazine, have the writer's father share child-rearing advice.

2. Do research to find out more information about modern Vietnamese culture. Present the information in a **chart** that compares Vietnamese and American cultures in terms of values, family unity, types of work, economy, and social customs.

Option: In a **letter** to a Vietnamese pen pal, explain what you have learned about the similarities and differences in the two cultures. Ask your pen pal to share his or her ideas.

3. This selection concerns the effects of war on the Vietnamese. Based on the anti-war message con-

veyed in this work, create an anti-war **handbill** that reveals the impact of war on families and family life.

Option: Write **song lyrics** that convey the anti-war theme of this work.

4. Read Le Ly Hayslip's entire autobiography. In a **book review,** explain whether she followed in the footsteps of her warrior ancestor, Phung Thi Chinh.

Option: Answer this question in a **biographical sketch** of Hayslip intended for a reference book on notable women.

From the Poets in the Kitchen

PAULE MARSHALL

A biography of Marshall appears on page 426.

Approaching the Essay

Paule Marshall is the author of several novels and short story collections. Marshall's writing is enriched by the use of "Bajan" English, the English spoken by the black people of Barbados, the West Indian island in the Caribbean from which her parents came. In this essay, originally published in the *New York Times Book Review,* Marshall explains the unique gift she received as a young child.

Building Vocabulary

These essential words are footnoted within the essay.

adversity (ad vʉr′ sə tē): Some people . . . didn't know how to deal with **adversity.** (page 33)

encompass (en kum′ pəs): Confronted . . . by a world they could not **encompass,** . . . they took refuge in language. (page 34)

exhorting (eg zôrt′ iŋ): They were always **exhorting** each other. (page 35)

infuse (in fyo͞oz′): They were always trying to **infuse** new life. (page 36)

aesthetic (es thet′ ik): This was their guiding **aesthetic.** (page 36)

voraciously (vô rā′ shəs lē), **indiscriminately** (in′ di skrim′ i nit lē): I sheltered from the storm of adolescence . . . . reading **voraciously, indiscriminately.** (page 36)

testimony (tes′ tə mō′ nē), **legacy** (leg′ ə sē): It stands as **testimony** to the rich **legacy** of language. (page 38)

Connecting Writing and Reading

If you hear a person describe something as "rad," what does this person mean? If someone is "out to lunch," is he or she really eating lunch? In your journal write down a few examples of words and phrases that communicate ideas in unusual ways. Keep in mind these expressions as you read about a writer's early experience with language.

From the Poets in the Kitchen

SOME YEARS AGO, when I was teaching a graduate seminar in fiction at Columbia University, a well-known male novelist visited my class to speak on his development as a writer. In discussing his formative years, he didn't realize it, but he seriously endangered his life by remarking that women writers are luckier than those of his sex because they usually spend so much time as children around their mothers and their mothers' friends in the kitchen.

What did he say that for? The women students immediately forgot about being in awe of him and began readying their attack for the question-and-answer period later on. Even I bristled. There again was that awful image of women locked away from the world in the kitchen with only each other to talk to, and their daughters locked in with them.

But my guest wasn't really being sexist or trying to be provocative or even spoiling for a fight. What he meant—when he got around to explaining himself more fully—was that, given the way children are (or were) raised in our society, with little girls kept closer to home and their mothers, the woman writer stands a better chance of being exposed, while growing up, to the kind of talk that goes on among women, more often than not in the kitchen; and that this experience gives her an edge over her male counterpart by instilling in her an appreciation for ordinary speech.

It was clear that my guest lecturer attached great importance to this, which is understandable. Common speech and the plain, workaday words that make it up are, after all, the stock in trade of some of the best fiction writers. They are the principal means by which characters in a novel or story reveal themselves and give voice sometimes to profound feelings and complex ideas about themselves and the world. Perhaps the proper measure of a writer's talent is skill in rendering everyday speech—when it is appropriate to the story—as well as the ability to tap, to exploit the beauty, poetry, and wisdom it often contains.

"If you say what's on your mind in the language that comes to you from your parents and your street and friends, you'll probably say something beautiful." Grace Paley tells this, she says, to her students at the beginning of every writing course.

It's all a matter of exposure and a training of the ear for the would-be writer in those early years of apprenticeship. And, according to my guest lecturer, this training, the best of it, often takes place in as unglamourous a setting as the kitchen.

He didn't know it, but he was essentially describing my experience as a little girl. I grew up among poets. Now they didn't look like poets—whatever that breed is supposed to look like. Nothing about them suggested that poetry was their calling. They were just a group of ordinary housewives and mothers, my mother included, who dressed in a way (shapeless housedresses, dowdy felt hats, and long, dark, solemn coats) that made it impossible for me to imagine they had ever been young.

Nor did they do what poets were supposed to do—spend their days in an attic room writing verses. They never put pen to paper except to write occasionally to their relatives in Barbados. "I take my pen in hand hoping these few lines will find you in health as they leave me fair for the time being," was the way their letters invariably began. Rather, their day was spent "scrubbing floor," as they described the work they did.

Several mornings a week these unknown bards would put an apron and a pair of old house shoes in a shopping bag and take the train or streetcar from our section of Brooklyn out to Flatbush. There, those who didn't have steady jobs would wait on certain designated corners for the white housewives in the neighborhood to come along and bargain with them over pay for a day's work cleaning their houses. This was the ritual even in the winter.

Later, armed with the few dollars they had earned, which in their vocabulary became "a few raw-mouth pennies," they made their way back to our neighborhood, where they would sometimes stop off to have a cup of tea or cocoa together before going home to cook dinner for their husbands and children.

The basement kitchen of the brownstone house where my family lived was the usual gathering place. Once inside the warm safety of its walls, the women threw off the drab coats and hats, seated themselves at the large center table, drank their cups of tea or cocoa, and talked. While my sister and I sat at a smaller table over in a corner doing our homework, they talked—endlessly, passionately, poetically, and with impressive range. No subject was beyond them. True, they would indulge in the usual gossip: whose husband was running with whom, whose daughter looked slightly "in the way" (pregnant) under her bridal gown as she walked down the aisle. That sort of thing. But they also tackled the great issues of the time. They were always, for example, discussing the state of the economy. It was the mid- and late thirties then, and the aftershock of the Depression, with its soup lines and suicides on Wall Street, was still being felt.

Some people, they declared, didn't know how to deal with adversity.[1] They didn't know that you had to "tie up your belly" (hold in the pain, that is) when things got rough and go on with life. They took their image from the bellyband that is tied around the stomach of a newborn baby to keep the navel pressed in.

They talked politics. Roosevelt[2] was their hero. He had come along and rescued the country with relief and jobs, and in gratitude they christened their sons Franklin and Delano and hoped they would live up to the names.

If F.D.R. was their hero, Marcus Garvey[3] was their God. The name of the fiery, Jamaican-born black nationalist of the twenties was constantly invoked around the table. For he had been their leader when they first came to the United States from the West Indies shortly after World War I. They had contributed to his organization, the United Negro Improvement Association (UNIA), out of their meager salaries, bought shares in his ill-fated Black Star Shipping Line, and at the height of the movement they had marched as members of his "nurses' brigade" in their white uniforms up Seventh Avenue in Harlem during the great Garvey Day parades. Garvey: he lived on through the power of their memories.

And their talk was of war and rumors of wars. They raged against World War II when it broke out in Europe, blaming it on the politicians. "It's these politicians. They're the ones always starting up all this lot of war. But what they care? It's the poor people got to suffer and mothers with their sons." If it was *their* sons,

---

1. **adversity** (ad vʉr′ sə tē): poverty and trouble.
2. **Roosevelt** (rō′ zə velt′): Franklin Delano (del′ ə nō′) Roosevelt (1882–1945), thirty-second President of the United States, who led the country through its worst economic depression.
3. **Garvey** (gär′ vē): Marcus Garvey (1887–1940), leader who believed that blacks should consider resettling in Africa in order to avoid oppression by whites. With funds collected from his followers, he set up several all-black businesses.

they swore they would keep them out of the army by giving them soap to eat each day to make their hearts sound defective. Hitler?[4] He was for them "the devil incarnate."

Then there was home. They reminisced often and at length about home. The old country. Barbados—or Bimshire, as they affectionately called it. The little Caribbean island in the sun they loved but had to leave. "Poor—poor but sweet" was the way they remembered it.

And naturally they discussed their adopted home. America came in for both good and bad marks. They lashed out at it for the racism they encountered. They took to task some of the people they worked for, especially those who gave them only a hard-boiled egg and a few spoonfuls of cottage cheese for lunch. "As if anybody can scrub floor on an egg and some cheese that don't have no taste to it!"

Yet although they caught H in "this man country," as they called America, it was nonetheless a place where "you could at least see your way to make a dollar." That much they acknowledged. They might even one day accumulate enough dollars, with both them and their husbands working, to buy the brownstone houses which, like my family, they were only leasing at that period. This was their consuming ambition: to "buy house" and to see the children through.

There was no way for me to understand it at the time, but the talk that filled the kitchen those afternoons was highly functional. It served as therapy, the cheapest kind available to my mother and her friends. Not only did it help them recover from the long wait on the corner that morning and the bargaining over their labor; it restored them to a sense of themselves and reaffirmed their self-worth. Through language they were able to overcome the humiliations of the workday.

But more than therapy, that freewheeling, wide-ranging, exuberant talk functioned as an outlet for the tremendous creative energy they possessed. They were women in whom the need for self-expression was strong, and since language was the only vehicle readily available to them, they made of it an art form that—in keeping with the African tradition in which art and life are one—was an integral part of their lives.

And their talk was a refuge. They never really ceased being baffled and overwhelmed by America—its vastness, complexity, and power. Its strange customs and laws. At a level beyond words, they remained fearful and in awe. Their uneasiness and fear were even reflected in their attitude toward the children they had given birth to in this country. They referred to those like myself, the little Brooklyn-born Bajans (Barbadians), as "these New York children" and complained that they couldn't discipline us properly because of the laws here. "You can't beat these children as you would like, you know, because the authorities in this place will dash you in jail for them. After all, these is New York children." Not only were we different, American, we had, as they saw it, escaped their ultimate authority.

Confronted therefore by a world they could not <u>encompass</u>,[5] which even limited their rights as parents, and at the same time finding themselves permanently separated from the world they had known, they took refuge in language. "Language is the only homeland," Czeslaw Milosz,[6] the emigre Polish writer and Nobel laureate, has said. This is what it became for the women at the kitchen table.

It served another purpose also, I suspect. My mother and her friends were after all the female counterpart of Ralph Ellison's invisible

---

4. Hitler (hit′ lər): Adolf Hitler (1889–1945), Nazi dictator of Germany.
5. encompass (en kum′ pəs): to bring within; comprehend.
6. Czeslaw Milosz (ches′ wäs mē′ lôsh).

man.[7] Indeed, you might say they suffered a triple invisibility, being black, female, and foreigners. They really didn't count in American society except as a source of cheap labor. But given the kind of women they were, they couldn't tolerate the fact of their invisibility, their powerlessness. And they fought back, using the only weapon at their command: the spoken word.

Those late afternoon conversations on a wide range of topics were a way for them to feel they exercised some measure of control over their lives and the events that shaped them. "Soully-gal, talk yuh talk!" they were always exhorting[8] each other. "In this man world you got to take yuh mouth and make a gun!" They were in control, if only verbally and if only for the two hours or so that they remained in our house.

For me, sitting over in the corner, being seen but not heard, which was the rule for children in those days, it wasn't only what the women talked about—the content—but the way they put things—their style. The insight, irony, wit, and humor they brought to their stories and discussions and their poet's inventiveness and daring with language—which of course I could only sense but not define back then.

They had taken the standard English taught them in the primary schools of Barbados and transformed it into an idiom, an instrument that more adequately described them— changing around the syntax and imposing their own rhythm and accent so that the sentences were more pleasing to their ears. They added the few African sounds and words that had survived, such as the derisive suck-teeth sound and the word *yam,* meaning "to eat." And to make it more vivid, more in keeping with their expressive quality, they brought to bear a raft of metaphors, parables, Biblical quotations, sayings, and the like:

"The sea ain' got no back door," they would say, meaning that it wasn't like a house, where if there was a fire, you could run out the back. Meaning that it was not to be trifled with. And meaning perhaps in a larger sense that man should treat all of nature with caution and respect.

"I has read hell by heart and called every generation blessed!" They sometimes went in for hyperbole.

A woman expecting a baby was never said to be pregnant. They never used that word. Rather, she was "in the way" or, better yet, "tumbling big." "Guess who I butt up on in the market the other day tumbling big again?"

And a woman with a reputation of being too free with her sexual favors was known in their book as a "thoroughfare"—the sense of men like a steady stream of cars moving up and down the road of her life. Or she might be dubbed "a free-bee," which was my favorite of the two. I liked the image it conjured up of a woman scandalous perhaps but independent, who flitted from one flower to another in a garden of male beauties, sampling their nectar, taking her pleasure at will, the roles reversed.

And nothing, no matter how beautiful, was ever described as simply beautiful. It was always "beautiful-ugly": the beautiful-ugly dress, the beautiful-ugly house, the beautiful-ugly car. Why the word "ugly," I used to wonder, when the thing they were referring to was beautiful, and they knew it. Why the antonym, the contradiction, the linking of opposites? It used to puzzle me greatly as a child.

There is the theory in linguistics which states that the idiom of a people, the way they use language, reflects not only the most fundamental views they hold of themselves and the world but their very conception of reality.

---

7. **Ralph Ellison's invisible man:** a reference to the novel *The Invisible Man,* in which writer Ellison depicts the plight of the black man in America.
8. **exhorting** (eg zôrt′ iŋ): urging; warning with advice.

Perhaps in using the term "beautiful-ugly" to describe nearly everything, my mother and her friends were expressing what they believed to be a fundamental dualism in life: the idea that a thing is at the same time its opposite, and that these opposites, these contradictions, make up the whole. But theirs was not a Manichaean[9] brand of dualism that sees matter, flesh, the body, as inherently evil, because they constantly addressed each other as "soully-gal"—*soul:* spirit; *gal:* the body, flesh, the visible self. And it was clear from their tone that they gave one as much weight and importance as the other. They had never heard of the mind-body split.

As for God, they summed up His essential attitude in a phrase. "God," they would say, "don' love ugly and He ain' stuck on pretty."

Using everyday speech, the simple commonplace words—but always with imagination and skill—they gave voice to the most complex ideas. Flannery O'Connor[10] would have approved of how they made ordinary language work, as she put it, "double-time," stretching, shading, deepening its meaning. Like Joseph Conrad[11] they were always trying to infuse[12] new life in the "old old words worn thin . . . by . . . careless usage." And the goals of their oral art were the same as his: "to make you hear, to make you feel . . . to make you see." This was their guiding aesthetic.[13]

By the time I was eight or nine, I graduated from the corner of the kitchen to the neighborhood library, and thus from the spoken to the written word. The Macon Street Branch of the Brooklyn Public Library was an imposing half-block-long edifice of heavy gray masonry, with glass-paneled doors at the front and two tall metal torches symbolizing the light that comes of learning flanking the wide steps outside.

The inside was just as impressive. More steps—of pale marble with gleaming brass railings at the center and sides—led up to the circulation desk, and a great pendulum clock gazed down from the balcony stacks that faced the entrance. Usually stationed at the top of the steps like the guards outside Buckingham Palace was the custodian, a stern-faced West Indian type, who for years, until I was old enough to obtain an adult card, would immediately shoo me with one hand into the Children's Room and with the other threaten me into silence, a finger to his lips. You would have thought he was the chief librarian and not just someone whose job it was to keep the brass polished and the clock wound. I put him in a story called "Barbados" years later and had terrible things happen to him at the end.

I sheltered from the storm of adolescence in the Macon Street library, reading voraciously,[14] indiscriminately,[15] everything from Jane Austen[16] to Zane Grey,[17] but with a special passion for the long, full-blown, richly detailed eighteenth- and nineteenth-century picaresque[18] tales: *Tom Jones, Great Expectations, Vanity Fair.*

But although I loved nearly everything I

---

9. Manichaean (man' i kē' ən): referring to a Near Eastern religion concerned with the conflict between the physical and spiritual aspects of human beings.
10. Flannery O'Connor: major American novelist and short story writer (1925–1964).
11. Joseph Conrad: major British novelist (1857–1924).
12. infuse (in fyo͞oz'): to impart; inspire.
13. aesthetic (es thet' ik): artistic viewpoint.
14. voraciously (vô rā' shəs lē): greedily; eagerly.
15. indiscriminately (in' di skrim' i nit lē): not making careful choices; randomly.
16. Jane Austen (ôs' tən): English novelist, often regarded as one of the greatest women novelists (1775–1817).
17. Zane Grey: American writer of popular Westerns (1875–1939).
18. picaresque (pik' ə resk'): describing a genre of literature in which the life and adventures of a hero are chronicled.

read and would enter fully into the lives of the characters—indeed, would cease being myself and become them—I sensed a lack after a time. Something I couldn't quite define was missing. And then one day, browsing in the poetry section, I came across a book by someone called Paul Laurence Dunbar, and opening it I found the photograph of a wistful, sad-eyed poet who to my surprise was black. I turned to a poem at random. "Little brown-baby wif spa'klin' / eyes / Come to yo' pappy an' set on his knee." Although I had a little difficulty at first with the words in dialect, the poem spoke to me as nothing I had read before of the closeness, the special relationship I had had with my father, who by then had become an ardent believer in Father Divine and gone to live in Father's "kingdom" in Harlem. Reading it helped to ease somewhat the tight knot of sorrow and longing I carried around in my chest that refused to go away. I read another poem. "'Lias! 'Lias! Bless de Lawd! / Don' you know de day's / erbroad? / Ef you don' get up, you scamp / Dey'll be trouble in dis camp." I laughed. It reminded me of the way my mother sometimes yelled at my sister and me to get out of bed in the mornings.

And another: "Seen my lady home las' night / Jump back, honey, jump back. / Hel' huh han' and sque'z it tight . . ." About love between a black man and a black woman. I had never seen that written about before, and it roused in me all kinds of delicious feelings and hopes.

And I began to search then for books and stories and poems about "The Race" (as it was put back then), about my people. While not abandoning Thackeray, Fielding, Dickens,[19] and the others, I started asking the reference librarian, who was white, for books by Negro writers, although I must admit I did so at first with a feeling of shame—the shame I and many others used to experience in those days whenever the word *Negro* or *colored* came up.

No grade school literature teacher of mine had ever mentioned Dunbar or James Weldon Johnson or Langston Hughes. I didn't know that Zora Neale Hurston existed and was busy writing and being published during those years. Nor was I made aware of people like Frederick Douglass[20] and Harriet Tubman—their spirit and example—or the great nineteenth-century abolitionist and feminist Sojourner Truth. There wasn't even Negro History Week when I attended P. S. 35 on Decatur Street!

What I needed, what all the kids—West Indian and native black American alike—with whom I grew up needed, was an equivalent of the Jewish shul,[21] someplace where we could go after school—the schools that were shortchanging us—and read works by those like ourselves and learn about our history.

It was around that time also that I began harboring the dangerous thoughts of someday trying to write myself. Perhaps a poem about an apple tree, although I had never seen one. Or the story of a girl who could magically transplant herself to wherever she wanted to be in the world—such as Father Divine's kingdom in Harlem. Dunbar—his dark, eloquent face, his large volume of poems—permitted me to dream that I might someday write, and with something of the power with words my mother and her friends possessed.

When people at readings and writers' conferences ask me who my major influences were, they are sometimes a little disappointed when I don't immediately name the usual literary giants. True, I am indebted to those writers, white and black, whom I read during my formative years and still read for instruction

---

19. **Thackeray,** (thak′ ər ē), **Fielding, Dickens:** authors of the three picaresque novels previously alluded to.
20. **Frederick Douglass:** American black leader, journalist, and statesman (1817–95).
21. **shul** (sho͞ol): synagogue.

and pleasure. But they were preceded in my life by another set of giants whom I always acknowledge before all others: the group of women around the table long ago. They taught me my first lessons in the narrative art. They trained my ear. They set a standard of excellence. This is why the best of my work must be attributed to them; it stands as testi-mony[22] to the rich legacy[23] of language and culture they so freely passed on to me in the wordshop of the kitchen.

---

22. **testimony** (tes′ tə mō′ nē): evidence; indication.
23. **legacy** (leg′ ə sē): anything handed down from, or as from, an ancestor.

Thinking About the Essay

A PERSONAL RESPONSE

sharing impressions

1. What thoughts and feelings do you have about the writer's experience growing up? Respond in your journal.

constructing interpretations

2. How would you describe the women in this essay?
Think about
- what they talked about
- the role of language in their lives
- how they made their living
- in what way they might be considered "poets"

3. What lessons do you think Marshall learned from her early experience with language?
Think about
- her reading as an adolescent
- her discovery of black writers
- the "legacy" passed to her by the mothers

A CREATIVE RESPONSE

4. If Marshall had been male instead of female, how might her childhood experiences have been different?

A CRITICAL RESPONSE

5. What insights might be gained from this essay about the immigrant experience? Explain your response.

6. Based on what you now know about Paule Marshall, would you want to read her novels or short stories? Give reasons for your answer.

7. In your opinion, could a young child today have the same kind of profound experience with language that Marshall had? Use details from the essay and your own observations to support your answer.

Analyzing the Writer's Craft

APHORISM AND THEME

Review the quotations from Grace Paley (page 32) and Czeslaw Milosz (page 34). Why do you think Marshall includes them?

Building a Literary Vocabulary. An aphorism is a brief statement that expresses a general observation about life in a clever or pointed way. An aphorism is often a sentence that is still meaningful when taken out of its original context. The quotations Marshall includes from Paley and Milosz could be viewed as aphorisms in that they express general truths about language and life. Marshall uses the aphorisms to support the theme—the central idea or message—of her essay.

Application: Analyzing Aphorism and Theme. In a small group, discuss the meaning of the quotations. Then hold a class discussion to explore the overall theme of the essay and to make connections between the theme and the two quotations.

Connecting Reading and Writing

1. Review this quotation from the selection: "It was around that time . . . that I began harboring the dangerous thoughts of someday trying to write myself" (page 37). Write a **diary entry** that Marshall might have written during this time in her life.

Option: Compose a **letter** that Marshall might have written to let a pen pal know of her growing interest in writing.

2. Write a **dramatic skit** about a childhood experience in which your parents or other adults were involved. Make sure that the dialogue captures the speech patterns of the adults as you recall those patterns. Perform the skit for the class.

Option: Create a **cartoon strip** for your friends based on the same childhood experience. Again, focus on the speech patterns of the adults.

3. Read a short story by Marshall and compile a **list** of expressions found in the story that seem to come from her West Indian roots. Share the list with your classmates, explaining the context in which each expression is used.

Option: Put together the lists from various classmates to create a **booklet** entitled "Gifts from the Poets in the Kitchen."

The Way It Is   GLORIA ODEN

Mother to Son   LANGSTON HUGHES

Biographies of Oden and Hughes appear on pages 427 and 424.

Approaching the Poems

One of the most important influences on a child growing up is the role model provided by a parent. The following poems are portraits of two mothers. The speaker in "The Way It Is" is a daughter talking about her mother, while the speaker in "Mother to Son" is a mother addressing her son.

Building Vocabulary

These essential words are defined alongside "The Way It Is."

commercial (kə mʉr′ shəl): such **commercial** virtues (line 7)

inaudible (in ôd′ ə bəl): an **inaudible** allegiance (line 37)

dominant (däm′ ə nənt): these are the **dominant** measures of / my sense of beauty (lines 41 and 42)

Connecting Writing and Reading

Choose one of your parents or another adult in your life whom you consider a role model. Think about how much you resemble that person—for example, in physical appearance and sense of humor. Then consider ways in which you would like to resemble that person more. Copy the following chart in your journal and fill it out with information about you and the person you resemble.

Ways I resemble _____	Ways I'd like to resemble _____

As you read, look for ways in which the two mothers in these poems provide role models for their children.

The Way It Is

I have always known
that had I been blonde
blue-eyed
with skin fabled white as the unicorn's
5   with cheeks tinted and pearled
as May morning on the lips of a rose
such commercial[1] virtues
could never have led me to assume myself
anywhere near as beautiful as
10 my mother
whose willow fall of black hair
—now pirate silver—
I brushed as a child
(earning five cents)
15 when shaken free from the bun
as wrapped round and pinned
it billowed in a fine mist
from her proud shoulders
to her waist.

20 Brown as I am, she is browner.
Walnut
like the satin leaves of the oak
that fallen overwinter in woods
where night comes quickly
25 and whose wind-peaked piles
deepen the shadows of
such seizure.

Moreover, she is tall.
At her side standing
30 I feel I am still
the scarecrow child of
yesteryear:
owl-eyed
toothed, boned, and angled
35 opposite to her
soft southern presence—
an inaudible[2] allegiance
but sweetening her attendance
upon strangers and friends.

1. commercial (kə mʉr′ shəl):
designed to have wide
popular appeal.

2. inaudible (in ôd′ ə bəl):
that cannot be heard.

40   Dark hair, dark skin
these are the <u>dominant</u>[3] measures of
my sense of beauty
which explains possibly
why being a black girl
45   in a country of white strangers
I am so pleased with myself.

3. dominant (däm′ ə nənt):
having superior force or
influence; ruling.

Thinking About the Poem

A PERSONAL RESPONSE

sharing impressions

1. Does this poem remind you of any emotions you have experienced? Write about those emotions in your journal.

constructing interpretations

2. Why do you think the speaker is pleased with herself?
   Think about
   • the "commercial virtues" expressed in lines 1-6
   • the sense of beauty the speaker gets from her mother

3. In what ways does the speaker compare herself to her mother?
   Think about
   • the physical aspects of each that the speaker chooses to highlight
   • how she feels standing by her mother's side in lines 28-36

4. Evaluate the mother in this poem as a model for her daughter.

A CRITICAL RESPONSE

5. How do the similes in lines 4-6 and lines 21-23 add to the contrast between the two standards of beauty?
   Think about
   • simile as a comparison, usually containing *like* or *as*
   • the objects that skin color is compared to
   • your associations with those objects

6. What message do you suppose this poet wants to communicate to society about role models?

Mother to Son

Well, Son, I'll tell you
Life for me ain't been no crystal stair
It's had tacks in it,
And splinters,
5   And boards torn up,
And places with no carpets on the floor,
Bare.
But all the time
I'se been climbin' on
10   And reachin' landin's
And turnin' corners
And sometimes goin' on in the dark
Where there ain't been no light.
So, Boy, don't you turn back.
15   Don't you set down on the steps
'Cause you find it's kinder hard.
Don't you fall now—
For I'se still goin', Honey,
I'se still climbin'
20   And life for me ain't been
                     no crystal stair.

The Mother, 1952, CHARLES WHITE.
Hirshhorn Museum and Sculpture Garden, Smithsonian Institution, Washington, D.C.
Gift of Joseph H. Hirshhorn, 1966.

Thinking About the Poem

A PERSONAL RESPONSE

sharing impressions

1. How do you feel about the speaker's observations about life? Describe your feelings in your journal.

constructing interpretations

2. What do you think the speaker means by saying that her life has not been a "crystal stair"?

Think about
- the comparison of life to a stairway
- the characteristics of crystal

3. What can you learn about the speaker from the way she refers to the stairway?

Think about
- what the descriptions in lines 3–7 reveal about her life
- what the descriptions in lines 8–13 indicate about how she has dealt with life
- what her advice to her son reveals about her character

4. What kind of role model do you think the speaker is for her son?

A CRITICAL RESPONSE

5. Why do you think Hughes created this particular mother as the speaker in his poem?

Think about
- how your feelings about her affect your acceptance of her message
- how her dialect relates to her message

6. Examine the portraits of the mothers in "The Way It Is" and "Mother to Son." Identify qualities of these mothers that you would like to imitate in your own life.

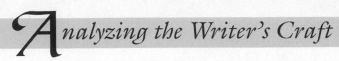

FIGURATIVE LANGUAGE: EXTENDED METAPHOR

What picture of the speaker's life can you imagine from the first seven lines of the poem?

Building a Literary Vocabulary. A metaphor makes a comparison between two things that have something in common. A metaphor either makes the comparison directly or implies it. An extended metaphor draws that comparison out and compares the two things in many ways. The extended metaphor in this poem reveals the obstacles and difficulties of the speaker's life. In the first seven lines, Langston Hughes includes realistic details—tacks, splinters, missing boards and carpets—that the speaker could have literally encountered while she was going up a flight of stairs to her apartment. In this way, Hughes builds on the idea of the speaker's struggle while at the same time realistically illustrating her life of poverty.

Application: Interpreting Extended Metaphor. In the remainder of the extended metaphor, the speaker explains how she has persevered through life and gives advice to her son. With a partner, make a chart similar to the one below and on it list an interpretation for each part of the extended metaphor. Two examples are provided for you. Then share the interpretations on your chart with another pair of students.

Part of the metaphor	Interpretation
1. "climbin' on"	keeping going, not giving up
2. "reachin' landin's"	reaching parts of life that have been restful, peaceful, or easy

Lineage   MARGARET WALKER

Women   ALICE WALKER

Biographies of Margaret Walker and Alice Walker appear on page 430.

Approaching the Poems

Some people are proud of their lineage—the people they descended from—because of rich or famous ancestors. In these two poems, the speakers are proud of their ancestors for more personal reasons. Both of the poets, Margaret Walker and Alice Walker, have published books of poetry, but they are more famous for writing fiction. Alice Walker's novel *The Color Purple* won the Pulitzer Prize and was made into a popular movie.

Connecting Writing and Reading

In your journal draw a family tree, filling in as many of your family members' names as you can. Use the chart below as a model.

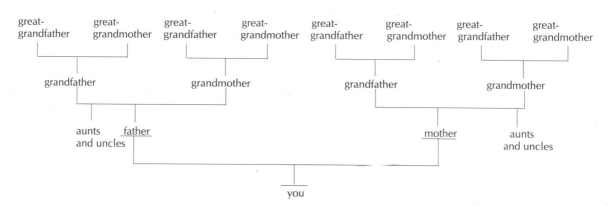

Once your family tree is complete, write a few sentences about the relative or ancestor you most admire. What similarities are there between you and this person? As you read, compare your feelings toward your relative or ancestor with the feelings expressed in the poems.

Lineage

My grandmothers were strong.
They followed plows and bent to toil.
They moved through fields sowing seed.
They touched earth and grain grew.
5   They were full of sturdiness and singing.
My grandmothers were strong.

My grandmothers are full of memories
Smelling of soap and onions and wet clay
With veins rolling roughly over quick hands
10   They have many clean words to say.
My grandmothers were strong.
Why am I not as they?

Thinking About the Poem

A PERSONAL RESPONSE

sharing impressions

1. What feelings or thoughts about your ancestors does the poem awaken in you? Write about these in your journal.

constructing interpretations

2. What effect does the last line have on your interpretation of the poem?

3. What do you think the speaker in the poem means by the word *strong?*
  Think about
  • the activities of the grandmothers
  • the outstanding qualities of the grandmothers

4. Why do you think the speaker's grandmothers were so strong?

5. How do the speaker's feelings about her ancestors compare with your feelings about the relative or ancestor you most admire?

A CREATIVE RESPONSE

6. How might the speaker feel if she knew nothing about her lineage?

7. Find several examples of alliteration and repetition in the poem and speculate about why Margaret Walker chose to use these techniques.

Think about
- alliteration as the repetition of initial consonant sounds
- the ideas emphasized by the repeated initial sounds, words, and lines
- the effect of the alliterative phrases and repetitions

Negress, 1946, ELIZABETH CATLETT.

Women

They were women then
My mama's generation
Husky of voice—Stout of
Step
5 With fists as well as
Hands
How they battered down
Doors
And ironed
10 Starched white
Shirts
How they led
Armies
Headragged Generals

15 Across mined
Fields
Booby-trapped
Ditches
To discover books
20 Desks
A place for us
How they knew what we
Must know
Without knowing a page
25 Of it
Themselves.

Thinking About the Poem

A PERSONAL RESPONSE

sharing impressions

1. Write a few words in your journal that tell how you picture the women described in the poem.

constructing interpretations

2. What do you think the speaker admires most about his or her mother's generation?

3. Why do you think the mothers are described as generals crossing "mined fields" and "booby-trapped ditches"?

Think about
- what the mothers were fighting for
- what obstacles they might have had to overcome

A CREATIVE RESPONSE

4. If this poem were about fathers instead of mothers, what kinds of battles do you think would be described?

A CRITICAL RESPONSE

5. Compare "Lineage" and "Women" as tributes to past generations of women.
Think about
- what the women described in each poem have in common
- how the speaker in each poem views the differences between his or her own generation and a past generation

Connecting Reading and Writing

1. Imagine what one of the ancestors in "Lineage" or one of the mothers in "Women" would say to the speaker in the poem. Write her reply as a **poem** directed to the speaker.

Option: Write the ancestor's or the mother's reply as a **letter** to the speaker.

2. Choose the ancestor or relative whom you described in your journal or a historical character whom you wish were an ancestor. Create a **storyboard** for a short documentary film showing scenes that reveal the person's admirable qualities.

Option: Write a **character sketch** for a children's magazine showing that person as someone to imitate.

3. Research your lineage by interviewing family members. Take notes for an **oral history** to be written about your family.

Option: Compare yourself to your ancestors in an **autobiographical sketch** to be given to your future children.

4. Imagine that you are an editor who must cut one of the four poems: "The Way It Is," "Mother to Son," "Lineage," or "Women." Make a chart listing pluses and minuses for each poem and then write your **recommendation** of which poem to cut.

Option: Write a **memo** to your boss explaining which poem you would cut and why.

Everyday Use

ALICE WALKER

A biography of Walker appears on page 430.

Approaching the Story

Alice Walker belongs to a generation of writers who benefited from the civil rights movement of the 1960's and the black pride movement of the 1970's. At the time that "Everyday Use" is set, many African Americans were not only discovering their African roots but also gaining a new appreciation for the heritage of the black experience in this country. As this story begins, the narrator waits with her daughter Maggie for her elder daughter, Dee, to return to the family farm in Georgia after a long absence.

Building Vocabulary

These essential words are footnoted within the story.

sidle (sīd' 'l): Have you ever seen a lame animal . . . **sidle** up to someone? (pages 52–53)

furtive (fur' tiv): **Furtive** boys in pink shirts hanging about on washday after school. (page 53)

Connecting Writing and Reading

What aspects of your family's heritage are especially important to you? In your journal, copy a chart similar to the one below. For each of the categories shown, fill in one or more examples relating to your heritage. For instance, under the category of language, you might write expressions that you have heard your parents and grandparents say. As you read, compare what you value in your heritage with what the characters in the story value.

Heritage

Family treasures	Traditional Foods
Holidays	Language

Everyday Use

I WILL WAIT for her in the yard that Maggie and I made so clean and wavy yesterday afternoon. A yard like this is more comfortable than most people know. It is not just a yard. It is like an extended living room. When the hard clay is swept clean as a floor and the fine sand around the edges lined with tiny, irregular grooves, anyone can come and sit and look up into the elm tree and wait for the breezes that never come inside the house.

Maggie will be nervous until after her sister goes. She will stand hopelessly in corners, homely and ashamed of the burn scars down her arms and legs, eyeing her sister with a mixture of envy and awe. She thinks her sister has held life always in the palm of one hand, that "no" is a word the world never learned to say to her.

You've no doubt seen those TV shows where the child who has "made it" is confronted, as a surprise, by her own mother and father, tottering in weakly from backstage. (A pleasant surprise, of course. What would they do if parent and child came on the show only to curse out and insult each other?) On TV, mother and child embrace and smile into each other's faces. Sometimes the mother and father weep, the child wraps them in her arms and leans across the table to tell how she would not have made it without their help. I have seen these programs.

Sometimes I dream a dream in which Dee and I are suddenly brought together on a TV program of this sort. Out of a dark and soft-seated limousine I am ushered into a bright room filled with many people. There I meet a smiling, gray, sporty man like Johnny Carson, who shakes my hand and tells me what a fine girl I have. Then we are on the stage and Dee is embracing me with tears in her eyes. She pins on my dress a large orchid, even though she had told me once that she thinks orchids are tacky flowers.

In real life I am a large, big-boned woman with rough, man-working hands. In the winter I wear flannel nightgowns to bed and overalls during the day. I can kill and clean a hog as mercilessly as a man. My fat keeps me hot in zero weather. I can work outside all day, breaking ice to get water for washing; I can eat pork liver cooked over the open fire minutes after it comes steaming from the hog. One winter I knocked a bull calf straight in the brain between the eyes with a sledge hammer and had the meat hung up to chill before nightfall. But of course all this does not show on television. I am the way my daughter would want me to be: a hundred pounds lighter, my skin like an uncooked barley pancake. My hair glistens in the hot bright lights. Johnny Carson has much to do to keep up with my quick and witty tongue.

But that is a mistake. I know even before I wake up. Who ever knew a Johnson with a quick tongue? Who can even imagine me looking a strange white man in the eye? It seems to me I have talked to them always with one foot raised in flight, with my head turned in whichever way is farthest from them. Dee, though. She would always look anyone in the eye. Hesitation was no part of her nature.

"How do I look, Mama?" Maggie says, showing just enough of her thin body enveloped in pink skirt and red blouse for me to know she's there, almost hidden by the door.

"Come out into the yard," I say.

Have you ever seen a lame animal, perhaps a dog run over by some careless person rich enough to own a car, <u>sidle</u>[1] up to someone who is ignorant enough to be kind to him? That is the way my Maggie walks. She has been like this, chin on chest, eyes on ground, feet in shuffle, ever since the fire that burned the other house to the ground.

Dee is lighter than Maggie, with nicer hair and a fuller figure. She's a woman now, though sometimes I forget. How long ago was it that the other house burned? Ten, twelve years? Sometimes I can still hear the flames and feel Maggie's arms sticking to me, her hair smoking and her dress falling off her in little black papery flakes. Her eyes seemed stretched open, blazed open by the flames reflected in them. And Dee. I see her standing off under the sweet gum tree she used to dig gum out of; a look of concentration on her face as she watched the last dingy gray board of the house fall in toward the red-hot brick chimney. Why don't you do a dance around the ashes? I'd wanted to ask her. She had hated the house that much.

I used to think she hated Maggie, too. But that was before we raised the money, the church and me, to send her to Augusta[2] to school. She used to read to us without pity; forcing words, lies, other folks' habits, whole lives upon us two, sitting trapped and ignorant underneath her voice. She washed us in a river of make-believe, burned us with a lot of knowledge we didn't necessarily need to know. Pressed us to her with the serious way she read, to shove us away at just the moment, like dimwits, we seemed about to understand.

Dee wanted nice things. A yellow organdy dress to wear to her graduation from high school; black pumps to match a green suit she'd made from an old suit somebody gave me. She was determined to stare down any disaster in her efforts. Her eyelids would not flicker for minutes at a time. Often I fought off the temptation to shake her. At sixteen she had a style of her own, and knew what style was.

I never had an education myself. After second grade the school was closed down. Don't ask me why; in 1927 blacks asked fewer questions than they do now. Sometimes Maggie reads to me. She stumbles along good-naturedly but can't see well. She knows she is not bright. Like good looks and money, quickness passed her by. She will marry John Thomas (who has mossy teeth in an earnest face), and then I'll be free to sit here and I guess just sing church songs to myself. Although I never was a good singer. Never could carry a tune. I was always better at a man's job. I used to love to milk till I was hooked in the side in '49. Cows are soothing and slow and don't bother you, unless you try to milk them the wrong way.

I have deliberately turned my back on the house. It is three rooms, just like the one that burned, except the roof is tin; they don't make shingle roofs any more. There are no real windows, just some holes cut in the sides, like the portholes in a ship, but not round and not square, with rawhide holding the shutters up on the outside. This house is in a pasture, too, like the other one. No doubt when Dee sees it, she will want to tear it down. She wrote me once that no matter where we "choose" to live, she will manage to come see us. But she will never bring her friends. Maggie and I thought about this and Maggie asked me, "Mama, when did Dee ever *have* any friends?"

She had a few. <u>Furtive</u>[3] boys in pink shirts hanging about on washday after school. Nervous girls who never laughed. Impressed with her, they worshiped the well-turned phrase, the cute shape, the scalding humor that erupted like bubbles in lye. She read to them.

When she was courting Jimmy T, she didn't have much time to pay to us, but turned all

---

1. sidle (sīd′ ′l): move sideways, especially in a way that does not draw attention.

2. Augusta: a city in Georgia.

3. furtive (fur′ tiv): stealthy, sneaky.

her faultfinding power on him. He *flew* to marry a cheap city girl from a family of ignorant, flashy people. She hardly had time to recompose herself.

When she comes I will meet—but there they are!

Maggie attempts to make a dash for the house, in her shuffling way, but I stay her with my hand. "Come back here," I say. And she stops and tries to dig a well in the sand with her toe.

It is hard to see them clearly through the strong sun. But even the first glimpse of leg out of the car tells me it is Dee. Her feet were always neat-looking, as if God himself had shaped them with a certain style. From the other side of the car comes a short, stocky man. Hair is all over his head a foot long and hanging from his chin like a kinky mule tail. I hear Maggie suck in her breath. "Uhnnnh," is what it sounds like. Like when you see the wriggling end of a snake just in front of your foot on the road. "Uhnnnh."

Dee next. A dress down to the ground, in this hot weather. A dress so loud it hurts my eyes. There are yellows and oranges enough to throw back the light of the sun. I feel my whole face warming from the heat waves it throws out. Earrings gold, too, and hanging down to her shoulders. Bracelets dangling and making noises when she moves her arm up to shake the folds of the dress out of her armpits. The dress is loose and flows, and as she walks closer, I like it. I hear Maggie go "Uhnnnh" again. It is her sister's hair. It stands straight up like the wool on a sheep. It is black as night and around the edges are two long pigtails that rope about like small lizards disappearing behind her ears.

"Wa-su-zo-Tean-o!" she says, coming on in that gliding way the dress makes her move. The short, stocky fellow with the hair to his navel is all grinning and he follows up with "Asalamalakim,[4] my mother and sister!" He moves to hug Maggie but she falls back, right up against the back of my chair. I feel her trembling there, and when I look up, I see the perspiration falling off her chin.

"Don't get up," says Dee. Since I am stout, it takes something of a push. You can see me trying to move a second or two before I make it. She turns, showing white heels through her sandals, and goes back to the car. Out she peeks next with a Polaroid. She stoops down quickly and lines up picture after picture of me sitting there in front of the house with Maggie cowering behind me. She never takes a shot without making sure the house is included. When a cow comes nibbling around the edge of the yard, she snaps it and me and Maggie *and* the house. Then she puts the Polaroid in the back seat of the car and comes up and kisses me on the forehead.

Meanwhile Asalamalakim is going through motions with Maggie's hand. Maggie's hand is as limp as a fish, and probably as cold, despite the sweat, and she keeps trying to pull it back. It looks like Asalamalakim wants to shake hands but wants to do it fancy. Or maybe he don't know how people shake hands. Anyhow, he soon gives up on Maggie.

"Well," I say. "Dee."

"No, Mama," she says. "Not 'Dee,'" Wangero Leewanika Kemanjo!"[5]

"What happened to 'Dee'?" I wanted to know.

"She's dead," Wangero said. "I couldn't bear it any longer, being named after the people who oppress me."

"You know as well as me you was named after your aunt Dicie," I said. Dicie is my sister. She named Dee. We called her "Big Dee" after Dee was born.

---

4. **Wa-su-zo-Tean-o . . . Asalamalakim** (wä sōō zō tēn′ ō, ä sə läm′ ä lī′ k∞m′): African greetings. The second, an Arabic greeting used among Muslims, means "Peace to you."

5. **Wangero Leewanika Kemanjo** (wän gᴜr′ ō lē wä′ nē kə ke män′ jō).

"But who was *she* named after?" asked Wangero.

"I guess after Grandma Dee," I said.

"And who was she named for?" asked Wangero.

"Her mother," I said, and saw Wangero was getting tired. "That's about as far back as I can trace it," I said. Though, in fact, I probably could have carried it back beyond the Civil War through the branches.

"Well," said Asalamalakim, "there you are."

"Uhnnnh," I heard Maggie say.

"There I was not," I said, "before 'Dicie' cropped up in our family, so why should I try to trace it that far back?"

He just stood there grinning, looking down on me like somebody inspecting a Model A car. Every once in a while he and Wangero sent eye signals over my head.

"How do you pronounce this name?" I asked.

"You don't have to call me by it if you don't want to," said Wangero.

"Why shouldn't I?" I asked. "If that's what you want us to call you, we'll call you."

"I know it might sound awkward at first," said Wangero.

"I'll get used to it," I said. "Ream it out again."

Well, soon we got the name out of the way. Asalamalakim had a name twice as long and three times as hard. After I tripped over it two or three times, he told me to just call him Hakim-a-barber.[6] I wanted to ask him was he a barber, but I really didn't think he was, so I didn't ask.

"You must belong to those beef-cattle peoples down the road," I said. They said "Asalamalakim" when they met you, too, but they didn't shake hands. Always too busy: feeding the cattle, fixing the fences, putting up salt lick shelters, throwing down hay. When the white folks poisoned some of the herd, the men stayed up all night with rifles in their hands. I walked a mile and a half just to see the sight.

Hakim-a-barber said, "I accept some of their doctrines, but farming and raising cattle is not my style." (They didn't tell me, and I didn't ask, whether Wangero (Dee) had really gone and married him.)

We sat down to eat, and right away he said he didn't eat collards and pork was unclean. Wangero, though, went on through the chitlins and corn bread, the greens, and everything else. She talked a blue streak over the sweet potatoes. Everything delighted her. Even the fact that we still used the benches her daddy made for the table when we couldn't afford to buy chairs.

"Oh, Mama!" she cried. Then turned to Hakim-a-barber. "I never knew how lovely these benches are. You can feel the rump prints," she said, running her hands underneath her and along the bench. Then she gave a sigh, and her hand closed over Grandma Dee's butter dish. "That's it!" she said. "I knew there was something I wanted to ask you if I could have." She jumped up from the table and went over in the corner where the churn stood, the milk in it clabber by now. She looked at the churn and looked at it.

"This churn top is what I need," she said. "Didn't Uncle Buddy whittle it out of a tree you all used to have?"

"Yes," I said.

"Uh huh," she said happily. "And I want the dasher, too."

"Uncle Buddy whittle that, too?" asked the barber.

Dee (Wangero) looked up at me.

"Aunt Dee's first husband whittled the dash," said Maggie so low you almost couldn't hear her. "His name was Henry, but they called him Stash."

"Maggie's brain is like an elephant's," Wangero said, laughing. "I can use the churn

---

6. **Hakim-a-barber** (hä kēm ä bär′ bər).

top as a centerpiece for the alcove table," she said, sliding a plate over the churn, "and I'll think of something artistic to do with the dasher."

When she finished wrapping the dasher, the handle stuck out. I took it for a moment in my hands. You didn't even have to look close to see where hands pushing the dasher up and down to make butter had left a kind of sink in the wood. In fact, there were a lot of small sinks; you could see where thumbs and fingers had sunk into the wood. It was beautiful light yellow wood, from a tree that grew in the yard where Big Dee and Stash lived.

After dinner Dee (Wangero) went to the trunk at the foot of my bed and started rifling through it. Maggie hung back in the kitchen over the dishpan. Out came Wangero with two quilts. They had been pieced by Grandma Dee, and then Big Dee and me had hung them on the quilt frames on the front porch and quilted them. One was in the Lone Star pattern. The other was Walk Around the Mountain. In both of them were scraps of dresses Grandma Dee had worn fifty and more years ago. Bits and pieces of Grandpa Jarrell's paisley shirts. And one teeny faded blue piece, about the size of a penny matchbox, that was from Great Grandpa Ezra's uniform that he wore in the Civil War.

"Mama," Wangero said, sweet as a bird. "Can I have these old quilts?"

I heard something fall in the kitchen, and a minute later the kitchen door slammed.

"Why don't you take one or two of the others?" I asked. "These old things was just done by me and Big Dee from some tops your grandma pieced before she died."

"No," said Wangero, "I don't want those. They are stitched around the borders by machine."

"That'll make them last better," I said.

"That's not the point," said Wangero. "These are all pieces of dresses Grandma used to wear. She did all this stitching by hand.

Imagine!" She held the quilts securely in her arms, stroking them.

"Some of the pieces, like those lavender ones, come from old clothes her mother handed down to her," I said, moving up to touch the quilts. Dee (Wangero) moved back just enough so that I couldn't reach the quilts. They already belonged to her.

"Imagine!" she breathed again, clutching them closely to her bosom.

"The truth is," I said, "I promised to give them quilts to Maggie, for when she marries John Thomas."

She gasped like a bee had stung her.

"Maggie can't appreciate these quilts!" she said. "She'd probably be backward enough to put them to everyday use."

"I reckon she would," I said. "God knows I been saving 'em long enough with nobody using 'em. I hope she will!" I didn't want to bring up how I had offered Dee (Wangero) a quilt when she went away to college. Then she had told me they were old-fashioned, out of style.

"But they're *priceless*!" she was saying now, furiously; for she has a temper. "Maggie would put them on the bed and in five years they'd be in rags. Less than that!"

"She can always make some more," I said. "Maggie knows how to quilt."

Dee (Wangero) looked at me with hatred. "You just will not understand. The point is these quilts, *these* quilts!"

"Well," I said, stumped. "What would you do with them?"

"Hang them," she said. As if that was the only thing you *could* do with quilts.

Maggie by now was standing in the door. I could almost hear the sound her feet made as they scraped over each other.

"She can have them, Mama," she said, like somebody used to never winning anything, or having anything reserved for her. "I can 'member Grandma Dee without the quilts."

I looked at her hard. She had filled her bot-

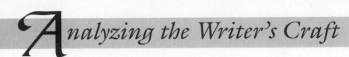

FOIL

Think about the contrast between Dee and her mother and sister.

Building a Literary Vocabulary. A foil is a character who provides a striking contrast to another character. A writer sometimes uses a foil to emphasize certain traits possessed by a character or simply to set off or enhance various characters through contrast. In "Everyday Use" Dee is a foil for both her mother and her sister. For example, as a child Dee hated the house in which they lived and watched it burn with "concentration." On the other hand, her mother values her home, no matter how humble it is. Maggie was scarred physically and emotionally by events in the house but does not hate either the old house or the new one.

Application: Analyzing Foil Characters. Working with a partner, go back through the story and find specific ways in which Dee and Maggie are different from each other. Then fill in a chart similar to the one below with details describing physical traits, personality, values, education, and lifestyle. After you have completed the chart, discuss what Walker achieves by using the sisters as foils for each other in this story about heritage.

	Dee	Maggie
Physical traits		
Personality		
Values		
Education		
Lifestyle		

Connecting Reading and Writing

1. Imagine that the narrator and Dee are, indeed, reunited on television after a long separation. Describe the scene in a **review** for a television guide advertising the show.

Option: Write the **dialogue** between mother and daughter as they are reunited on television.

2. Research quilts and quilting in America. Then write **informational footnotes** for terms in the story such as "pieced," "quilt frame," "tops," and "stitching by hand" as well as for the quilt patterns mentioned.

Options: Mount several photos or drawings of quilt patterns, including those mentioned in the story. Write **captions** explaining the names of the patterns and something about their history or technique for a brochure distributed at a community craft fair.

3. If you were going to direct a film based on this short story, whom would you choose to play the narrator, Maggie, Dee, and Hakim-a-barber? Write a **memo** to the producer of the film explaining your choices.

Option: Indicate your choices and the reasons for them in a **press release** for movie reviewers.

4. Provide information about what happens to Dee, Maggie, and the narrator in a **booklet** prepared for the Johnson family reunion.

Option: Write a **sequel** for the story to share with a creative writing club. Set the story at the family reunion.

INSIGHT

from Generations: A Memoir

Lucille Clifton

Things don't fall apart. Things hold. Lines connect in thin ways that last and last and lives become generations made out of pictures and words just kept. "We come out of it [slavery] better than they [enslavers] did, Lue," my Daddy said, and I watch my six children and know we did. They walk with confidence through the world, free sons and daughters of free folk, for my Mama told me that slavery was a temporary thing, mostly we was free and she was right. And she smiled when she said it and Daddy smiled too and saw that my sons are as strong as my daughters and it had been made right.

And I could tell you about things we been through, some awful ones, some wonderful, but I know that the things that make us are more than that, our lives are more than the days in them, our lives are our line and we go on.

My Mother Pieced Quilts

TERESA PALOMO ACOSTA

My Father's Song   SIMON ORTIZ

Biographies of Acosta and Ortiz appear on pages 418 and 428.

Approaching the Poems

In the poems that follow, Teresa Palomo Acosta and Simon Ortiz capture meaningful moments from childhood. Acosta draws upon her Mexican-American heritage to recall her mother's designing and sewing of quilts and the feelings she experienced while observing her mother. Ortiz, a Native American writer, remembers a tender moment with his father when he was a child.

Connecting Writing and Reading

In your journal, copy and complete the following statements:

- My most vivid memory of a parent or other adult from my childhood is _____.

- At the time, I remember feeling _____ about the experience.

- Now I feel _____ about the experience.

As you read the poems, compare your memory and your feelings about it with the memory and feelings portrayed in each poem.

My Mother Pieced Quilts

they were just meant as covers
in winters
as weapons
against pounding january winds

5 but it was just that every morning I awoke to these
october ripened canvases
passed my hand across their cloth faces
and began to wonder how you pieced
all these together
10 these strips of gentle communion cotton and flannel
nightgowns
wedding organdies
dime store velvets

how you shaped patterns square and oblong and round
positioned
15 balanced
then cemented them
with your thread
a steel needle
a thimble

20 how the thread darted in and out
galloping along the frayed edges, tucking them in
as you did us at night
oh how you stretched and turned and re-arranged
your michigan spring faded curtain pieces
25 my father's santa fe work shirt[1]
the summer denims, the tweeds of fall

in the evening you sat at your canvas
—our cracked linoleum floor the drawing board
me lounging on your arm
30 and you staking out the plan:
whether to put the lilac purple of easter against the red
plaid of winter-going-
into-spring
whether to mix a yellow with blue and white and paint the
corpus christi[2] noon when my father held your hand

1. Santa Fe work shirt: work clothes named after the Santa Fe Railroad.

2. Corpus Christi: a city and port in southern Texas.

35   whether to shape a five-point star from the
somber black silk you wore to grandmother's funeral

you were the river current
carrying the roaring notes
forming them into pictures of a little boy reclining
40   a swallow flying
you were the caravan master at the reins
driving your threaded needle artillery across the mosaic
    cloth bridges
delivering yourself in separate testimonies.

oh mother you plunged me sobbing and laughing
45   into our past
into the river crossing at five
into the spinach fields
into the plainview[3] cotton rows
into tuberculosis wards
50   into braids and muslin dresses
sewn hard and taut to withstand the thrashings of
    twenty-five years

stretched out they lay
armed/ready/shouting/celebrating

knotted with love
55   the quilts sing on

3. Plainview: a Texas cotton town.

My Father's Song

Wanting to say things,
I miss my father tonight.
His voice, the slight catch,
the depth from his thin chest,
5   the tremble of emotion
in something he has just said
to his son, his song:

We planted corn one spring at Acu—
we planted several times
10   but this one particular time
I remember the soft damp sand
in my hand.

father had stopped at one point
to show me an overturned furrow;
15   the plowshare had unearthed
the burrow nest of a mouse
in the soft moist sand.

Very gently, he scooped tiny pink animals
into the palm of his hand
20   and told me to touch them.
We took them to the edge
of the field and put them in the shade
of a sand moist clod.

I remember the very softness
25   of cool and warm sand and tiny alive mice
and my father saying things.

Thinking About the Poems

A PERSONAL RESPONSE

sharing impressions

1. What feelings and memories did these poems evoke in you? Briefly describe your responses in your journal.

constructing interpretations

2. Why do you think the memory described in each poem is so important to the speaker?

Think about
- the physical sensations described in "My Father's Song" in lines 11–12, 17, 21–26
- why the father might have wanted his son to see and touch the mice
- how the memory captures aspects of his father that the speaker now misses
- the practical use of the quilts described in lines 1–4 of "My Mother Pieced Quilts"
- how the quilts relate to the past in lines 7–12, 21–26, 31–36, 44–51
- the artistry of the quilts in lines 6, 13–19, 27–43

3. What do you think the references to songs or singing mean in the poems?

Think about
- why the memory of finding the mice is described as a song
- what the speaker means by saying the quilts "sing on"

A CREATIVE RESPONSE

4. If these poems had included some unhappy memories of the speakers' childhoods, how might your responses to the poems differ?

A CRITICAL RESPONSE

5. Explain whether the poets are successful in making their memories vivid and intimate for you as a reader.

Think about
- the things quilts and quilting are compared to in "My Mother Pieced Quilts"
- the senses appealed to in each of the poems
- the speakers' emotions as revealed in the poems
- your own emotional responses to the poems

6. In colonial America, quilting was born of necessity: women pieced together otherwise unusable fabric scraps to create warm bedcoverings. Today, quilting is considered an important form of artistic expression. What was the most important reason that the speaker's mother created quilts—necessity, desire for expression, or some other reason? Cite lines from the poem to support your opinion.

7. In Native American cultures, parents are revered for the passing on of tradition to their children. Critic Brian Swann claims that no other Native American poet surpasses Simon Ortiz in "parent-reverence." Using specific references to the poem, explain how this judgment might apply to "My Father's Song."

Analyzing the Writer's Craft

SOUND DEVICES: ALLITERATION, CONSONANCE, ASSONANCE

Think about the ways in which both Acosta and Ortiz give unity and a musical quality to their free verse poems.

Building a Literary Vocabulary. Poets use the sound devices of alliteration, consonance, and assonance to impart a musical quality to their poems, to create mood, to reinforce meaning, to emphasize words, and to unify lines or stanzas. Alliteration is the repetition of consonant sounds at the beginnings of words. In the first stanza of "My Mother Pieced Quilts," the alliteration of *w* sounds emphasizes the importance of quilts "in winters / as weapons / against pounding january winds." Consonance is the repetition of consonant sounds within and at the ends of words. The mother's act of sewing in lines 13–18 is given added firmness and purpose by the consonance of the hard *d* sounds: *shaped, round, positioned, balanced, cemented, thread,* and *needle.* Assonance is the repe-

tition of a vowel sound within words. In "My Father's Song," the assonance of the short *o* sounds lends a gentleness to the last two lines of the first stanza: "in something he has just said / to his son, his song."

Application: Identifying Sound Devices. Working with a partner, create a chart similar to the one below. Go back through the poems and look for two examples each of alliteration, consonance, and assonance from both poems. Then briefly list your examples in the appropriate columns of the chart, including line numbers. Two examples are given for you. After your chart is completed, decide which effect or effects the sound devices in each poem have: add to the musical quality of the poems, create mood, reinforce meaning, emphasize words, or unify stanzas. Share your conclusions with the class.

Poem	Alliteration	Consonance	Assonance
"My Mother Pieced Quilts"	lines 1–4 were, winters weapons, winds	lines 13–18 repetition of *d* sound	

Sweet Potato Pie

EUGENIA COLLIER

A biography of Collier appears on page 420.

Approaching the Story

The narrator of this story is the successful son of parents who were Southern share-croppers. A sharecropper is a tenant farmer who works someone else's land in exchange for a portion of the earnings from the crop. The story consists of two flashbacks, in which the narrator recalls scenes from events that happened before the beginning of the story.

FROM UP HERE on the fourteenth floor, my brother Charley looks like an insect scurrying among other insects. A deep feeling of love surges through me. Despite the distance, he seems to feel it, for he turns and scans the upper windows, but failing to find me, continues on his way. I watch him moving quickly— gingerly, it seems to me—down Fifth Avenue and around the corner to his shabby taxicab. In a moment he will be heading back uptown.

I turn from the window and flop down on the bed, shoes and all. Perhaps because of what happened this afternoon or maybe just because I see Charley so seldom, my thoughts hover over him like hummingbirds. The cheerful, impersonal tidiness of this room is a world away from Charley's walk-up flat in Harlem and a hundred worlds from the bare, noisy shanty where he and the rest of us spent what there was of childhood. I close my eyes, and side by side I see the Charley of my boyhood and the Charley of this afternoon, as clearly as if I were looking at a split TV screen. Another surge of love, seasoned with gratitude, wells up in me.

As far as I know, Charley never had any childhood at all. The oldest children of share-croppers never do. Mama and Pa were shadowy figures whose voices I heard vaguely in the morning when sleep was shallow and whom I glimpsed as they left for the field before I was fully awake or as they trudged wearily into the house at night when my lids were irresistibly heavy.

They came into sharp focus only on special occasions. One such occasion was the day when the crops were in and the sharecroppers were paid. In our cabin there was so much excitement in the air that even I, the "baby," responded to it. For weeks we had been running out of things that we could neither grow nor get on credit. On the evening of that day we waited anxiously for our parents' return. Then we would cluster around the rough wooden table—I on Lil's lap or clinging to Charley's neck, little Alberta nervously tugging her plait,[1] Jamie crouched at Mama's elbow, like a panther about to spring, and all

---

1. **plait** (plāt): a braid of hair.

seven of us silent for once, waiting. Pa would place the money on the table—gently, for it was made from the sweat of their bodies and from their children's tears. Mama would count it out in little piles, her dark face stern and, I think now, beautiful. Not with the hollow beauty of well-modeled features but with the strong radiance of one who has suffered and never yielded.

"This for store bill," she would mutter, making a little pile. "This for c'llection. This for piece o' gingham . . ." and so on, stretching the money as tight over our collective needs as Jamie's outgrown pants were stretched over my bottom. "Well, that's the crop." She would look up at Pa at last. "It'll do." Pa's face would relax, and a general grin flitted from child to child. We would survive, at least for the present.

The other time when my parents were solid entities[2] was at church. On Sundays we would don our threadbare Sunday-go-to-meeting clothes and tramp, along with neighbors similarly attired, to the Tabernacle Baptist Church, the frail edifice of bare boards held together by God knows what, which was all that my parents ever knew of security and future promise.

Being the youngest and therefore the most likely to err, I was plopped between my father and my mother on the long wooden bench. They sat huge and eternal like twin mountains at my sides. I remember my father's still, black profile silhouetted against the sunny window, looking back into dark recesses of time, into some dim antiquity, like an ancient ceremonial mask. My mother's face, usually sternly set, changed with the varying nuances of her emotion, its planes shifting, shaped by the soft highlights of the sanctuary, as she progressed from a subdued "amen" to a loud "Help me, Jesus" wrung from the depths of her gaunt frame.

My early memories of my parents are associated with special occasions. The contours of my everyday were shaped by Lil and Charley,

the oldest children, who rode herd on the rest of us while Pa and Mama toiled in fields not their own. Not until years later did I realize that Lil and Charley were little more than children themselves.

Lil had the loudest, screechiest voice in the county. When she yelled, "Boy, you better git yourself in here!" you *got* yourself in there. It was Lil who caught and bathed us, Lil who fed us and sent us to school, Lil who punished us when we needed punishing and comforted us when we needed comforting. If her voice was loud, so was her laughter. When she laughed, everybody laughed. And when Lil sang, everybody listened.

Charley was taller than anybody in the world, including, I was certain, God. From his shoulders, where I spent considerable time in the earliest years, the world had a different perspective. I looked down at tops of heads rather than at the undersides of chins. As I grew older, Charley became more father than brother. Those days return in fragments of splintered memory: Charley's slender, dark hands whittling a toy from a chunk of wood, his face thin and intense, brown as the loaves Lil baked when there was flour. Charley's quick fingers guiding a stick of charred kindling over a bit of scrap paper, making a wondrous picture take shape—Jamie's face or Alberta's rag doll or the spare figure of our bony brown dog. Charley's voice low and terrible in the dark, telling ghost stories so delightfully dreadful that later in the night the moan of the wind through the chinks in the wall sent us scurrying to the security of Charley's pallet, Charley's sleeping form.

Some memories are more than fragmentary. I can still feel the *whap* of the wet dishrag across my mouth. Somehow I developed a stutter, which Charley was determined to cure.

_____

2. **entities** (en' tə tēz): things or beings that have a real existence, as distinguished from a mere function.

Someone had told him that an effective cure was to slap the stutterer across the mouth with a sopping wet dishrag. Thereafter, whenever I began, "Let's g-g-g—," *whap!* from nowhere would come the ubiquitous[3] rag. Charley would always insist, "I don't want hurt you none, Buddy—" and *whap* again. I don't know when or why I stopped stuttering. But I stopped.

Already laid waste by poverty, we were easy prey for ignorance and superstition, which hunted us like hawks. We sought education feverishly—and, for most of us, futilely, for the sum total of our combined energies was required for mere brute survival. Inevitably each child had to leave school and bear his share of the eternal burden.

Eventually the family's hopes for learning fastened on me, the youngest. I remember—I *think* I remember, for I could not have been more than five—one frigid day Pa huddled on a rickety stool before the coal stove, took me on his knee and studied me gravely. I was a skinny little thing, they tell me, with large, solemn eyes.

"Well, boy," Pa said at last, "if you got to depend on your looks for what you get out'n this world, you just as well lay down right now." His hand was rough from the plow, but gentle as it touched my cheek. "Lucky for you, you got a *mind*. And that's something ain't everybody got. You go to school, boy, get yourself some learning. Make something out'n yourself. Ain't nothing you can't do if you got learning."

Charley was determined that I would break the chain of poverty, that I would "be somebody." As we worked our small vegetable garden in the sun or pulled a bucket of brackish water from the well, Charley would tell me, "You ain gon be no poor farmer, Buddy. You gon be a teacher or maybe a doctor or a lawyer. One thing, bad as you is, you ain gon be no preacher."

I loved school with a desperate passion, which became more intense when I began to realize what a monumental struggle it was for my parents and brothers and sisters to keep me there. The cramped, dingy classroom became a battleground where I was victorious. I stayed on top of my class. With glee I outread, outfigured, and outspelled the country boys who mocked my poverty, calling me "the boy with eyes in back of his head"—the "eyes" being the perpetual holes in my hand-me-down pants.

As the years passed, the economic strain was eased enough to make it possible for me to go on to high school. There were fewer mouths to feed, for one thing. Alberta went North to find work at sixteen; Jamie died at twelve.

I finished high school at the head of my class. For Mama and Pa and each of my brothers and sisters, my success was a personal triumph. One by one they came to me the week before commencement, bringing crumpled dollar bills and coins long hoarded, muttering, "Here, Buddy, put this on your gradiation clothes." My graduation suit was the first suit that was all my own.

On graduation night our cabin (less crowded now) was a frantic collage of frayed nerves. I thought Charley would drive me mad.

"Buddy, you ain pressed out them pants right. . . . Can't you git a better shine on them shoes? . . . Lord, you done messed up that tie!"

Overwhelmed by the combination of Charley's nerves and my own, I finally exploded. "Man, cut it out!" Abruptly he stopped tugging at my tie, and I was afraid I had hurt his feelings. "It's okay, Charley. Look, you're strangling me. The tie's okay."

Charley relaxed a little and gave a rather sheepish chuckle. "Sure, Buddy." He gave my

---

3. ubiquitous (yo͞o bik′ wə təs): present, or seeming to be present, everywhere at the same time.

Let's Walk Together (detail) 1953-1954, CHARLES WHITE.
Collection of Tom Pedi, New York. Courtesy of Heritage Gallery, Los Angeles.

shoulder a rough joggle. "But you gotta look good. You *somebody*."

My valedictory address[4] was the usual idealistic, sentimental nonsense. I have forgotten what I said that night, but the sight of Mama and Pa and the rest is like a lithograph burned on my memory; Lil, her round face made beautiful by her proud smile; Pa, his head held high, eyes loving and fierce; Mama radiant. Years later when her shriveled hands were finally still, my mind kept coming back to her as she was now. I believe this moment was the <u>apex</u>[5] of her entire life. All of them, even Alberta down from Baltimore—different now, but united with them in her pride. And Charley, on the end of the row, still somehow the protector of them all. Charley, looking as if he were in the presence of something sacred.

As I made my way through the carefully rehearsed speech, it was as if part of me were standing outside watching the whole thing—their proud, work-weary faces, myself wearing the suit that was their combined strength and love and hope: Lil with her lovely, low-pitched voice, Charley with the hands of an artist, Pa and Mama with God knows what potential lost with their sweat in the fields. I realized in that moment that I wasn't necessarily the smartest—only the youngest.

And the luckiest. The war came along, and I exchanged three years of my life (including a fair amount of my blood and a great deal of pain) for the GI Bill[6] and a college education. Strange how time can slip by like water flowing through your fingers. One by one the changes came—the old house empty at last, the rest of us scattered; for me, marriage, graduate school, kids, a professorship, and by now a thickening waistline and thinning hair. My mind spins off the years, and I am back to this afternoon and today's Charley—still long and lean, still gentle-eyed, still my greatest fan, and still determined to keep me on the ball.

I didn't tell Charley I would be at a profes-sional meeting in New York and would surely visit; he and Bea would have spent days in fixing up, and I would have had to be company. No, I would drop in on them, take them by surprise before they had a chance to stiffen up. I was eager to see them—it had been so long. Yesterday and this morning were taken up with meetings in the posh Fifth Avenue hotel—a place we could not have dreamed in our boyhood. Late this afternoon I shook loose and headed for Harlem, hoping that Charley still came home for a few hours before his evening run. Leaving the glare and glitter of downtown, I entered the subway that lurks like the dark, inscrutable *id*[7] beneath the surface of the city. When I emerged, I was in Harlem.

Whenever I come to Harlem I feel somehow as if I were coming home—to some mythic ancestral home. The problems are real, the people are real—yet there is some mysterious epic quality about Harlem, as if all black people began and ended there, as if each had left something of himself. As if in Harlem the very heart of Blackness pulsed its beautiful, tortured rhythms. Joining the throngs of people that saunter Lenox Avenue late afternoons, I headed for Charley's apartment. Along the way I savored the panorama of Harlem—women with shopping bags trudging wearily home; little kids flitting saucily through the crowd; groups of adolescent boys striding boldly along—some boisterous, some ominously silent; tables of merchandise spread on the

---

4. **valedictory** (val′ ə dik′ tər ē) **address:** a farewell speech, usually made by the top student in a graduating class.
5. **apex:** the highest point.
6. **GI Bill:** United States government program to help veterans. It includes education at government expense.
7. ***id:*** in psychoanalysis, the part of the mind associated with instinctual drives and primitive urges.

sidewalks with hawkers singing their siren songs of irresistible bargains; a blaring microphone sending forth waves of words to draw passersby into a restless bunch around a slender young man whose eyes have seen Truth; defeated men standing around on street corners or sitting on steps, heads down, hands idle; posters announcing Garvey Day;[8] "Buy Black" stamped on pavements; store windows bright with things African; stores still boarded up, a livid scar from last year's rioting. There was a terrible tension in the air; I thought of how quickly dry timber becomes a roaring fire from a single spark.

I mounted the steps of Charley's building—old and in need of paint, like all the rest—and pushed the button to his apartment. The graffiti on the dirty wall recorded the fantasies of past visitors. Some of it was even a dialogue of sorts. Someone had scrawled, "Call Lola" and a telephone number, followed by a catalog of Lola's friends. Someone else had written, "I called Lola and she is a Dog." Charley's buzzer rang. I pushed open the door and mounted the urine-scented stairs.

"Well, do Jesus—it's Buddy!" roared Charley as I arrived on the third floor. "Bea! Bea! Come here, girl, it's Buddy!" And somehow I was simultaneously shaking Charley's hand, getting clapped on the back, and being buried in the fervor of Bea's gigantic hug. They swept me from the hall into their dim apartment.

"Lord, Buddy, what you doing here? Whyn't you tell me you was coming to New York?" His face was so lit up with pleasure that in spite of the inroads of time, he still looked like the Charley of years gone by, excited over a new litter of kittens.

"The place look a mess! Whyn't you let us know?" put in Bea, suddenly distressed.

"Looks fine to me, girl. And so do you!"

And she did. Bea is a fine-looking woman, plump and firm still, with rich brown skin and thick black hair.

"Mary, Lucy, look, Uncle Buddy's here!" Two neat little girls came shyly from the TV. Uncle Buddy was something of a celebrity in this house.

I hugged them heartily, much to their discomfort. "Charley, where you getting all these pretty women?"

We all sat in the warm kitchen, where Bea was preparing dinner. It felt good there. Beautiful odors mingled in the air. Charley sprawled in a chair near mine, his long arms and legs akimbo. No longer shy, the tinier girl sat on my lap, while her sister darted here and there like a merry little water bug. Bea bustled about, managing to keep up with both the conversation and the cooking.

I told them about the conference I was attending, and, knowing it would give them pleasure, I mentioned that I had addressed the group that morning. Charley's eyes glistened.

"You hear that, Bea?" he whispered. "Buddy done spoke in front of all them professors!"

"Sure I hear," Bea answered briskly, stirring something that was making an aromatic steam. "I bet he weren't even scared. I bet them professors learnt something, too."

We all chuckled. "Well anyway," I said, "I hope they did."

We talked about a hundred different things after that—Bea's job in the school cafeteria, my Jess and the kids, our scattered family.

"Seem like we don't git together no more, not since Mama and Pa passed on," said Charley sadly. "I ain't even got a Christmas card from Alberta for three-four year now."

"Well, ain't no two a y'all in the same city. An' everybody scratchin' to make ends meet," Bea replied. "Ain't nobody got time to git together."

"Yeah, that's the way it goes, I guess," I said.

"But it sure is good to see you, Buddy. Say,

---

8. **Garvey Day:** a day commemorating black nationalist leader Marcus Garvey.

look, Lil told me bout the cash you sent the children last winter when Jake was out of work all that time. She sure 'preciated it."

"Lord, man, as close as you and Lil stuck to me when I was a kid, I owed her that and more. Say, Bea, did I ever tell you about the time—" and we swung into the usual reminiscences.

They insisted that I stay for dinner. Persuading me was no hard job: fish fried golden, ham hocks and collard greens, corn bread—if I'd *tried* to leave, my feet wouldn't have taken me. It was good to sit there in Charley's kitchen, my coat and tie flung over a chair, surrounded by soul food and love.

"Say, Buddy, a couple months back I picked up a kid from your school."

"No stuff."

"I axed him did he know you. He say he was in your class last year."

"Did you get his name?"

"No, I didn't ax him that. Man he told me you were the best teacher he had. He said you were one smart cat!"

"He told you that cause you're my brother."

"Your *brother*—I didn't tell him I was your brother. I said you was a old friend of mine."

I put my fork down and leaned over. "What you tell him *that* for?"

Charley explained patiently as he had explained things when I was a child and had missed an obvious truth. "I didn't want your students to know your brother wasn't nothing but a cab driver. You *somebody*."

"You're a nut," I said gently. "You should've told that kid the truth." I wanted to say, I'm proud of you, you've got more on the ball than most people I know, I wouldn't have been anything at all except for you. But he would have been embarrassed.

Bea brought in the dessert—homemade sweet potato pie! "Buddy, I must of knew you were coming! I just had a mind I wanted to make sweet potato pie."

There's nothing in this world I like better than Bea's sweet potato pie! "Lord, girl, how you expect me to eat all that?"

The slice she put before me was outrageously big—and moist and covered with a light, golden crust—I ate it all.

"Bea, I'm gonna have to eat and run," I said at last.

Charley guffawed. "Much as you et, I don't see how you gonna *walk*, let alone *run*." He went out to get his cab from the garage several blocks away.

Bea was washing the tiny girl's face. "Wait a minute, Buddy, I'm gon give you the rest of that pie to take with you."

"Great!" I'd eaten all I could hold, but my *spirit* was still hungry for sweet potato pie.

Bea got out some waxed paper and wrapped up the rest of the pie. "That'll do you for a snack tonight." She slipped it into a brown paper bag.

I gave her a long goodbye hug. "Bea, I love you for a lot of things. Your cooking is one of them!" We had a last comfortable laugh together. I kissed the little girls and went outside to wait for Charley, holding the bag of pie reverently.

In a minute Charley's ancient cab limped to the curb. I plopped into the seat next to him, and we headed downtown. Soon we were assailed by the garish lights of New York on a sultry spring night. We chatted as Charley skillfully managed the heavy traffic. I looked at his long hands on the wheel and wondered what they could have done with artists' brushes.

We stopped a bit down the street from my hotel. I invited him in, but he said he had to get on with his evening run. But as I opened the door to get out, he commanded in the old familiar voice, "Buddy, you wait!"

For a moment I thought my coat was torn or something. "What's wrong?"

"What's that you got there?"

I was bewildered. "That? You mean this bag? That's a piece of sweet potato pie Bea fixed for me."

"You ain't going through the lobby of no big hotel carrying no brown paper bag."

"Man, you *crazy!* Of course I'm going—Look, Bea fixed it for me—*That's my pie*—"

Charley's eyes were miserable. "Folks in that hotel don't go through the lobby carrying no brown paper bags. That's *country*. And you can't neither. You *somebody*, Buddy. You got to be *right*. Now gimme that bag."

"I want that pie, Charley. I've got nothing to prove to anybody—"

I couldn't believe it. But there was no point in arguing. Foolish as it seemed to me, it was important to him.

"You got to look *right*, Buddy. Can't nobody look dignified carrying a brown paper bag."

So finally, thinking how tasty it would have been and how seldom I got a chance to eat anything that good, I handed over my bag of sweet potato pie. If it was that important to him—

I tried not to show my irritation. "Okay, man—take care now." I slammed the door harder than I had intended, walked rapidly to the hotel, and entered the brilliant, crowded lobby.

"That Charley!" I thought. Walking slower now, I crossed the carpeted lobby toward the elevator, still thinking of my lost snack. I had to admit that of all the herd of people who jostled each other in the lobby, not one was carrying a brown paper bag. Or anything but expensive attaché cases or slick packages from exclusive shops. I suppose we all operate according to the symbols that are meaningful to us, and to Charley a brown paper bag symbolizes the humble life he thought I had left. I was *somebody*.

I don't know what made me glance back, but I did. And suddenly the tears of laughter, toil, and love of a lifetime burst around me like fireworks in a night sky.

For there, following a few steps behind, came Charley, proudly carrying a brown paper bag full of sweet potato pie.

Reviewing Concepts

PARENTS AND CHILDREN: TRANSMITTING CULTURAL VALUES

making connections

In the selections in this unit, the writers celebrate their heritage and communicate appreciation for their cultural values. Parents and parent figures serve as links to heritage and transmitters of values. For example, in the excerpt from *When Heaven and Earth Changed Places,* Bay Ly's father imparts to his daughter love of country and respect for ancestors: "Your job is to stay alive—to keep an eye on things and keep the village safe. . . . Most of all, it is to live in peace and tend the shrine of our ancestors." Bay Ly's relationship with her father is a channel through which the values of her heritage flow to her.

Think about the relationships between parents and children presented in the selections in this unit. Then create a chart similar to the one below. For each selection you have read, identify the parent or parent figure and the cultural values transmitted. A model for the excerpt from *When Heaven and Earth Changed Places* is given.

Title	Parent	Values
from *When Heaven and Earth Changed Places*	Bay Ly's father	survival, duty to others, love for country, respect for ancestors

describing connections

Review the information on your chart. Then think about your own cultural values. Write an **essay** comparing your values with those the writers chose to portray. Share your essay with your classmates.

J. L. Balldwin, Civil War soldier, date and photographer unknown. Chicago Historical Society.

Opposing Injustice

"One function of serious literature is to deal with the moral core of a given society."

RALPH ELLISON

Opposing Injustice

Writers sometimes serve as a nation's conscience. They examine the fabric of society, point out wrongs, and call for redress, and in the process they stir the mind and touch the heart.

In taking a stand against injustice, writers display a wide range of attitudes. Some writers seem concerned about injustice but remain emotionally detached; others are passionately committed to social reform. Even within a single work, the tone of opposition may vary greatly from beginning to end.

The writers represented in this unit use different strategies to oppose injustice. Some writers subtly hint at underlying wrongs while portraying real-life or fictional situations. In the excerpt from *Farewell to Manzanar,* for example, Jeanne Wakatsuki Houston recalls her experiences as a member of a Japanese-American family interned during World War II. In recalling these experiences, Houston sometimes alludes to the underlying injustice of the situation: the violation of human rights in consigning thousands of Japanese Americans to detention camps. In the short story "Blues Ain't No Mockin Bird," Toni Cade Bambara similarly provides clues about a social evil. The speech and conduct of some of the characters in her story suggest deep-rooted racist attitudes.

The writers in this unit who are associated with the Harlem Renaissance often used poetry as a vehicle to oppose injustice. The Harlem Renaissance, an awakening of creativity in African-American literature and the other arts that centered in Harlem shortly after World War I, included the poets Langston Hughes, Countee Cullen, Jean Toomer, and Arna Bontemps. In presenting African-American life truthfully, these poets suggest messages about the plight of their people.

Other writers represented in this unit address injustice directly. Julius Lester describes the atrocities of the slave trade in colonial America. Frederick Douglass tells about the vicious beatings inflicted on him in a futile attempt to break his spirit. Martin Luther

King, Jr., in defending civil disobedience as a tool for change, cites instances of racial intolerance. In her short story "The Censors," the Argentinian writer Luisa Valenzuela warns against the threat of government censorship in a high-tech society.

As you read each selection in this unit, ask yourself how the writer makes you feel about the situation presented. Think about the strength of spirit required to oppose injustice, about the profound changes in American society wrought by the writers of the past, and about the lingering injustices that must be addressed by writers today and in the future.

Literary Vocabulary

INTRODUCED IN THIS UNIT

Autobiography. An autobiography is the story of a person's life written by that person. Generally, an autobiographer uses the first-person point of view and combines objective description with the expression of personal feelings. In *Narrative of the Life,* for example, Frederick Douglass provides details about slavery in general and also expresses his feelings about his own physical and psychological ordeal.

Persuasion. Persuasion is a technique used by speakers and writers to convince an audience to adopt a particular opinion, perform an action, or both. Effective persuasion often appeals to both the emotions and the intellect of the listener or reader. For example, campaign speeches by political candidates and editorials in local and school newspapers often combine logical arguments and emotionally charged words and details.

Irony. Irony is a contrast between what is expected and what actually exists or happens. For example, in "From the Poets in the Kitchen," Paule Marshall underscores an irony when she points out that the major influence on her writing came not from the great writers she had read but from the cleaning women who had gathered in her mother's kitchen.

REVIEWED IN THIS UNIT

Figurative Language

Theme

from To Be a Slave

JULIUS LESTER

A biography of Lester appears on page 426.

*A*pproaching the Selection

The majority of black Africans arrived in America as slaves. In the following selection Julius Lester presents a brief history of the slave trade and then quotes at length from the autobiography of the grandson of a slave to give a gripping account of captured Africans shipped to America in chains.

*B*uilding Vocabulary

The following words are footnoted within the selection.

susceptible (sə sep′ tə bəl): They also proved to be very **susceptible** to the diseases of the colonists. (page 81)

inexhaustible (in′ eg zôs′ tə bəl): And finally, the supply was **inexhaustible.** (page 81)

align (ə līn′): One African chief would **align** with another chief. (page 82)

stupor (stoō′ pər): "I was knocked down . . . and when I recovered from the **stupor** that followed, I found myself tied fast." (page 82)

*C*onnecting Writing and Reading

What words and phrases come to mind when you think of the ideas of freedom and slavery? Create two cluster diagrams in which you brainstorm words and phrases that you associate with each concept. Then while you read this selection, think about what these concepts meant to the Africans brought to America as slaves.

THE AFRICAN SLAVE trade was already over a hundred years old when the Dutch ship landed twenty Africans at the Jamestown colony in 1619. Portugal had introduced Africans to Europe in the early sixteenth century. The slave trade soon extended into England and Spain and to their colonies in the New World of the Americas when it was discovered. Africans accompanied Spanish explorers on their journeys to the New World. There were thirty blacks with Balboa when he discovered the Pacific Ocean; blacks accompanied Pizarro to Peru, Coronado to New Mexico, Narvaez and Cabeza de Vaca in their explorations of what is now Arizona and New Mexico. Blacks also accompanied the French explorers to Canada and the Mississippi River valley. Thus blacks were a part of the New World long before the *Mayflower*, even before the settling of Jamestown in 1609.

Yet even with the existence of the slave trade and the early presence of blacks in what was to become the United States, slavery was not introduced immediately. The English colonists were in great need of labor to help settle their colonies. At first they tried to use the Indians. This proved impossible. The Indians came from a society and a way of life that was relatively uncomplicated. This background did not prepare them for the disciplined and complex way of life and work necessary for the plantation system. They also proved to be very susceptible[1] to the diseases of the colonists. Everywhere Indian labor was used, it proved to be highly unsuccessful.

England then tried sending poor whites, prisoners, and debtors from England and Ireland to the American colonies. Men, women, and children were often kidnapped and sent to America to work. These whites were held as indentured servants for seven years and then released. This soon created the need for a continual supply of people to work.

Another disadvantage was simply the fact that a white indentured servant could run away, and because he was white, he could go to another place, change his name, and have no fear of being caught.

Gradually the English colonists turned to Africans as the ideal solution. Because they were black, it would be difficult for them to run away and escape detection. Too, they could be bought outright and held for as long as they lived. And, finally, the supply was inexhaustible.[2]

Eighteen years after the first Africans came to the Jamestown colony, the first American-built slave ship sailed from Marblehead, Massachusetts. Its name was the *Desire*. The slave ships sailed to the west coast of Africa, and there the captains of the slave vessels went about their job of loading the ship with blacks to bring to America.

When the slave trade began, West Africa had a highly developed civilization, with complex economic and political institutions. It was because of their sophisticated civilization that West Africans could be used so easily in the rapidly growing economy of America.

Generally the slave trade was carried out in one of three ways. The first and easiest was simply to lie in wait until somebody came by, and then capture him. This method soon gave way to an alliance between white slave traders and black African tribal chiefs. The African chief would make war on another tribe for the purpose of capturing as many people as possible. He would turn them over to the white slave traders in exchange for various items the chief wanted—tobacco, guns, ammunition, liquor. This arrangement evolved into a more complicated one in which one African chief

---

1. **susceptible** (sə sep′ tə bəl): easily affected; sensitive; unresistant.
2. **inexhaustible** (in′ eg zôs′ tə bəl): incapable of being used up.

would align[3] with another chief, who would agree to sell some of his own tribesmen or others he had captured in a battle. He would be paid in goods for these soon-to-be slaves by the first African chief, who in turn would sell them to a white slave trader.

Charles Bell, a slave during the early nineteenth century, came into contact with many Africans who had been brought to America. His own grandfather had come from Africa, and as a child Bell had heard many stories about Africa from him. In his autobiography he recorded the story of one slave who was brought from Africa to America.

We were alarmed one morning, just at the break of day, by the horrible uproar caused by mingled shouts of men, and blows given with heavy sticks, upon large wooden drums. The village was surrounded by enemies, who attacked us with clubs, long wooden spears, and bows and arrows. After fighting for more than an hour, those who were not fortunate enough to run away were made prisoners. It was not the object of our enemies to kill; they wished to take us alive and sell us as slaves. I was knocked down by a heavy blow of a club, and when I recovered from the stupor[4] that followed, I found myself tied fast with the long rope I had brought from the desert. . . .

We were immediately led away from this village, through the forest, and were compelled to travel all day as fast as we could walk. . . . We traveled three weeks in the woods—sometimes without any path at all—and arrived one day at a large river with a rapid current. Here we were forced to help our conquerors to roll a great number of dead trees into the water from a vast pile that had been thrown together by high floods.

These trees, being dry and light, floated high out of the water; and when several of them were fastened together with the tough branches of young trees, [they] formed a raft, upon which we all placed ourselves, and descended the river for three days, when we came in sight of what appeared to me the most wonderful object in the world; this was a large ship at anchor in the river. When our raft came near the ship, the white people—for such they were on board—assisted to take us on the deck, and the logs were suffered to float down the river.

I had never seen white people before and they appeared to me the ugliest creatures in the world. The persons who brought us down the river received payment for us of the people in the ship, in various articles, of which I remember that a keg of liquor and some yards of blue and red cotton cloth were the principal.

Once on board, the slaves were taken below the deck and chained together in what was called the slave galley. It was here that they were kept throughout the long voyage from Africa to America. And it was here that millions died from the conditions on board the ship.

At the time we came into this ship, she was full of black people, who were all confined in a dark and low place, in irons.[5] The women were in irons as well as the men.

About twenty persons were seized in our village at the time I was; and amongst these were three children so young that they were not able to walk or to eat any hard substance. The mothers of these children had brought them all the way with them and had them in their arms when we were taken on board this ship.

---

3. **align** (ə līn′): cooperate or take sides with.
4. **stupor** (stōō′ pər): a state in which the mind and senses are numbed.
5. **irons** (ī′ ərnz): chains or shackles.

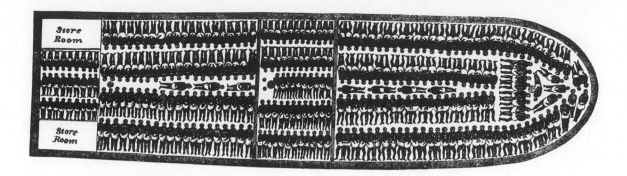

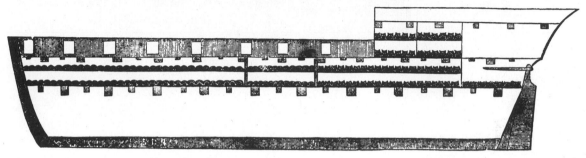

Slave ship diagram, 1798. Courtesy of the Newberry Library, Chicago.

When they put us in irons to be sent to our place of confinement in the ship, the men who fastened the irons on these mothers took the children out of their hands and threw them over the side of the ship into the water. When this was done, two of the women leaped overboard after the children—the third was already confined by a chain to another woman and could not get into the water, but in struggling to disengage herself, she broke her arm and died a few days after of a fever. One of the two women who were in the river was carried down by the weight of her irons before she could be rescued; but the other was taken up by some men in a boat and brought on board. This woman threw herself overboard one night when we were at sea.

The weather was very hot whilst we lay in the river and many of us died every day; but the number brought on board greatly exceeded those who died, and at the end of two weeks, the place in which we were confined was so full that no one could lie down; and we were obliged to sit all the time, for the room was not high enough for us to stand. When our prison could hold no more, the ship sailed down the river; and on the night of the second day after she sailed, I heard the roaring of the ocean as it dashed against her sides.

After we had been at sea some days, the irons were removed from the women and they were permitted to go upon deck; but whenever the wind blew high, they were driven down amongst us.

We had nothing to eat but yams, which were thrown amongst us at random—and of these we had scarcely enough to support life. More than a third of us died on the passage and when we arrived at Charleston, I was not able to stand. It was more than a week after I left the ship before I could straighten my limbs. I was bought by a trader with several others, brought up the country and sold to my present master. I have been here five years.

It is estimated that some fifty million people were taken from the continent during the years of the slave trade. These fifty million were, of course, the youngest, the strongest, those most capable of bringing great profit, first to the slave trader, and later to the slave owner. These Africans were scattered throughout South America, the islands of the West Indies, and the United States. Africa's citizens became the laboring backbone of much of the Western hemisphere.

Slavery differed from country to country. But it was in the United States that a system of slavery evolved that was more cruel and total than almost any other system of slavery devised by one group of men against another. No other country where blacks were enslaved destroyed African culture to the extent that it was destroyed here. Today there still exist, in South America and the Caribbean Islands, African religions, music, and language, which came over on the slave ships. Only fragments of Africa remain among the blacks of th United States.

Thinking About the Selection

A PERSONAL RESPONSE

sharing impressions

1. What impressions of the slave trade does this account give you? Jot down your ideas in your journal.

constructing interpretations

2. What was the most surprising or shocking thing you learned about the slave trade from this selection?

3. Besides the loss of freedom, what other losses were suffered by the Africans sold into slavery? Explain your answer.

4. What qualities do you think the captured Africans needed in order to survive the passage to America? Explain your answer.

A CREATIVE RESPONSE

5. How might this selection be different if Lester had included the point of view of a slave trader?

6. What do you think Lester gains by interweaving his history of the slave trade with a firsthand account by a captured African?

7. Why do you think it is important for Americans today to learn about the slave trade in their study of American history? Refer to details from Lester's essay in supporting your opinion.

Connecting Reading and Writing

1. Imagine that a Puritan colonist and the slave quoted in Lester's essay were to meet as guests on a daytime TV talk show to discuss the topic, "The Bible and the Auction Block: Freedom and Slavery in Daily America." Write a **transcript** of the show that includes questions from the host and the audience as well as responses from the guests.

Option: Compare Puritan and slave experiences in an **essay** to appear in an American history magazine.

2. What do you imagine went through the mind of a captured African while chained below deck on the passage to America? Write a **monologue** expressing one African's thoughts and feelings as told to his or her grandchild.

Option: Express his or her thoughts and feelings in a **poem** or **song** that a folklorist might record.

3. Imagine that you are preparing an oral report for Black History Month on the sufferings of Africans as a result of the slave trade. Using the information derived from Lester's history and from other accounts, write **notes** for a classroom presentation.

Option: Create an **informal outline** highlighting the important points that your speech will cover.

from Narrative of the
Life of Frederick Douglass,
an American Slave

FREDERICK DOUGLASS

A biography of Douglass appears on page 421.

Approaching the Selection

The escaped slave Frederick Douglass was such an intelligent and eloquent speaker that many doubted he could have ever been a slave. Douglass decided to write his autobiography *Narrative of the Life* to convince skeptics. As a boy, he was a servant in the home of Hugh Auld of Baltimore, where Mrs. Auld illegally taught Douglass the alphabet. After Mr. Auld commanded his wife to stop educating the boy, Douglass taught himself to read with the help of white playmates. When he was sixteen, Douglass was sent to live with Hugh Auld's brother, Thomas. Thomas Auld decided it was necessary to break the spirit of the young Douglass, whom he believed had been too spoiled as a house slave to be useful on a plantation. Auld rented Douglass for a year to Edward Covey, who had a reputation as a slave breaker. The following excerpt covers the time that Douglass spent with Covey.

Building Vocabulary

These essential words are footnoted within the selection.

elasticity (ē′ las tis′ ə tē), **languished** (laŋ′ gwisht): My natural **elasticity** was crushed [and] my intellect **languished.** (page 88)

epoch (ep′ ək): The circumstances leading to the change in Mr. Covey's course toward me form an **epoch** in my humble history. (page 89)

Connecting Writing and Reading

In your journal describe what you think life must have been like for a plantation slave in the early nineteenth century. Jot down your ideas about such areas as

- work required
- methods of punishment
- relationship of master and slave
- daily life

Then as you read this excerpt, see if Douglass's account of life as a slave fits your ideas about slavery.

I LEFT MASTER Thomas's house, and went to live with Mr. Covey, on the 1st of January, 1833. I was now, for the first time in my life, a field hand. In my new employment, I found myself even more awkward than a country boy appeared to be in a large city. I had been at my new home but one week before Mr. Covey gave me a very severe whipping, cutting my back, causing the blood to run, and raising ridges on my flesh as large as my little finger. The details of this affair are as follows: Mr. Covey sent me, very early in the morning of one of our coldest days in the month of January, to the woods, to get a load of wood. He gave me a team of unbroken oxen. He told me which was the in-hand ox, and which the off-hand one. He then tied the end of a large rope around the horns of the in-hand ox, and gave me the other end of it, and told me, if the oxen started to run, that I must hold on upon the rope. I had never driven oxen before, and of course I was very awkward. I, however, succeeded in getting to the edge of the woods with little difficulty; but I had got a very few rods into the woods, when the oxen took fright, and started full tilt, carrying the cart against trees, and over stumps, in the most frightful manner. I expected every moment that my brains would be dashed out against the trees. After running thus for a considerable distance, they finally upset the cart, dashing it with great force against a tree, and threw themselves into a dense thicket. How I escaped death, I do not know. There I was, entirely alone, in a thick wood, in a place new to me. My cart was upset and shattered, my oxen were entangled among the young trees, and there was none to help me. After a long spell of effort, I succeeded in getting my cart righted, my oxen disentangled, and again yoked to the cart. I now proceeded with my team to the place where I had, the day before, been chopping wood, and loaded my cart pretty heavily, thinking in this way to tame my oxen. I then proceeded on my way home. I had now consumed one-half of the day. I got out of the woods safely, and now felt out of danger. I stopped my oxen to open the woods gate; and just as I did so, before I could get hold of my ox rope, the oxen again started, rushed through the gate, catching it between the wheel and the body of the cart, tearing it to pieces, and coming within a few inches of crushing me against the gatepost. Thus twice, in one short day, I escaped death by the merest chance. On my return, I told Mr. Covey what had happened, and how it happened. He ordered me to return to the woods again immediately. I did so, and he followed on after me. Just as I got into the woods, he came up and told me to stop my cart, and that he would teach me how to trifle away my time, and break gates. He then went to a large gum tree, and with his axe cut three large switches, and, after trimming them up neatly with his pocketknife, he ordered me to take off my clothes. I made him no answer, but stood with my clothes on. He repeated his order. I still made him no answer, nor did I move to strip myself. Upon this he rushed at me with the fierceness of a tiger, tore off my clothes, and lashed me till he had worn out his switches, cutting me so savagely as to leave the marks visible for a long time after. This whipping was the first of a number just like it, and for similar offenses.

I lived with Mr. Covey one year. During the first six months of that year, scarce a week passed without his whipping me. I was seldom free from a sore back. My awkwardness was almost always his excuse for whipping me. We were worked fully up to the point of endurance. Long before day we were up, our horses fed, and by the first approach of day we were off to the field with our hoes and ploughing teams. Mr. Covey gave us enough to eat, but scarce time to eat it. We were often less than five minutes taking our meals. We were often in the field from the first approach of day till its last lingering ray had left us; and at saving-fodder time, midnight often caught us in the field binding blades.

Covey would be out with us. The way he used to stand it, was this. He would spend the most of his afternoons in bed. He would then come out fresh in the evening, ready to urge us on with his words, example, and frequently with the whip. Mr. Covey was one of the few slaveholders who could and did work with his hands. He was a hardworking man. He knew by himself just what a man or a boy could do. There was no deceiving him. His work went on in his absence almost as well as in his presence; and he had the faculty of making us feel that he was ever present with us. This he did by surprising us. He seldom approached the spot where we were at work openly, if he could do it secretly. He always aimed at taking us by surprise. Such was his cunning, that we used to call him, among ourselves, "the snake." When we were at work in the cornfield, he would sometimes crawl on his hands and knees to avoid detection, and all at once he would rise nearly in our midst, and scream out, "Ha, ha! Come, come! Dash on, dash on!" This being his mode of attack, it was never safe to stop a single minute. His comings were like a thief in the night. He appeared to us as being ever at hand. He was under every tree, behind every stump, in every bush, and at every window, on the plantation. He would sometimes mount his horse, as if bound to St. Michael's, a distance of seven miles, and in half an hour afterwards you would see him coiled up in the corner of the wood fence, watching every motion of the slaves. He would, for this purpose, leave his horse tied up in the woods. Again, he would sometimes walk up to us, and give us orders as though he was upon the point of starting on a long journey, turn his back upon us, and make as though he was going to the house to get ready; and, before he would get

halfway thither, he would turn short and crawl into a fence corner, or behind some tree, and there watch us till the going down of the sun. . . .

If at any one time of my life more than another, I was made to drink the bitterest dregs of slavery, that time was during the first six months of my stay with Mr. Covey. We were worked in all weathers. It was never too hot or too cold; it could never rain, blow, hail, or snow, too hard for us to work in the field. Work, work, work, was scarcely more the order of the day than of the night. The longest days were too short for him, and the shortest nights too long for him. I was somewhat unmanageable when I first went there, but a few months of this discipline tamed me. Mr. Covey succeeded in breaking me. I was broken in body, soul, and spirit. My natural elasticity[1] was crushed, my intellect languished,[2] the disposition to read departed, the cheerful spark that lingered about my eye died; the dark night of slavery closed in upon me; and behold a man transformed into a brute!

Sunday was my only leisure time. I spent this in a sort of beastlike stupor, between sleep and wake, under some large tree. At times I would rise up, a flash of energetic freedom would dart through my soul, accompanied with a faint beam of hope, that flickered for a moment, and then vanished. I sank down again, mourning over my wretched condition. I was sometimes prompted to take my life, and that of Covey, but was prevented by a combination of hope and fear. My sufferings on this plantation seem now like a dream rather than a stern reality. . . .

I have already intimated that my condition was much worse, during the first six months of my stay at Mr. Covey's, than in the last six. The circumstances leading to the change in

---

1. **elasticity** (ē′ las tis′ ə tē): the quality of being able to recover quickly.
2. **languished** (laŋ′ gwisht): became weak.

Mr. Covey's course toward me form an epoch[3] in my humble history. You have seen how a man was made a slave; you shall see how a slave was made a man. On one of the hottest days of the month of August, 1833, Bill Smith, William Hughes, a slave named Eli, and myself, were engaged in fanning wheat.[4] Hughes was clearing the fanned wheat from before the fan. Eli was turning, Smith was feeding, and I was carrying wheat to the fan. The work was simple, requiring strength rather than intellect; yet, to one entirely unused to such work, it came very hard. About three o' clock of that day, I broke down; my strength failed me; I was seized with a violent aching of the head, attended with extreme dizziness; I trembled in every limb. Finding what was coming, I nerved myself up, feeling it would never do to stop work. I stood as long as I could stagger to the hopper with grain. When I could stand no longer, I fell, and felt as if held down by an immense weight. The fan of course stopped; every one had his own work to do; and no one could do the work of the other, and have his own go on at the same time.

Mr. Covey was at the house, about one hundred yards from the treading-yard where we were fanning. On hearing the fan stop, he left immediately, and came to the spot where we were. He hastily inquired what the matter was. Bill answered that I was sick, and there was no one to bring wheat to the fan. I had by this time crawled away under the side of the post and rail fence by which the yard was enclosed, hoping to find relief by getting out of the sun. He then asked where I was. He was told by one of the hands. He came to the spot, and, after looking at me awhile, asked me what was the matter. I told him as well as I could, for I scarce had strength to speak. He then gave me a savage kick in the side, and told me to get up. I tried to do so, but fell back in the attempt. He gave me another kick, and again told me to rise. I again tried, and suc-

ceeded in gaining my feet; but, stooping to get the tub with which I was feeding the fan, I again staggered and fell. While down in this situation, Mr. Covey took up the hickory slat with which Hughes had been striking off the half-bushel measure, and with it gave me a heavy blow upon the head, making a large wound, and the blood ran freely; and with this again told me to get up. I made no effort to comply, having now made up my mind to let him do his worst. In a short time after receiving this blow, my head grew better. Mr. Covey had now left me to my fate. At this moment I resolved, for the first time, to go to my master, enter a complaint, and ask his protection. In order to do this, I must that afternoon walk seven miles; and this, under the circumstances, was truly a severe undertaking. I was exceedingly feeble; made so as much by the kicks and blows which I received, as by the severe fit of sickness to which I had been subjected. I, however, watched my chance, while Covey was looking in an opposite direction, and started for St. Michael's. I succeeded in getting a considerable distance on my way to the woods, when Covey discovered me, and called after me to come back, threatening what he would do if I did not come. I disregarded both his calls and his threats, and made my way to the woods as fast as my feeble state would allow; and thinking I might be overhauled by him if I kept the road, I walked through the woods, keeping far enough from the road to avoid detection, and near enough to prevent losing my way. I had not gone far before my little strength again failed me. I could go no farther. I fell down, and lay for a considerable time. The blood was yet oozing from the wound on my head. For a time I thought I should bleed

---

3. **epoch** (ep′ ək): beginning of a new and important period in the history of something.
4. **fanning wheat:** using a machine to separate the grain from the unusable chaff.

to death; and think now that I should have done so, but that the blood so matted my hair as to stop the wound. After lying there about three-quarters of an hour, I nerved myself up again, and started on my way, through bogs and briers, barefooted and bareheaded, tearing my feet sometimes at nearly every step; and after a journey of about seven miles, occupying some five hours to perform it, I arrived at master's store. I then presented an appearance enough to affect any but a heart of iron. From the crown of my head to my feet, I was covered with blood. My hair was all clotted with dust and blood; my shirt was stiff with blood. My legs and feet were torn in sundry places with briers and thorns, and were also covered with blood. I suppose I looked like a man who had escaped a den of wild beasts, and barely escaped them. In this state I appeared before my master, humbly entreating him to interpose his authority for my protection. I told him all the circumstances as well as I could, and it seemed, as I spoke, at times to affect him. He would then walk the floor, and seek to justify Covey by saying he expected I deserved it. He asked me what I wanted. I told him, to let me get a new home; that as sure as I lived with Mr. Covey again, I should live with but to die with him; that Covey would surely kill me; he was in a fair way for it. Master Thomas ridiculed the idea that there was any danger of Mr. Covey's killing me, and said that he knew Mr. Covey; that he was a good man, and that he could not think of taking me from him; that, should he do so, he would lose the whole year's wages; that I belonged to Mr. Covey for one year, and that I must go back to him, come what might; and that I must not trouble him with any more stories, or that he would himself *get hold of me.* After threatening me thus, he gave me a very large dose of salts, telling me that I might remain in St. Michael's that night (it being quite late), but that I must be off back to Mr. Covey's early in the morning; and

that if I did not, he would *get hold of me,* which meant that he would whip me. I remained all night, and, according to his orders, I started off to Covey's in the morning (Saturday morning), wearied in body and broken in spirit. I got no supper that night, or breakfast that morning. I reached Covey's about nine o' clock; and just as I was getting over the fence that divided Mrs. Kemp's fields from ours, out ran Covey with his cowskin, to give me another whipping. Before he could reach me, I succeeded in getting to the cornfield; and as the corn was very high, it afforded me the means of hiding. He seemed very angry, and searched for me a long time. My behavior was altogether unaccountable. He finally gave up the chase, thinking, I suppose, that I must come home for something to eat; he would give himself no further trouble in looking for me. I spent that day mostly in the woods, having the alternative before me—to go home and be whipped to death, or stay in the woods and be starved to death. That night, I fell in with Sandy Jenkins, a slave with whom I was somewhat acquainted. Sandy had a free wife who lived about four miles from Mr. Covey's; and it being Saturday, he was on his way to see her. I told him my circumstances, and he very kindly invited me to go home with him. I went home with him, and talked this whole matter over, and got his advice as to what course it was best for me to pursue. I found Sandy an old adviser. He told me, with great solemnity, I must go back to Covey; but that before I went, I must go with him into another part of the woods, where there was a certain *root,* which, if I would take some of it with me, carrying it *always on my right side,* would render it impossible for Mr. Covey, or any other white man, to whip me. He said he had carried it for years; and since he had done so, he had never received a blow, and never expected to while he carried it. I at first rejected the idea, that the simple carrying of a root in my pocket would have any such effect as he had said, and was not disposed to take it; but Sandy impressed the necessity with much earnestness, telling me it could do no harm, if it did no good. To please him, I at length took the root, and, according to his direction, carried it upon my right side. This was Sunday morning. I immediately started for home; and upon entering the yard gate, out came Mr. Covey on his way to meeting. He spoke to me very kindly, bade me drive the pigs from a lot near by, and passed on toward the church. Now, this singular conduct of Mr. Covey really made me begin to think that there was something in the *root* which Sandy had given me; and had it been on any other day than Sunday, I could have attributed the conduct to no other cause than the influence of that root; and as it was, I was half inclined to think the *root* to be something more than I at first had taken it to be. All went well till Monday morning. On this morning, the virtue of the *root* was fully tested. Long before daylight, I was called to go and rub, curry, and feed, the horses. I obeyed, and was glad to obey. But whilst thus engaged, whilst in the act of throwing down some blades from the loft, Mr. Covey entered the stable with a long rope; and just as I was half out of the loft, he caught hold of my legs, and was about tying me. As soon as I found what he was up to, I gave a sudden spring, and as I did so, he holding to my legs, I was brought sprawling on the stable floor. Mr. Covey seemed now to think he had me, and could do what he pleased; but at this moment—from whence came the spirit I don't know—I resolved to fight; and, suiting my action to the resolution, I seized Covey hard by the throat; and as I did so, I rose. He held on to me, and I to him. My resistance was so entirely unexpected, that Covey seemed taken all aback. He trembled like a leaf. This gave me assurance, and I held him uneasy, causing the blood to run where I touched him with the ends of my fingers. Mr. Covey soon called out to Hughes for help. Hughes came, and, while Covey held me, attempted to tie my right hand. While he was in the act of doing so, I watched my chance, and gave him a heavy kick close under the ribs. This kick fairly sickened Hughes, so that he left me in the hands of Mr. Covey. This kick had the effect of not only weakening Hughes, but Covey also. When he saw Hughes bending over with pain, his courage quailed. He asked me if I meant to persist in my resistance. I told him I did, come what might; that he had used me like a brute for six months, and that I was determined to be used so no longer. With that, he strove to drag me to a stick that was lying just out of the stable door. He meant to knock me down. But just as he was leaning over to get the stick, I seized him with both hands by his collar, and brought him by a sudden snatch to the ground. By this time, Bill came. Covey called upon him for assistance. Bill wanted to know what he could do. Covey said, "Take hold of him, take hold of him!" Bill said his master hired him out to work, and not to help whip me; so he left Covey and myself to fight our own battle out. We were at it for nearly two hours. Covey at length let me go, puffing and blowing at a great rate, saying that if I had not resisted, he would not have whipped me half so much. The truth was, that he had not whipped me at all. I considered him as getting entirely the worst end of the bargain; for he had drawn no blood from me, but I had from him. The whole six months afterwards, that I spent with Mr. Covey, he never laid the weight of his finger upon me in anger. He would occasionally say, he didn't want to get hold of me again. "No," thought I, "you need not; for you will come off worse than you did before."

This battle with Mr. Covey was the turning point in my career as a slave. It rekindled the few expiring embers of freedom, and revived within me a sense of my own manhood. It recalled the departed self-confidence, and inspired me again with a determination to be free. The gratification afforded by the triumph was a full compensation for whatever else might follow, even death itself. He only can understand the deep satisfaction which I experienced, who has himself repelled by force the bloody arm of slavery. I felt as I never felt before. It was a glorious resurrection, from the tomb of slavery, to the heaven of freedom. My long-crushed spirit rose, cowardice departed, bold defiance took its place; and I now resolved that, however long I might remain a slave in form, the day had passed forever when I could be a slave in fact. I did not hesitate to let it be known of me, that the white man who expected to succeed in whipping, must also succeed in killing me.

From this time I was never again what might be called fairly whipped, though I remained a slave four years afterwards. I had several fights, but was never whipped.

$\mathcal{T}$hinking About the Selection

A PERSONAL RESPONSE

sharing impressions

1. After reading the selection, what impression do you have of Frederick Douglass? In your journal describe your impressions.

constructing interpretations

2. Why do you think Douglass emphasizes the distinction between fighting and being whipped at the end of this excerpt?

3. What do the choices that Douglass makes reveal about his character?
   Think about
   • his resolve to ask Master Thomas for protection
   • his agreeing to take the root from Sandy
   • his decision to fight Covey

4. Describe the relationship that Master Thomas and Covey each has with Douglass.

5. Explain how this excerpt has increased your understanding of the life of a plantation slave.

A CREATIVE RESPONSE

6. How do you think that Douglass's life might have been different if Master Thomas had not sent him back to Covey?

A CRITICAL RESPONSE

7. What do the conflicts between Douglass and Covey reveal about the way slavery affects both master and slave? Go back through the excerpt and find specific examples to support your answer.

8. Which of Douglass's qualities do you think would be most valuable in fighting injustice today? Give reasons for your answer.

Analyzing the Writer's Craft

AUTOBIOGRAPHY

In the next-to-last paragraph, what words and phrases does Douglass use to convey his feelings about his experience with Covey?

Building a Literary Vocabulary. An autobiography is the story of a person's life written by that person. Generally an autobiographer uses the first-person point of view. One of the challenges of writing a good autobiography is to combine objective description with the expression of subjective feelings. In *Narrative of the Life,* Frederick Douglass describes the circumstances of his service with Covey in surprisingly objective, unemotional language: "We were worked fully up to the point of endurance. Long before day we were up, our horses fed, and by the first approach of day we were off to the field with our hoes and ploughing teams. Mr. Covey gave us enough to eat, but scarce time to eat it. We were often less than five minutes taking our meals." In contrast, when Douglass relates his own feelings, he uses emotionally charged words and figurative expressions that convey the experience of being a slave. For example, "It was a glorious resurrection, from the tomb of slavery, to the heaven of freedom."

Application: Evaluating Autobiography. In a small group, go back through the selection and select three passages that you think give an especially vivid picture of slavery. Then determine whether each passage is primarily an objective description of Douglass's life as a slave, a subjective expression of his feelings, or a combination of both. As a group, decide whether you think the most effective passages are primarily objective, subjective, or a combination. Share your conclusions with the class.

Connecting Reading and Writing

1. On the basis of what you know from this excerpt, write an **introduction** to Douglass's autobiography trying to convince a nineteenth-century audience that the work is a legitimate portrayal of the life of a slave.

Option: Retell this episode from the autobiography in a short **speech** Douglass might have delivered to the Anti-Slavery Society.

2. Research Douglass's life after the incident recounted in this excerpt. Write a **eulogy** summarizing his life that might be delivered at a public meeting after his death.

Option: Create a **time line** that could accompany Douglass's autobiography showing specific events as he moved from slave to free man to national figure.

3. Think of an incident from your life that you would describe as a turning point the way that Douglass's fight with Covey was a turning point for him. Write about the incident in an **autobiographical sketch,** explaining why it changed your life.

Option: Write notes for an **oral history** relating the incident. Then make a recording of your history for your children to listen to someday.

4. Read the complete *Narrative of the Life of Frederick Douglass, an American Slave.* Choose another excerpt that you think next year's class should read along with the excerpt included in this book. Write a **recommendation** to your teacher explaining your choice.

Option: Choose several excerpts from the autobiography that you think reveal important aspects of Douglass's character. Write **director's notes** explaining how you would combine these episodes in a brief documentary about Douglass's life.

Frederick Douglass

Robert Hayden

When it is finally ours, this freedom, this liberty, this beautiful
and terrible thing, needful to man as air,
usable as earth; when it belongs at last to all,
when it is truly instinct, brain matter, diastole, systole,
reflex action; when it is finally won; when it is more
than the gaudy mumbo jumbo of politicians:
this man, this Douglass, this former slave, this Negro
beaten to his knees, exiled, visioning a world
where none is lonely, none hunted, alien,
this man, superb in love and logic, this man
shall be remembered. Oh, not with statues' rhetoric,
not with legends and poems and wreaths of bronze alone,
but with the lives grown out of his life, the lives
fleshing his dream of the beautiful, needful thing.

As I Grew Older   LANGSTON HUGHES

Any Human to Another   COUNTEE CULLEN

Biographies of Hughes and Cullen appear on pages 424 and 420.

Approaching the Poems

According to the poet Arna Bontemps, the "twin stars of the black Awakening in literature" (the Harlem Renaissance) were Langston Hughes and Countee Cullen. In their works these "twin stars" explore issues especially important to African Americans. One of these issues is the dream of a better future, free from the shackles of oppression and racism. In the following poems Hughes and Cullen express their ideas about this dream.

Building Vocabulary

The following essential words are defined alongside "Any Human to Another."

marrow (mar′ ō): Pierce to the **marrow,** (line 4)

diverse (də vʉrs′): **Diverse** yet single, (line 11)

unsheathed (un shē *th*d′): Like a blade / Shining and **unsheathed** (lines 26–27)

Connecting Writing and Reading

What are your dreams for the future? Do you want to discover a cure for cancer? explore the solar system? fight injustices in the world? live on a farm? break a sports record? In your journal make a chart with two columns. In the first column describe two or three dreams. In the second column list any obstacles that you might have to overcome in order to achieve these dreams. As you read, keep in mind these dreams and obstacles as you consider the ideas presented in the following poems.

As I Grew Older

It was a long time ago.
I have almost forgotten my dream.
But it was there then,
In front of me,
5   Bright like a sun—
My dream.

And then the wall rose,
Rose slowly,
Slowly,
10   Between me and my dream.
Rose slowly, slowly,
Dimming,
Hiding,
The light of my dream.
15   Rose until it touched the sky—
The wall.

Shadow.
I am black.

I lie down in the shadow.
20   No longer the light of my dream before me,
Above me.
Only the thick wall.
Only the shadow.

My hands!
25   My dark hands!
Break through the wall!
Find my dream!
Help me to shatter this darkness,
To smash this night,
30   To break this shadow
Into a thousand lights of sun,
Into a thousand whirling dreams
Of sun!

Don't You Turn Back (L. Hughes), ANN GRIFALCONI.
© Ann Grifalconi, New York.

Any Human to Another

The ills I sorrow at
Not me alone
Like an arrow,
Pierce to the <u>marrow</u>,[1]
5   Through the fat
And past the bone.

Your grief and mine
Must intertwine
Like sea and river,
10   Be fused and mingle,
<u>Diverse</u>[2] yet single,
Forever and forever.

Let no man be so proud
And confident,
15   To think he is allowed
A little tent
Pitched in a meadow
Of sun and shadow
All his little own.

20   Joy may be shy, unique,
Friendly to a few,
Sorrow never scorned to speak
To any who
Were false or true.

25   Your every grief
Like a blade
Shining and <u>unsheathed</u>[3]
Must strike me down.
Of bitter aloes[4] wreathed,
30   My sorrow must be laid
On your head like a crown.

1. **marrow** (mar′ ō): the soft tissue that fills the cavities of most bones.

2. **diverse** (də vʉrs′): different; varying.

3. **unsheathed** (un shē*th*d′): removed from a scabbard, or case.
4. **bitter aloes** (al′ ōz): a plant of the lily family; an unpleasant-tasting medicine made from this plant.

Thinking About the Poems

A PERSONAL RESPONSE

sharing impressions

1. How do the ideas expressed in these poems make you feel? Respond in your journal.

constructing interpretations

2. What is your opinion of the speaker's ideas in "Any Human to Another"?
Think about
- the response to suffering envisioned by the speaker (lines 7–12 and lines 25–31)
- the bonds that join all humans (lines 20–24)
- what human relationships might be like if the speaker's dream were to come true

3. How would you explain the meaning of the wall in "As I Grew Older"?
Think about
- when and how the wall rose
- the effect of the wall upon the speaker
- what will happen if the wall is destroyed

4. Which speaker might have to overcome greater obstacles to achieve his or her dream? Explain your answer.

A CREATIVE RESPONSE

5. How do you think you might respond to these poems if the speakers expressed a defeatist attitude?

A CRITICAL RESPONSE

6. Read the following quotation from Dr. Martin Luther King, Jr.: "True altruism is more than the capacity to pity; it is the capacity to empathize. . . . Empathy is fellow feeling for the person in need—his pain, agony, and burdens." How would you relate this definition of altruism to the ideas presented in these two poems? Cite lines from the poems in explaining your answer.

7. Which of the two poems do you think is more relevant to African Americans today, and why?

FIGURATIVE LANGUAGE

Think about lines 4 and 5 of the poem "Frederick Douglass" (page 95): "when it [freedom] is truly instinct, brain matter, diastole, systole,/ reflex action." What impressions do the words create in your mind?

Building a Literary Vocabulary. Figurative language is language that communicates ideas beyond the literal meanings of words. The words in a figurative expression are not literally true; rather, they create impressions in the reader's mind.

Two of the most common kinds of figurative language are metaphor and simile. For example, the words "instinct, brain matter, diastole, systole,/ reflex action" are metaphors that compare freedom to inherent characteristics of human organisms. The words create impressions of naturalness and essentiality. A simile compares two things in a phrase that contains *like* or *as*, such as the phrase "this freedom . . . needful to man as air" in "Frederick Douglass." The comparison of freedom to air suggests that both are necessary conditions for human survival.

Personification is a form of figurative language in which human qualities are attributed to an object, animal, or idea. An example of this technique is the final line in "My Mother Pieced Quilts" (page 63): "the quilts sing on."

Application: Interpreting Figurative Language. Working with a small group, find three or four examples of figurative language in "Any Human to Another." List the examples on a chart similar to the one below, which presents the central metaphor in "As I Grew Older." Share your examples with other groups.

Example	Form	Impressions
"the wall rose"	metaphor	insurmountable obstacles, separation, racism

from Letter from Birmingham Jail

MARTIN LUTHER KING, JR.

A biography of King appears on page 425.

*A*pproaching the Selection

In 1963 the Rev. Martin Luther King, Jr., led a massive civil rights campaign in Birmingham, Alabama, involving drives for black voter registration and for desegregation in education and housing. During this nonviolent action, King was arrested and imprisoned several times. During one imprisonment he wrote the "Letter from Birmingham Jail," which has become a classic statement in support of civil disobedience. It was written in response to a published letter by eight local clergymen criticizing King's actions as "unwise and untimely." In the part of the letter that follows, King defends his actions by drawing upon the ideas of philosophers, religious scholars, biblical figures, and political thinkers with whom his audience, as clergymen, would have been familiar.

*B*uilding Vocabulary

These essential words are footnoted within the selection.

moratorium (môr′ ə tôr′ ē əm): The leaders . . . agreed to a **moratorium** on all demonstrations. (page 103)

rabid (rab′ id), **anarchy** (an′ ər kē): In no sense do I advocate evading or defying the law, as would the **rabid** segregationist. That would lead to **anarchy.** (page 106)

paternalistically (pə tʉr′ nəl is′ tik lē): The white moderate . . . **paternalistically** believes he can set the timetable for another man's freedom. (page 106)

*C*onnecting Writing and Reading

How far would you go to stand up for an issue that you believe in? Would you march in a demonstration, risk suspension from school, go to jail? In your journal, briefly explain the issue and what you would do to support it. As you read, think about whether you are willing to go as far as King to stand up for what you believe in.

from Letter from Birmingham Jail

April 16, 1963

My Dear Fellow Clergymen:

While confined here in the Birmingham city jail, I came across your recent statement calling my present activities "unwise and untimely." Seldom do I pause to answer criticism of my work and ideas. If I sought to answer all the criticisms that cross my desk, my secretaries would have little time for anything other than such correspondence in the course of the day, and I would have no time for constructive work. But since I feel that you are men of genuine goodwill and that your criticisms are sincerely set forth, I want to try to answer your statement in what I hope will be patient and reasonable terms.

I think I should indicate why I am here in Birmingham, since you have been influenced by the view which argues against "outsiders coming in." I have the honor of serving as president of the Southern Christian Leadership Conference, an organization operating in every Southern state, with headquarters in Atlanta, Georgia. We have some eighty-five affiliated organizations across the South, and one of them is the Alabama Christian Movement for Human Rights. Frequently we share staff, educational, and financial resources with our affiliates. Several months ago the affiliate here in Birmingham asked us to be on call to engage in a nonviolent direct-action program if such were deemed necessary. We readily consented, and when the hour came, we lived up to our promise. So I, along with several members of my staff, am here because I was invited here. I am here because I have organizational ties here.

But more basically, I am in Birmingham because injustice is here. Just as the prophets of the eighth century B.C. left their villages and carried their "thus saith the Lord" far beyond the boundaries of their hometowns, and just as the Apostle Paul left his village of Tarsus and carried the gospel of Jesus Christ to the far corners of the Greco-Roman world, so am I compelled to carry the gospel of freedom beyond my own hometown. Like Paul, I must constantly respond to the Macedonian call for aid.

Moreover, I am cognizant of the interrelatedness of all communities and states. I cannot sit idly by in Atlanta and not be concerned about what happens in Birmingham. Injustice anywhere is a threat to justice everywhere. We are caught in an inescapable network of mutuality, tied in a single garment of destiny. Whatever affects one directly, affects all indirectly. Never again can we afford to live with the narrow, provincial "outside agitator" idea. Anyone who lives inside the United States can never be considered an outsider anywhere within its bounds.

You deplore the demonstrations taking place in Birmingham. But your statement, I am sorry to say, fails to express a similar concern for the conditions that brought about the demonstrations. I am sure that none of you would want to rest content with the superficial kind of social analysis that deals merely with effects and does not grapple with underlying causes. It is unfortunate that demonstrations are taking place in Birmingham, but it is even more unfortunate that the city's white power structure left the Negro community with no alternative.

In any nonviolent campaign there are four basic steps: collection of the facts to determine whether injustices exist; negotiation; self-purification; and direct action. We have gone through all these steps in Birmingham. There can be no gainsaying the fact that racial injustice engulfs this community. Birmingham is probably the most thoroughly segregated city in the United States. Its ugly record of brutality is widely known. Negroes have experienced grossly unjust treatment in the courts. There have been more unsolved bombings of Negro homes and churches in Birmingham than in any other city in the nation. These are the hard, brutal facts of the case. On the basis of these conditions, Negro leaders sought to negotiate with the city fathers. But the latter consistently refused to engage in good-faith negotiations.

Then, last September, came the opportunity to talk with leaders of Birmingham's economic community. In the course of the negotiations, certain promises were made by the merchants —for example, to remove the stores' humiliating racial signs.[1] On the basis of these promises, The Reverend Fred Shuttlesworth and the leaders of the Alabama Christian Movement for Human Rights agreed to a moratorium[2] on all demonstrations. As the weeks and months went by, we realized that we were the victims of a broken promise. A few signs, briefly removed, returned; the others remained.

As in so many past experiences, our hopes had been blasted, and the shadow of deep disappointment settled upon us. We had no alternative except to prepare for direct action, whereby we would present our very bodies as a means of laying our case before the conscience of the local and the national community. Mindful of the difficulties involved, we decided to undertake a process of self-purification. We began a series of workshops on nonviolence, and we repeatedly asked ourselves: "Are you able to accept blows without retaliating?" "Are you able to endure the ordeal of jail?" We decided to schedule our direct-action program for the Easter season, realizing

that except for Christmas, this is the main shopping period of the year. Knowing that a strong economic-withdrawal program would be the by-product of direct action, we felt that this would be the best time to bring pressure to bear on the merchants for the needed change.

Then it occurred to us that Birmingham's mayoral election was coming up in March, and we speedily decided to postpone action until after election day. When we discovered that the Commissioner of Public Safety, Eugene "Bull" Connor, had piled up enough votes to be in the runoff, we decided again to postpone action until the day after the runoff so that the demonstrations could not be used to cloud the issues. Like many others, we waited to see Mr. Connor defeated, and to this end we endured postponement after postponement. Having aided in this community need, we felt that our direct-action program could be delayed no longer.

You may well ask: "Why direct action? Why sit-ins, marches, and so forth? Isn't negotiation a better path?" You are quite right in calling for negotiation. Indeed, this is the very purpose of direct action. Nonviolent direct action seeks to create such a crisis and foster such a tension that a community which has constantly refused to negotiate is forced to confront the issue. It seeks so to dramatize the issue that it can no longer be ignored. My citing the creation of tension as part of the work of the nonviolent-resister may sound rather shocking. But I must confess that I am not afraid of the word "tension." I have earnestly opposed violent tension, but there is a type of constructive, nonviolent tension which is necessary for

---

1. **racial signs:** a reference to signs once used throughout the South to label public facilities and services for use by white people or black people only.
2. **moratorium** (môr′ ə tôr′ ē əm): an authorized delay or stopping of some specified activity.

growth. Just as Socrates felt that it was necessary to create a tension in the mind so that individuals could rise from the bondage of myths and half-truths to the unfettered realm of creative analysis and objective appraisal, so must we see the need for nonviolent gadflies to create the kind of tension in society that will help men rise from the dark depths of prejudice and racism to the majestic heights of understanding and brotherhood.

The purpose of our direct-action program is to create a situation so crisis-packed that it will inevitably open the door to negotiation. I therefore concur with you in your call for negotiation. Too long has our beloved Southland been bogged down in a tragic effort to live in monologue rather than dialogue.

One of the basic points in your statement is that the action that I and my associates have taken in Birmingham is untimely. Some have asked: "Why didn't you give the new city administration time to act?" The only answer that I can give to this query is that the new Birmingham administration must be prodded about as much as the outgoing one before it will act. . . . My friends, I must say to you that we have not made a single gain in civil rights without determined legal and nonviolent pressure. Lamentably, it is a historical fact that privileged groups seldom give up their privileges voluntarily. Individuals may see the moral light and voluntarily give up their unjust posture; but, as Reinhold Niebuhr has reminded us, groups tend to be more immoral than individuals.

We know through painful experience that freedom is never voluntarily given by the oppressor; it must be demanded by the oppressed. Frankly, I have yet to engage in a direct-action campaign that was "well-timed" in the view of those who have not suffered unduly from the disease of segregation. For years now I have heard the word "Wait!" It rings in the ear of every Negro with piercing familiarity. This "Wait" has almost always meant "Never." We

must come to see, with one of our distinguished jurists, that "justice too long delayed is justice denied."

We have waited for more than 340 years for our constitutional and God-given rights. The nations of Asia and Africa are moving with jetlike speed toward gaining political independence, but we still creep at horse-and-buggy pace toward gaining a cup of coffee at a lunch counter. Perhaps it is easy for those who have never felt the stinging darts of segregation to say, "Wait." But when you have seen vicious mobs lynch your mothers and fathers at will and drown your sisters and brothers at whim; when you have seen hate-filled policemen curse, kick, and even kill your black brothers and sisters; when you see the vast majority of your twenty million Negro brothers smothering in an airtight cage of poverty in the midst of an affluent society; when you suddenly find your tongue twisted and your speech stammering as you seek to explain to your six-year-old daughter why she can't go to the public amusement park that has just been advertised on television, and see tears welling up in her eyes when she is told that Funtown is closed to colored children, and see ominous clouds of inferiority beginning to form in her little mental sky, and see her beginning to distort her personality by developing an unconscious bitterness toward white people; when you have to concoct an answer for a five-year-old son who is asking: "Daddy, why do white people treat colored people so mean?"; when you take a cross-country drive and find it necessary to sleep night after night in the uncomfortable corners of your automobile because no motel will accept you; when you are humiliated day in and day out by nagging signs reading "white" and "colored"; when your first name becomes "nigger," your middle name becomes "boy" (however old you are) and your last name becomes "John," and your wife and mother are never given the respected title "Mrs."; when you are harried by day and haunted by night by the fact that you are a Negro, living constantly at tiptoe stance, never quite knowing what to expect next, and are plagued with inner fears and outer resentments; when you are forever fighting a degenerating sense of "nobodiness"—then you will understand why we find it difficult to wait. There comes a time when the cup of endurance runs over, and men are no longer willing to be plunged into the abyss of despair. I hope, sirs, you can understand our legitimate and unavoidable impatience.

You express a great deal of anxiety over our willingness to break laws. This is certainly a legitimate concern. Since we so diligently urge people to obey the Supreme Court's decision of 1954 outlawing segregation in the public schools, at first glance it may seem rather paradoxical for us consciously to break laws. One may well ask: "How can you advocate breaking some laws and obeying others?" The answer lies in the fact that there are two types of laws: just and unjust. I would be the first to advocate obeying just laws. One has not only a legal but a moral responsibility to obey just laws. Conversely, one has a moral responsibility to disobey unjust laws. I would agree with St. Augustine that "an unjust law is no law at all."

Now, what is the difference between the two? How does one determine whether a law is just or unjust? A just law is a man-made code that squares with the moral law or the law of God. An unjust law is a code that is out of harmony with the moral law. To put it in the terms of St. Thomas Aquinas: An unjust law is a human law that is not rooted in eternal law and natural law. Any law that uplifts human personality is just. Any law that degrades human personality is unjust. All segregation statutes are unjust because segregation distorts the soul and damages the personality. It gives the segregator a false sense of superiority and the segregated a false sense of inferiority. Segregation, to use the terminology of the Jewish philosopher Martin Buber, substitutes an "I-it"

relationship for an "I-thou" relationship and ends up relegating persons to the status of things. Hence segregation is not only politically, economically, and sociologically unsound, it is morally wrong and sinful. Paul Tillich has said that sin is separation. Is not segregation an existential expression of man's tragic separation, his awful estrangement, his terrible sinfulness? Thus it is that I can urge men to obey the 1954 decision of the Supreme Court, for it is morally right; and I can urge them to disobey segregation ordinances, for they are morally wrong.

Let us consider a more concrete example of just and unjust laws. An unjust law is a code that a numerical or power majority group compels a minority group to obey but does not make binding on itself. This is *difference* made legal. By the same token, a just law is a code that a majority compels a minority to follow and that it is willing to follow itself. This is *sameness* made legal.

Let me give another explanation. A law is unjust if it is inflicted on a minority that, as a result of being denied the right to vote, had no part in enacting or devising the law. Who can say that the legislature of Alabama which set up that state's segregation laws was democratically elected? Throughout Alabama all sorts of devious methods are used to prevent Negroes from becoming registered voters, and there are some counties in which, even though Negroes constitute a majority of the population, not a single Negro is registered. Can any law enacted under such circumstances be considered democratically structured?

Sometimes a law is just on its face and unjust in its application. For instance, I have been arrested on a charge of parading without a permit. Now, there is nothing wrong in having an ordinance which requires a permit for a parade. But such an ordinance becomes unjust when it is used to maintain segregation and to deny citizens the First Amendment privilege of peaceful assembly and protest.

I hope you are able to see the distinction I am trying to point out. In no sense do I advocate evading or defying the law, as would the rabid[3] segregationist. That would lead to anarchy.[4] One who breaks an unjust law must do so openly, lovingly, and with a willingness to accept the penalty. I submit that an individual who breaks a law that conscience tells him is unjust, and who willingly accepts the penalty of imprisonment in order to arouse the conscience of the community over its injustice, is in reality expressing the highest respect for law.

Of course, there is nothing new about this kind of civil disobedience. It was evidenced sublimely in the refusal of Shadrach, Meshach, and Abednego to obey the laws of Nebuchadnezzar, on the ground that a higher moral law was at stake. It was practiced superbly by the early Christians, who were willing to face hungry lions and the excruciating pain of chopping blocks rather than submit to certain unjust laws of the Roman Empire. To a degree, academic freedom is a reality today because Socrates practiced civil disobedience. In our own nation, the Boston Tea Party represented a massive act of civil disobedience.

We should never forget that everything Adolf Hitler did in Germany was "legal" and everything the Hungarian freedom fighters did in Hungary was "illegal." It was "illegal" to aid and comfort a Jew in Hitler's Germany. Even so, I am sure that, had I lived in Germany at the time, I would have aided and comforted my Jewish brothers. If today I lived in a Communist country where certain principles dear to the Christian faith are suppressed, I would openly advocate disobeying that country's antireligious laws.

I must make two honest confessions to you, my Christian and Jewish brothers. First, I must confess that over the past few years I have been gravely disappointed with the white moderate. I have almost reached the regrettable conclusion that the Negro's great stumbling block in his stride toward freedom is not the White Citizen's Counciler or the Ku Klux Klanner,[5] but the white moderate, who is more devoted to "order" than to justice; who prefers a negative peace which is the absence of tension to a positive peace which is the presence of justice; who constantly says: "I agree with you in the goal you seek, but I cannot agree with your methods of direct action"; who paternalistically[6] believes he can set the timetable for another man's freedom; who lives by a mythical concept of time and who constantly advises the Negro to wait for a "more convenient season." Shallow understanding from people of goodwill is more frustrating than absolute misunderstanding from people of ill will. Lukewarm acceptance is much more bewildering than outright rejection.

I had hoped that the white moderate would understand that law and order exist for the purpose of establishing justice and that when they fail in this purpose, they become the dangerously structured dams that block the flow of social progress. I had hoped that the white moderate would understand that the present tension in the South is a necessary phase of the transition from an obnoxious negative peace, in which the Negro passively accepted his unjust plight, to a substantive and positive peace, in which all men will respect the dignity and worth of human personality. Actually, we who engage in nonviolent direct action are not the creators of tension. We merely bring to the surface the hidden tension that is already

---

3. **rabid** (rab′ id): extreme.
4. **anarchy** (an′ ər kē): political disorder and violence; lawlessness.
5. **White Citizen's Counciler . . . Ku Klux Klanner:** references to people who participate in one of several white supremacist groups committed to the exclusion and persecution of African Americans and other minority groups.
6. **paternalistically** (pə tʉr′ nəl is′ tik lē): in a manner suggesting a father's relationship with his children.

alive. We bring it out in the open, where it can be seen and dealt with. Like a boil that can never be cured so long as it is covered up but must be opened with all its ugliness to the natural medicines of air and light, injustice must be exposed, with all the tension its exposure creates, to the light of human conscience and the air of national opinion before it can be cured.

In your statement you assert that our actions, even though peaceful, must be condemned because they precipitate violence. But is this a logical assertion? Isn't this like condemning a robbed man because his possession of money precipitated the evil act of robbery? Isn't this like condemning Socrates because his unswerving commitment to truth and his philosophical inquiries precipitated the act by the misguided populace in which they made him drink hemlock? Isn't this like condemning Jesus because his unique God-consciousness and never-ceasing devotion to God's will precipitated the evil act of crucifixion? We must come to see that, as the federal courts have consistently affirmed, it is wrong to urge an individual to cease his efforts to gain his basic constitutional rights because the quest may precipitate violence. Society must protect the robbed and punish the robber. . . .

Oppressed people cannot remain oppressed forever. The yearning for freedom eventually manifests itself, and that is what has happened to the American Negro. Something within has reminded him of his birthright of freedom, and something without has reminded him that it can be gained. Consciously or unconsciously, he has been caught up by the *Zeitgeist*,[7] and with his black brothers of Africa and his brown and yellow brothers of Asia, South America, and the Caribbean, the United States Negro is moving with a sense of great urgency toward the promised land of racial justice. If one recognizes this vital urge that has engulfed the Negro community, one should readily understand why public demonstrations are taking place. The Negro has many pent-up resentments and latent frustrations, and he must release them. So let him march; let him make prayer pilgrimages to the city hall; let him go on freedom rides—and try to understand why he must do so. If his repressed emotions are not released in nonviolent ways, they will seek expression through violence; this is not a threat but a fact of history. So I have not said to my people: "Get rid of your discontent." Rather, I have tried to say that this normal and healthy discontent can be channeled into the creative outlet of nonviolent direct action. And now this approach is being termed extremist.

But though I was initially disappointed at being categorized as an extremist, as I continued to think about the matter, I gradually gained a measure of satisfaction from the label. Was not Jesus an extremist for love: "Love your enemies, bless them that curse you, do good to them that hate you, and pray for them which despitefully use you, and persecute you." Was not Amos an extremist for justice: "Let justice roll down like waters and righteousness like an ever-flowing stream." Was not Paul an extremist for the Christian gospel: "I bear in my body the marks of the Lord Jesus." Was not Martin Luther an extremist: "Here I stand; I cannot do otherwise, so help me God." And John Bunyan: "I will stay in jail to the end of my days before I make a butchery of my conscience." And Abraham Lincoln: "This nation cannot survive half slave and half free." And Thomas Jefferson: "We hold these truths to be self-evident, that all men are created equal. . . ." So the question is not whether we will be extremists, but what kind of extremists we will be. Will we be extremists for hate or for love? Will we be extremists for the preservation of injustice or for the extension of justice? In that dramatic scene on Cavalry's hill three men

---

7. ***Zeitgeist*** (tsīt′ gīst′) *German:* the spirit of the age; trend of thought and feeling in a period of history.

were crucified. We must never forget that all three were crucified for the same crime—the crime of extremism. Two were extremists for immorality, and thus fell below their environment. The other, Jesus Christ, was an extremist for love, truth, and goodness, and thereby rose above his environment. Perhaps the South, the nation and the world are in dire need of creative extremists. . . .

I wish you had commended the Negro sit-inners and demonstrators of Birmingham for their sublime courage, their willingness to suffer, and their amazing discipline in the midst of great provocation. One day the South will recognize its real heroes. They will be the James Merediths,[8] with the noble sense of purpose that enables them to face jeering and hostile mobs, and with the agonizing loneliness that characterizes the life of the pioneer. They will be old, oppressed, battered Negro women, symbolized in a seventy-two-year-old woman in Montgomery, Alabama, who rose up with a sense of dignity and with her people decided not to ride segregated buses, and who responded with ungrammatical profundity to one who inquired about her weariness: "My feets is tired, but my soul is at rest." They will be the young high school and college students, the young ministers of the gospel and a host of their elders, courageously and nonviolently sitting in at lunch counters and willingly going to jail for conscience' sake. One day the South will know that when these disinherited children of God sat down at lunch counters, they were in reality standing up for what is best in the American dream and for the most sacred values in our Judeo-Christian heritage, thereby bringing our nation back to those great wells of democracy which were dug deep by the founding fathers in their formulation of the Constitution and the Declaration of Independence.

Never before have I written so long a letter. I'm afraid it is much too long to take your precious time. I can assure you that it would have been much shorter if I had been writing from a comfortable desk, but what else can one do when he is alone in a narrow jail cell, other than write long letters, think long thoughts, and pray long prayers?

If I have said anything in this letter that overstates the truth and indicates an unreasonable impatience, I beg you to forgive me. If I have said anything that understates the truth and indicates my having a patience that allows me to settle for anything less than brotherhood, I beg God to forgive me.

I hope this letter finds you strong in the faith. I also hope that circumstances will soon make it possible for me to meet each of you, not as an integrationist or a civil-rights leader but as a fellow clergyman and a Christian brother. Let us all hope that the dark clouds of racial prejudice will soon pass away and the deep fog of misunderstanding will be lifted from our fear-drenched communities, and in some not too distant tomorrow the radiant stars of love and brotherhood will shine over our great nation with all their scintillating beauty.

Yours for the cause of Peace and Brotherhood,

Martin Luther King, Jr.

---

8. **James Meredith:** the first black man to attend the University of Mississippi, despite violent protests from local whites.

Thinking About the Selection

A PERSONAL RESPONSE

sharing impressions

1. What ideas and emotions expressed in the letter had the greatest impact on you? Briefly note them in your journal.

constructing interpretations

2. How do you think the clergymen felt after they read King's letter? Point out specific passages that may have particularly influenced their reactions.

3. Explain whether you think King was wise to criticize the white moderate in his letter.

4. Do you agree with King's methods of standing up for his beliefs?
Think about
- the four steps of a nonviolent campaign
- specific kinds of nonviolent direct action that he advocates
- his belief in the need to create "tension"
- his distinction between just and unjust laws
- whether you think he is an extremist

5. How realistic do you find the vision of America that King would like to bring about? Explain your answer.

A CREATIVE RESPONSE

6. How might this letter be different if King had written it today rather than in 1963?

A CRITICAL RESPONSE

7. Of the many points that King makes to support his argument, choose four or five and explain why you find them particularly convincing.

8. How effective do you think King would be in opposing injustice in a totalitarian country: for example, in China or Cuba? Support your answer.

Analyzing the Writer's Craft

PERSUASION

Think about the way that King goes about convincing his audience of the validity of civil disobedience.

Building a Literary Vocabulary. Persuasion is a technique used by speakers and writers to convince an audience to adopt a particular opinion, perform an action, or both. Effective persuasion often appeals to both the emotions and the intellect of the reader or listener. Sometimes persuasion also appeals to ethics—the sense of right and wrong. In the "Letter from Birmingham Jail," King appeals to the reader's intellect by pointing out that his methods have historical precedent in the stance of the early Christians who resisted unjust Roman laws. He appeals to the reader's emotions when he recounts his daughter's tearful response upon learning that an amusement park is closed to black people. When King points out that it is not right to criticize the Birmingham demonstrations while ignoring the conditions that caused the demonstrators to act, he appeals to the reader's ethics.

Application: Analyzing Persuasion. Working with two or three classmates, go back through the selection and find specific examples of each kind of persuasive appeal. Record these examples on a chart similar to the one below. You may use some of the points you cited for question 7, if they are appropriate. Then, decide which method of persuasion was most effective at convincing your group to agree with King's ideas. Share your chart and conclusions with another group of students.

Appeal to reason	Appeal to emotion	Appeal to ethics

Connecting Reading and Writing

1. Imagine that King is on trial in Birmingham for parading without a permit. Choose to be either the prosecuting attorney or the defense attorney and write **notes** as to how you would use King's letter as evidence.

Option: Imagine that you are the judge at King's trial. Write your **verdict,** citing evidence from King's letter.

2. Write a **letter** to King in which you explain whether you find his ideas and methods of standing up for his beliefs applicable today.

Option: Write an **editorial** for your school newspaper in which you assess the applicability of King's ideas to contemporary society.

3. Go back through the selection and write down several of King's aphorisms. Compile them into a **booklet** of quotations to use as a resource for planning the celebration of King's birthday.

Option: Use the aphorisms you identify as **captions** for illustrations for the "Letter" that could be added to this textbook.

4. Read more about the civil rights movement, particularly the years from 1955 to 1968. Create a **time line** of events that could be part of a school display on the U.S. civil rights movement.

Option: Use your findings to create a **photo essay** on the civil rights movement for the same school display.

from Farewell to Manzanar

JEANNE WAKATSUKI HOUSTON AND JAMES D. HOUSTON

A biography of the Houstons appears on page 424.

*A*pproaching the Selection

On December 7, 1941, Japanese planes attacked Pearl Harbor, the U.S. naval base in the Hawaiian Islands. The United States consequently declared war on Japan, thereby entering World War II. Two months later, on February 19, 1942, President Franklin D. Roosevelt signed Executive Order 9066, which gave the War Department the authority to define military areas in the Western states and to exclude from them anyone who might threaten the war effort. Believing that 110,000 people of Japanese ancestry living on the West Coast posed a security threat, the government forcibly removed them to ten inland detention camps for the duration of the war. People had to abandon their property and possessions, much of which would never be regained. Approximately two-thirds of these people were American citizens. Manzanar was the first of the camps to open. It held 10,200 people.

This selection is taken from the memoirs of Jeanne Wakatsuki Houston, who was seven years old when her family was evacuated to Manzanar. As the selection begins, Jeanne and her family have been living in the camp for about a year. Some families are being allowed to leave the camp if they sign an oath promising loyalty to the United States.

*C*onnecting Writing and Reading

Imagine yourself confronted with one of the following situations:

- Your family is evicted from your home.
- Your family loses its source of income.
- Your parents divorce.
- A family member suffers a serious illness.

How well do you think you would cope? Respond in your journal. As you read, compare your ideas with the way the people in this selection cope with a situation beyond their control.

from Farewell to Manzanar

IN SPANISH, _manzanar_ means "apple orchard." Great stretches of Owens Valley were once green with orchards and alfalfa fields. It has been a desert ever since its water started flowing south into Los Angeles, sometime during the twenties. But a few rows of untended pear and apple trees were still growing there when the camp opened, where a shallow water table had kept them alive. In the spring of 1943 we moved to Block 28, right up next to one of the old pear orchards. That's where we stayed until the end of the war, and those trees stand in my memory for the turning of our life in camp, from the outrageous to the tolerable.

Papa pruned and cared for the nearest trees. Late that summer we picked the fruit green and stored it in a root cellar he had dug under our new barracks. At night the wind through the leaves would sound like the surf had sounded in Ocean Park, and while drifting off to sleep I could almost imagine we were still living by the beach.

Mama had set up this move. Block 28 was also close to the camp hospital. For the most part, people lived there who had to have easy access to it. Mama's connection was her job as dietitian. A whole half of one barracks had fallen empty when another family relocated. Mama hustled us in there almost before they'd snapped their suitcases shut.

For all the pain it caused, the loyalty oath finally did speed up the relocation program. One result was a gradual easing of the congestion in the barracks. A shrewd house hunter like Mama could set things up fairly comfortably—by Manzanar standards—if she kept her eyes open. But you had to move fast. As soon as the word got around that so-and-so had been cleared to leave, there would be a kind of tribal restlessness, a nervous rise in the level of neighborhood gossip as wives jockeyed for position to see who would get the empty cubicles.

In Block 28 we doubled our living space— four rooms for the twelve of us. Ray and Woody walled them with sheetrock. We had ceilings this time, and linoleum floors of solid maroon. You had three colors to choose from—maroon, black, and forest green—and there was plenty of it around by this time. Some families would vie with one another for the most elegant floor designs, obtaining a roll of each color from the supply shed, cutting it into diamonds, squares, or triangles, shining it with heating oil, then leaving their doors open so that passers-by could admire the handiwork.

Papa brought his still with him when we moved. He set it up behind the door, where he continued to brew his own sake and brandy. He wasn't drinking as much now, though. He spent a lot of time outdoors. Like many of the older Issei[1] men, he didn't take a regular job in camp. He puttered. He had been working hard for thirty years and, bad as it was for him in some ways, camp did allow him time to dabble with hobbies he would never have found time for otherwise.

Once the first year's turmoil cooled down, the authorities started letting us outside the wire for recreation. Papa used to hike along the creeks that channeled down from the base

---

1. Issei (ē′ sā′): referring to a Japanese person who emigrated to the United States after the Oriental exclusion proclamation of 1907 and was thus ineligible to become a U. S. citizen.

of the Sierras.[2] He brought back chunks of driftwood, and he would pass long hours sitting on the steps carving myrtle limbs into benches, table legs, and lamps, filling our rooms with bits of gnarled, polished furniture.

He hauled stones in off the desert and built a small rock garden outside our doorway, with succulents and a patch of moss. Near it he laid flat steppingstones leading to the stairs.

He also painted watercolors. Until this time I had not known he could paint. He loved to sketch the mountains. If anything made that country habitable it was the mountains themselves, purple when the sun dropped and so sharply etched in the morning light the granite dazzled almost more than the bright snow lacing it. The nearest peaks rose ten thousand feet higher than the valley floor, with Whitney, the highest, just off to the south. They were important for all of us, but especially for the Issei. Whitney reminded Papa of Fujiyama,[3] that is, it gave him the same kind of spiritual sustenance. The tremendous beauty of those peaks was inspirational, as so many natural forms are to the Japanese (the rocks outside our doorway could be those mountains in miniature). They also represented those forces in nature, those powerful and inevitable forces that cannot be resisted, reminding a man that sometimes he must simply endure that which cannot be changed.

Subdued, resigned, Papa's life—all our lives—took on a pattern that would hold for the duration of the war. Public shows of resentment pretty much spent themselves over the loyalty oath crises. *Shikata ga nai*[4] again became the motto, but under altered circumstances. What had to be endured was the climate, the confinement, the steady crumbling away of family life. But the camp itself had been made livable. The government provided for our physical needs. My parents and older brothers and sisters, like most of the internees, accepted their lot and did what they could to make the best of a bad situation. "We're here," Woody would say. "We're here, and there's no use moaning about it forever."

Gardens had sprung up everywhere, in the firebreaks, between the rows of barracks—rock gardens, vegetable gardens, cactus and flower gardens. People who lived in Owens Valley during the war still remember the flowers and lush greenery they could see from the highway as they drove past the main gate. The soil around Manzanar is alluvial and very rich. With water siphoned off from the Los Angeles-bound aqueduct, a large farm was under cultivation just outside the camp, providing the mess halls with lettuce, corn, tomatoes, eggplant, string beans, horseradish, and cucumbers. Near Block 28 some of the men who had been professional gardeners built a small park, with mossy nooks, ponds, waterfalls, and curved wooden bridges. Sometimes in the evenings we could walk down the raked gravel paths. You could face away from the barracks, look past a tiny rapids toward the darkening mountains, and for a while not be a prisoner at all. You could hang suspended in some odd, almost lovely land you could not escape from yet almost didn't want to leave.

As the months at Manzanar turned to years, it became a world unto itself, with its own logic and familiar ways. In time, staying there seemed far simpler than moving once again to another, unknown place. It was as if the war were forgotten, our reason for being there forgotten. The present, the little bit of busywork you had right in front of you, became the most

---

2. Sierras (sē er′ əz): the Sierra Nevada, a mountain range in eastern California.

3. Fujiyama (fo͞o′ jē yä′ mə): the highest mountain in Japan.

4. *Shikata ga nai* (shē kä′ tə gä nī): a Japanese phrase meaning "it cannot be helped" or "it must be done."

Grandfather and Grandchildren Awaiting Evacuation Bus,
Hayward, California, 1942, DOROTHEA LANGE.
National Archives, Washington, D.C.

urgent thing. In such a narrowed world, in order to survive, you learn to contain your rage and your despair, and you try to re-create, as well as you can, your normality, some sense of things continuing. The fact that America had accused us, or excluded us, or imprisoned us, or whatever it might be called, did not change the kind of world we wanted. Most of us were born in this country; we had no other models. Those parks and gardens lent it an Oriental character, but in most ways it was a totally equipped American small town, complete with schools, churches, Boy Scouts, beauty parlors, neighborhood gossip, fire and police departments, glee clubs, softball leagues, Abbott and Costello movies, tennis courts, and traveling shows. (I still remember an Indian who turned up one Saturday billing himself as a Sioux chief, wearing bear claws and head feathers. In the firebreak he sang songs and danced his tribal dances while hundreds of us watched.)

In our family, while Papa puttered, Mama made her daily rounds to the mess halls, helping young mothers with their feeding, planning diets for the various ailments people suffered from. She wore a bright yellow, long-billed sun hat she had made herself and always kept stiffly starched. Afternoons I would see her coming from blocks away, heading home, her tiny figure warped by heat waves and that bonnet a yellow flower wavering in the glare.

In their disagreement over serving the country, Woody and Papa had struck a kind of compromise. Papa talked him out of volunteering; Woody waited for the army to induct him. Meanwhile he clerked in the co-op general store. Kiyo, nearly thirteen by this time, looked forward to the heavy winds. They moved the sand around and uncovered obsidian arrowheads he could sell to old men in camp for fifty cents apiece. Ray, a few years older, played in the six-man touch football league, sometimes against Caucasian teams who would come in from Lone Pine or Independence. My sister Lillian was in high school and singing with a hillbilly band called The Sierra Stars—jeans, cowboy hats, two guitars, and a tub bass. And my oldest brother, Bill, led a dance band called The Jive Bombers—brass and rhythm, with cardboard foldout music stands lettered "J.B." Dances were held every weekend in one of the recreation halls. Bill played trumpet and took vocals on Glenn Miller arrangements of such tunes as "In the Mood," "String of Pearls," and "Don't Fence Me In." He didn't sing "Don't Fence Me In" out of protest, as if trying quietly to mock the authorities. It just happened to be a hit song one year, and they all wanted to be an up-to-date American swing band. They would blast it out into recreation barracks full of bobby-soxed, jitterbugging couples:

> Oh, give me land, lots of land
> Under starry skies above,
> Don't fence me in.
> Let me ride through the wide
> Open country that I love . . .

Pictures of the band, in their bow ties and jackets, appeared in the high school yearbook for 1943–1944, along with pictures of just about everything else in camp that year. It was called *Our World*. In its pages you see school kids with armloads of books, wearing cardigan sweaters and walking past rows of tar-papered shacks. You see chubby girl yell leaders, pompons flying as they leap with glee. You read about the school play, called *Growing Pains*, ". . . the story of a typical American home, in this case that of the McIntyres. They see their boy and girl tossed into the normal awkward growing up stage, but can offer little assistance or direction in their turbulent course. . . ," with Shoji Katayama as George McIntyre, Takudo

Ando as Terry McIntyre, and Mrs. McIntyre played by Kazuko Nagai.

All the class pictures are in there, from the seventh grade through twelfth, with individual head shots of seniors, their names followed by the names of the high schools they would have graduated from on the outside: Theodore Roosevelt, Thomas Jefferson, Herbert Hoover, Sacred Heart. You see pretty girls on bicycles, chicken yards full of fat pullets, patients back-tilted in dental chairs, lines of laundry, and finally, two large blowups, the first of a high tower with a searchlight, against a Sierra backdrop, the next a two-page endsheet showing a wide path that curves among rows of elm trees. White stones border the path. Two dogs are following an old woman in gardening clothes as she strolls along. She is in the middle distance, small beneath the trees, beneath the snowy peaks. It is winter. All the elms are bare. The scene is both stark and comforting. This path leads toward one edge of camp, but the wire is out of sight, or out of focus. The tiny woman seems very much at ease. She and her tiny dogs seem almost swallowed by the landscape, or floating in it.

Postscript

The Manzanar War Relocation Center officially closed in November 1945. The older Wakatsuki children moved to the East Coast to avoid the prejudice they felt they would encounter on the West Coast. Jeanne, her parents, and her youngest brother, however, returned to the coastal area of southern California. Jeanne eventually graduated from high school in San Jose and studied sociology and journalism at San Jose State College, where she and her husband, James Houston, met.

Thinking About the Selection

A PERSONAL RESPONSE

sharing impressions

1. What mood, or feeling, does this selection leave you with? Describe this mood in your journal.

constructing interpretations

2. How would you describe Jeanne Wakatsuki Houston's feelings about Manzanar as she wrote this memoir?

Think about
- her description of the high school yearbook
- her description of her family's activities
- her description of the physical surroundings
- the pear trees she mentions at the beginning of the selection

3. Who do you think probably had the hardest time coping with the situation of internment—the parents, the older children, or the younger children? Use details from the selection to explain your answer.

4. How do you think the experience of detention affected Japanese Americans later in life?

5. What relationship do you see between the setting and the mood of this selection?
   Think about
   • the qualities you associate with a desert
   • the presence of the Sierra Nevada in the distance
   • your response to question 1

6. What do you think is the main reason why Jeanne Wakatsuki Houston wrote this memoir? Cite examples to support your response.

7. Many now feel that the internment of Japanese Americans during World War II was irresponsible, unnecessary, and a violation of human rights. In your opinion, could something like it ever happen again? Explain.

Analyzing the Writer's Craft

IRONY

Think about the details of life in Manzanar that are highlighted in the yearbook. Why do so many of these details seem absurd or out of place?

Building a Literary Vocabulary. Irony is the contrast between what is expected and what actually exists or happens. In *Farewell to Manzanar*, details about camp life point out the differences between appearance or expectation and the reality of the situation. For example, the Japanese Americans in Manzanar were sent to the camp because the United States government feared they might be more loyal to Japan. In reality, the society created in the camp by the Japanese Americans was decidedly American.

Application: Interpreting Irony. Working in small groups, list other examples of irony found in the selection. For each example write a sentence explaining what is ironic. Then discuss which examples of irony had the greatest impact on the members of the group. Share your results with the rest of the class.

Connecting Reading and Writing

1. Imagine that you are leaving your own community. Describe in a **memoir** various places in your community that you want to remember. Use the selection as a model for the kinds of details to include.

Option: Write a **poem** using images to capture the sights, sounds, and smells of one of these places.

2. Read later chapters of *Farewell to Manzanar* in order to gain insights into the long-term effects of this experience on Jeanne Wakatsuki Houston. Then write a possible **conversation** in which Houston explains to her child what her experience at Manzanar was like and how it affected her life in later years. Make sure to include questions that the child might pose as the conversation develops.

Option: Write this conversation as a **dramatic scene.**

3. Prepare a **collage** that visually represents the various thoughts and feelings evoked by this selection. Include quotations from the selection that evoked strong feelings in you.

Option: Write a **personal essay** in your journal that explains how this selection affected you.

4. Read another account of confinement, such as one by an Indian removed to a reservation, a survivor of a Nazi concentration camp, a prisoner of war, or a refugee detained in a camp. Compare the account to the Houstons' in an **expository essay** to be shared with a history class studying human rights.

Option: Present this information in a **report** to be submitted to an organization crusading for human rights.

Blues Ain't No Mockin Bird

TONI CADE BAMBARA

A biography of Bambara appears on page 418.

Approaching the Story

This story is one of many that Toni Cade Bambara has written about the experiences of African Americans. Like much of her work, the story presents the perceptions of children and is written in a dialect appropriate to the narrator. The reader must make an effort to understand the implications of the details given and to become attuned to the rhythms of African-American speech.

Connecting Writing and Reading

Which of the following situations would you find intrusive? Copy this chart in your journal and indicate your responses.

	Yes	No
• someone smiles at you	☐	☐
• someone gives you a gift	☐	☐
• someone pays you a compliment	☐	☐
• someone photographs you	☐	☐
• someone interviews you	☐	☐
• someone enters your home	☐	☐
• someone goes through your dresser drawers or luggage	☐	☐

For every "yes" answer, explain the circumstances in which the situation would seem intrusive. Continue to consider what makes an action intrusive as you read about one family's encounter with strangers.

Blues Ain't No Mockin Bird

HE PUDDLE HAD frozen over, and me and Cathy went stompin in it. The twins from next door, Tyrone and Terry, were swingin so high out of sight we forgot we were waitin our turn on the tire. Cathy jumped up and came down hard on her heels and started tap-dancin. And the frozen patch splinterin every which way underneath kinda spooky. "Looks like a plastic spider web," she said. "A sort of weird spider, I guess, with many mental problems." But really it looked like the crystal paperweight Granny kept in the parlor. She was on the back porch Granny was, making the cakes drunk. The old ladle dripping rum into the Christmas tins, like it used to drip maple syrup into the pails when we lived in the Judsons' woods, like it poured cider into the vats when we were on the Cooper place, like it used to scoop buttermilk and soft cheese when we lived at the dairy.

"Go tell that man we ain't a bunch of trees."

"Ma'am?"

"I said to tell that man to get away from here with that camera." Me and Cathy look over toward the meadow where the men with the station wagon'd been roamin around all mornin. The tall man with a huge camera lassoed to his shoulder was buzzin our way.

"They're makin movie pictures," yelled Tyrone, stiffenin his legs and twistin so the tire'd come down slow so they could see.

"They're makin movie pictures," sang out Terry.

"That boy don't never have anything original to say," say Cathy grown-up.

By the time the man with the camera had cut across our neighbor's yard, the twins were out of the trees swingin low and Granny was onto the steps, the screen door bammin soft and scratchy against her palms. "We thought we'd get a shot or two of the house and everything and then—"

"Good mornin," Granny cut him off. And smiled that smile.

"Good mornin," he said, head all down the way Bingo does when you yell at him about the bones on the kitchen floor. "Nice place you got here, aunty. We thought we'd take a—"

"Did you?" said Granny with her eyebrows. Cathy pulled up her socks and giggled.

"Nice things here," said the man, buzzin his camera over the yard. The pecan barrels, the sled, me and Cathy, the flowers, the printed stones along the driveway, the trees, the twins, the toolshed.

"I don't know about the thing, the it, and the stuff," said Granny, still talkin with her eyebrows. "Just people here is what I tend to consider."

Camera man stopped buzzin. Cathy giggled into her collar.

"Mornin, ladies," a new man said. He had come up behind us when we weren't lookin. "And gents," discoverin the twins givin him a nasty look. "We're filmin for the county," he said with a smile. "Mind if we shoot a bit around here?"

"I do indeed," said Granny with no smile. Smilin man was smiling up a storm. So was Cathy. But he didn't seem to have another word to say, so he and the camera man backed on out of the yard, but you could hear the camera buzzin still. "Suppose you just shut that machine off," said Granny real low through her teeth, and took a step down off the porch and then another.

"Now, aunty," Camera said, pointin the thing straight at her.

"Your mama and I are not related."

Smilin man got his notebook out and a chewed-up pencil. "Listen," he said, movin back into our yard, "we'd like to have a statement from you . . . for the film. We're filmin for the county, see. Part of the food stamp[1] campaign. You know about the food stamps?"

Granny said nuthin.

"Maybe there's somethin you want to say for the film. I see you grow your own vegetables," he smiled real nice. "If more folks did that, see, there'd be no need—"

Granny wasn't sayin nuthin. So they backed on out, buzzin at our clothesline and the twins' bicycles, then back on down to the meadow. The twins were danglin in the tire, lookin at Granny. Me and Cathy were waitin, too, cause Granny always got something to say. She teaches steady with no let-up. "I was on this bridge one time," she started off. "Was a crowd cause this man was goin to jump, you understand. And a minister was there and the police and some other folks. His woman was there, too."

"What was they doin?" asked Tyrone.

"Tryin to talk him out of it was what they was doin. The minister talkin about how it was a mortal sin, suicide. His woman takin bites out of her own hand and not even knowin it, so nervous and cryin and talkin fast."

"So what happened?" asked Tyrone.

"So here comes . . . this person . . . with a camera, takin pictures of the man and the minister and the woman. Takin pictures of the man in his misery about to jump, cause life so bad and people been messin with him so bad. This person takin up the whole roll of film practically. But savin a few, of course."

"Of course," said Cathy, hatin the person. Me standin there wonderin how Cathy knew it was "of course" when I didn't and it was *my* grandmother.

After a while Tyrone say, "Did he jump?"

"Yeh, did he jump?" say Terry all eager.

And Granny just stared at the twins till their faces swallow up the eager and they don't even care any more about the man jumpin. Then she goes back onto the porch and lets the screen door go for itself. I'm lookin to Cathy to finish the story cause she knows Granny's whole story before me even. Like she knew how come we move so much and Cathy ain't but a third cousin we picked up on the way last Thanksgivin visitin. But she knew it was on account of people drivin Granny crazy till she'd get up in the night and start packin. Mumblin and packin and wakin everybody up sayin, "Let's get away from here before I kill me somebody." Like people wouldn't pay her for things like they said they would. Or Mr. Judson bringin us boxes of old clothes and raggedy magazines. Or Mrs. Cooper comin in our kitchen and touchin everything and sayin how clean it all was. Granny goin crazy, and Granddaddy Cain pullin her off the people, sayin, "Now, now, Cora." But next day loadin up the truck, with rocks all in his jaw, madder than Granny in the first place.

"I read a story once," said Cathy, soundin like Granny teacher. "About this lady Goldilocks who barged into a house that wasn't even hers. And not invited, you understand. Messed over the people's groceries and broke up the people's furniture. Had the nerve to sleep in the folks' bed."

"Then what happened?" asked Tyrone. "What they do, the folks, when they come in to all this mess?"

"Did they make her pay for it?" asked Terry, makin a fist. "I'd've made her pay me."

I didn't even ask. I could see Cathy actress was very likely to just walk away and leave us

1. **food stamp:** any of the federal coupons given to qualifying low-income persons for use in buying food.

in mystery about this story which I heard was about some bears.

"Did they throw her out?" asked Tyrone, like his father sounds when he's bein extra nasty-plus to the washin-machine man.

"Woulda," said Terry. "I woulda gone upside her head with my fist and—"

"You woulda done whatcha always do—go cry to Mama, you big baby," said Tyrone. So naturally Terry starts hittin on Tyrone and next thing you know they tumblin out the tire and rollin on the ground. But Granny didn't say a thing or send the twins home or step out on the steps to tell us about how we can't afford to be fightin among ourselves. She didn't say nuthin. So I get into the tire to take my turn. And I could see her leanin up against the pantry table, starin at the cakes she was puttin up for the Christmas sale, mumblin real low and grumpy and holdin her forehead like it wanted to fall off and mess up the rum cakes.

Behind me I hear before I can see Granddaddy Cain comin through the woods in his field boots. Then I twist around to see the shiny black oilskin[2] cuttin through what little left there was of yellows, reds, and oranges. His great white head not quite round cause of this bloody thing high on his shoulder, like he was wearin a cap sideways. He takes the shortcut through the pecan grove, and the sound of twigs snappin overhead and underfoot travels clear and cold all the way up to us. And here comes Smilin and Camera up behind him like they was goin to do somethin. Folks like to go for him sometimes. Cathy say it's because he's so tall and quiet and like a king. And people just can't stand it. But Smilin and Camera don't hit him in the head or nuthin. They just buzz on him as he stalks by with the chicken hawk slung over his shoulder, squawkin, drippin red down the back of the oilskin. He passes the porch and stops a second for Granny to see he's caught

the hawk at last, but she's just starin and mumblin, and not at the hawk. So he nails the bird to the toolshed door, the hammerin crackin through the eardrums. And the bird flappin himself to death and droolin down the door to paint the gravel in the driveway red, then brown, then black. And the two men movin up on tiptoe like they was invisible or we were blind, one.

"Get them persons out of my flower bed, Mister Cain," says Granny, moanin real low like at a funeral.

"How come your grandmother calls her husband 'Mister Cain' all the time?" Tyrone whispers all loud and noisy and from the city and don't know no better. Like his mama, Miss Myrtle, tell us never mind the formality as if we had no better breedin than to call her Myrtle, plain. And then this awful thing—a giant hawk—come wailin up over the meadow, flyin low and tilted and screamin, zigzaggin through the pecan grove, breakin branches and hollerin, snappin past the clothesline, flyin every which way, flyin into things reckless with crazy.

"He's come to claim his mate," say Cathy fast, and ducks down. We all fall quick and flat into the gravel driveway, stones scrapin my face. I squinch my eyes open again at the hawk on the door, tryin to fly up out of her death like it was just a sack flown into by mistake. Her body holdin her there on that nail, though. The mate beatin the air overhead and clutchin for hair, for heads, for landin space.

The camera man duckin and bendin and runnin and fallin, jigglin the camera and scared. And Smilin jumpin up and down swipin at the huge bird, tryin to bring the hawk down with just his raggedy ole cap. Granddaddy Cain straight up and silent,

---

2. **oilskin:** a garment made waterproof by treatment with oil.

watchin the circles of the hawk, then aimin the hammer off his wrist. The giant bird fallin, silent and slow. Then here comes Camera and Smilin all big and bad now that the awful screechin thing is on its back and broken, here they come. And Granddaddy Cain looks up at them like it was the first time noticin, but not payin them too much mind cause he's listenin, we all listenin, to that low groanin music comin from the porch. And we figure any minute now, Granny gonna bust through that screen with somethin in her hand and murder on her mind. So Granddaddy say above the buzzin, but quiet, "Good day, gentlemen." Just like that. Like he's invited them in to play cards and they'd stayed too long and all the sandwiches were gone and Reverend Webb was droppin by and it was time to go.

They didn't know what to do. But like Cathy say, folks can't stand Granddaddy tall and silent and like a king. They can't neither. The smile the men smilin is pullin the mouth back and showin the teeth. Lookin like the wolf man, both of them. Then Granddaddy holds his hand out—this huge hand I used to sit in when I was a baby and he'd carry me through the house to my mother like I was a gift on a tray. Like he used to on the trains. They called the other men just waiters. But they spoke of Granddaddy separate and said, The Waiter. And said he had engines in his feet and motors in his hands and couldn't no train throw him off and couldn't nobody turn him round. They were big enough for motors, his hands were. He held that one hand out all still and it gettin to be not at all a hand but a person in itself.

"He wants you to hand him the camera," Smilin whispers to Camera, tiltin his head to talk secret like they was in the jungle or somethin and come upon a native that don't speak the language. The men start untyin the straps, and they put the camera into that great hand speckled with the hawk's blood all black and crackly now. And the hand don't even drop with the weight, just the fingers move, curl up around the machine. But Granddaddy lookin straight at the men. They lookin at each other and everywhere but at Granddaddy's face.

"We filmin for the county, see," say Smilin. "We puttin together a movie for the food stamp program . . . filmin all around these parts. Uhh, filmin for the county."

"Can I have my camera back?" say the tall man with no machine on his shoulder, but still keepin it high like the camera was still there or needed to be. "Please, sir."

Then Granddaddy's other hand flies up like a sudden and gentle bird, slaps down fast on top of the camera and lifts off half like it was a calabash[3] cut for sharing.

"Hey," Camera jumps forward. He gathers up the parts into his chest and everything unrollin and fallin all over. "Whatcha tryin to do? You'll ruin the film." He looks down into his chest of metal reels and things like he protectin a kitten from the cold.

"You standin in the missis' flower bed," say Granddaddy. "This is our own place."

The two men look at him, then at each other, then back at the mess in the camera man's chest, and they just back off. One sayin over and over all the way down to the meadow, "Watch it, Bruno. Keep ya fingers off the film." Then Granddaddy picks up the hammer and jams it into the oilskin pocket, scrapes his boots, and goes into the house. And you can hear the squish of his boots headin though the house. And you can see the funny shadow he throws from the parlor window onto the ground by the string bean patch. The hammer draggin the pocket of the oilskin out so Granddaddy looked even wider. Granny was hummin now—high, not low

---

3. **calabash** (kal′ ə bash′): a gourdlike fruit.

and grumbly. And she was doin the cakes again, you could smell the molasses from the rum.

"There's this story I'm goin to write one day," say Cathy dreamer. "About the proper use of the hammer."

"Can I be in it?" Tyrone say, with his hand up like it was a matter of first come, first served.

"Perhaps," say Cathy, climbin onto the tire to pump us up. "If you there and ready."

Thinking About the Story

A PERSONAL RESPONSE

sharing impressions

1. Jot down words and phrases in your journal that describe your impression of Granny, Granddaddy, and the other members of the family.

constructing interpretations

2. What do you suppose is Cathy's idea of "the proper use of the hammer"?

Think about
- how Granddaddy Cain uses the hammer in dealing with the chicken hawks
- what this incident reveals to the filmmakers about Granddaddy Cain's character

3. Do you think Granny and Granddaddy Cain are right to react to the filmmakers as they do? Explain.

Think about
- how the filmmakers address them and treat their property
- why the film is being made
- whether you consider the filmmakers' actions intrusive

4. Summarize the Cains' beliefs about the proper way to treat people.

Think about
- the point of Granny's story about the man on the bridge
- the reasons the family has moved so often
- how Granny addresses her husband and how the narrator and Cathy address the twins' mother

A CREATIVE RESPONSE

5. What might have happened if Granddaddy Cain had not come home when he did?

A CRITICAL RESPONSE

6. Based on what you know about the narrator, explain why this person is or is not a good choice to tell the story.

7. How do you think the title relates to the story?
   Think about
   • blues as a type of African-American folk music characterized by a slow tempo and melancholy words
   • characteristics one might associate with mockingbirds

8. Discuss which story has the more important message for your community: "Blues Ain't No Mockin Bird" or "Everyday Use."

nalyzing the Writer's Craft

THEME

Think about the brief stories embedded within the main story in "Blues Ain't No Mockin Bird." What might be the point of including these stories?

Building a Literary Vocabulary. Theme is a central idea or message in a work of literature. Theme should not be confused with subject, or what the work is about. Rather, theme is a perception about life or human nature that the writer shares with the reader. In Alice Walker's "Everyday Use," for example, the subject is family relationships. The main theme is that family relationships may be complex, unpredictable, and far from ideal. Walker includes two episodes that convey themes related to this main theme. In one episode the narrator describes a fantasy in which her daughter Dee embraces her on a TV talk show. The theme of this episode is that people sometimes dream about storybook relationships denied them in real life. In another episode the narrator recalls how Dee seemed pleased when the family home was destroyed even though her sister Maggie was severely burned. The theme of this episode is that even in times of great crisis a family member may be aloof rather than loving.

Application: Identifying Theme. Working in small groups, decide what themes are conveyed by these brief stories or episodes within "Blues Ain't No Mockin Bird": the story Granny tells about the man on the bridge, Cathy's retelling of the Goldilocks tale, and the episode involving the chicken hawks.

Consider how these themes relate to the family's encounter with the filmmakers and try to determine the theme of the story as a whole.

Present your ideas in a diagram similar to the one below.

Blues Ain't No Mockin Bird

Story of man on bridge	Goldilocks tale	Hawk incident
Theme:_____	**Theme:**_____	**Theme:** _____
_____	_____	_____
_____	_____	_____

Overall theme: _____

_____

_____

_____

Connecting Reading and Writing

1. Add another **episode** to the story, describing the incident that made the family leave the Judsons' woods or the Cooper place. Read your episode to classmates.

Option: Perform the incident as a **dramatic scene** for the class.

2. Use the Cains' experience to create a set of **guidelines** for reporters and for directors of documentary films.

Option: Write a **letter of complaint** that you would send to the county on the Cains' behalf.

3. Toni Cade Bambara defines her reasons for writing as follows: "Through writing, I attempt to celebrate the tradition of resistance, attempt to tap Black potential, and try to join the chorus of voices that argues exploitation and misery are neither inevitable nor necessary." In an **evaluation** that you would send to Bambara, comment on how these purposes are reflected in her story.

Option: Write a **recommendation** for including this story in a forthcoming anthology of resistance literature.

from **To Be Young, Gifted, and Black**

Lorraine Hansberry

O, the things that we have learned in this unkind house that we have to tell the world about!

Despair? Did someone say despair was a question in the world? Well then, listen to the sons of those who have known little else if you wish to know the resiliency of this thing you would so quickly resign to mythhood, this thing called the human spirit. . . .

Life? Ask those who have tasted of it in pieces rationed out by enemies.

Love? Ah, ask the troubadours who come from those who have loved when all reason pointed to the uselessness and foolhardiness of love. Perhaps we shall be the teachers when it is done. Out of the depths of pain we have thought to be our sole heritage in this world—O, we know about love!

And that is why I say to *you* that, though it be a thrilling and marvelous thing to be merely young and gifted in such times, it is doubly so, doubly dynamic—to be young, gifted, *and black.*

Look at the work that awaits you!

Write if you will: but write about the world as it is and as you think it *ought* to be and must be—if there is to be a world.

Write about all the things that men have written about since the beginning of writing and talking—but write *to a point.* Work hard at it, *care* about it.

Write about *our people:* tell their story. You have something glorious to draw on begging for attention. Don't pass it up. *Use* it.

Good luck to you. This Nation needs your gifts.

Perfect them!

November Cotton Flower   JEAN TOOMER

A Note of Humility   ARNA BONTEMPS

Biographies of Toomer and Bontemps appear on pages 430 and 419.

Approaching the Poems

These two poems reflect important concerns of the Harlem Renaissance. In "November Cotton Flower," Jean Toomer draws upon the folk culture of African Americans in the South. Toomer had sojourned in Georgia in 1921, returning to Harlem with a new admiration for "the Negro peasant, strong with the tang of fields and soil." The boll weevil mentioned in the first line of his poem is a particularly harmful beetle, capable in large numbers of destroying an entire cotton crop. In "A Note of Humility," Arna Bontemps expresses the disillusionment of many African Americans whose circumstances ultimately frustrated their potential.

November Cotton Flower

Boll weevil's coming, and the winter's cold,
Made cotton stalks look rusty, seasons old,
And cotton, scarce as any southern snow,
Was vanishing; the branch, so pinched and slow,
5   Failed in its function as the autumn rake;
Drought fighting soil had caused the soil to take
All water from the streams; dead birds were found
In wells a hundred feet below the ground—
Such was the season when the flower bloomed.
10   Old folks were startled, and it soon assumed[1]
Significance. Superstition saw
Something it had never seen before:
Brown eyes that loved without a trace of fear,
Beauty so sudden for that time of year.

1. **assumed** (ə so͞omd′): took on.

A Note of Humility

When all our hopes are sown on stony ground,
And we have yielded up the thought of gain,
Long after our last songs have lost their sound,
We may come back, we may come back again.

5   When thorns have choked the last green thing we loved,
And we have said all there is to say,
When love that moved us once leaves us unmoved,
Then men like us may come to have a day.

For it will be with us as with the bee,
10 The meager[1] ant, the sea-gull and the loon;
We may come back to triumph mournfully
An hour or two, but it will not be soon.

1. meager (mē′ gər): thin, lean, emaciated.

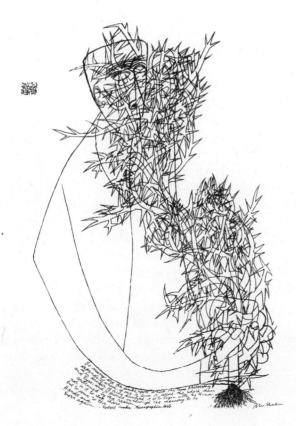

Blind Botanist, 1961, BEN SHAHN.

The Censors

LUISA VALENZUELA

A biography of Valenzuela appears on page 430.

Approaching the Story

Writers can reveal injustice by creating cautionary tales that exaggerate dangerous tendencies in the modern world. In Luisa Valenzuela's (loo e' sä vä len zwe' lä) "The Censors," set in a fictitious Latin American country, censorship has reached new bureaucratic heights.

Note as you read that the names Juan and Juancito, the diminutive form of Juan, refer to the same person.

POOR JUAN! ONE day they caught him with his guard down before he could even realize that what he had taken as a stroke of luck was really one of fate's dirty tricks. These things happen the minute you're careless and you let down your guard, as one often does. Juancito let happiness—a feeling you can't trust—get the better of him when he received from a confidential source Mariana's new address in Paris and he knew that she hadn't forgotten him. Without thinking twice, he sat down at his table and wrote her a letter. *The* letter that keeps his mind off his job during the day and won't let him sleep at night (what had he scrawled, what had he put on that sheet of paper he sent to Mariana?).

Juan knows there won't be a problem with the letter's contents, that it's irreproachable, harmless. But what about the rest? He knows that they examine, sniff, feel, and read between the lines of each and every letter, and check its tiniest comma and most accidental stain. He knows that all letters pass from hand to hand and go through all sorts of tests in the huge censorship offices and that, in the end, very few continue on their way. Usually it takes months, even years, if there aren't any snags; all this time the freedom, maybe even the life, of both sender and receiver is in jeopardy. And that's why Juan's so down in the dumps: thinking that something might happen to Mariana because of his letters. Of all people, Mariana, who must finally feel safe there where she always dreamed she'd live. But he knows that the Censor's Secret Command operates all over the world and cashes in on the discount in air rates; there's nothing to stop them from going as far as that hidden Paris neighborhood, kidnapping Mariana, and returning to their cozy homes, certain of having fulfilled their noble mission.

Well, you've got to beat them to the punch, do what everyone tries to do: sabotage the machinery, throw sand in its gears, get to the bottom of the problem so as to stop it.

This was Juan's sound plan when he, like many others, applied for a censor's job—not because he had a calling or needed a job: no, he applied simply to intercept his own letter, a consoling but unoriginal idea. He was hired immediately, for each day more and more censors are needed and no one would bother to check on his references.

Ulterior motives couldn't be overlooked by the Censorship Division, but they needn't be too strict with those who applied. They knew how hard it would be for those poor guys to find the letter they wanted and even if they did, what's a letter or two when the new censor would snap up so many others? That's how Juan managed to join the Post Office's Censorship Division, with a certain goal in mind.

The building had a festive air on the outside which contrasted with its inner staidness. Little by little, Juan was absorbed by his job and he felt at peace since he was doing everything he could to get his letter for Mariana. He didn't even worry when, in his first month, he was sent to Section K where envelopes are very carefully screened for explosives.

It's true that on the third day, a fellow worker had his right hand blown off by a letter, but the division chief claimed it was sheer negligence on the victim's part. Juan and the other employees were allowed to go back to their work, albeit feeling less secure. After work, one of them tried to organize a strike to demand higher wages for unhealthy work, but Juan didn't join in; after thinking it over, he reported him to his superiors and thus got promoted.

You don't form a habit by doing something once, he told himself as he left his boss's office. And when he was transferred to Section J, where letters are carefully checked for poison dust, he felt he had climbed a rung in the ladder.

By working hard, he quickly reached Section E where the work was more interesting, for he could now read and analyze the letters' contents. Here he could even hope to get hold of his letter which, judging by the time that had elapsed, had gone through the other sections and was probably floating around in this one.

Soon his work became so absorbing that his noble mission blurred in his mind. Day after day he crossed out whole paragraphs in red ink, pitilessly chucking many letters into the censored basket. These were horrible days when he was shocked by the subtle and conniving ways employed by people to pass on subversive messages; his instincts were so sharp that he found behind a simple "the weather's unsettled" or "prices continue to soar" the wavering hand of someone secretly scheming to overthrow the Government.

His zeal brought him swift promotion. We don't know if this made him happy. Very few letters reached him in Section B—only a handful passed the other hurdles—so he read them over and over again, passed them under a magnifying glass, searched for microprint with an electronic microscope, and tuned his sense of smell so that he was beat by the time he made it home. He'd barely manage to warm up his soup, eat some fruit, and fall into bed, satisfied with having done his duty. Only his darling mother worried, but she couldn't get him back on the right road. She'd say, though it wasn't always true: Lola called, she's at the bar with the girls, they miss you, they're waiting for you. Or else she'd leave a bottle of red wine on the table. But Juan wouldn't overdo it: any distraction could make him lose his edge and the perfect censor had to be alert, keen, attentive, and sharp to nab cheats. He had a truly patriotic task, both self-denying and uplifting.

His basket for censored letters became the best fed as well as the most cunning basket in the whole Censorship Division. He was about to congratulate himself for having finally discovered his true mission, when his letter to Mariana reached his hands. Naturally, he censored it without regret. And just as naturally, he couldn't stop them from executing him the following morning, another victim of his devotion to his work.

Reviewing Concepts

LITERARY PROTEST: ENGAGING THE READER

*making
connections*

The writers represented in this unit appeal to both the mind and the heart of the reader. They use a variety of techniques to do so, including use of vivid details, choice of words charged with emotional power, and logical argument. For example, in the excerpt from *To Be a Slave,* Julius Lester quotes from a narrative that tells about distraught slaves struggling to rescue their drowning children: "Two of the women leaped overboard after the children—the third was already confined by a chain to another woman and could not get into the water, but in struggling to disengage herself, she broke her arm and died a few days after of a fever." Details such as the leaping of the two women into the water and the desperate attempt of the third woman to break free re-create for the reader the horror of the mothers' plight. Phrases such as "confined by a chain" and "struggling to disengage herself" reinforce the mood of horror.

Analyze the techniques that the writers in this unit use to appeal to the emotions and the intellect of the reader. For each selection you have read, create a bar graph on which you can indicate, on a scale of 0 to 5, the relative appeal of the details used, the words chosen, and the arguments presented. A sample bar graph has been done for the excerpt from *To Be a Slave.*

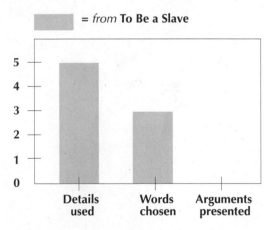

*describing
connections*

Draw some conclusions from the information on your bar graphs. Write **notes** for an oral presentation on literary protest in which you state some generalizations about the selections in this unit.

> ### Think about
> • which selections appeal primarily to the emotions
> • which selections appeal primarily to the intellect

African Mask, Congo Region

Affirming Identity

"*I am my mother's daughter, and the drums of Africa beat in my heart.*"

MARY McLEOD BETHUNE

Affirming Identity

Since the 1970's, minority cultures have become increasingly important in American life. Today, films directed by African Americans earn critical and popular acclaim. Books by Asian-American writers grace bookstore windows. Hispanic and Native American poets frequently read their works in libraries, lecture halls, and cultural centers. More than ever before, minority voices are exploring their experiences and affirming their cultural identities.

The unique features of any culture foster in its members a sense of identity as a special people, distinct from other cultural groups. These features may include language, traditions, values, and perspectives on life events as well as special holidays, customs, clothing, hairstyles, and cuisine. Mexican Americans, for example, speak Spanish. Many observe a holiday known as *Cinco de Mayo* (the Fifth of May), which commemorates of a victory by the Mexican army in 1862. On festive occasions, Mexican-American children often take turns trying to break open a piñata filled with candy, coins, and toys—a custom drawn from Mexican festivals. By keeping alive their cultural heritage, Mexican Americans retain the sense of who they are as a people.

The writers represented in this unit all explore the interplay between cultural and personal identity. Some writers do so mainly by dealing with issues that are unique to their culture. The issue of discrimination, for example, is a key to the African-American experience. Zora Neale Hurston, Martin Luther King, Jr., and Maya Angelou all address this issue—Hurston, by affirming her identity in confident and ringing tones; King, by firmly asserting the rights of African Americans to freedom and justice; and Angelou, by describing her struggle against prejudice as a young woman. A key to the Hispanic experience is the issue of acquiring English as a second language. Ernesto Galarza and Richard Rodriguez address this issue in recalling their experiences in American schools.

Other writers focus more directly on personal identity as it evolves in a specific cultural context. In "High Horse's Courting," for example, the main character must prove his worth according to the traditions of the Sioux culture. In the stories by Alberto Ríos and Toni Cade Bambara, the way the narrators experience their worlds is determined in part by the cultures to which they belong.

As you read the selections that follow, think about the degree to which culture influences the behavior, perceptions, expectations, and values of individuals. Compare yourself to the individuals in the selections to get a clearer idea of how culture affects your own sense of self and your relationship to the rest of the world.

Literary Vocabulary

INTRODUCED IN THIS UNIT

Oral literature. Oral literature is literature that is passed from one generation to another by performance or word-of-mouth. Oral literature is often performed for a specific purpose, such as to teach, to worship, or to entertain, and is sometimes accompanied by music and dancing. Folk tales, fables, myths, chants, and legends are part of the oral literature of cultures throughout the world.

Diction. Diction is a writer's choice of words, a significant component of his or her style. Diction encompasses both vocabulary (individual words) and syntax (the order or arrangement of words). Diction can be described in such terms as formal or informal, technical or common, abstract or concrete. For example, in *Narrative of the Life,* Frederick Douglass's diction often is concrete, as in this sentence: "My hair was all clotted with dust and blood; my shirt was stiff with blood."

Setting. Setting is the time and place of the action of a story. Setting may have a major or a minor influence on the plot of a story. For example, in "The Legend of Gregorio Cortez," the setting is Texas near the turn of the century, when Mexicans and Anglos fought each other in border skirmishes. This setting greatly influences the conflict between Gregorio Cortez and the sheriffs.

Tone. Tone is the attitude a writer takes toward a subject. Style and description in a work of literature help create tone, which might be described as formal, ironic, angry, serious, or playful. For example, the tone of Martin Luther King, Jr.'s "Letter from Birmingham Jail" might be described as formal, serious, and indignant.

REVIEWED IN THIS UNIT

Autobiography **Persuasion** **Theme**

How It Feels to Be Colored Me

ZORA NEALE HURSTON

A biography of Hurston appears on page 424.

*A*pproaching the Essay

From the time she moved to Harlem in 1925 until her death in 1960, Zora Neale Hurston was the most prolific African-American woman writer. Like the other writers in the Harlem Renaissance, she searched within herself for the clues to her identity rather than defining herself according to the racial stereotypes current in her day. In the following essay, first published in 1928, she presents her feelings about herself as an African American.

*B*uilding Vocabulary

These essential words are footnoted within the selection.

extenuating (ek sten′ yo͞o āt′ iŋ): I am colored but I offer nothing in the way of **extenuating** circumstances. (page 139)

pigmentation (pig′ mən tā′ shən): I have seen that the world is to the strong regardless of a little **pigmentation** more or less. (page 140)

veneer (və nir′): I creep back slowly to the **veneer** we call civilization. (page 140)

*C*onnecting Writing and Reading

Imagine that you are filling out a college application and that one of the questions asks you to describe what makes you a unique individual. In your journal, list three or four qualities that you would attribute to yourself in such a description. As you read this essay, notice that Hurston too has a sense of herself as a unique individual.

I AM COLORED but I offer nothing in the way of extenuating[1] circumstances except the fact that I am the only Negro in the United States whose grandfather on the mother's side was *not* an Indian chief.

I remember the very day that I became colored. Up to my thirteenth year I lived in the little Negro town of Eatonville, Florida. It is exclusively a colored town. The only white people I knew passed through the town going to or coming from Orlando. The native whites rode dusty horses; the Northern tourists chugged down the sandy village road in automobiles. The town knew the Southerners and never stopped cane chewing when they passed. But the Northerners were something else again. They were peered at cautiously from behind curtains by the timid. The more venturesome would come out on the porch to watch them go past and got just as much pleasure out of the tourists as the tourists got out of the village.

The front porch might seem a daring place for the rest of the town, but it was a gallery seat for me. My favorite place was atop the gatepost. Proscenium box for a born first-nighter.[2] Not only did I enjoy the show, but I didn't mind the actors knowing that I liked it. I usually spoke to them in passing. I'd wave at them and when they returned my salute, I would say something like this: "Howdy-do-well-I-thank-you-where-you-goin'?" Usually the automobile or the horse paused at this, and after a queer exchange of compliments, I would probably "go a piece of the way" with them, as we say in farthest Florida. If one of my family happened to come to the front in time to see me, of course, negotiations would be rudely broken off. But even so, it is clear that I was the first "welcome-to-our-state" Floridian, and I hope the Miami Chamber of Commerce will please take notice.

During this period, white people differed from colored to me only in that they rode through town and never lived there. They liked to hear me "speak pieces" and sing and wanted to see me dance the parse-me-la, and gave me generously of their small silver for doing these things, which seemed strange to me, for I wanted to do them so much that I needed bribing to stop. Only they didn't know it. The colored people gave no dimes. They deplored any joyful tendencies in me, but I was their Zora nevertheless. I belonged to them, to the nearby hotels, to the county—everybody's Zora.

But changes came in the family when I was thirteen, and I was sent to school in Jacksonville. I left Eatonville, the town of the oleanders,[3] as Zora. When I disembarked from the riverboat at Jacksonville, she was no more. It seemed that I had suffered a sea change. I was not Zora of Orange County any more, I was now a little colored girl. I found it out in certain ways. In my heart as well as in the mirror, I became a fast brown—warranted not to rub nor run.

But I am not tragically colored. There is no great sorrow dammed up in my soul, nor lurking behind my eyes. I do not mind at all. I do not belong to the sobbing school of Negrohood who hold that nature somehow has given them a lowdown dirty deal and whose feelings are all hurt about it. Even in the helter-skelter skirmish that is my life, I have seen that the world is to the strong

---

1. **extenuating** (ek sten′ yo͞o āt′ iŋ): lessening or seeming to lessen the seriousness of by giving excuses.
2. **first-nighter:** a person who attends the opening performance of a play, opera, or similar production.
3. **oleanders** (ō′ lē an′ dərz): evergreen shrubs with fragrant flowers of white, pink, or red.

regardless of a little pigmentation[4] more or less. No, I do not weep at the world—I am too busy sharpening my oyster knife.[5]

Someone is always at my elbow reminding me that I am the granddaughter of slaves. It fails to register depression with me. Slavery is sixty years in the past. The operation was successful and the patient is doing well, thank you. The terrible struggle that made me an American out of a potential slave said, "On the line!" The Reconstruction said, "Get set!" and the generation before said, "Go!" I am off to a flying start and I must not halt in the stretch to look behind and weep. Slavery is the price I paid for civilization, and the choice was not with me. It is a bully adventure and worth all that I have paid through my ancestors for it. No one on earth ever had a greater chance for glory. The world to be won and nothing to be lost. It is thrilling to think—to know that for any act of mine, I shall get twice as much praise or twice as much blame. It is quite exciting to hold the center of the national stage, with the spectators not knowing whether to laugh or to weep.

The position of my white neighbor is much more difficult. No brown specter pulls up a chair beside me when I sit down to eat. No dark ghost thrusts its leg against mine in bed. The game of keeping what one has is never so exciting as the game of getting.

I do not always feel colored. Even now I often achieve the unconscious Zora of Eaton-ville before the Hegira.[6] I feel most colored when I am thrown against a sharp white background.

For instance at Barnard.[7] "Beside the waters of the Hudson" I feel my race. Among the thousand white persons, I am a dark rock surged upon, and overswept, but through it all, I remain myself. When covered by the waters, I am; and the ebb but reveals me again.

Sometimes it is the other way around. A white person is set down in our midst, but the contrast is just as sharp for me. For instance, when I sit in the drafty basement that is The New World Cabaret with a white person, my color comes. We enter chatting about any little nothing that we have in common and are seated by the jazz waiters. In the abrupt way that jazz orchestras have, this one plunges into a number. It loses no time in circumlocutions, but gets right down to business. It constricts the thorax and splits the heart with its tempo and narcotic harmonies. This orchestra grows rambunctious, rears on its hind legs and attacks the tonal veil with primitive fury, rending it, clawing it until it breaks through to the jungle beyond. I follow those heathen—follow them exultingly. I dance wildly inside myself; I yell within, I whoop; I shake my assegai[8] above my head, I hurl it true to the mark *yeeeeooww!* I am in the jungle and living in the jungle way. My face is painted red and yellow and my body is painted blue. My pulse is throbbing like a war drum. I want to slaughter something—give pain, give death to what, I do not know. But the piece ends. The men of the orchestra wipe their lips and rest their fingers. I creep back slowly to the veneer[9] we call civilization with the last tone and find the white friend sitting motionless in his seat, smoking calmly.

---

4. pigmentation (pig′ mən tā′ shən): coloration due to the presence of pigment in the tissue.
5. oyster knife: a reference to the saying "The world is my oyster."
6. Hegira (hi jī′ rə): Mohammed's flight from Mecca to Medina in A.D. 622; hence, any trip or journey, especially one made to escape a dangerous or undesirable situation.
7. Barnard: the college in New York City from which Hurston graduated in 1928.
8. assegai (as′ ə gī′): a slender spear or javelin with an iron tip, used in southern Africa.
9. veneer (və nir′): a thin surface layer of fine wood or costly material laid over a base of common material; any attractive but superficial appearance.

"Good music they have here," he remarks, drumming the table with his fingertips.

Music. The great blobs of purple and red emotion have not touched him. He has only heard what I felt. He is far away and I see him but dimly across the ocean and the continent that have fallen between us. He is so pale with his whiteness then and I am so colored.

At certain times I have no race. I am *me*. When I set my hat at a certain angle and saunter down Seventh Avenue, Harlem City, feeling as snooty as the lions in front of the Forty-Second Street Library, for instance. So far as my feelings are concerned, Peggy Hopkins Joyce on the Boule Mich with her gorgeous raiment, stately carriage, knees knocking together in a most aristocratic manner, has nothing on me. The cosmic Zora emerges. I belong to no race nor time. I am the eternal feminine with its string of beads.

I have no separate feeling about being an American citizen and colored. I am merely a fragment of the Great Soul that surges within the boundaries. My country, right or wrong.

Sometimes, I feel discriminated against, but it does not make me angry. It merely astonishes me. How *can* any deny themselves the pleasure of my company? It's beyond me.

But in the main, I feel like a brown bag of miscellany propped against a wall. Against a wall in company with other bags, white, red, and yellow. Pour out the contents, and there is discovered a jumble of small things priceless and worthless. A first-water[10] diamond, an empty spool, bits of broken glass, lengths of string, a key to a door long since crumbled away, a rusty knife blade, old shoes saved for a road that never was and never will be, a nail bent under the weight of things too heavy for any nail, a dried flower or two still a little fragrant. In your hand is the brown bag. On the ground before you is the jumble it held—so much like the jumble in the bags, could they be emptied, that all might be dumped in a single heap and the bags refilled without altering the content of any greatly. A bit of colored glass more or less would not matter. Perhaps that is how the Great Stuffer of Bags filled them in the first place—who knows?

---

10. **first-water:** of the best quality and purest luster.

Untitled drawing, 1959, IRENE CLARK.

Irene Clark -59

Thinking About the Essay

A PERSONAL RESPONSE

sharing impressions

1. What mental picture do you have of the writer of this essay? Respond in your journal.

constructing interpretations

2. How does Hurston's description of herself as a brown bag influence your final impression of her?

Think about

- how the contents of the brown bag compare with the contents of the other bags
- what the description conveys about the similarities and differences among races
- what your impression of her might have been if you had not read this description

3. What words and phrases would you use to describe Hurston as a unique individual?

Think about

- the meaning of her statement "I am not tragically colored"
- her views on slavery
- the times when she is most aware of her color
- the times when she forgets about her color
- her response to discrimination

A CREATIVE RESPONSE

4. How might Hurston have been different if she had grown up in an integrated community?

A CRITICAL RESPONSE

5. How much do you think Hurston's being female determined her experiences and attitudes? Explain your opinion, referring to details in the essay.

6. How would you relate Hurston's views of her African-American heritage to those suggested by Hughes in "As I Grew Older" (page 97) and by Cullen in "Any Human to Another" (page 98)? Cite lines from Hurston's essay and the two poems in explaining your answer.

Analyzing the Writer's Craft

TONE AND DICTION

What words and phrases in this essay suggest how Hurston feels about herself?

Building a Literary Vocabulary. Tone is the attitude a writer takes toward a subject. Hurston's attitude in this essay is breezy, confident, exuberant, and optimistic. This tone is conveyed through her choice of memories to relate and through her word choice, or diction. For example, instead of describing a negative or painful experience from her childhood, she relates her childish zest for observing the tourists and for performing for them. The phrase "proscenium box for a born first-nighter" communicates her expectations of a thrilling spectacle.

Application: Examining Tone and Diction. Get together in a small group and identify key words and phrases that convey the tone of Hurston's description of her experience of jazz. Next rewrite the passage and change the tone by substituting other words and phrases for the ones identified. Then prepare an oral reading of Hurston's passage and the rewritten passage to present before other groups.

Connecting Reading and Writing

1. Write a **proposal** to a committee planning a school assembly in honor of famous African Americans. In your proposal, present reasons why Hurston's essay should be read at the assembly.

Option: Write **program notes** for Hurston's essay, explaining why it is included in the assembly program.

2. Imagine that an organization whose purpose is to foster racial or ethnic identity will award a scholarship to the applicant who best expresses an appreciation of his or her heritage. Write an **autobiographical essay,** modeled after Hurston's, expressing your views about your heritage.

Option: Explore your heritage in an **article** to appear with other articles in a feature for the magazine section of a weekend newspaper.

3. Imagine that you are the host for a radio show that will feature a panel discussion with Hurston and two other writers included in this book. Write a **script** in which you include questions that you might ask and comments that the writers might make in response.

Option: Write an **introduction** that you might read to present the writers to your audience.

4. Alice Walker wrote that she admires Zora Neale Hurston for "her devoted appreciation of her own culture." Read additional writing by Hurston: for example, an excerpt from her folklore collection *Mules and Men* or from her autobiography *Dust Tracks on a Road.* Then write **notes** for a class report in which you support Walker's statement by citing examples from these works and the essay "How It Feels to Be Colored Me."

Option: In your journal write a **personal response** to these works by Hurston.

I Have a Dream

MARTIN LUTHER KING, JR.

A biography of King appears on page 425.

Approaching the Speech

Nineteen sixty-three. A century had passed since Lincoln had freed the slaves, but local laws in the South barred most African Americans from registering to vote and from staying in hotels. Public beaches, parks, drinking fountains, restrooms, and lunch counters bore signs reading For Whites Only. The North did not have the same discriminatory laws as the South but shared similar discriminatory attitudes. The civil rights movement emerged in the 1950's to protest discrimination and gained momentum under the inspired leadership of Martin Luther King, Jr., an eloquent minister from Atlanta. King urged African Americans to use nonviolent protest to gain equality, and early in 1963 he helped organize a series of peaceful demonstrations in Birmingham, Alabama. Birmingham police reacted violently to the demonstrations, unleashing attack dogs and aiming fire hoses on the crowds, which included women and children. As television coverage drew national attention to the struggle in the South, President Kennedy proposed a civil rights bill to Congress. King and other leaders organized a mass march on Washington, D.C., to pressure Congress to pass the bill. In the sweltering heat of August 1963, King delivered his impassioned "I Have a Dream" speech on the steps of the Lincoln Memorial, where more than 200,000 demonstrators had gathered.

The following year, Congress passed the Civil Rights Act, and King received the Nobel Prize for peace. King continued to work for justice and equality until he was assassinated in 1968.

Bob Adelman/Magnum Photos, Inc., New York.

Building Vocabulary

These essential words are footnoted within the selection.

manacles (man´ ə kəls), **segregation** (seg´ rə gā´ shən),
 discrimination (di skrim´ i nā´ shən): The Negro is still sadly crippled
 by the **manacles** of **segregation** and the chains of **discrimination**.
 (page 146)

languishing (laŋ´ gwish iŋ): The Negro is still **languishing** in the corners
 of American society. (page 146)

degenerate (de jen´ ər āt): We must not allow our creative protests to
 degenerate into physical violence. (page 147)

militancy (mil´ i tənt sē): The marvelous new **militancy**, which has
 engulfed the Negro community, must not lead us to a distrust of all
 white people. (page 147)

tribulations (trib´ yōō lā´ shəns): I am not unmindful that some of you
 have come here out of great trials and **tribulations**. (page 147)

discords (dis´ kôrdz): We will be able to transform the jangling **discords**
 of our nation into a beautiful symphony of brotherhood. (page 148)

Connecting Writing and Reading

What would you identify as the most pressing problems in our country today? In
your journal, list these problems in a chart similar to the one below. As you read
King's speech, jot down the specific problems that King identifies in 1963.

Problems today	Problems in 1963

I Have a Dream

*I*AM HAPPY to join with you today in what will go down in history as the greatest demonstration for freedom in the history of our nation.

Five score years ago, a great American, in whose symbolic shadow we stand today, signed the Emancipation Proclamation.[1] This momentous decree came as a great beacon light of hope to millions of Negro slaves who had been seared in the flames of withering injustice. It came as a joyous daybreak to end the long night of their captivity.

But one hundred years later, the Negro still is not free; one hundred years later, the life of the Negro is still sadly crippled by the manacles[2] of segregation[3] and the chains of discrimination;[4] one hundred years later, the Negro lives on a lonely island of poverty in the midst of a vast ocean of material prosperity; one hundred years later, the Negro is still languishing[5] in the corners of American society and finds himself in exile in his own land.

So we've come here today to dramatize a shameful condition. In a sense we've come to our nation's capital to cash a check. When the architects of our republic wrote the magnificent words of the Constitution and the Declaration of Independence, they were signing a promissory note[6] to which every American was to fall heir. This note was the promise that all men, yes, black men as well as white men, would be guaranteed the unalienable rights of life, liberty, and the pursuit of happiness.

It is obvious today that America has defaulted on this promissory note insofar as her citizens of color are concerned. Instead of honoring this sacred obligation, America has given the Negro people a bad check, a check which has come back marked "insufficient funds." But we refuse to believe that the bank of justice is bankrupt. We refuse to believe that there are insufficient funds in the great vaults of opportunity of this nation. And so we've come to cash this check, a check that will give us upon demand the riches of freedom and the security of justice.

We have also come to this hallowed spot to remind America of the fierce urgency of now. This is no time to engage in the luxury of cooling off or to take the tranquilizing drug of gradualism. Now is the time to make real the promises of democracy; now is the time to rise from the dark and desolate valley of segregation to the sunlit path of racial justice; now is the time to lift our nation from the quicksands of racial injustice to the solid rock of brotherhood; now is the time to make justice a reality for all of God's children. It would be fatal for

---

1. Emancipation Proclamation (ē man′ sə pā′ shan präk′ lə mā′ shən): document signed by President Lincoln during the Civil War, freeing slaves in the Confederate states.

2. manacles (man′ ə kəls): handcuffs.

3. segregation (seg′ rə gā′ shən): the policy of forcing racial groups to live apart from each other, go to separate schools, and so on.

4. discrimination (di skrim′ i nā′ shən): a showing of favoritism or prejudice in treatment.

5. languishing (laŋ′ gwish iŋ): living under distressing conditions or in a state of suffering.

6. promissory note (präm′ i sôr′ ē): a written promise to repay a debt.

the nation to overlook the urgency of the moment. This sweltering summer of the Negro's legitimate discontent will not pass until there is an invigorating autumn of freedom and equality.

Nineteen sixty-three is not an end, but a beginning. And those who hope that the Negro needed to blow off steam and will now be content will have a rude awakening if the nation returns to business as usual. There will be neither rest nor tranquility in America until the Negro is granted his citizenship rights. The whirlwinds of revolt will continue to shake the foundations of our nation until the bright day of justice emerges.

But there is something that I must say to my people, who stand on the worn threshold which leads into the palace of justice. In the process of gaining our rightful place, we must not be guilty of wrongful deeds. Let us not seek to satisfy our thirst for freedom by drinking from the cup of bitterness and hatred. We must forever conduct our struggle on the high plain of dignity and discipline. We must not allow our creative protests to degenerate[7] into physical violence. Again and again we must rise to the majestic heights of meeting physical force with soul force. The marvelous new militancy,[8] which has engulfed the Negro community, must not lead us to a distrust of all white people. For many of our white brothers, as evidenced by their presence here today, have come to realize that their destiny is tied up with our destiny. And they have come to realize that their freedom is inextricably bound to our freedom. We cannot walk alone. And as we walk, we must make the pledge that we shall always march ahead. We cannot turn back.

There are those who are asking the devotees of civil rights, "When will you be satisfed?" We can never be satisfied as long as the Negro is the victim of the unspeakable horrors of police brutality; we can never be satisfied as long as our bodies, heavy with the fatigue of travel, cannot gain lodging in the motels of the highways and the hotels of the cities; we cannot be satisfied as long as the Negro's basic mobility is from a smaller ghetto to a larger one; we can never be satisfied as long as our children are stripped of their selfhood and robbed of their dignity by signs stating For Whites Only; we cannot be satisfied as long as the Negro in Mississippi cannot vote and a Negro in New York believes he has nothing for which to vote. No! No, we are not satisfied, and we will not be satisfied until "justice rolls down like waters and righteousness like a mighty stream."

I am not unmindful that some of you have come here out of great trials and tribulations.[9] Some of you have come fresh from narrow jail cells. Some of you have come from areas where your quest for freedom left you battered by the storms of persecution and staggered by the winds of police brutality. You have been the veterans of creative suffering. Continue to work with the faith that unearned suffering is redemptive.[10] Go back to Mississippi. Go back to Alabama. Go back to South Carolina. Go back to Georgia. Go back to Louisiana. Go back to the slums and ghettos of our Northern cities, knowing that somehow this situation can and will be changed. Let us not wallow in the valley of despair.

I say to you today, my friends, even though we face the difficulties of today and tomorrow, I still have a dream. It is a dream deeply rooted in the American dream. I have a dream that

---

7. degenerate (dē jen′ ər āt): to become less moral, cultured, and so on.

8. militancy (mil′ i tənt sē): the state of being ready and willing to fight, especially, aggressively active in support of a cause.

9. tribulations (trib′ yo͞o lā′ shəns): the causes of great misery and distress; deep sorrows.

10. redemptive (ri demp′ tiv): having the power to restore one by making up for wrongdoing.

one day this nation will rise up and live out the true meaning of its creed, "We hold these truths to be self-evident; that all men are created equal." I have a dream that one day on the red hills of Georgia, sons of former slaves and the sons of former slave owners will be able to sit down together at the table of brotherhood. I have a dream that one day even the state of Mississippi, a state sweltering with the heat of injustice, sweltering with the heat of oppression, will be transformed into an oasis of freedom and justice. I have a dream that my four little children will one day live in a nation where they will not be judged by the color of their skin, but by the content of their character.

I have a dream today!

I have a dream that one day down in Alabama—with its vicious racists, with its Governor having his lips dripping with the words of interposition and nullification[11]—one day right there in Alabama, little black boys and black girls will be able to join hands with little white boys and white girls as sisters and brothers.

I have a dream today!

I have a dream that one day every valley shall be exalted, and every hill and mountain shall be made low. The rough places will be plain and the crooked places will be made straight, "and the glory of the Lord shall be revealed, and all flesh shall see it together."

This is our hope. This is the faith that I go back to the South with. With this faith we will be able to hew out of the mountain of despair a stone of hope. With this faith we will be able to transform the jangling discords[12] of our nation into a beautiful symphony of brotherhood. With this faith we will be able to work together, to pray together, to struggle together, to go to jail together, to stand up for freedom together, knowing that we will be free one day. And this will be the day. This will be the day when all of God's children will be able to sing with new meaning, "My country 'tis of thee, sweet land of liberty, of thee I sing. Land where my fathers died, land of the pilgrims' pride, from every mountainside, let freedom ring." And if America is to be a great nation, this must become true.

So let freedom ring from the prodigious hilltops of New Hampshire; let freedom ring from the mighty mountains of New York; let freedom ring from the heightening Alleghenies of Pennsylvania; let freedom ring from the snowcapped Rockies of Colorado; let freedom ring from the curvaceous slopes of California. But not only that. Let freedom ring from Stone Mountain of Georgia; let freedom ring from Lookout Mountain of Tennessee; let freedom ring from every hill and molehill of Mississippi. "From every mountainside, let freedom ring."

And when this happens, and when we allow freedom to ring, when we let it ring from every village and every hamlet, from every state and every city, we will be able to speed up that day when all of God's children—black men and white men, Jews and Gentiles, Protestants and Catholics—will be able to join hands and sing in the words of the old Negro spiritual, "Free at last. Free at last. Thank God Almighty, we are free at last."

---

11. **interposition** (in′ tər pə zish′ ən) and **nullification** (nul′ ə fi kā′ shən): acts taken by state officials to undermine the enforcement of federal laws.

12. **discords** (dis′ kôrdz): tones sounded together that lack harmony.

Thinking About the Speech

A PERSONAL RESPONSE

sharing impressions

1. What sentences and phrases from this speech stand out in your mind? Jot these down in your journal.

constructing interpretations

2. How does King's dream at the end of this speech offer a solution to the problems he identifies?

> **Think about**
> • specific examples of discrimination he gives
> • the groups of people that he wants to join hands together

3. Why do you think King quotes from the Declaration of Independence, the United States Constitution, the national anthem, and an old spiritual in his speech?

4. What do you think the words *freedom* and *justice* mean to King?

A CREATIVE RESPONSE

5. If this speech were delivered today, what problems might it address?

A CRITICAL RESPONSE

6. To what extent do you think this speech is specific to the problems of a single time and place and to what extent is it not limited to any one time or place? Go back to the speech and find passages that support your answer.

7. This speech is King's most famous and is considered by critics to be one of the great speeches of the twentieth century. Tell whether you agree with this view and give examples from the speech that influence your opinion.

Analyzing the Writer's Craft

PERSUASION

Think about King's audience for this speech—the 200,000 marchers gathered to hear him, the legislators in the Capitol, and the rest of the country who learned of the speech through the news media. What do you think King wanted to accomplish with this speech?

Building a Literary Vocabulary. Persuasion is a technique used by speakers and writers to convince an audience to adopt a particular opinion, perform an action, or both. King probably has several persuasive aims for his speech. First, he is trying to persuade Congress to pass the civil rights bill to end injustice and discrimination. Second, he wants to convince the marchers to persist in nonviolent action to put the spotlight on inequality. Finally, King eloquently unfolds his dream in order to inspire all Americans to end injustice and racial discrimination.

Application: Identifying Persuasion. Working in a small group, choose a passage that you think is particularly persuasive. Make a tape recording of one of your group members reading this passage. Then, from your school or public library, obtain a recording of King delivering the speech. As a class, listen to and compare the two recordings. Discuss how delivery affects the persuasiveness of a speech.

Connecting Reading and Writing

1. Read media accounts of the march on Washington in August 1963. Create **cue cards** for a television news report about that day.

Option: Write an **editorial** expressing your opinion about the events of that day.

2. Using your prereading notes that describe a national problem, write your own "I Have a Dream" **speech** that expresses your hopes for the future of the country.

Option: Draw pictures or find magazine pictures that represent your hopes for the future of the country. Write **captions** that explain the pictures.

3. Analyze how King's use of metaphor adds to the impact of the speech. Using examples from King's speech, write **instructions** teaching a classmate how to use figurative language in a speech.

Option: Present your analysis in a **review** of the speech for a literary magazine.

4. Imagine that you are at the Lincoln Memorial listening to King's speech. Write a **letter** to your family describing your reactions.

Option: Think of a national law that should be changed or passed. Using persuasive language similar to King's, write a **petition** calling for that change and circulate the petition among your classmates.

Getting a Job

from I Know Why the Caged Bird Sings

MAYA ANGELOU

A biography of Angelou appears on page 418.

*A*pproaching the Selection

I Know Why the Caged Bird Sings is the first in a series of autobiographical works written by Maya Angelou. Angelou, born Marguerite Johnson, was raised by her grandmother in Arkansas, but during World War II, at the age of fifteen, she moved to San Francisco to live with her mother. As this excerpt begins, Marguerite faces adjustments to her new surroundings.

*B*uilding Vocabulary

These essential words are footnoted within the selection.

supercilious (soo′ pər sil′ ē əs): I spoke in **supercilious** accents. (page 153)

hypocrisy (hi päk′ rə sē): We were firmly joined in the **hypocrisy** to play out the scene. (page 153)

aphorisms (af′ ə riz′ əmz): She had a store of **aphorisms** that she dished out as the occasion demanded. (page 154)

*C*onnecting Writing and Reading

Think of a job that you might want if you went out looking for work today. Copy the following application into your journal and fill it out as if you were applying for this job.

> Position applying for: _____
> Name: _____
> Address: _____
> Date of birth: _____
> Number of years of school: _____
> Previous work experience: _____
> Other qualifications: _____

In your journal describe how you felt as you completed the application. Did you consider yourself qualified? Were you tempted to lie? Recall your own feelings as you read about a fifteen-year-old's determination to get a job.

Getting a Job

MY ROOM HAD all the cheeriness of a dungeon and the appeal of a tomb. It was going to be impossible to stay there, but leaving held no attraction for me either. The answer came to me with the suddenness of a collision. I would go to work. Mother wouldn't be difficult to convince; after all, in school I was a year ahead of my grade and Mother was a firm believer in self-sufficiency. In fact, she'd be pleased to think that I had that much gumption, that much of her in my character. (She liked to speak of herself as the original "do-it-yourself girl.")

Once I had settled on getting a job, all that remained was to decide which kind of job I was most fitted for. My intellectual pride had kept me from selecting typing, shorthand, or filing as subjects in school, so office work was ruled out. War plants and shipyards demanded birth certificates, and mine would reveal me to be fifteen, and ineligible for work. So the well-paying defense jobs were also out. Women had replaced men on the streetcars as conductors and motormen, and the thought of sailing up and down the hills of San Francisco in a dark-blue uniform, with a money changer at my belt, caught my fancy.

Mother was as easy as I had anticipated. The world was moving so fast, so much money was being made, so many people were dying in Guam[1] and Germany that hordes of strangers became good friends overnight. Life was cheap and death entirely free. How could she have the time to think about my academic career?

To her question of what I planned to do, I replied that I would get a job on the streetcars.

She rejected the proposal with "They don't accept black people on the streetcars."

I would like to claim an immediate fury that was followed by the noble determination to break the restricting tradition. But the truth is, my first reaction was one of disappointment. I'd pictured myself dressed in a neat blue serge suit, my money changer swinging jauntily at my waist, and a cheery smile for the passengers that would make their own work day brighter.

From disappointment I gradually ascended the emotional ladder to haughty indignation, and finally to that state of stubbornness where the mind is locked like the jaws of an enraged bulldog.

I would go to work on the streetcars and wear a blue serge suit. Mother gave me her support with one of her usual terse asides: "That's what you want to do? Then nothing beats a trial but a failure. Give it everything you've got. I've told you many times, 'Can't Do is like Don't Care.' Neither of them has a home."

Translated, that meant there is nothing a person can't do, and there should be nothing a human being doesn't care about. It was the most positive encouragement I could have hoped for.

In the offices of the Market Street Railway Company, the receptionist seemed as surprised to see me there as I was surprised to find the interior dingy and drab. Somehow I had expected waxed surfaces and carpeted floors. If I had met no resistance, I might have decided against working for such a poor-mouth-looking concern. As it was, I explained

---

1. **Guam** (gwäm): an island in the west Pacific, a scene of fighting during World War II.

that I had come to see about a job. She asked, was I sent by an agency, and when I replied that I was not, she told me they were only accepting applicants from agencies.

The classified pages of the morning papers had listed advertisements for motorettes and conductorettes, and I reminded her of that. She gave me a face full of astonishment that my suspicious nature would not accept.

"I am applying for the job listed in this morning's *Chronicle*, and I'd like to be presented to your personnel manager." While I spoke in supercilious² accents and looked at the room as if I had an oil well in my own backyard, my armpits were being pricked by millions of hot pointed needles. She saw her escape and dived into it.

"He's out. He's out for the day. You might call him tomorrow, and if he's in, I'm sure you can see him." Then she swiveled her chair around on its rusty screws, and with that I was supposed to be dismissed.

"May I ask his name?"

She half turned, acting surprised to find me still there.

"His name? Whose name?"

"Your personnel manager."

We were firmly joined in the hypocrisy³ to play out the scene.

"The personnel manager? Oh, he's Mr. Cooper, but I'm not sure you'll find him here tomorrow. He's . . . oh, but you can try."

"Thank you."

"You're welcome."

And I was out of the musty room and into the even mustier lobby. In the street I saw the receptionist and myself going faithfully through paces that were stale with familiarity, although I had never encountered that kind of situation before and, probably, neither had she. We were like actors who, knowing the play by heart, were still able to cry afresh over the old tragedies and laugh spontaneously at the comic situations.

The miserable little encounter had nothing to do with me, the me of me, any more than it had to do with that silly clerk. The incident was a recurring dream concocted years before by whites, and it eternally came back to haunt us all. The secretary and I were like people in a scene where, because of harm done by one ancestor to another, we were bound to duel to the death. Also, because the play must end somewhere.

I went further than forgiving the clerk; I accepted her as a fellow victim of the same puppeteer.

On the streetcar I put my fare into the box, and the conductorette looked at me with the usual hard eyes of white contempt. "Move into the car, please move on in the car." She patted her money changer.

Her Southern nasal accent sliced my meditation, and I looked deep into my thoughts. All lies, all comfortable lies. The receptionist was not innocent and neither was I. The whole charade we had played out in that waiting room had directly to do with me, black, and her, white.

I wouldn't move into the streetcar but stood on the ledge over the conductor, glaring. My mind shouted so energetically that the announcement made my veins stand out and my mouth tighten into a prune.

I WOULD HAVE THE JOB. I WOULD BE A CONDUCTORETTE AND SLING A FULL MONEY CHANGER FROM MY BELT. I WOULD.

The next three weeks were a honeycomb of determination with apertures for the days to go in and out. The black organizations to whom I appealed for support bounced me back and forth like a shuttlecock on a badminton

---

2. supercilious (so͞o′ pər sil′ ē əs): looking down on others; characterized by pride or scorn.
3. hypocrisy (hi päk′ rə sē): a pretending to be what one is not or to believe what one does not.

court. Why did I insist on that particular job? Openings were going begging that paid nearly twice the money. The minor officials with whom I was able to win an audience thought me mad. Possibly I was.

Downtown San Francisco became alien and cold, and the streets I had loved in a personal familiarity were unknown lanes that twisted with malicious intent. My trips to the streetcar office were of the frequency of a person on salary. The struggle expanded. I was no longer in conflict only with the Market Street Railway but with the marble lobby of the building that housed its offices, and elevators and their operators.

During this period of strain, Mother and I began our first steps on the long path toward mutual adult admiration. She never asked for reports and I didn't offer any details. But every morning she made breakfast, gave me carfare and lunch money, as if I were going to work. She comprehended that in the struggle lies the joy. That I was no glory seeker was obvious to her, and that I had to exhaust every possibility before giving in was also clear.

On my way out of the house one morning she said, "Life is going to give you just what you put in it. Put your whole heart in everything you do, and pray; then you can wait." Another time she reminded me that "God helps those who help themselves." She had a store of aphorisms[4] that she dished out as the occasion demanded. Strangely, as bored as I was with clichés, her inflection gave them something new and set me thinking for a little while at least. Later, when asked how I got my job, I was never able to say exactly. I only knew that one day, which was tiresomely like all the others before it, I sat in the Railway office, waiting to be interviewed. The receptionist called me to her desk and shuffled a bundle of papers to me. They were job application forms. She said they had to be filled in [in] triplicate. I had little time to wonder if I

had won or not, for the standard questions reminded me of the necessity for lying. How old was I? List my previous jobs, starting from the last job held and go backward to the first. How much money did I earn, and why did I leave the position? Give two references (not relatives). I kept my face blank (an old art) and wrote quickly the fable of Marguerite Johnson, aged nineteen, former companion and driver for Mrs. Annie Henderson (a White Lady) in Stamps, Arkansas.

I was given blood tests, aptitude tests, and physical coordination tests; then, on a blissful day, I was hired as the first black on the San Francisco streetcars.

Mother gave me the money to have my blue serge suit tailored, and I learned to fill out work cards, operate the money changer, and punch transfers. The time crowded together, and at an End of Days I was swinging on the back of the rackety trolley, smiling sweetly and persuading my charges to "step forward in the car, please."

For one whole semester the streetcars and I shimmied up and scooted down the sheer hills of San Francisco. I lost some of my need for the black ghetto's shielding-sponge quality as I clanged and cleared my way down Market Street, with its honky-tonk homes for homeless sailors, past the quiet retreat of Golden Gate Park, and along closed undwelled-in-looking dwellings of the Sunset District.

My work shifts were split so haphazardly that it was easy to believe that my superiors had chosen them maliciously. Upon mentioning my suspicions to Mother, she said, "Don't you worry about it. You ask for what you want, and you pay for what you get. And I'm going to show you that it ain't no trouble when you pack double."

She stayed awake to drive me out to the car

---

4. aphorisms (af′ ə riz′ əmz): short sentences expressing wise observations or general truths.

barn at four-thirty in the mornings or to pick me up when I was relieved just before dawn. Her awareness of life's perils convinced her that while I would be safe on the public conveyances, she "wasn't about to trust a taxi driver with her baby."

When the spring classes began, I resumed my commitment to formal education. I was so much wiser and older, so much more independent, with a bank account and clothes that I had bought for myself, that I was sure I had learned and earned the magic formula that would make me a part of the life my contemporaries led.

Not a bit of it. Within weeks, I realized that my schoolmates and I were on paths moving away from each other. They were concerned and excited over the approaching football games. They concentrated great interest on who was worthy of being student body president and when the metal bands would be removed from their teeth, while I remembered conducting a streetcar in the uneven hours of the morning.

Cable Car, c. 1949, photographer unknown.
Underwood Photo Archives, San Francisco.

Thinking About the Selection

A PERSONAL RESPONSE

sharing impressions

1. What is your impression of Marguerite? In your journal jot down words and phrases that describe her.

constructing interpretations

2. Why do you think Marguerite is so determined to become a conductorette?
   Think about
   • her reaction to her mother's comment "They don't accept black people on the streetcars."
   • the image she has of the job
   • her interactions with the receptionist
   • her encounter with the white conductorette
   • the dilemma she faces as the selection begins

3. In your opinion, why does Marguerite finally get the job?

4. What do you think of the mother's attitude toward her daughter and toward life? Explain.

A CREATIVE RESPONSE

5. Speculate about the kind of future Marguerite will have, based on what you learn about her from the selection.

A CRITICAL RESPONSE

6. What similarities do you see between this selection and a short story?
   Think about
   • whether the selection has a beginning, middle, and end
   • the literary elements of a short story, specifically plot, setting, character, conflict, and theme

7. Based on this excerpt, how would you explain the meaning of the title *I Know Why the Caged Bird Sings?*

8. The experience described by Angelou took place in the 1940's. What situations can you imagine a fifteen-year-old today handling with the same determination? Explain.

Analyzing the Writer's Craft

What are Marguerite's outstanding qualities and what events reveal these qualities?

Building a Literary Vocabulary. An autobiography is the story of a person's life written by that person, usually from the first-person point of view. The writer of an autobiography includes events that are personally significant. In *I Know Why the Caged Bird Sings,* Maya Angelou focuses specifically on the important events of her childhood and adolescence. As she recalls her experiences and feelings and comments on them from her present-day perspective, the reader is given a unique opportunity to understand the kind of person she is.

Application: Examining Autobiography. Together with two or three other students, create a poem that reflects the group's feelings and impressions of Marguerite. As a starting point, you might want to refer to your responses to question 1, where you were asked to record words and phrases that describe Marguerite. Share your poem with the class.

Connecting Reading and Writing

1. Imagine that Marguerite decides to run for president of the student council upon returning to high school. Create a **campaign poster** that describes her qualifications.

Option: Write a **campaign speech** that Marguerite might deliver to the student body.

2. Think of a person you know or have read about in books or news articles who, like Marguerite, has overcome obstacles with his or her personal determination. Write a **character sketch** of the person, to be read by a fellow-student or younger person who lacks self-confidence.

Option: Write a **ballad** that sings the praises of this person's determination and accomplishments.

3. Write three or four **aphorisms** that reflect your personal attitude toward life, to be compiled with other students' aphorisms in a booklet for incoming freshmen.

Option: Think of a situation in real life that illustrates one of the aphorisms in this selection. Create **storyboards** for a public service message that uses the aphorism and depicts this situation.

4. Read an excerpt from one of Angelou's later autobiographical works, *Gather Together in My Name, Singin' and Swingin' and Gettin' Merry Like Christmas,* or *The Heart of a Woman.* Based on the information revealed in this additional reading, modify the **poem** you composed earlier to describe Marguerite. Share the poem with students who have not yet read Angelou's later works.

Option: Use information from these sources to write a paragraph or two of a **biographical sketch** of Angelou intended for a reference book on twentieth-century women authors.

Sympathy

Paul Laurence Dunbar

I know what the caged bird feels, alas!
　　When the sun is bright on the upland slopes;
When the wind stirs soft through the springing grass,
And the river flows like a stream of glass;
　　When the first bird sings and the first bud opes,
And the faint perfume from its chalice steals—
I know what the caged bird feels!

I know why the caged bird beats his wing
　　Till its blood is red on the cruel bars;
For he must fly back to his perch and cling
When he fain[1] would be on the bough a-swing;
　　And a pain still throbs in the old, old scars
And they pulse again with a keener sting—
I know why he beats his wing!

I know why the caged bird sings, ah me,
　　When his wing is bruised and his bosom sore,—
When he beats his bars and he would be free;
It is not a carol of joy or glee,
　　But a prayer that he sends from his heart's deep core,
But a plea, that upward to Heaven he flings—
I know why the caged bird sings!

1. *fain*: gladly or willingly.

from Barrio Boy

ERNESTO GALARZA

A biography of Galarza appears on page 422.

Approaching the Selection

This selection is an excerpt from Ernesto Galarza's autobiography, in which he recalls his early years. In order to escape the violence of the Mexican revolution in the early 1900's, he and his family moved to the United States, arriving first in Tucson, Arizona, and then settling in Sacramento, California. In this selection he recounts some of his earliest experiences of America—in particular, being a Spanish-speaking immigrant child attending school in Sacramento.

Building Vocabulary

These essential words are footnoted within the selection.

boisterous (bɔis′ tər əs): You could hardly tell whether the **boisterous** Americans were roaring mad or roaring happy. (page 160)

formidable (fôr′ mə də bəl): Miss Hopley did a **formidable** thing. (page 162)

alien (āl′ ē ən): Miss Hopley . . . never let us forget why we were at Lincoln: for those who were **alien,** to become good Americans. (page 164)

indignation (in′ dig nā′ shən): Miss Hopley was now standing at the rail . . . , the words coming down to us . . . loaded with **indignation.** (page 165)

reverie (rev′ ər ē): Miss Campbell read to us . . . about King Arthur, . . . and Daniel Boone, who came to life in the **reverie** of the class through the magic of her voice. (page 165)

Connecting Writing and Reading

Imagine that you have just arrived in a country totally different from your own—perhaps a country in Southeast Asia, South America, or Africa—where you will now live. Think about the difficulties you might have adjusting to your new country. How would you handle communication in a different language? What foods would you miss? what recreational activities? What other cultural differences might make life difficult? Record your thoughts in your journal. Keep these ideas in mind as you read about a young boy's experience adjusting to a new country.

WE FOUND THE Americans as strange in their customs as they probably found us. Immediately we discovered that there were no _mercados_[1] and that when shopping, you did not put groceries in a _chiquihuite_.[2] Instead, everything was in cans or in cardboard boxes, or each item was put into a brown paper bag. There were neighborhood grocery stores at the corners and some big ones uptown, but no _mercado_. The grocers did not give children a _pilón_;[3] they did not stand at the door and coax you to come in and buy, as they did in Mazatlán.[4] The fruits and vegetables were displayed on counters instead of being piled up on the floor. The stores smelled of fly spray and oiled floors, not of fresh pineapple and limes.

Neither was there a plaza, only parks that had no bandstands, no concerts every Thursday, no Judases exploding on Holy Week, and no promenades of boys going one way and girls the other. There were no parks in the _barrio_;[5] and the ones uptown were cold and rainy in winter, and in summer there was no place to sit except on the grass. When there were celebrations, nobody set off rockets in the parks, much less on the street in front of your house to announce to the neighborhood that a wedding or a baptism was taking place. Sacramento did not have a _mercado_ and a plaza with the cathedral to one side and the _Palacio de Gobierno_[6] on another to make it obvious that there and nowhere else was the center of town.

It was just as puzzling that the Americans did not live in _vecindades_,[7] like our block on Leandro Valle. Even in the alleys, where people knew one another better, the houses were fenced apart, without central courts to wash clothes, talk, and play with the other children. Like the city, the Sacramento _barrio_ did not have a place which was the middle of things for everyone.

In more personal ways we had to get used to the Americans. They did not listen if you did not speak loudly, as they always did. In the Mexican style, people would know that you were enjoying their jokes tremendously if you merely smiled and shook a little, as if you were trying to swallow your mirth. In the American style there was little difference between a laugh and a roar, and until you got used to them, you could hardly tell whether the boisterous[8] Americans were roaring mad or roaring happy. . . .

America was all around us, in and out of the

---

1. _mercados_ (mer kä′ dôs) _Spanish:_ marketplaces.
2. _chiquihuite_ (chē kē hwē′ tā) _Mexican Spanish:_ a wicker, reed, or willow basket with a looped handle, used for shopping in a _mercado_.
3. _pilón_ (pē lôn′) _Spanish:_ a treat, such as a piece of brown sugar or a jelly bean.
4. **Mazatlán** (mä sät län′): a seaport on the Pacific coast of Mexico.
5. _barrio_ (bä′ ryô) _Spanish:_ a section of a city in the United States inhabited primarily by a Spanish-speaking population.
6. _Palacio de Gobierno_ (pä lä′ syô dā gô byer′ nô) _Spanish:_ Palace of Government.
7. _vecindades_ (ve sēn dä′ des): _Spanish:_ neighborhoods.
8. **boisterous** (bois′ tər əs): noisy and unruly.

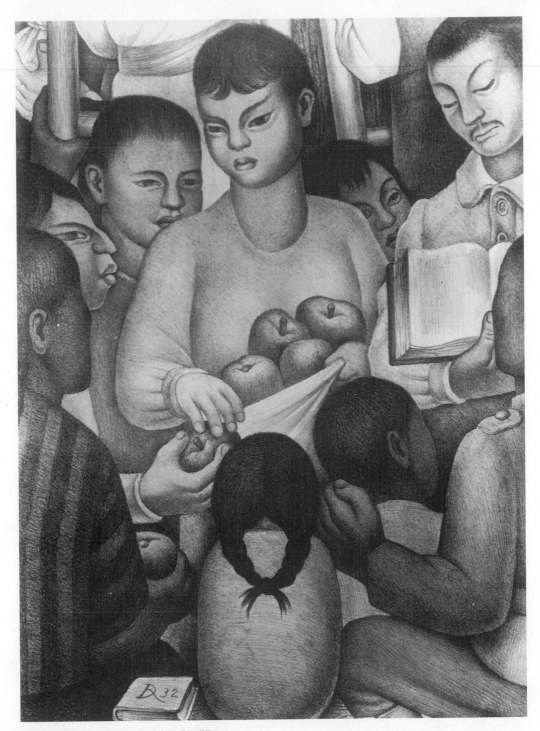

Fruits of Labor, 1932, DIEGO RIVERA.
Giraudon / Art Resource, New York.

barrio. Abruptly we had to forget the ways of shopping in a *mercado* and learn those of shopping in a corner grocery or in a department store. The Americans paid no attention to the Sixteenth of September,[9] but they made a great commotion about the Fourth of July. In Mazatlán, Don Salvador had told us, saluting and marching as he talked to our class, that the *Cinco de Mayo*[10] was the most glorious date in human history. The Americans had not even heard about it.

In Tucson, when I had asked my mother again if the Americans were having a revolution, the answer was, "No, but they have good schools, and you are going to one of them." We were by now settled at 418 L Street, and the time had come for me to exchange a revolution for an American education.

The two of us walked south on Fifth Street one morning to the corner of Q Street and turned right. Half of the block was occupied by the Lincoln School. It was a three-story wooden building, with two wings that gave it the shape of a double-T connected by a central hall. It was a new building, painted yellow, with a shingled roof that was not like the red tile of the school in Mazatlán. I noticed other differences, none of them very reassuring.

We walked up the wide staircase hand in hand and through the door, which closed by itself. A mechanical contraption screwed to the top shut it behind us quietly.

Up to this point the adventure of enrolling me in the school had been carefully rehearsed. Mrs. Dodson had told us how to find it, and we had circled it several times on our walks. Friends in the *barrio* explained that the director was called a principal, and that it was a lady and not a man. They assured us that there was always a person at the school who could speak Spanish.

Exactly as we had been told, there was a sign on the door in both Spanish and English,

"Principal." We crossed the hall and entered the office of Miss Nettie Hopley.

Miss Hopley was at a roll-top desk to one side, sitting in a swivel chair that moved on wheels. There was a sofa against the opposite wall, flanked by two windows and a door that opened on a small balcony. Chairs were set around a table, and framed pictures hung on the walls of a man with long white hair and another with a sad face and a black beard.

The principal half turned in the swivel chair to look at us over the pinch glasses that crossed the ridge of her nose. To do this she had to duck her head slightly as if she were about to step through a low doorway.

What Miss Hopley said to us we did not know, but we saw in her eyes a warm welcome, and when she took off her glasses and straightened up, she smiled wholeheartedly, like Mrs. Dodson. We were, of course, saying nothing, only catching the friendliness of her voice and the sparkle in her eyes while she said words we did not understand. She signaled us to the table. Almost tiptoeing across the office, I maneuvered myself to keep my mother between me and the *gringo*[11] lady. In a matter of seconds I had to decide whether she was a possible friend or a menace. We sat down.

Then Miss Hopley did a formidable[12] thing. She stood up. Had she been standing when we entered, she would have seemed tall. But rising from her chair, she soared. And what she carried up and up with her was a buxom superstructure, firm shoulders, a straight sharp nose,

---

9. Sixteenth of September: Mexican Independence Day.
10. *Cinco de Mayo* (sēn′ kô dā mä′ yô) *Spanish:* Fifth of May, a Mexican national holiday to celebrate the defeat of the French troops in 1862.
11. *gringo* (griŋ′ gô) *Mexican Spanish:* in Latin America, a foreigner, especially American or British.
12. formidable (fôr′ mə də bəl): causing fear; awe-inspiring; strikingly impressive.

full cheeks slightly molded by a curved line along the nostrils, thin lips that moved like steel springs and a high forehead topped by hair gathered in a bun. Miss Hopley was not a giant in body, but when she mobilized it to a standing position, she seemed a match for giants. I decided I liked her.

She strode to a door in the far corner of the office, opened it, and called a name. A boy of about ten years appeared in the doorway. He sat down at one end of the table. He was brown like us, a plump kid with shiny black hair combed straight back, neat, cool, and faintly obnoxious.

Miss Hopley joined us with a large book and some papers in her hand. She, too, sat down and the questions and answers began by way of our interpreter. My name was Ernesto. My mother's name was Henriqueta.[13] My birth certificate was in San Blas. Here was my last report card from the *Escuela Municipal Numero 3 para Varones*[14] of Mazatlán, and so forth. Miss Hopley put things down in the book, and my mother signed a card.

As long as the questions continued, Doña[15] Henriqueta could stay and I was secure. Now that they were over, Miss Hopley saw her to the door, dismissed our interpreter, and without further ado took me by the hand and strode down the hall to Miss Ryan's first grade.

Miss Ryan took me to a seat at the front of the room, into which I shrank—the better to survey her. She was—to skinny, somewhat runty me—of a withering height when she patrolled the class. And when I least expected it, there she was, crouching by my desk, her blond radiant face level with mine, her voice patiently maneuvering me over the awful idiocies of the English language.

During the next few weeks Miss Ryan overcame my fears of tall, energetic teachers as she bent over my desk to help me with a word in the preprimer. Step by step, she loosened me and my classmates from the safe anchorage of the desks for recitations at the blackboard and consultations at her desk. Frequently she burst into happy announcements to the whole class. "Ito can read a sentence," and small Japanese Ito, squint-eyed and shy, slowly read aloud while the class listened in wonder: "Come, Skipper come. Come and run." The Korean, Portuguese, Italian, and Polish first graders had similar moments of glory no less shining than mine the day I conquered *butterfly*, which I had been persistently pronouncing in standard Spanish as *boo-ter-flee*. "Children," Miss Ryan called for attention. "Ernesto has learned how to pronounce *butterfly*!" And I proved it with a perfect imitation of Miss Ryan. From that celebrated success, I was soon able to match Ito's progress as a sentence reader with "Come, butterfly, come fly with me."

Like Ito and several other first graders who did not know English, I received private lessons from Miss Ryan in the closet, a narrow hall off the classroom with a door at each end. Next to one of these doors Miss Ryan placed a large chair for herself and a small one for me. Keeping an eye on the class through the open door, she read with me about sheep in the meadow and a frightened chicken going to see the king, coaching me out of my phonetic ruts in words like *pasture*, *bow-wow-wow*, *hay*, and *pretty*, which to my Mexican ear and eye had so many unnecessary sounds and letters. She made me watch her lips and then close my eyes as she repeated words I found hard to read. When we came to know each other better, I tried interrupting to tell Miss Ryan how we said it in Spanish. It didn't work. She only

---

13. Henriqueta (en *rē* kä′ tä).

14. *Escuela Municipal Numero 3 para Varones* (es kwe′ lä mōō nē sē päl′ nōō′ me *rô̄* tres pä′ rä vä *rô̄*′ nes) *Spanish:* Municipal School Number Three for Males.

15. *Doña* (dô̄′ nyä) *Spanish:* Madam, a Spanish title of respect, used with a woman's name.

said "oh" and went on with *pasture, bow-wow-wow,* and *pretty*. It was as if in that closet we were both discovering together the secrets of the English language and grieving together over the tragedies of Bo-Peep. The main reason I was graduated with honors from the first grade was that I had fallen in love with Miss Ryan. Her radiant, no-nonsense character made us either afraid not to love her or love her so we would not be afraid; I am not sure which. It was not only that we sensed she was with it, but also that she was with us.

Like the first grade, the rest of the Lincoln School was a sampling of the lower part of town where many races made their home. My pals in the second grade were Kazushi, whose parents spoke only Japanese; Matti, a skinny Italian boy; and Manuel, a fat Portuguese who would never get into a fight but wrestled you to the ground and just sat on you. Our assortment of nationalities included Koreans, Yugoslavs, Poles, Irish, and home-grown Americans.

Miss Hopley and her teachers never let us forget why we were at Lincoln: for those who were <u>alien</u>,[16] to become good Americans; for those who were so born, to accept the rest of us. Off the school grounds we traded the same insults we heard from our elders. On the playground we were sure to be marched up to the principal's office for calling someone a wop, a chink, a dago,[17] or a greaser. The school was not so much a melting pot as a griddle, where Miss Hopley and her helpers warmed knowledge into us and roasted racial hatreds out of us.

At Lincoln, making us into Americans did not mean scrubbing away what made us originally foreign. The teachers called us as our parents did or as close as they could pronounce our names in Spanish or Japanese. No one was ever scolded or punished for speaking in his native tongue on the playground. Matti told the class about his mother's down quilt, which she had made in Italy with the fine feathers of a thousand geese. Encarnación[18] acted out how

boys learned to fish in the Philippines. I astounded the third grade with the story of my travels on a stagecoach, which nobody else in the class had seen except in the museum at Sutter's Fort. After a visit to the Crocker Art Gallery and its collection of heroic paintings of the golden age of California, someone showed a silk scroll with a Chinese painting. Miss Hopley herself had a way of expressing wonder over these matters before a class, her eyes wide open until they popped slightly. It was easy for me to feel that becoming a proud American, as she said we should, did not mean feeling ashamed of being a Mexican.

The Americanization of Mexican me was no smooth matter. I had to fight one lout who made fun of my travels on the *diligencia*[19] and my barbaric translation of the word into "diligence." He doubled up with laughter over the word until I straightened him out with a kick. In class I made points explaining that in Mexico roosters said "qui-qui-ri-qui" and not "cock-a-doodle-doo," but after school I had to put up with the taunts of a big Yugoslav who said Mexican roosters were crazy.

But it was Homer who gave me the most lasting lesson for a future American.

Homer was a chunky Irishman who dressed as if every day was Sunday. He slicked his hair between a crew cut and a pompadour. And Homer was smart, as he clearly showed when he and I ran for president of the third grade.

Everyone understood that this was to be a demonstration of how the American people vote for President. In an election, the teacher explained, the candidates could be generous and vote for each other. We cast our ballots in

---

16. alien (āl′ ē ən): belonging to another country or people; foreign.
17. wop, chink, dago: derogatory terms for persons of Italian (wop, dago) and Chinese (chink) descent.
18. Encarnación (en kär nä syôn′).
19. *diligencia* (dē lē hen′ syä) *Spanish:* stagecoach.

a shoe box and Homer won by two votes. I polled my supporters and I came to the conclusion that I had voted for Homer and, so had he. After class he didn't deny it, reminding me of what the teacher had said—we could vote for each other but didn't have to.

The lower part of town was a collage of nationalities in the middle of which Miss Nettie Hopley kept school with discipline and compassion. She called assemblies in the upper hall to introduce celebrities like the police sergeant or the fire chief, to lay down the law of the school, to present awards to our athletic champions, and to make important announcements. One of these was that I had been proposed by my school and accepted as a member of the newly formed Sacramento Boys' Band. "Now, isn't that a wonderful thing?" Miss Hopley asked the assembled school, all eyes on me. And everyone answered in a chorus, including myself, "Yes, Miss Hopley."

It was not only the parents who were summoned to her office and boys and girls who served sentences there who knew that Nettie Hopley meant business. The entire school witnessed her sizzling Americanism in its awful majesty one morning at flag salute.

All the grades, as usual, were lined up in the courtyard between the wings of the building, ready to march to classes after the opening bell. Miss Shand was on the balcony of the second floor of Miss Hopley's office, conducting us in our lusty singing of "My Country tiz-a-thee." Our principal, as always, stood there like us, at attention, her right hand over her heart, joining in the song.

Halfway through the second stanza she stepped forward, held up her arm in a sign of command, and called loud and clear, "Stop the singing." Miss Shand looked flabbergasted. We were frozen with shock.

Miss Hopley was now standing at the rail of the balcony, her eyes sparkling, her voice low and resonant, the words coming down to us distinctly and loaded with indignation.[20]

"There are two gentlemen walking on the school grounds with their hats on while we are singing," she said, sweeping our ranks with her eyes. "We will remain silent until the gentlemen come to attention and remove their hats." A minute of awful silence ended when Miss Hopley, her gaze fixed on something behind us, signaled Miss Shand, and we began once more the familiar hymn. That afternoon, when school was out, the word spread. The two gentlemen were the Superintendent of Schools and an important guest on an inspection.

I came back to the Lincoln School after every summer, moving up through the grades with Miss Campbell, Miss Beakey, Mrs. Wood, Miss Applegate, and Miss Delahunty. I sat in the classroom adjoining the principal's office and had my turn answering her telephone when she was about the building repeating the message to the teacher, who made a note of it. Miss Campbell read to us during the last period of the week about King Arthur, Columbus, Buffalo Bill, and Daniel Boone, who came to life in the reverie[21] of the class through the magic of her voice. And it was Miss Campbell who introduced me to the public library on Eye Street, where I became a regular customer.

All of Lincoln School mourned together when Eddie, the blond boy everybody liked, was killed by a freight train as he crawled across the tracks going home one day. We assembled to say goodbye to Miss Applegate, who was off to Alaska to be married. Now it was my turn to be excused from class to interpret for a parent enrolling a new student fresh

---

20. **indignation** (in′ dig nā′ shən): anger at something that seems unjust.
21. **reverie** (rev′ ər ē): the condition of being lost in thought; daydreaming.

from Mexico. Graduates from Lincoln came back now and then to tell us about high school. A naturalist entertained us in assembly, imitating the calls of the meadowlark, the water ouzel, the oriole, and the killdeer. I decided to become a bird man after I left Lincoln.

In the years we lived in the lower part of town, La Leen-Con, as my family called it, became a benchmark in our lives, like the purple light of the Lyric Theater and the golden dome of the *Palacio de Gobierno* gleaming above Capitol Park.

Thinking About the Selection

A PERSONAL RESPONSE

sharing impressions

1. How did you react to Ernesto's experiences? Describe your reactions in your journal.

constructing interpretations

2. How difficult does Ernesto's adjustment to a new country seem to be?
   Think about
   • what you wrote in your journal in the prereading activity
   • his experience learning English
   • his relationships with other students
   • the support he receives
   • his apparent attitude toward school as a young boy
   • the cultural differences he observes

3. Why do you think Galarza chose to relate this experience? Explain.

4. Analyze your impression of Miss Hopley.
   Think about
   • her reaction to the superintendent and his guest when they do not remove their hats during the singing of "My Country tiz-a-thee"
   • her goal of having the immigrant students become "good Americans"
   • Galarza's encounter with her on the first day of school
   • how important she appears to be to Galarza

A CREATIVE RESPONSE

5. If Galarza were a young immigrant in the 1990's, how might his experience adjusting to a new country be different?

6. How would you describe the tone of this selection?
Think about
- tone as the attitude a writer takes toward a subject
- your answer to question 3

7. In what what ways might each of the following people benefit from the lessons presented in this selection: an educator, a young person new to this country, a young person born in this country?

Analyzing the Writer's Craft

THEME

What does Galarza want the reader to understand about his early experiences?

Building a Literary Vocabulary. Theme, as you know, is the central idea or message in a work of literature. It is the writer's perception about life or humanity that is shared with the reader. A work of literature can have several minor themes in addition to the major theme.

Throughout *Barrio Boy* Galarza describes the positive influences that school had on his life. This theme might be simply stated, "Education is an important tool for self-improvement." While it is fairly easy to recognize this as the major theme, a deeper look at Galarza's early life leads the reader to note additional themes relating to the plight of immigrants.

Application: Analyzing Themes. Working with a partner, decide what theme each of the following quotations communicates. If necessary, refer to the

selection to refresh your memory about the context of each quotation.

"We found the Americans as strange in their customs as they probably found us." (page 160)

"The school was not so much a melting pot as a griddle. . . ." (page 164)

"It was easy for me to feel that becoming a proud American, as she [Miss Hopley] said we should, did not mean feeling ashamed of being a Mexican." (page 164)

"In the years we lived in the lower part of town, La Leen-Con [Lincoln School] . . . became a benchmark in our lives, like . . . the golden dome of the *Palacio de Gobierno* gleaming above Capitol Park." (page 166)

Get together with other classmates and share your analysis of these themes.

Connecting Reading and Writing

1. Write a **human interest story** about Miss Hopley that Galarza might have written for a local newspaper.

Option: Compose a **tribute** that Galarza might have delivered at Miss Hopley's retirement dinner.

2. Using information gathered from your parents and/or other relatives, create a **family tree** that indicates who immigrated to this country, when they came, and from what country they came.

Option: Create **notes** for an oral presentation on the immigration experiences of your family. Assume that you will use a map or globe in your presentation.

3. Write an **anecdote** about an experience you had as a newcomer to a school, neighborhood, or class. Share the anecdote with your classmates.

Option: Create a **booklet** that presents tips for adjusting successfully to a new place.

4. In an **editorial** for the school newspaper, discuss whether you think your school promotes or discourages cultural diversity.

Option: Prepare a set of **questions** to be used in an interview with your principal in which you discuss your school's policy toward the promotion of cultural diversity.

5. Create a **program** for a cultural festival that might take place at your school. Your program might include plans for various activities involving history, music, art, food, and any other aspects of culture that would encourage multicultural awareness.

Option: Compile a **cookbook** featuring recipes of various ethnic groups represented in your school.

from Hunger of Memory

RICHARD RODRIGUEZ

A biography of Rodriguez appears on page 428.

Approaching the Selection

The son of Mexican immigrants, Richard Rodriguez spoke barely fifty words of English when he entered school at the age of six. He worked hard at learning the language, though, and ultimately became a rising star in an educational system that encouraged him with scholarships. By the time he was in fourth grade, Rodriguez had concluded that reading was the key to his success. In this excerpt from his autobiography, Rodriguez describes the progress and results of the reading program he devised for himself.

Building Vocabulary

These essential words are footnoted within the selection.

grandiose (gran′ dē ōs′): I embarked upon a **grandiose** reading program. (page 170)

appraisals (ə prāz′ elz): Rereading these brief moralistic **appraisal**s usually left me disheartened. (page 170)

epigrams (ep′ ə gramz′): I vacuumed books for **epigrams.** (page 171)

Connecting Writing and Reading

In your journal, list three books that you have read and enjoyed. Next to each title, jot down a brief descriptive phrase telling what you remember from the book.

1. _____

2. _____

3. _____

As you read, notice whether Rodriguez describes similar memories from his reading.

*I*N FOURTH GRADE I embarked upon a <u>grandiose</u>[1] reading program. "Give me the names of important books," I would say to startled teachers. They soon found out that I had in mind "adult books." I ignored their suggestion of anything I suspected was written for children. (Not until I was in college, as a result, did I read *Huckleberry Finn* or *Alice's Adventures in Wonderland*.) Instead, I read *The Scarlet Letter* and Franklin's *Autobiography*. And whatever I read I read for extra credit. Each time I finished a book, I reported the achievement to a teacher and basked in the praise my effort earned. Despite my best efforts, however, there seemed to be more and more books I needed to read. At the library I would literally tremble as I came upon whole shelves of books I hadn't read. So I read and I read and I read: *Great Expectations*; all the short stories of Kipling; *The Babe Ruth Story*; the entire first volume of the *Encyclopaedia Britannica* (A–ANSTEY); the *Iliad*; *Moby-Dick*; *Gone with the Wind*; *The Good Earth*; *Ramona*; *Forever Amber*; *The Lives of the Saints*; *Crime and Punishment*; *The Pearl*. . . . Librarians who initially frowned when I checked out the maximum ten books at a time started saving books they thought I might like. Teachers would say to the rest of the class, "I only wish the rest of you took reading as seriously as Richard obviously does."

But at home I would hear my mother wondering, "What do you see in your books?" (Was reading a hobby like her knitting? Was so much reading even healthy for a boy? Was it the sign of "brains"? Or was it just a convenient excuse for not helping around the house on Saturday mornings?) Always, "What do you see . . . ?"

What *did* I see in my books? I had the idea that they were crucial for my academic success, though I couldn't have said exactly how or why. In the sixth grade I simply concluded that what gave a book its value was some major idea or theme it contained. If that core essence could be mined and memorized, I would become learned like my teachers. I decided to record in a notebook the themes of the books that I read. After reading *Robinson Crusoe, I* wrote that its theme was "the value of learning to live by oneself." When I completed *Wuthering Heights,* I noted the danger of "letting emotions get out of control." Rereading these brief moralistic <u>appraisals</u>[2] usually left me disheartened. I couldn't believe that they were really the source of reading's value. But for many more years, they constituted the only means I had of describing to myself the educational value of books.

In spite of my earnestness, I found reading a pleasurable activity. I came to enjoy the lonely good company of books. Early on weekday mornings, I'd read in my bed. I'd feel a mysterious comfort then, reading in the dawn quiet —the blue-gray silence interrupted by the occasional churning of the refrigerator motor a few rooms away or the more distant sounds of a city bus beginning its run. On weekends I'd go to the public library to read, surrounded by old men and women. Or, if the weather was fine, I would take my books to the park and read in the shade of a tree. A warm summer evening was my favorite reading time.

---

1. grandiose (gran′ dē ōs′): impressive; on a large scale.
2. appraisals (ə prāz′ elz): judgments of quality or worth.

Neighbors would leave for vacation and I would water their lawns. I would sit through the twilight on the front porches or in backyards, reading to the cool, whirling sounds of the sprinklers.

I also had favorite writers. But often those writers I enjoyed most I was least able to value. When I read William Saroyan's *The Human Comedy,* I was immediately pleased by the narrator's warmth and the charm of his story. But as quickly I became suspicious. A book so enjoyable to read couldn't be very "important." Another summer I determined to read all the novels of Dickens. Reading his fat novels, I loved the feeling I got—after the first hundred pages—of being at home in a fictional world where I knew the names of the characters and cared about what was going to happen to them. And it bothered me that I was forced away at the conclusion, when the fiction closed tight, like a fortune-teller's fist—the futures of all the major characters neatly resolved. I never knew how to take such feelings seriously, however. Nor did I suspect that these experiences could be part of a novel's meaning. Still, there were pleasures to sustain me after I'd finish my books. Carrying a volume back to the library, I would be pleased by its weight. I'd run my fingers along the edge of the pages and marvel at the breadth of my achievement. Around my room, growing stacks of paperback books reinforced my assurance.

I entered high school having read hundreds of books. My habit of reading made me a confident speaker and writer of English. Reading also enabled me to sense something of the shape, the major concerns, of Western thought. (I was able to say something about Dante and Descartes and Engels and James Baldwin in my high school term papers.) In these various ways, books brought me academic success as I hoped that they would. But I was not a good reader. Merely bookish, I lacked a point of view when I read. Rather, I read in order to acquire a point of view. I vacuumed books for epigrams,[3] scraps of information, ideas, themes—anything to fill the hollow within me and make me feel educated. When one of my teachers suggested to his drowsy tenth-grade English class that a person could not have a "complicated idea" until he had read at least two thousand books, I heard the remark without detecting either its irony or its very complicated truth. I merely determined to compile a list of all the books I had ever read. Harsh with myself, I included only once a title I might have read several times. (How, after all, could one read a book more than once?) And I included only those books over a hundred pages in length. (Could anything shorter be a book?)

There was yet another high school list I compiled. One day I came across a newspaper article about the retirement of an English professor at a nearby state college. The article was accompanied by a list of the "hundred most important books of Western Civilization." "More than anything else in my life," the professor told the reporter with finality, "these books have made me all that I am." That was the kind of remark I couldn't ignore. I clipped out the list and kept it for the several months it took me to read all of the titles. Most books, of course, I barely understood. While reading Plato's *Republic*, for instance, I needed to keep looking at the book jacket comments to remind myself what the text was about. Nevertheless, with the special patience and superstition of a scholarship boy, I looked at every word of the text. And by the time I reached the last word, relieved, I convinced myself that I had read *The Republic*. In a ceremony of great pride, I solemnly crossed Plato off my list.

---

3. epigrams (ep′ ə gramz′): short, witty, pointed statements.

The scholarship boy pleases most when he is young—the working-class child struggling for academic success. To his teachers, he offers great satisfaction; his success is their proudest achievement. Many other persons offer to help him. A businessman learns the boy's story and promises to underwrite part of the cost of his college education. A woman leaves him her entire library of several hundred books when she moves. His progress is featured in a newspaper article. Many people seem happy for him. They marvel. "How did you manage so fast?" From all sides, there is lavish praise and encouragement.

In his grammar school classroom, however, the boy already makes students around him uneasy. They scorn his desire to succeed. They scorn him for constantly wanting the teacher's attention and praise. . . . Later, when he makes it to college, no one will mock him aloud. But he detects annoyance on the faces of some students and even some teachers who watch him. It puzzles him often. In college, then in graduate school, he behaves much as he always has. If anything is different about him, it is that he dares to anticipate the successful conclusion of his studies. At last he feels that he belongs in the classroom, and this is exactly the source of the dissatisfaction he causes. To many persons around him, he appears too much the academic. There may be some things about him that recall his beginnings—his shabby clothes; his persistent poverty; or his dark skin (in those cases when it symbolizes his parents' disadvantaged condition)—but they only make clear how far he has moved from his past. He has used education to remake himself. . . . If, because of my schooling, I had grown culturally separated from my parents, my education finally [after several years] had given me ways of speaking and caring about that fact.

*T*hinking *About the Selection*

A PERSONAL RESPONSE

sharing impressions

1. What is your reaction to Rodriguez's reading program? Jot down your reaction in your journal.

constructing interpretations

2. In your opinion are the effects of Rodriguez's reading primarily positive or negative?

Think about

- how he remakes himself
- how teachers and other adults in the community respond to him
- how his reading affects his relationships with family and fellow students
- your own experiences with reading and with those who read a lot

3. Which of Rodriguez's beliefs about reading come closest to your own?

Think about

- his belief that books are crucial to academic success
- how he views his childhood idea that understanding themes provides "the educational value of books"

- whether he still believes that enjoyable books are not very important
- his later understanding that the feeling of "being at home" in a fictional world "could be part of a novel's meaning"
- his explanation of why he was not a good reader

A CREATIVE RESPONSE

4. If Rodriguez could live his life over again, how do you think he might conduct his reading program?

A CRITICAL RESPONSE

5. What similarities and differences do you find between Richard Rodriguez and students in your school? Cite details from the selection in explaining your answer.

6. Would you consult Ernesto Galarza or Richard Rodriguez for advice about the problems faced by non-native speakers of English in American schools? Use details from both selections to support your choice.

Analyzing the Writer's Craft

AUTOBIOGRAPHY

Note places where Rodriguez uses direct quotations in this excerpt. How do those quotations help to convey an impression of Rodriguez's life?

Building a Literary Vocabulary. An autobiography is the story of a person's life written by that person. Generally an autobiographer uses the first-person point of view. Rodriguez not only uses first person but occasionally quotes himself and others directly. In the first paragraph, for example, Rodriguez says to his teachers, "Give me the names of important books." This statement, startling from a nine-year-old boy, conveys how serious and determined Rodriguez was as a child. Other techniques that Rodriguez uses to convey a sense of his early life include revealing his thoughts as a child, interpreting his past experiences from his perspective as an adult, and reporting how other people viewed him.

Application: Analyzing Autobiography. Working in a group with two or three classmates, copy the following chart on a sheet of paper. Go back through the selection to find examples of each technique listed on the chart. Then fill out the chart with examples and brief descriptions of the qualities revealed by each example. When you have finished, write a statement explaining what you think are the most effective techniques used by Rodriguez.

Technique	Examples	Quality revealed
Using direct quotations from self and others	"Give me the names of important books."	A determined personality
Revealing his thoughts as a child		
Interpreting from an adult perspective		
Reporting how others viewed him		

Connecting Reading and Writing

1. Write at least five **slogans** that Rodriguez might compose on the value of reading to be displayed on posters in your school library during National Library Week.

Option: Write a **script** for a public service announcement that Rodriguez might make encouraging people to read.

2. Using your prereading journal entry as a model, survey at least ten people—both adults and students—about three books they have read. Compile your findings with those of the rest of the class in a **report** that can be used as a resource by librarians.

Option: Ask at least twenty people how many books they estimate they have read in the last twelve months. Compile your findings with those of the rest of the class and create a **graph** that could be printed in a journal for reading teachers.

3. Choosing one or more of the techniques listed in Analyzing the Writer's Craft, write an **autobiographical sketch,** modeled on any of the ones in this section, in which you describe a project you carried out as a child.

Option: Write about that project in a **diary entry,** expressing the perspective you had at the time you completed the project.

High Horse's Courting

BLACK ELK

As told through JOHN G. NEIHARDT (FLAMING RAINBOW)

A biography of Black Elk appears on page 419.

Approaching the Story

"High Horse's Courting" is a story that Black Elk learned from an older member of his tribe and passed on to his biographer, John Neihardt. The story deals with the universal themes of love and courtship in the context of the distinctive customs and beliefs of the Sioux. The story is told in Black Elk's own words, as though he were talking to someone sitting next to him.

Connecting Writing and Reading

What methods would you be most likely to use to make someone feel romantic toward you? In your journal, copy the following chart and rate how likely you would be to use the courtship methods listed.

Method of courtship	Not likely	Somewhat likely	Very likely
Going out to a fancy place			
Sending flowers			
Giving presents			
Cooking dinner			
Declaring your love			
Other: _____			

As you read the story, compare the courtship methods you would use to those of High Horse.

High Horse's Courting

YOU KNOW, IN the old days, it was not so very easy to get a girl when you wanted to be married. Sometimes it was hard work for a young man and he had to stand a great deal. Say I am a young man and I have seen a young girl who looks so beautiful to me that I feel all sick when I think about her. I can not just go and tell her about it and then get married if she is willing. I have to be a very sneaky fellow to talk to her at all, and after I have managed to talk to her, that is only the beginning.

Probably for a long time I have been feeling sick about a certain girl because I love her so much, but she will not even look at me, and her parents keep a good watch over her. But I keep feeling worse and worse all the time; so maybe I sneak up to her tepee in the dark and wait until she comes out. Maybe I just wait there all night and don't get any sleep at all and she does not come out. Then I feel sicker than ever about her.

Maybe I hide in the brush by a spring where she sometimes goes to get water, and when she comes by, if nobody is looking, then I jump out and hold her and just make her listen to me. If she likes me too, I can tell that from the way she acts, for she is very bashful and maybe will not say a word or even look at me the first time. So I let her go, and then maybe I sneak around until I can see her father alone, and I tell him how many horses I can give him for his beautiful girl,[1] and by now I am feeling so sick that maybe I would give him all the horses in the world if I had them.

Well, this young man I am telling about was called High Horse, and there was a girl in the village who looked so beautiful to him that he was just sick all over from thinking about her so much and he was getting sicker all the time. The girl was very shy, and her parents thought a great deal of her because they were not young any more and this was the only child they had. So they watched her all day long, and they fixed it so that she would be safe at night too when they were asleep. They thought so much of her that they had made a rawhide bed for her to sleep in, and after they knew that High Horse was sneaking around after her, they took rawhide thongs and tied the girl in bed at night so that nobody could steal her when they were asleep, for they were not sure but that their girl might really want to be stolen.

Well, after High Horse had been sneaking around a good while and hiding and waiting for the girl and getting sicker all the time, he finally caught her alone and made her talk to him. Then he found out that she liked him maybe a little. Of course this did not make him feel well. It made him sicker than ever, but now he felt as brave as a bison bull, and so he went right to her father and said he loved the girl so much that he would give two good horses for her—one of them young and the other one not so very old.

But the old man just waved his hand, meaning for High Horse to go away and quit talking foolishness like that.

High Horse was feeling sicker than ever about it; but there was another young fellow who said he would loan High Horse two ponies and when he got some more horses,

---

1. **how many . . . girl:** Like other cultures around the world, many Native American tribes had the custom of exchanging something of value for a bride. Among the Sioux, the "bride price" was often horses.

why, he could just give them back for the ones he had borrowed.

Then High Horse went back to the old man and said he would give four horses for the girl—two of them young and the other two not hardly old at all. But the old man just waved his hand and would not say anything.

So High Horse sneaked around until he could talk to the girl again, and he asked her to run away with him. He told her he thought he would just fall over and die if she did not. But she said she would not do that; she wanted to be bought like a fine woman. You see she thought a great deal of herself too.

That made High Horse feel so very sick that he could not eat a bite, and he went around with his head hanging down as though he might just fall down and die any time.

Red Deer was another young fellow, and he and High Horse were great comrades, always doing things together. Red Deer saw how High Horse was acting, and he said: "Cousin, what is the matter? Are you sick in the belly? You look as though you were going to die."

Then High Horse told Red Deer how it was, and said he thought he could not stay alive much longer if he could not marry the girl pretty quick.

Red Deer thought awhile about it, and then he said: "Cousin, I have a plan, and if you are man enough to do as I tell you, then everything will be all right. She will not run away with you; her old man will not take four horses; and four horses are all you can get. You must steal her and run away with her. Then afterwhile you can come back and the old man cannot do anything because she will be your woman. Probably she wants you to steal her anyway."

So they planned what High Horse had to do, and he said he loved the girl so much that he was man enough to do anything Red Deer or anybody else could think up.

So this is what they did.

That night late they sneaked up to the girl's tepee and waited until it sounded inside as though the old man and the old woman and the girl were sound asleep. Then High Horse crawled under the tepee with a knife. He had to cut the rawhide thongs first, and then Red Deer, who was pulling up the stakes around that side of the tepee, was going to help drag the girl outside and gag her. After that, High Horse could put her across his pony in front of him and hurry out of there and be happy all the rest of his life.

When High Horse had crawled inside, he felt so nervous that he could hear his heart drumming, and it seemed so loud he felt sure it would 'waken the old folks. But it did not, and afterwhile he began cutting the thongs. Every time he cut one it made a pop and nearly scared him to death. But he was getting along all right and all the thongs were cut down as far as the girl's thighs, when he became so nervous that his knife slipped and stuck the girl. She gave a big, loud yell. Then the old folks jumped up and yelled too. By this time High Horse was outside, and he and Red Deer were running away like antelope. The old man and some other people chased the young men but they got away in the dark and nobody knew who it was.

Well, if you ever wanted a beautiful girl you will know how sick High Horse was now. It was very bad the way he felt, and it looked as though he would starve even if he did not drop over dead sometime.

Red Deer kept thinking about this, and after a few days he went to High Horse and said: "Cousin, take courage! I have another plan, and I am sure, if you are man enough, we can steal her this time." And High Horse said: "I am man enough to do anything anybody can think up, if I can only get that girl."

So this is what they did.

They went away from the village alone, and Red Deer made High Horse strip naked. Then he painted High Horse solid white all over, and after that he painted black stripes all over the white and put black rings around High Horse's eyes. High Horse looked terrible. He looked so terrible that when Red Deer was through painting and took a good look at what he had done, he said it scared even him a little.

"Now," Red Deer said, "if you get caught again, everybody will be so scared they will think you are a bad spirit and will be afraid to chase you."

So when the night was getting old and everybody was sound asleep, they sneaked back to the girl's tepee. High Horse crawled in with his knife, as before, and Red Deer waited outside, ready to drag the girl out and gag her when High Horse had all the thongs cut.

High Horse crept up by the girl's bed and began cutting at the thongs. But he kept thinking, "If they see me they will shoot me because I look so terrible." The girl was restless and kept squirming around in bed, and when a thong was cut, it popped. So High Horse worked very slowly and carefully.

But he must have made some noise, for suddenly the old woman awoke and said to her old man: "Old Man, wake up! There is somebody in this tepee!" But the old man was sleepy and didn't want to be bothered. He said: "Of course there is somebody in this tepee. Go to sleep and don't bother me." Then he snored some more.

But High Horse was so scared by now that he lay very still and as flat to the ground as he could. Now, you see, he had not been sleeping very well for a long time because he was so sick about the girl. And while he was lying there waiting for the old woman to snore, he just forgot everything, even how beautiful the girl was. Red Deer, who was lying outside ready to do his part, wondered and wondered what had happened in there, but he did not dare call out to High Horse.

Afterwhile the day began to break and Red Deer had to leave with the two ponies he had staked there for his comrade and girl, or somebody would see him.

So he left.

Now when it was getting light in the tepee, the girl awoke and the first thing she saw was a terrible animal, all white with black stripes on it, lying asleep beside her bed. So she screamed, and then the old woman screamed and the old man yelled. High Horse jumped up, scared almost to death, and he nearly knocked the tepee down getting out of there.

People were coming running from all over the village with guns and bows and axes, and everybody was yelling.

By now High Horse was running so fast that he hardly touched the ground at all, and he looked so terrible that the people fled from him and let him run. Some braves wanted to shoot at him, but the others said he might be some sacred being and it would bring bad trouble to kill him.

High Horse made for the river that was near, and in among the brush he found a hollow tree and dived into it. Afterwhile some braves came there and he could hear them saying that it was some bad spirit that had come out of the water and gone back in again.

That morning the people were ordered to break camp and move away from there. So they did, while High Horse was hiding in his hollow tree.

Now Red Deer had been watching all this from his own tepee and trying to look as though he were as much surprised and scared as all the others. So when the camp moved, he sneaked back to where he had seen his comrade disappear. When he was down there in the brush, he called, and High Horse answered, because he knew his friend's voice. They washed off the paint from High Horse and sat down on the river bank to talk about their troubles.

High Horse said he never would go back to the village as long as he lived and he did not care what happened to him now. He said he was going to go on the warpath all by himself. Red Deer said: "No, cousin, you are not going on the warpath alone, because I am going with you."

So Red Deer got everything ready, and at night they started out on the warpath all alone. After several days they came to a Crow camp just about sundown, and when it was dark they sneaked up to where the Crow horses were grazing, killed the horse guard, who was not thinking about enemies because he thought all the Lakotas were far away, and drove off about a hundred horses.

They got a big start because all the Crow horses stampeded and it was probably morning before the Crow warriors could catch any horses to ride. Red Deer and High Horse fled with their herd three days and nights before they reached the village of their people. Then they drove the whole herd right into the village and up in front of the girl's tepee. The old man was there, and High Horse called out to him and asked if he thought maybe that would be enough horses for his girl. The old man did not wave him away that time. It was not the horses that he wanted. What he wanted was a son who was a real man and good for something.

So High Horse got his girl after all, and I think he deserved her.

Thinking About the Story

A PERSONAL RESPONSE

sharing impressions

1. How did you react when High Horse finally got his girl? Describe your reaction in your journal.

constructing interpretations

2. Compare the motivations of High Horse, the girl, the girl's father, and Red Deer.
Think about
- why High Horse perseveres in trying different courtship methods
- why the girl refuses to run away with High Horse
- why the girl's father waves High Horse away the first two times but not the last time
- why Red Deer helps High Horse

3. How do you think High Horse is changed by his courtship?

A CREATIVE RESPONSE

4. If High Horse had succeeded in stealing the girl, how might his relationship to the tribe have been different?

A CRITICAL RESPONSE

5. What tribal values can you infer from this story? Use specific details from the story to support your answer.

6. What do you think a contemporary reader can identify with in this story?

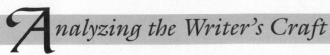

Analyzing the Writer's Craft

ORAL LITERATURE ───────────────────────

"High Horse's Courting" was passed down from a man named Watanye to Black Elk, who told it to his biographer. What purpose do you think Watanye and Black Elk had for telling this story?

Building a Literary Vocabulary. Oral literature is literature that is passed from one generation to another by performance or word-of-mouth. Folk tales, fables, myths, chants, and legends are part of the oral tradition of cultures throughout the world. All North American Indian literature originated in the oral tradition.

Oral literature is often performed for a specific purpose, such as to teach, to pray, or to entertain. In his book, *Black Elk Speaks*, Black Elk states that Watanye most often told him funny stories—such

as "High Horse's Courting," with its exaggerated descriptions of lovesickness. In addition to being entertaining, the story reinforces tribal values, such as persistence and the need for a young brave to prove that he will be a good provider for his wife and tribe before he is considered a man. Perhaps Black Elk, who saw the Sioux way of life destroyed by the white settlers, wanted to pass on this story in order to preserve tribal values and memories.

Application: Performing Oral Literature. With three or four classmates, present "High Horse's Courting" as a skit or dramatic reading for the class. You may want to incorporate instrumental music, costumes, props, or photographs in your performance.

Connecting Reading and Writing

1. Write an amusing **story**, similar to "High Horse's Courting," recounting a young person's obstacles to romance in contemporary America. Collect the stories of several classmates into a magazine called *Courtship Today*.

Option: Create **notes** for telling such a story in an oral presentation for your class.

2. In many Native American tribes it was customary to name a person after a strong character trait or significant event in his or her life. Imagine that you are a holy man of the tribe and decide to rename High Horse following the adventure in this story. Write a **speech** in which

you tell the tribe what his new name will be and explain why you chose that name.

Option: Responding as the girl's father, write an **explanation** of what you would name your new son-in-law.

3. Research Black Elk's tribe, the Oglala Sioux. Create a poster that illustrates several aspects of their life, with explanatory **captions** beneath the pictures. Display your poster in class.

Option: Write a formal **outline** that you could use to write a research paper on the Oglala Sioux.

The Secret Lion

ALBERTO ALVARO RÍOS

A biography of Ríos appears on page 428.

Approaching the Story

"The Secret Lion" centers on two important episodes in the life of a boy growing up in southern Arizona. In his own words, the boy recalls things he did and how he felt as a twelve-year-old entering junior high school and earlier, at the age of five. The style of the story is informal and conversational, as though the reader were right at the boy's side listening to his recollections.

Connecting Writing and Reading

What do you remember about starting junior high school or middle school? Think about how junior high or middle school was different from elementary school and about any changes you experienced during the transition. Jot down at least five things that you remember from that time in your life. Then, while you read, compare changes you remember with the changes described in "The Secret Lion."

Two Children Singing, 1957, ADOLFO MEXIAC.
Courtesy of the artist and the Mexican Fine Arts Center Museum, Chicago.

The Secret Lion

I WAS TWELVE and in junior high school and something happened that we didn't have a name for, but it was there nonetheless like a lion, and roaring, roaring that way the biggest things do. Everything changed. Just like that. Like the rug, the one that gets pulled—or better, like the tablecloth those magicians pull where the stuff on the table stays the same but the gasp! from the audience makes the staying-the-same part not matter. Like that.

What happened was there were teachers now, not just one teacher, teach-erz, and we felt personally abandoned somehow. When a person had all these teachers now, he didn't get taken care of the same way, even though six was more than one. Arithmetic went out the door when we walked in. And we saw girls now, but they weren't the same girls we used to know because we couldn't talk to them anymore, not the same way we used to, certainly not to Sandy, even though she was my neighbor, too. Not even to her. She just played the piano all the time. And there were words, oh there were words in junior high school, and we wanted to know what they were, and how a person did them—that's what school was supposed to be for. Only, in junior high school, school wasn't school, everything was backwardlike. If you went up to a teacher and said the word to try and find out what it meant you got in trouble for saying it. So we didn't. And we figured it must have been that way about other stuff, too, so we never said anything about anything—we weren't stupid.

But my friend Sergio and I, we solved junior high school. We would come home from school on the bus, put our books away, change shoes, and go across the highway to the arroyo.[1] It was the one place we were not supposed to go. So we did. This was, after all, what junior high had at least shown us. It was our river, though, our personal Mississippi, our friend from long back, and it was full of stories and all the branch forts we had built in it when we were still the Vikings of America, with our own symbol, which we had carved everywhere, even in the sand, which let the water take it. That was good, we had decided; whoever was at the end of this river would know about us.

At the very very top of our growing lungs, what we would do down there was shout every dirty word we could think of, in every combination we could come up with, and we would yell about girls, and all the things we wanted to do with them, as loud as we could—we didn't know what we wanted to do with them, just things—and we would yell about teachers, and how we loved some of them, like Miss Crevelone, and how we wanted to dissect some of them, making signs of the cross, like priests, and we would yell this stuff over and over because it felt good, we couldn't explain why, it just felt good and for the first time in our lives there was nobody to tell us we couldn't. So we did.

One Thursday we were walking along shouting this way, and the railroad, the Southern Pacific, which ran above and along the far side of the arroyo, had dropped a grinding ball down there, which was, we found out later, a cannonball thing used in mining. A bunch of them were put in a big vat which turned around and crushed the ore. One had

---

1. **arroyo** (ə rōi′ ō): a dry creek bed.

been dropped, or thrown—what do caboose men do when they get bored—but it got down there regardless and as we were walking along yelling about one girl or another, a particular Claudia, we found it, one of these things, looked at it, picked it up, and got very very excited, and held it and passed it back and forth, and we were saying, "Guythisis, this is, geeGuythis . . .": we had this perception about nature then, that nature is imperfect and that round things are perfect: we said, "GuyGodthis is perfect, thisisthis is perfect, it's round, round and heavy, it'sit's the best thing we'veeverseen. Whatisit?" We didn't know. We just knew it was great. We just, whatever, we played with it, held it some more.

And then we had to decide what to do with it. We knew, because of a lot of things, that if we were going to take this and show it to anybody, this discovery, this best thing, was going to be taken away from us. That's the way it works with little kids, like all the polished quartz, the tons of it we had collected piece by piece over the years. Junior high kids too. If we took it home, my mother, we knew, was going to look at it and say, "Throw that dirty thing in the, get rid of it." Simple like, like that. "But ma it's the best thing I" "Getridofit." Simple.

So we didn't. Take it home. Instead, we came up with the answer. We dug a hole and we buried it. And we marked it secretly. Lots of secret signs. And came back the next week to dig it up and, we didn't know, pass it around some more or something, but we didn't find it. We dug up that whole bank, and we never found it again. We tried.

Sergio and I talked about that ball or whatever it was when we couldn't find it. All we used were small words, neat, good. Kid words. What we were really saying, but didn't know the words, was how much that ball was like that place, that whole arroyo: couldn't tell anybody about it, didn't understand what it was, didn't have a name for it. It just felt good. It

was just perfect in the way it was that place, that whole going to that place, that whole junior high school lion. It was just iron-heavy, it had no name, it felt good or not, we couldn't take it home to show our mothers, and once we buried it, it was gone forever.

The ball was gone, like the first reasons we had come to that arroyo years earlier, like the first time we had seen the arroyo, it was gone like everything else that had been taken away. This was not our first lesson. We stopped going to the arroyo after not finding the thing, the same way we had stopped going there years earlier and headed for the mountains. Nature seemed to keep pushing us around one way or another, teaching us the same thing every place we ended up. Nature's gang was tough that way, teaching us stuff.

When we were young we moved away from town, me and my family. Sergio's was already out there. Out in the wilds. Or at least the new place seemed like the wilds since everything looks bigger the smaller a man is. I was five, I guess, and we had moved three miles north of Nogales,[2] where we had lived, three miles north of the Mexican border. We looked across the highway in one direction and there was the arroyo; hills stood up in the other direction. Mountains, for a small man.

When the first summer came the very first place we went to was of course the one place we weren't supposed to go, the arroyo. We went down in there and found water running, summer rainwater mostly, and we went swimming. But every third or fourth or fifth day, the sewage treatment plant that was, we found out, upstream, would release whatever it was that it released, and we would never know exactly what day that was, and a person really couldn't tell right off by looking at the water, not every time, not so a person could get out

---

2. **Nogales** (nō gal′ əs).

in time. So, we went swimming that summer and some days we had a lot of fun. Some days we didn't. We found a thousand ways to explain what happened on those other days, constructing elaborate stories about neighborhood dogs, and hadn't she, my mother, miscalculated her step before, too? But she knew something was up because we'd come running into the house those days, wanting to take a shower, even—if this can be imagined—in the middle of the day.

That was the first time we stopped going to the arroyo. It taught us to look the other way. We decided, as the second side of summer came, we wanted to go into the mountains. They were still mountains then. We went running in one summer Thursday morning, my friend Sergio and I, into my mother's kitchen, and said, well, what'zin, what'zin those hills over there—we used her word so she'd understand us—and she said nothingdon'tworryaboutit. So we went out, and we weren't dumb, we thought with our eyes to each other, ohhoshe'stryingtokeep somethingfromus. We knew adults.

We had read the books, after all; we knew about bridges and castles and wildtreacherousraging alligatormouth rivers. We wanted them. So we were going to go out and get them. We went back that morning into that kitchen and we said, "We're going out there, we're going into the hills, we're going away for three days, don't worry." She said, "All right."

"You know," I said to Sergio, "if we're going to go away for three days, well, we ought to at least pack a lunch."

But we were two young boys with no patience for what we thought at the time was mom-stuff: making sa-and-wiches. My mother didn't offer. So we got our little kid knapsacks that my mother had sewn for us, and into them we put the jar of mustard. A loaf of bread. Knivesforksplates, bottles of Coke, a can opener. This was lunch for the two of us.

And we were weighed down, humped over to be strong enough to carry this stuff. But we started walking, anyway, into the hills. We were going to eat berries and stuff otherwise. "Goodbye." My mom said that.

After the first hill we were dead. But we walked. My mother could still see us. And we kept walking. We walked until we got to where the sun is straight overhead, noon. That place. Where that is doesn't matter; it's time to eat. The truth is we weren't anywhere close to that place. We just agreed that the sun was overhead and that it was time to eat, and by tilting our heads a little we could make that the truth.

"We really ought to start looking for a place to eat."

"Yeah. Let's look for a good place to eat." We went back and forth saying that for fifteen minutes, making it lunch time because that's what we always said back and forth before lunch times at home. "Yeah, I'm hungry all right." I nodded my head. "Yeah, I'm hungry all right too. I'm hungry." He nodded his head. I nodded my head back. After a good deal more nodding, we were ready, just as we came over a little hill. We hadn't found the mountains yet. This was a little hill.

And on the other side of this hill we found heaven.

It was just what we thought it would be.

Perfect. Heaven was green, like nothing else in Arizona. And it wasn't a cemetery or like that because we had seen cemeteries and they had gravestones and stuff and this didn't. This was perfect, had trees, lots of trees, had birds, like we had never seen before. It was like *The Wizard of Oz*, like when they got to Oz and everything was so green, so emerald, they had to wear those glasses, and we ran just like them, laughing, laughing that way we did that moment, and we went running down to this clearing in it all, hitting each other that good way we did.

We got down there, we kept laughing, we kept hitting each other, we unpacked our stuff, and we started acting "rich." We knew all about how to do that, like blowing on our nails, then rubbing them on our chests for the shine. We made our sandwiches, opened our Cokes, got out the rest of the stuff, the salt and pepper shakers. I found this particular hole and I put my Coke right into it, a perfect fit, and I called it my Coke-holder. I got down next to it on my back, because everyone knows that rich people eat lying down, and I got my sandwich in one hand and put my other arm around the Coke in its holder. When I wanted a drink, I lifted my neck a little, put out my lips, and tipped my Coke a little with the crook of my elbow. Ah.

We were there, lying down, eating our sandwiches, laughing, throwing bread at each other and out for the birds. This was heaven. We were laughing and we couldn't believe it. My mother *was* keeping something from us, ah ha, but we had found her out. We even found water over at the side of the clearing to wash our plates with—we had brought plates. Sergio started washing his plates when he was done, and I was being rich with my Coke, and this day in summer was right.

When suddenly these two men came, from around a corner of trees and the tallest grass we had ever seen. They had bags on their backs, leather bags, bags and sticks.

We didn't know what clubs were, but I learned later, like I learned about the grinding balls. The two men yelled at us. Most specifically, one wanted me to take my Coke out of my Coke-holder so he could sink his golf ball into it.

Something got taken away from us that moment. Heaven. We grew up a little bit, and couldn't go backward. We learned. No one had ever told us about golf. They had told us about heaven. And it went away. We got golf in exchange.

We went back to the arroyo for the rest of that summer, and tried to have fun the best we could. We learned to be ready for finding the grinding ball. We loved it, and when we buried it we knew what would happen. The truth is, we didn't look so hard for it. We were two boys and twelve summers then, and not stupid. Things get taken away.

We buried it because it was perfect. We didn't tell my mother, but together it was all we talked about, till we forgot. It was the lion.

Thinking About the Story

A PERSONAL RESPONSE

sharing impressions

1. What is your overall impression of the experiences the boys have in this story? Jot down some of your thoughts and feelings in your journal.

constructing interpretations

2. How does the boys' experience at the golf course relate to their later experience with the grinding ball?

Think about

- what they think the golf course is at first, and why
- what the grinding ball means to them
- what they learn from each experience and how they change

3. What do you think the "lion" represents?

> ***Think about***
> - what the boy telling the story says in the first and last paragraphs
> - why the lion is "secret"
> - how the title applies to the story as a whole

4. The boy telling the story says at the beginning, "We solved junior high school." Explain how you think he and Sergio did it.

> ***Think about***
> - how he describes the differences between grade school and junior high
> - how his interactions with others change during junior high
> - why the boys go back to the arroyo during this time
> - what they do at the arroyo

5. How do your memories of junior high school or middle school compare with the boys' experience in this story?

A CREATIVE RESPONSE

6. If the boys lived in an urban environment, how would you expect this story to be different?

A CRITICAL RESPONSE

7. Go back through the story and find elements of style that you think add to the story.

> ***Think about***
> - the definition of style as the way in which a piece of literature is written
> - some of the comparisons in the story
> - word choice, including the use of informal language to reflect the boy's speech
> - sentence lengths and patterns

8. One of the issues explored in "The Secret Lion" and in the excerpts from *Hunger of Memory* and *Barrio Boy* is the relationship between young people and adults. Compare the ways in which adults respond to the needs of young people in these selections.

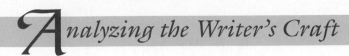

Analyzing the Writer's Craft

SETTING

How important do you think time and place are to this story?

Building a Literary Vocabulary. Setting refers to the time and place of the action of a story. Time in "The Secret Lion" is important in terms of the boys' ages. Place is essential to the events in the story because the arroyo and the hills determine the nature of the boys' experiences.

Application: Imagining Setting. Working with a group of classmates, carefully look through the story and write down all the locations that make up the setting, such as the narrator's home and the highway. Then use a large sheet of paper to draw a map showing these locations. Keep in mind that some locations in the story are described in relation to others. For example, the Southern Pacific railroad is located near the arroyo. For other locations, such as the school, you may have to guess where to put them on the map. After you have completed the map, trace the pattern of events in the story by drawing a line from location to location. You might use different-colored lines for the boys' experiences at different ages. Compare your map with the maps created by other groups.

Connecting Reading and Writing

1. "Things get taken away" is a realization that the narrator and Sergio come to as they grow out of childhood. Compile other words of wisdom they might share in a **handbook** for incoming junior high or middle school students.

Option: Write a **speech** that the boys might make to younger students about what they must learn in life.

2. What does the grinding ball symbolize for the boys? Give your views in a **letter** from the narrator as an adult writing to his own son.

Option: Imagine that this question appears on an essay exam and write an **interpretive essay** on the symbolism.

3. The style of this story is vivid and distinctive. Imitate this style in writing about an experience you remember having with a friend. Write a humorous **autobiographical sketch** that might appear in a magazine.

Option: Write a **dramatic monologue** retelling your experience, and deliver it to the class.

My Delicate Heart Condition

TONI CADE BAMBARA

A biography of Bambara appears on page 418.

Approaching the Story

"My Delicate Heart Condition" features Harriet Watkins, a girl who tells the story in her own words. Harriet has an especially colorful, often humorous way of talking. She begins her story abruptly, and because she sometimes refers to people, locations, and events without explaining who or what they are, the reader has to infer a great deal.

M Y COUSIN JOANNE has not been allowed to hang out with me for some time because she went and told Aunt Hazel that I scare her to death whenever she sleeps over at our house or I spend the weekend at hers. The truth is I sometimes like to tell stories about bloodthirsty vampires or ugly monsters that lurk in clothes closets or giant beetles that eat their way through the shower curtain, like I used to do at camp to entertain the kids in my bunk. But Joanne always cries and that makes the stories even weirder, like background music her crying. And too—I'm not going to lie about it—I get spookier on purpose until all the little crybabies are stuffing themselves under their pillows and throwing their sneakers at me and making such a racket that Mary the counselor has to come in and shine her flashlight around the bunkhouse. I play like I'm asleep. The rest of them are too busy blub-

bering and finding their way out from under blankets to tell Mary that it's me. Besides, once they get a load of her standing against the moonlight in that long white robe of hers looking like a ghost, they just start up again and pretty soon the whole camp is awake. Anyway, that's what I do for fun. So Joanne hasn't been around. And this year I'll have to go to the circus by myself and to camp without her. My mother said on the phone to Aunt Hazel—"Good, keep Jo over there and maybe Harriet'll behave herself if she's got no one to show off to." For all the years my mother's known me, she still doesn't understand that my behaving has got nothing to do with who I hang out with. A private thing between me and me or maybe between me and the Fly family since they were the ones that first got me to sit through monster movies and with-stand all the terror I could take.

For four summers now, me and the Fly family have had this thing going. A battle of nerves, you might say. Each year they raise the rope closer and closer to the very top of the tent—I hear they're going to perform outdoors this year and be even higher—and they stretch the rope further across the rings where the clowns and the pony riders perform. Each year they get bolder and more daring with their rope dancing and swinging by the legs and flinging themselves into empty space making everyone throw up their hands and gasp for air until Mr. Fly at the very last possible second swings out on his bar to catch them up by the tips of their heels. Everyone just dies and clutches at their hearts. Everybody but me. I sit there calmly. I've trained myself. Joanne used to die and duck her head under the benches and stay there till it was all over.

Last summer they really got bold. On the final performance just before the fair closed, and some revival type tent show comes in and all the kids go off to camp, the Fly family performed without a net. I figured they'd be up to something so I made sure my stomach was like steel. I did ten push-ups before breakfast, twenty sit-ups before lunch, skipped dinner altogether. My brother Teddy kidded me all day—"Harriet's trying out for the Olympics." I passed up the icie man on the corner and the pizza and sausage stand by the schoolyard and the cotton candy and jelly apple lady and the pickle and penny candy boy, in fact I passed up all the stands that lead from the street down the little roadway to the fair grounds that used to be a swamp when we first moved from Baltimore to Jamaica, Long Island. It wasn't easy, I'm not going to lie, but I was taking no chances. Between the balloon man and the wheel of fortune was the usual clump of ladies from church who came night after night to try to win the giant punch bowl set on the top shelf above the wheel, but had to settle night after night for a jar of gumdrops or salt and pepper shakers or some other little thing from the bottom shelf. And from the wheel of for-

tune to the tent was at least a million stands selling B. B. bats and jawbreakers and gingerbread and sweet potato pie and frozen custard and—like I said it wasn't easy. A million ways to tempt you, to unsettle your stomach, and make you lose the battle with the Fly family.

I sat there almost enjoying the silly clowns who came tumbling out of a steamer trunk no bigger than the one we have in the basement where my mother keeps my old report cards and photographs and letters and things. And I almost enjoyed the fire-eater and the knife thrower, but I was so close up I could see how there wasn't any real thrill. I almost enjoyed the fat-leg girls who rode the ponies two at a time and standing up, but their costumes weren't very pretty—just an ordinary polo shirt like you get if you run in the PAL meets[1] and short skirts you can wear on either side like the big girls wear at the roller rink. And I almost enjoyed the jugglers except that my Uncle Bubba can juggle the dinner plates better any day of the week so long as Aunt Hazel isn't there to stop him. I was impatient and started yawning. Finally all the clowns hitched up their baggy pants and tumbled over each other out of the ring and into the dark, the jugglers caught all the things that were up in the air and yawning just like me went off to the side. The pony girls brought their horses to a sudden stop that raised a lot of dust, then jumped down into the dirt and bowed. Then the ringmaster stepped into the circle of light and tipped his hat which was a little raggedy from where I was sitting and said—"And now, Ladieeez and Gentlemen, what you've alll been waiting forrr, the Main aTTRACtion, the FLY FAMILEEE." And everyone jumped up to shout like crazy as they came running out on their toes to stand in the light and then climb the ropes. I took a deep breath and fold-

1. **PAL meets:** sports events organized for neighborhood children by the Police Athletic League.

ed my arms over my chest and a kid next to me went into hiding, acting like she was going to tie her shoelaces.

There used to be four of them—the father, a big guy with a bald head and a bushy mustache and shoulders and arms like King Kong; a tall lanky mother whom you'd never guess could even climb into a high chair or catch anything heavier than a Ping-Pong ball to look at her; the oldest son who looked like his father except he had hair on his head but none on his face and a big face it was, so that no matter how high up he got you could always tell whether he was smiling or frowning or counting; the younger boy about thirteen, maybe, had a vacant stare like he was a million miles away feeding his turtles or something, anything but walking along a tightrope or flying through the air with his family. I had always liked to watch him because he was as cool as I was. But last summer the little girl got into the act. My grandmother says she's probably a midget 'cause no self-respecting mother would allow her child to be up there acting like a bird. "Just a baby," she'd say. "Can't be more than six years old. Should be home in bed. Must be a midget." My grandfather would give me a look when she started in and we'd smile at her together.

They almost got to me that last performance, dodging around with new routines and two at a time so that you didn't know which one Mr. Fly was going to save at the last minute. But he'd fly out and catch the little boy and swing over to the opposite stand where the big boy was flying out to catch them both by the wrists and the poor woman would be left kind of dangling there, suspended, then she'd do this double flip which would kill off everyone in the tent except me, of course, and swing out on the very bar she was on in the first place. And then they'd mess around two or three flying at once just to confuse you until the big drum roll started and out steps the lit-

tle girl in a party dress and a huge blindfold wrapped around her little head and a pink umbrella like they sell down in Chinatown. And I almost—I won't lie about it—I almost let my heart thump me off the bench. I almost thought I too had to tie my shoelaces. But I sat there. Stubborn. And the kid starts bouncing up and down on the rope like she was about to take off and tear through the canvas roof. Then out swings her little brother, and before you know it, Fly Jr. like a great eagle with his arms flapping grabs up the kid, eyeband in his teeth, and swoops her off to the bar that's already got Mrs., Mr., and Big Bro on it, and surely there's no room for him. And everyone standing on their feet clutching at their faces. Everyone but me. Cause I know from the getgo[2] that Mr. and Mrs. are going to leave the bar to give Jr. room and fly over to the other side. Which is exactly what they do. The lady in front of me, Mrs. Perez, who does all the sewing in our neighborhood, gets up and starts shaking her hands like ladies do to get the fingernail polish dry and she says to me with her eyes jammed shut "I must go finish the wedding gowns. Tell me later who died." And she scoots through the aisle, falling all over everybody with her eyes still shut and never looks up. And Mrs. Caine taps me on the back and leans over and says, "Some people just can't take it." And I smile at her and at her twins who're sitting there with their mouths open. I fold my arms over my chest and just dare the Fly family to do their very worst.

The minute I got to camp, I ran up to the main house where all the counselors gather to say hello to the parents and talk with the directors. I had to tell Mary the latest doings with the Fly family. But she put a finger to her mouth like she sometimes does to shush me. "Let's not have any scary stuff this summer,

_____

2. **getgo** (get′ gō): start; beginning.

Harriet," she said, looking over my shoulder at a new kid. This new kid, Willie, was from my old neighborhood in Baltimore so we got friendly right off. Then he told me that he had a romantic heart so I quite naturally took him under my wing and decided not to give him a heart attack with any ghost tales. Mary said he meant "rheumatic"[3] heart, but I don't see any difference. So I told Mary to move him out of George's tent and give him a nicer counselor who'd respect his romantic heart. George used to be my play boyfriend when I first came to camp as a little kid and didn't know any better. But he's not a nice person. He makes up funny nicknames for people which aren't funny at all. Like calling Eddie Michaels the Watermelon Kid or David Farmer Charcoal Plenty which I really do not appreciate and especially from a counselor. And once he asked Joanne, who was the table monitor, to go fetch a pail of milk from the kitchen. And the minute she got up, he started hatching a plot, trying to get the kids to hide her peanut butter sandwich and put spiders in her soup. I had to remind everyone at the table that Joanne was my first cousin by blood, and I would be forced to waste the first bum that laid a hand on her plate. And ole George says, "Oh don't be a dumbhead, Harriet. Jo's so stupid she won't even notice." And I told him right then and there that I was not his play girlfriend anymore and would rather marry the wolfman than grow up and be his wife. And just in case he didn't get the message, that night around the campfire when we were all playing Little Sally Walker sittin' in a saucer and it was my turn to shake it to the east and to shake it to the west and to shake it to the very one that I loved the best—I shook straight for Mr. Nelson the lifeguard, who was not only the ugliest person in camp but the arch enemy of ole George.

And that very first day of camp last summer when Willie came running up to me to get in line for lunch, here comes George talking some simple stuff about "What a beautiful head you have, Willie. A long, smooth, streamlined head. A sure sign of superior gifts. Definitely genius proportions." And poor Willie went for it, grinning and touching his head, which if you want to know the truth is a bullet head and that's all there is to it. And he's turning to me every which way, like he's modeling his head in a fashion show. And the minute his back is turned, ole George makes a face about Willie's head and all the kids in the line bust out laughing. So I had to beat up a few right then and there and finish off the rest later in the shower for being so stupid, laughing at a kid with a romantic heart.

One night in the last week of August when the big campfire party is held, it was very dark and the moon was all smoky, and I just couldn't help myself and started in with a story about the great caterpillar who was going to prowl through the tents and nibble off everybody's toes. And Willie started this whimpering in the back of his throat so I had to switch the story real quick to something cheerful. But before I could do that, ole George picked up my story and added a wicked witch who puts spells on city kids who come to camp, and a hunchback dwarf that chopped up tents and bunk beds, and a one-eyed phantom giant who gobbled up the hearts of underprivileged kids. And every time he got to the part where the phantom ripped out a heart, poor Willie would get louder and louder until finally he started rolling around in the grass and screaming and all the kids went crazy and scattered behind the rocks almost kicking the fire completely out as they dashed off into the darkness yelling bloody murder. And the counselors could hardly round us all up—me, too, I'm not going to lie about it. Their little circles of flashlight bobbing in and out of the bushes along the

---

3. **rheumatic** (r$\overline{oo}$ mat′ ik): painfully inflamed.

patches of pine, bumping into each other as they scrambled for us kids. And poor Willie rolling around something awful, so they took him to the infirmary.

I was sneaking some gingersnaps in to him later that night when I hear Mary and another senior counselor fussing at ole George in the hallway.

"You've been picking on that kid ever since he got here, George. But tonight was the limit——"

"I wasn't picking on him, I was just trying to tell a story——"

"All that talk about hearts, gobblin' up hearts, and underpriv——"

"Yeh, you were directing it all at the little kid. You should be——"

"I wasn't talking about him. They're all underprivileged kids, after all. I mean all the kids are underprivileged."

I huddled back into the shadows and almost banged into Willie's iron bed. I was hoping he'd open his eyes and wink at me and tell me he was just fooling. That it wasn't so bad to have an underprivileged heart. But he just slept. "I'm an underprivileged kid too," I thought to myself. I knew that it was a special camp, but I'd never realized. No wonder Aunt Hazel screamed so about my scary stories and my mother flicked off the TV when the monsters came on and Mary was always shushing me. We all had bad hearts. I crawled into the supply cabinet to wait for Willie to wake up so I could ask him about it all. I ate all the gingersnaps but I didn't feel any better. You have a romantic heart, I whispered to myself settling down among the bandages. You will have to be very careful.

It didn't make any difference to Aunt Hazel that I had changed, that I no longer told scary stories or dragged my schoolmates to the latest creature movie, or raced my friends to the edge of the roof, or held my breath, or ran under the train rail when the train was already in sight. As far as she was concerned, I was still the same ole spooky kid I'd always been. So Joanne was kept at home. My mother noticed the difference, but she said over the phone to my grandmother, "She's acting very ladylike these days, growing up." I didn't tell her about my secret, that I knew about my heart. And I was kind of glad Joanne wasn't around 'cause I would have blabbed it all to her and scared her to death. When school starts again, I decided, I'll ask my teacher how to outgrow my underprivileged heart. I'll train myself, just like I did with the Fly family.

"Well, I guess you'll want some change to go to the fair again, hunh?" my mother said coming into my room and dumping things in her pocketbook.

"No," I said. "I'm too grown up for circuses."

She put the money on the dresser anyway. I was lying, of course. I was thinking what a terrible strain it would be for Mrs. Perez and everybody else if while sitting there, with the Fly family zooming around in the open air a million miles above the ground, little Harriet Watkins should drop dead with a fatal heart attack behind them.

"I lost," I said out loud.

"Lost what?"

"The battle with the Fly family."

She just stood there a long time looking at me, trying to figure me out, the way mothers are always doing but should know better. Then she kissed me goodbye and left for work.

Reviewing Concepts

MINORITY VOICES: CONVEYING ATTITUDES

*making
connections*

In this unit, writers treat a variety of subjects related to the theme of identity. In each selection the writer's tone, or attitude toward the subject, influences the readers' perceptions of what the writer is saying, both directly and indirectly.

As you may recall from your study of Zora Neale Hurston's essay "How It Feels to Be Colored Me," one way that a writer conveys tone is through diction, or word choice. For example, Hurston uses phrases such as "proscenium box for a born first-nighter," "the first 'welcome-to-our-state Floridian,'" "busy sharpening my oyster knife," and "Great Stuffer of Bags" to convey an attitude that you might call breezy, confident, zestful, or exuberant.

Review the selections you have read in this unit. Identify the tone of each and find examples of the writer's diction that helped create the tone. Make a chart similar to the one below on which you can record your findings. For each selection, describe the tone and list at least three examples of words or phrases that suggest that tone. You may find that in certain selections more than one tone is conveyed.

Selection	Tone	Diction
"How It Feels to Be Colored Me"	breezy confident zestful exuberant	"proscenium box for a born first-nighter" "the first 'welcome-to-our-state-Floridian'" "busy sharpening my oyster knife" "Great Stuffer of Bags"

*describing
connections*

After you have completed your chart, choose two selections that you think convey markedly different tones. Then write **instructions** that you might give to two students preparing oral interpretations of the two selections. The instructions should include the information recorded on your chart. Have two students present oral interpretations of the selections based on your instructions.

© 1990, Phillip Cantor, Chicago.

Exploring
Cultural
Conflicts

"I grew up victim to a disabling confusion. As I grew fluent in English, I no longer could speak Spanish with confidence. . . . A powerful guilt blocked my spoken words."

RICHARD RODRIGUEZ

Exploring Cultural Conflicts

Imagine yourself as an exchange student living in a household in Korea. The cultural differences between Korea and the United States might take some getting used to. You would have to learn how to eat with chopsticks, for instance. Instead of having cereal, toast, or eggs for breakfast, you might be served pickled cabbage. You would have to observe different rules of etiquette, such as the practice of belching to compliment fine cooking. Your American habit of speaking your mind during class would clash with the Korean practice of deferring to teachers.

Cultural differences become cultural conflicts when a person of one culture feels at odds with a dominant culture or torn between the value systems of different cultures. The writers in this unit explore cultural conflicts by focusing on individuals in conflict. In the first four selections, the conflict is centered in the family. In "Two Kinds," for example, the conflict between a Chinese mother and her American-born daughter epitomizes the contrast between two value systems. Both "Seventeen Syllables" and the excerpt from *Kaffir Boy* reveal the anguish of children whose parents clash in a struggle that is both personal and cultural. The speaker's conflict with his mother in "Hiccups" involves the tension between African and French cultures in French Guiana. In the fifth selection, the context shifts from the family to a broader scope. In the excerpt from *Arctic Dreams*, Barry Lopez reflects on the march of progress in the Arctic, empathizing with a native culture threatened with extinction. In the final two selections, two African-American writers explain their struggles to find a place in a discriminatory society.

In exploring cultural conflicts, the writers bring to light complex questions that defy simple answers: To what extent can cultural conflicts ever be resolved? Should they be resolved? What is gained and what is lost by choosing the values of one culture over those of another? Consider these questions as you read the following selections. Also empathize with the individuals in conflict.

Literary Vocabulary

Plot. Plot refers to the actions and events in a literary work. For example, in "My Delicate Heart Condition," Harriet Watkins, claims that she has inured herself to terror by watching a family of acrobats perform death-defying stunts. At summer camp, Harriet meets Willie and concludes that he has a "romantic heart," a misunderstanding of *rheumatic,* and tries to protect him from George, an insensitive counselor. Later, when Harriet overhears George refer to all the kids at camp as "underprivileged," she concludes that she, like Willie, has an "underprivileged heart." This realization makes her avoid activities that are frightening.

Dialogue. Dialogue is written conversation between two or more characters. The use of dialogue brings characters to life and gives the reader insights into their qualities, or personality traits. For example, in the excerpt from *I Know Why the Caged Bird Sings,* Maya Angelou uses dialogue to reveal the hypocrisy of the receptionist at the Market Street Railway Company:

> "I am applying for the job listed in this morning's *Chronicle,* and I'd like to be presented to your personnel manager." . . .
> "He's out. He's out for the day. You might call him tomorrow, and if he's in, I'm sure you can see him." . . .
> "May I ask his name?" . . .
> "His name? Whose name?"

Description. Description is writing that helps a reader to picture scenes, events, and characters. Imagery, figures of speech, and carefully selected detail create effective description. For example, in "How It Feels to Be Colored Me," Zora Neale Hurston uses imagery and figurative language to convey her impressions of a jazz orchestra: "This orchestra grows rambunctious, rears on its hind legs and attacks the tonal veil with primitive fury, rending it, clawing it until it breaks through to the jungle beyond."

Conflict. Conflict is a struggle between opposing forces. A conflict may be external, involving a character pitted against an outside force—nature, society, a physical obstacle, or another character. A conflict may also be internal, occurring within a character. For example, an external conflict in the excerpt from *I Know Why the Caged Bird Sings* involves Maya Angelou's struggle against the forces of discrimination. An internal conflict is her inner struggle to stay determined.

Figurative Language: Simile   **Theme**

Two Kinds

AMY TAN

A biography of Tan appears on page 429.

Approaching the Story

During the 1930's and 1940's China was invaded by the Japanese and was racked by political upheavals that led to a bitter civil war. Some Chinese citizens escaped these dangers by emigrating to the United States. Here they settled in California, primarily in San Francisco, their point of entry. To many Chinese immigrants life in the United States was so different from life in war-torn China that anything seemed possible, especially for their children. The children were expected to pursue the American dream of material success, without sacrificing the traditional Chinese values of obedience and respect for one's elders. "Two Kinds" is told by a young woman who, like Amy Tan herself, is the daughter of Chinese immigrants.

Building Vocabulary

These essential words are footnoted within the story.

prodigy (präd′ ə jē): "Of course, you can be **prodigy**, too." (page 199)

preludes (prel′ yo̅o̅dz), **discordant** (dis kôrd′ 'nt): I learned to play only the most ear-splitting **preludes**, the most **discordant** hymns. (page 202)

devastated (dev′ əs tāt′ ed): But my mother's expression was what **devastated** me: a quiet, blank look that said she had lost everything. (page 204)

fiasco (fē äs′ kō): I assumed my talent-show **fiasco** meant I never had to play the piano again. (page 204)

Connecting Writing and Reading

Imagine that your mother has decided that you should study to be a concert violinist. She tells you that you must practice for two hours after school every day, even though you would rather spend that time with your friends. How would you respond to your mother's expectations? Write a few phrases in your journal describing your probable response. Then during your reading of "Two Kinds," notice how the narrator responds to her mother's expectations.

MY MOTHER BELIEVED you could be anything you wanted to be in America. You could open a restaurant. You could work for the government and get good retirement. You could buy a house with almost no money down. You could become rich. You could become instantly famous.

"Of course, you can be prodigy,[1] too," my mother told me when I was nine. "You can be best anything. What does Auntie Lindo know? Her daughter, she is only best tricky."

America was where all my mother's hopes lay. She had come to San Francisco in 1949 after losing everything in China: her mother and father, her family home, her first husband, and two daughters, twin baby girls. But she never looked back with regret. There were so many ways for things to get better.

We didn't immediately pick the right kind of prodigy. At first my mother thought I could be a Chinese Shirley Temple.[2] We'd watch Shirley's old movies on TV as though they were training films. My mother would poke my arm and say, *"Ni kan"*—You watch. And I would see Shirley tapping her feet, or singing a sailor song, or pursing her lips into a very round O while saying, "Oh my goodness."

"Ni kan," said my mother as Shirley's eyes flooded with tears. "You already know how. Don't need talent for crying!"

Soon after my mother got this idea about Shirley Temple, she took me to a beauty training school in the Mission district and put me in the hands of a student who could barely hold the scissors without shaking. Instead of getting big fat curls, I emerged with an uneven mass of crinkly black fuzz. My mother dragged me off to the bathroom and tried to wet down my hair.

"You look like Negro Chinese," she lamented, as if I had done this on purpose.

The instructor of the beauty training school had to lop off these soggy clumps to make my hair even again. "Peter Pan is very popular these days," the instructor assured my mother. I now had hair the length of a boy's, with straight-across bangs that hung at a slant two inches above my eyebrows. I liked the haircut and it made me actually look forward to my future fame.

In fact, in the beginning, I was just as excited as my mother, maybe even more so. I pictured this prodigy part of me as many different images, trying each one on for size. I was a dainty ballerina girl standing by the curtains, waiting to hear the right music that would send me floating on my tiptoes. I was like the Christ child lifted out of the straw manger, crying with holy indignity. I was Cinderella stepping from her pumpkin carriage with sparkly cartoon music filling the air.

In all of my imaginings, I was filled with a sense that I would soon become *perfect*. My mother and father would adore me. I would be beyond reproach. I would never feel the need to sulk for anything.

But sometimes the prodigy in me became impatient. "If you don't hurry up and get me out of here, I'm disappearing for good," it warned. "And then you'll always be nothing."

Every night after dinner, my mother and I would sit at the Formica kitchen table. She would present new tests, taking her examples from stories of amazing children she had read in *Ripley's Believe It or Not*, or *Good Housekeeping*, *Reader's Digest*, and a dozen other magazines she kept in a pile in our bathroom. My mother got these magazines from people whose houses she cleaned. And since she cleaned many houses each week, we had a great assortment. She would look through them all, searching for stories about remarkable children.

---

1. **prodigy** (präd′ ə jē): a child who is amazingly talented or intelligent.
2. **Shirley Temple:** a popular child movie star of the 1930's.

The first night she brought out a story about a three-year-old boy who knew the capitals of all the states and even most of the European countries. A teacher was quoted as saying the little boy could also pronounce the names of the foreign cities correctly.

"What's the capital of Finland?" my mother asked me, looking at the magazine story.

All I knew was the capital of California, because Sacramento was the name of the street we lived on in Chinatown. "Nairobi!" I guessed, saying the most foreign word I could think of. She checked to see if that was possibly one way to pronounce "Helsinki" before showing me the answer.

The tests got harder—multiplying numbers in my head, finding the queen of hearts in a deck of cards, trying to stand on my head without using my hands, predicting the daily temperatures in Los Angeles, New York, and London.

One night I had to look at a page from the Bible for three minutes and then report everything I could remember. "Now Jehoshaphat had riches and honor in abundance and . . . that's all I remember, Ma," I said.

And after seeing my mother's disappointed face once again, something inside of me began to die. I hated the tests, the raised hopes and failed expectations. Before going to bed that night, I looked in the mirror above the bathroom sink and when I saw only my face staring back—and that it would always be this ordinary face—I began to cry. Such a sad, ugly girl! I made high-pitched noises like a crazed animal, trying to scratch out the face in the mirror.

And then I saw what seemed to be the prodigy side of me—because I had never seen that face before. I looked at my reflection, blinking so I could see more clearly. The girl staring back at me was angry, powerful. This girl and I were the same. I had new thoughts, willful thoughts, or rather thoughts filled with lots of won'ts. I won't let her change me, I promised myself. I won't be what I'm not.

So now on nights when my mother presented her tests, I performed listlessly, my head propped on one arm. I pretended to be bored. And I was. I got so bored I started counting the bellows of the foghorns out on the bay while my mother drilled me in other areas. The sound was comforting and reminded me of the cow jumping over the moon. And the next day, I played a game with myself, seeing if my mother would give up on me before eight bellows. After a while I usually counted only one, maybe two bellows at most. At last she was beginning to give up hope.

Two or three months had gone by without any mention of my being a prodigy again. And then one day my mother was watching *The Ed Sullivan Show*[3] on TV. The TV was old and the sound kept shorting out. Every time my mother got halfway up from the sofa to adjust the set, the sound would go back on and Ed would be talking. As soon as she sat down, Ed would go silent again. She got up, the TV broke into loud piano music. She sat down. Silence. Up and down, back and forth, quiet and loud. It was like a stiff embraceless dance between her and the TV set. Finally she stood by the set with her hand on the sound dial.

She seemed entranced by the music, a little frenzied piano piece with this mesmerizing quality, sort of quick passages and then teasing lilting ones before it returned to the quick playful parts.

"*Ni kan*," my mother said, calling me over with hurried hand gestures, "Look here."

I could see why my mother was fascinated by the music. It was being pounded out by a little Chinese girl, about nine years old, with a Peter Pan haircut. The girl had the sauciness

---

3. *The Ed Sullivan Show:* a weekly variety-program television series of the 1950's and 1960's.

of a Shirley Temple. She was proudly modest like a proper Chinese child. And she also did this fancy sweep of a curtsy, so that the fluffy skirt of her white dress cascaded slowly to the floor like the petals of a large carnation.

In spite of these warning signs, I wasn't worried. Our family had no piano and we couldn't afford to buy one, let alone reams of sheet music and piano lessons. So I could be generous in my comments when my mother bad-mouthed the little girl on TV.

"Play note right, but doesn't sound good! No singing sound," complained my mother.

"What are you picking on her for?" I said carelessly. "She's pretty good. Maybe she's not the best, but she's trying hard." I knew almost immediately I would be sorry I said that.

"Just like you," she said. "Not the best. Because you not trying." She gave a little huff as she let go of the sound dial and sat down on the sofa.

The little Chinese girl sat down also to play an encore of "Anitra's Dance" by Grieg. I remember the song, because later on I had to learn how to play it.

Three days after watching *The Ed Sullivan Show*, my mother told me what my schedule would be for piano lessons and piano practice. She had talked to Mr. Chong, who lived on the first floor of our apartment building. Mr. Chong was a retired piano teacher and my mother had traded housecleaning services for weekly lessons and a piano for me to practice on every day, two hours a day, from four until six.

When my mother told me this, I felt as though I had been sent to hell. I whined and then kicked my foot a little when I couldn't stand it anymore.

"Why don't you like me the way I am? I'm *not* a genius! I can't play the piano. And even if I could, I wouldn't go on TV if you paid me a million dollars!" I cried.

My mother slapped me. "Who ask you be genius?" she shouted. "Only ask you be your best. For you sake. You think I want you be genius? Hnnh! What for! Who ask you!"

"So ungrateful," I heard her mutter in Chinese. "If she had as much talent as she has temper, she would be famous now."

Mr. Chong, whom I secretly nicknamed Old Chong, was very strange, always tapping his fingers to the silent music of an invisible orchestra. He looked ancient in my eyes. He had lost most of the hair on top of his head and he wore thick glasses and had eyes that always looked tired and sleepy. But he must have been younger than I thought, since he lived with his mother and was not yet married.

I met Old Lady Chong once and that was enough. She had this peculiar smell like a baby that had done something in its pants. And her fingers felt like a dead person's, like an old peach I once found in the back of the refrigerator; the skin just slid off the meat when I picked it up.

I soon found out why Old Chong had retired from teaching piano. He was deaf. "Like Beethoven!" he shouted to me. "We're both listening only in our head!" And he would start to conduct his frantic silent sonatas.

Our lessons went like this. He would open the book and point to different things, explaining their purpose: "Key! Treble! Bass! No sharps or flats! So this is C major! Listen now and play after me!"

And then he would play the C scale a few times, a simple chord, and then, as if inspired by an old, unreachable itch, he gradually added more notes and running trills and a pounding bass until the music was really something quite grand.

I would play after him, the simple scale, the simple chord, and then I just played some nonsense that sounded like a cat running up and down on top of garbage cans. Old Chong smiled and applauded and then said, "Very good! But now you must learn to keep time!"

So that's how I discovered that Old Chong's eyes were too slow to keep up with the wrong notes I was playing. He went through the motions in half-time. To help me keep rhythm, he stood behind me, pushing down on my right shoulder for every beat. He balanced pennies on top of my wrists so I would keep them still as I slowly played scales and arpeggios. He had me curve my hand around an apple and keep that shape when playing chords. He marched stiffly to show me how to make each finger dance up and down, staccato like an obedient little soldier.

He taught me all these things, and that was how I also learned I could be lazy and get away with mistakes, lots of mistakes. If I hit the wrong notes because I hadn't practiced enough, I never corrected myself. I just kept playing in rhythm. And Old Chong kept conducting his own private reverie.

So maybe I never really gave myself a fair chance. I did pick up the basics pretty quickly, and I might have become a good pianist at that young age. But I was so determined not to try, not to be anybody different that I learned to play only the most ear-splitting preludes,[4] the most discordant[5] hymns.

Over the next year, I practiced like this, dutifully in my own way. And then one day I heard my mother and her friend Lindo Jong both talking in a loud bragging tone of voice so others could hear. It was after church, and I was leaning against the brick wall wearing a dress with stiff white petticoats. Auntie Lindo's daughter, Waverly, who was about my age, was standing farther down the wall about five feet away. We had grown up together and shared all the closeness of two sisters squabbling over crayons and dolls. In other words, for the most part, we hated each other. I thought she was snotty. Waverly Jong had gained a certain amount of fame as "Chinatown's Littlest Chinese Chess Champion."

"She bring home too many trophy," lamented Auntie Lindo that Sunday. "All day she play chess. All day I have no time do nothing but dust off her winnings." She threw a scolding look at Waverly, who pretended not to see her.

"You lucky you don't have this problem," said Auntie Lindo with a sigh to my mother.

And my mother squared her shoulders and bragged: "Our problem worser than yours. If we ask Jing-mei wash dish, she hear nothing but music. It's like you can't stop this natural talent."

And right then, I was determined to put a stop to her foolish pride.

A few weeks later, Old Chong and my mother conspired to have me play in a talent show which would be held in the church hall. By then, my parents had saved up enough to buy me a secondhand piano, a black Wurlitzer spinet with a scarred bench. It was the showpiece of our living room.

For the talent show, I was to play a piece called "Pleading Child" from Schumann's *Scenes from Childhood*. It was a simple, moody piece that sounded more difficult than it was. I was supposed to memorize the whole thing, playing the repeat parts twice to make the piece sound longer. But I dawdled over it, playing a few bars and then cheating, looking up to see what notes followed. I never really listened to what I was playing. I daydreamed about being somewhere else, about being someone else.

The part I liked to practice best was the fancy curtsy: right foot out, touch the rose on the carpet with a pointed foot, sweep to the side, left leg bends, look up and smile.

My parents invited all the couples from the

---

4. preludes (prel′ yo͞odz): introductory musical works.
5. discordant (dis kôrd′ ′nt): not in harmony; clashing.

Joy Luck Club[6] to witness my debut. Auntie Lindo and Uncle Tin were there. Waverly and her two older brothers had also come. The first two rows were filled with children both younger and older than I was. The littlest ones got to go first. They recited simple nursery rhymes, squawked out tunes on miniature violins, twirled Hula Hoops, pranced in pink ballet tutus, and when they bowed or curtsied, the audience would sigh in unison, "Awww," and then clap enthusiastically.

When my turn came, I was very confident. I remember my childish excitement. It was as if I knew, without a doubt, that the prodigy side of me really did exist. I had no fear whatsoever, no nervousness. I remember thinking to myself, This is it! This is it! I looked out over the audience, at my mother's blank face, my father's yawn, Auntie Lindo's stiff-lipped smile, Waverly's sulky expression. I had on a white dress layered with sheets of lace, and pink bow in my Peter Pan haircut. As I sat down I envisioned people jumping to their feet and Ed Sullivan rushing up to introduce me to everyone on TV.

And I started to play. It was so beautiful. I was so caught up in how lovely I looked that at first I didn't worry how I would sound. So it was a surprise to me when I hit the first wrong note and I realized something didn't sound quite right. And then I hit another and another followed that. A chill started at the top of my head and began to trickle down. Yet I couldn't stop playing, as though my hands were bewitched. I kept thinking my fingers would adjust themselves back, like a train switching to the right track. I played this strange jumble through two repeats, the sour notes staying with me all the way to the end.

When I stood up, I discovered my legs were shaking. Maybe I had just been nervous and the audience, like Old Chong, had seen me go through the right motions and had not heard anything wrong at all. I swept my right foot out, went down on my knee, looked up and smiled. The room was quiet, except for Old Chong, who was beaming and shouting, "Bravo! Bravo! Well done!" But then I saw my mother's face, her stricken face. The audience clapped weakly, and as I walked back to my chair, with my whole face quivering as I tried not to cry, I heard a little boy whisper loudly to his mother, "That was awful," and the mother whispered back, "Well, she certainly tried."

And now I realized how many people were in the audience, the whole world it seemed. I was aware of eyes burning into my back. I felt the shame of my mother and father as they sat stiffly throughout the rest of the show.

We could have escaped during intermission. Pride and some strange sense of honor must have anchored my parents to their chairs. And so we watched it all: the eighteen-year-old boy with a fake mustache who did a magic show and juggled flaming hoops while riding a unicycle. The girl with white makeup who sang from *Madama Butterfly* and got honorable mention. And the eleven-year-old boy who won first prize playing a tricky violin song that sounded like a busy bee.

After the show, the Hsus, the Jongs, and the St. Clairs from the Joy Luck Club came up to my mother and father.

"Lots of talented kids," Auntie Lindo said vaguely, smiling broadly.

"That was somethin' else," said my father, and I wondered if he was referring to me in a humorous way, or whether he even remembered what I had done.

Waverly looked at me and shrugged her shoulders. "You aren't a genius like me," she said matter-of-factly. And if I hadn't felt so bad, I would have pulled her braids and punched her stomach.

---

6. **Joy Luck Club:** the social group to which the family in this story belongs.

But my mother's expression was what devastated[7] me: a quiet, blank look that said she had lost everything. I felt the same way, and it seemed as if everybody were now coming up, like gawkers at the scene of an accident, to see what parts were actually missing. When we got on the bus to go home, my father was humming the busy-bee tune and my mother was silent. I kept thinking she wanted to wait until we got home before shouting at me. But when my father unlocked the door to our apartment, my mother walked in and then went to the back, into the bedroom. No accusations. No blame. And in a way, I felt disappointed. I had been waiting for her to start shouting, so I could shout back and cry and blame her for all my misery.

I assumed my talent-show fiasco[8] meant I never had to play the piano again. But two days later, after school, my mother came out of the kitchen and saw me watching TV.

"Four clock," she reminded me as if it were any other day. I was stunned, as though she were asking me to go through the talent-show torture again. I wedged myself more tightly in front of the TV.

"Turn off TV," she called from the kitchen five minutes later.

I didn't budge. And then I decided. I didn't have to do what my mother said anymore. I wasn't her slave. This wasn't China. I had listened to her before and look what happened. She was the stupid one.

She came out from the kitchen and stood in the arched entryway of the living room. "Four clock," she said once again, louder.

"I'm not going to play anymore," I said nonchalantly. "Why should I? I'm not a genius."

She walked over and stood in front of the TV. I saw her chest was heaving up and down in an angry way.

"No!" I said, and I now felt stronger, as if my true self had finally emerged. So this was what had been inside me all along.

"No! I won't!" I screamed.

She yanked me by the arm, pulled me off the floor snapped off the TV. She was frighteningly strong, half pulling, half carrying me toward the piano as I kicked the throw rugs under my feet. She lifted me up and onto the hard bench. I was sobbing by now, looking at her bitterly. Her chest was heaving even more and her mouth was open, smiling crazily as if she were pleased I was crying.

"You want me to be someone that I'm not!" I sobbed. "I'll never be the kind of daughter you want me to be!"

"Only two kinds of daughters," she shouted in Chinese. "Those who are obedient and those who follow their own mind! Only one kind of daughter can live in this house. Obedient daughter!"

"Then I wish I wasn't your daughter. I wish you weren't my mother," I shouted. As I said these things I got scared. It felt like worms and toads and slimy things crawling out of my chest, but it also felt good, as if this awful side of me had surfaced, at last.

"Too late change this," said my mother shrilly.

And I could sense her anger rising to its breaking point. I wanted to see it spill over. And that's when I remembered the babies she had lost in China, the ones we never talked about. "Then I wish I'd never been born!" I shouted. "I wish I were dead! Like them."

It was as if I had said the magic words. Alakazam!—and her face went blank, her mouth closed, her arms went slack, and she backed out of the room, stunned, as if she were blowing away like a small brown leaf, thin, brittle, lifeless.

It was not the only disappointment my

---

7. **devastated** (dev′ əs tāt′ ed): destroyed completely.
8. **fiasco** (fē äs′ kō): a complete or ridiculous failure.

mother felt in me. In the years that followed, I failed her so many times, each time asserting my own will, my right to fall short of expectations. I didn't get straight As. I didn't become class president. I didn't get into Stanford. I dropped out of college.

For unlike my mother, I did not believe I could be anything I wanted to be. I could only be me.

And for all those years, we never talked about the disaster at the recital or my terrible accusations afterward at the piano bench. All that remained unchecked, like a betrayal that was now unspeakable. So I never found a way to ask her why she had hoped for something so large that failure was inevitable.

And even worse, I never asked her what frightened me the most: Why had she given up hope?

For after our struggle at the piano, she never mentioned my playing again. The lessons stopped. The lid to the piano was closed, shutting out the dust, my misery, and her dreams.

So she surprised me. A few years ago, she offered to give me the piano, for my thirtieth birthday. I had not played in all those years. I saw the offer as a sign of forgiveness, a tremendous burden removed.

"Are you sure?" I asked shyly. "I mean, won't you and Dad miss it?"

"No, this your piano," she said firmly. "Always your piano. You only one can play."

"Well, I probably can't play anymore," I said. "It's been years."

"You pick up fast," said my mother, as if she knew this was certain. "You have natural talent. You could been genius if you want to."

"No I couldn't."

"You just not trying," said my mother. And she was neither angry nor sad. She said it as if to announce a fact that could never be disproved. "Take it," she said.

But I didn't at first. It was enough that she had offered it to me. And after that, every time I saw it in my parents' living room, standing in front of the bay windows, it made me feel proud, as if it were a shiny trophy I had won back.

Last week I sent a tuner over to my parents' apartment and had the piano reconditioned, for purely sentimental reasons. My mother had died a few months before and I had been getting things in order for my father, a little bit at a time. I put the jewelry in special silk pouches. The sweaters she had knitted in yellow, pink, bright orange—all the colors I hated—I put those in moth-proof boxes. I found some old Chinese silk dresses, the kind with little slits up the sides. I rubbed the old silk against my skin, then wrapped them in tissue and decided to take them home with me.

After I had the piano tuned, I opened the lid and touched the keys. It sounded even richer than I remembered. Really, it was a very good piano. Inside the bench were the same exercise notes with handwritten scales, the same secondhand music books with their covers held together with yellow tape.

I opened up the Schumann book to the dark little piece I had played at the recital. It was on the left-hand side of the page, "Pleading Child." It looked more difficult than I remembered. I played a few bars, surprised at how easily the notes came back to me.

And for the first time, or so it seemed, I noticed the piece on the right-hand side. It was called "Perfectly Contented." I tried to play this one as well. It had a lighter melody but the same flowing rhythm and turned out to be quite easy. "Pleading Child" was shorter but slower; "Perfectly Contented" was longer, but faster. And after I played them both a few times, I realized they were two halves of the same song.

Thinking About the Story

A PERSONAL RESPONSE

sharing impressions

1. What words describe your feelings about the two main characters in the story? Write these words in your journal.

constructing interpretations

2. What might the narrator mean when she says that "Pleading Child" and "Perfectly Contented" are "two halves of the same song"?

> **Think about**
> - why she plays the piano again after her mother dies
> - how the songs might express her feelings about her relationship with her mother

3. Why do you think the narrator's feelings about being a prodigy change during the story?

> **Think about**
> - her daydreams at the beginning of the story
> - her response to her mother's expectations
> - her own opinions about herself

4. Who do you think is right in the story, the mother or the daughter?

> **Think about**
> - how realistic the mother's expectations are
> - how the mother treats the daughter
> - how the daughter treats the mother

A CREATIVE RESPONSE

5. How might this story be different if the mother had not lost the two babies in China?

A CRITICAL RESPONSE

6. Explain to what extent the conflict between the narrator and her mother is resolved in the story. Support your interpretation with examples from the story.

7. Do you think "Two Kinds" is an appropriate title for this story? Explain your opinion.

> ***Think about***
> - the pieces the narrator plays at the end of the story
> - her mother's expectations and the narrator's response to them
> - the cultural conflict experienced by the narrator

8. Amy Tan wrote the following about the book from which "Two Kinds" is taken: "When I was writing, it was so much for my mother and myself. I wanted her to know what I thought about China and what I thought about growing up in this country. And I wanted those words to almost fall off the page so that she could just see the story, almost like a little curtain that would fall away." Analyze to what extent you think Tan succeeded at writing a story that can be easily visualized by all readers.

Analyzing the Writer's Craft

FIGURATIVE LANGUAGE: SIMILE

Comparisons often capture feelings and sensations better than direct descriptions do. For example, the narrator describes Old Lady Chong's fingers in two comparisons: "And her fingers felt like a dead person's, like an old peach I once found in the back of the refrigerator; the skin just slid off the meat when I picked it up." What effect do these comparisons have on you?

Building a Literary Vocabulary. Figurative language is language that communicates ideas beyond the literal meanings of the words. The comparisons of Old Lady Chong's fingers to those of a corpse and to a rotten peach are figurative expressions called similes. A simile compares two things in a phrase that contains *like* or *as*. The similes in the description of Old Lady Chong's fingers help the reader to imagine the feeling of loose skin over cold, shrunken flesh. The similes also show in a humorous way the perspective of a child who considers old age creepy.

Application: Identifying Similes. Working in a group, find at least five similes in the story. For each example, create a diagram similar to the one that follows.

Example from story

"And her fingers felt like a dead person's, like an old peach I once found in the back of the refrigerator; the skin just slid off the meat when I picked it up."

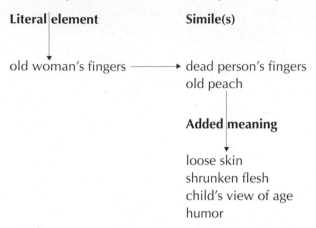

Literal element

old woman's fingers ———→

Simile(s)

dead person's fingers
old peach

Added meaning

loose skin
shrunken flesh
child's view of age
humor

After you have diagramed five examples, choose the one simile that your group likes best and diagram it for your class on the board or on a large sheet of paper.

Connecting Reading and Writing

1. Imagine that you are a school counselor and the narrator has come to you with her problem. How will you respond when she tells you about her conflict with her mother? Create a **dialogue** between yourself and the narrator.

Option: Write a **letter** of concern and advice to the mother, in the voice of a school counselor.

2. Review your prereading notes about how you would react to your parents' expectations for you to be a violinist. Write a **dramatic skit** that more fully portrays your response to your parents.

Option: Write about your response to your parents in a brief **story**.

3. In newspaper and magazine articles research the adjustments that children of immigrants must make. Use the information to create a set of **guidelines** for your school to follow in dealing with students from immigrant families.

Option: Write a **summary** of what you have learned.

Saying Yes

Diana Chang

"Are you Chinese?"
"Yes."

"American?"
"Yes."

"*Really* Chinese?"
"No . . . not quite."

"*Really* American?"
"Well, actually, you see . . ."

But I would rather say
yes

Not neither-nor,
not maybe,
but both, and not only

The homes I've had,
the ways I am

I'd rather say it
twice,
yes

Seventeen Syllables

HISAYE YAMAMOTO

A biography of Yamamoto appears on page 431.

*A*pproaching the Story

Like the character Rosie in this story, Hisaye Yamamoto (hē sä′ ye yä mä mô′ tô) was born in the United States to parents who emigrated from Japan. Much of her fiction, including "Seventeen Syllables," portrays the contrast between the thoughts and feelings of the two generations.

*B*uilding Vocabulary

These essential words are footnoted within the story.

vernaculars (vər nak′ yə lərz): Several Japanese **vernaculars** were printed there. (page 211)

anaesthetic (an′ əs thet′ ik): Rosie found the greater part of the evening practically **anaesthetic.** (page 212)

garrulous (gar′ ə ləs): Haru, the **garrulous** one, said . . .,"Oh, you must see my new coat!" (page 212)

infinitesimal (in′ fin i tes′ i məl), **repartee** (rep′ ər tē′): They laughed a great deal together over **infinitesimal repartee**. (page 214)

rapt: Mr. Kuroda was in his shirtsleeves expounding some *haiku* theory . . . , and her mother was **rapt.** (page 217)

vacillating (vas′ ə lāt′ iŋ): Frightened and **vacillating,** Rosie saw her father enter the house. (page 218)

indiscretion (in′ di skresh′ ən): She could no longer project herself . . . without refreshing in them the memory of her **indiscretion.** (page 218)

glib (glib): For an instant she turned away, and her mother, hearing the familiar **glib** agreement, released her. (page 219)

*C*onnecting Writing and Reading

Think of a time when you witnessed a major conflict between two people close to you—friends, for example, or family members. In your journal, describe the conflict and how it made you feel. As you read, compare your feelings about the conflict you witnessed with Rosie's feelings about the conflict between her parents.

*T*HE FIRST ROSIE knew that her mother had taken to writing poems was one evening when she finished one and read it aloud for her daughter's approval. It was about cats, and Rosie pretended to understand it thoroughly and appreciate it to no end, partly because she hesitated to disillusion her mother about the quantity and quality of Japanese she had learned in all the years now that she had been going to Japanese school every Saturday (and Wednesday, too, in the summer). Even so, her mother must have been skeptical about the depth of Rosie's understanding, because she explained afterwards about the kind of poem she was trying to write.

See, Rosie, she said, it was a haiku, a poem in which she must pack all her meaning into seventeen syllables only, which were divided into three lines of five, seven, and five syllables. In the one she had just read, she had tried to capture the charm of a kitten, as well as comment on the superstition that owning a cat of three colors meant good luck.

"Yes, yes, I understand. How utterly lovely," Rosie said, and her mother, either satisfied or seeing through the deception and resigned, went back to composing.

The truth was that Rosie was lazy; English lay ready on the tongue but Japanese had to be searched for and examined, and even then put forth tentatively (probably to meet with laughter). It was so much easier to say yes, yes, even when one meant no, no. Besides, this was what was in her mind to say: I was looking through one of your magazines from Japan last night, Mother, and toward the back I found some haiku in English that delighted me. There was one that made me giggle off and on until I fell asleep—

It is morning, and lo!
I lie awake, *comme il faut*,[1]
sighing for some dough.

Now, how to reach her mother, how to communicate the melancholy song? Rosie knew formal Japanese by fits and starts, her mother had even less English, no French. It was much more possible to say yes, yes.

It developed that her mother was writing the haiku for a daily newspaper, the *Mainichi Shimbun*,[2] that was published in San Francisco. Los Angeles, to be sure, was closer to the farming community in which the Hayashi[3] family lived and several Japanese vernaculars[4] were printed there, but Rosie's parents said they preferred the tone of the northern paper. Once a week, the *Mainichi* would have a section devoted to haiku, and her mother became an extravagant contributor, taking for herself the blossoming pen name, Ume Hanazono.[5]

So Rosie and her father lived for a while with two women, her mother and Ume Hanazono. Her mother (Tome Hayashi by name) kept house, cooked, washed, and, along with her husband and the Carrascos, the Mexican family hired for the harvest, did her ample share of picking tomatoes out in the sweltering fields and boxing them in tidy strata in the cool packing shed. Ume Hanazono, who came to life after the dinner dishes were done, was an earnest, muttering stranger who often neglected speaking when spoken to and stayed busy at the parlor table as late as midnight scribbling with pencil on scratch paper or carefully copying characters on good paper with her fat, pale green Parker.

---

1. *comme il faut* (kôm ēl fō) *French:* as one does.
2. *Mainichi Shimbun* (mä ē nē′ chē shēm′ bun).
3. **Hayashi** (hä yä′ shē).
4. **vernaculars** (vər nak′ ye lərz): newspapers printed in a native language.
5. **Ume Hanazono** (o͞o′ me hä nä zô′ nô).

The new interest had some repercussions on the household routine. Before, Rosie had been accustomed to her parents and herself taking their hot baths early and going to bed almost immediately afterward unless her parents challenged each other to a game of flower cards or unless company dropped in. Now if her father wanted to play cards, he had to resort to solitaire (at which he always cheated fearlessly), and if a group of friends came over, it was bound to contain someone who was also writing haiku, and the small assemblage would be split in two, her father entertaining the non-literary members and her mother comparing ecstatic notes with the visiting poet.

If they went out, it was more of the same thing. But Ume Hanazono's life span, even for a poet's, was very brief—perhaps three months at most.

One night they went over to see the Hayano family in the neighboring town to the west, an adventure both painful and attractive to Rosie. It was attractive because there were four Hayano girls, all lovely and each one named after a season of the year (Haru, Natsu, Aki, Fuyu),[6] painful because something had been wrong with Mrs. Hayano ever since the birth of her first child. Rosie would sometimes watch Mrs. Hayano, reputed to have been the belle of her native village, making her way about a room, stooped, slowly shuffling, violently trembling (*always* trembling), and she would be reminded that this woman, in this same condition, had carried and given issue to three babies. She would look wonderingly at Mr. Hayano, handsome, tall, and strong, and she would look at her four pretty friends. But it was not a matter she could come to any decision about.

On this visit, however, Mrs. Hayano sat all evening in the rocker, as motionless and unobtrusive as it was possible for her to be, and Rosie found the greater part of the evening practically anaesthetic.[7] Too, Rosie spent most

of it in the girls' room, because Haru, the garrulous[8] one, said almost as soon as the bows and other greetings were over, "Oh, you must see my new coat!"

It was a pale plaid of gray, sand, and blue, with an enormous collar, and Rosie, seeing nothing special in it, said, "Gee, how nice."

"Nice?" said Haru, indignantly. "Is that all you can say about it? It's gorgeous! And so cheap, too. Only seventeen-ninety-eight, because it was a sale. The saleslady said it was twenty-five dollars regular."

"Gee," said Rosie. Natsu, who never said much and when she said anything said it shyly, fingered the coat covetously and Haru pulled it away.

"Mine," she said, putting it on. She minced in the aisle between the two large beds and smiled happily. "Let's see how your mother likes it."

She broke into the front room and the adult conversation and went to stand in front of Rosie's mother, while the rest watched from the door. Rosie's mother was properly envious. "May I inherit it when you're through with it?"

Haru, pleased, giggled and said yes, she could, but Natsu reminded gravely from the door, "You promised me, Haru."

Everyone laughed but Natsu, who shame-facedly retreated into the bedroom. Haru came in laughing, taking off the coat. "We were only kidding, Natsu," she said. "Here, you try it on now."

After Natsu buttoned herself into the coat, inspected herself solemnly in the bureau mirror, and reluctantly shed it, Rosie, Aki, and Fuyu got their turns, and Fuyu, who was eight, drowned in it while her sisters and Rosie dou-

---

6. Haru, Natsu, Aki, Fuyu (hä′ ro͞o, nä′ tso͞o, ä′ kē, fo͞o′ yo͞o).

7. anaesthetic (an′ əs thet′ ik): numbing; making one fall asleep; dull.

8. garrulous (gar′ ə ləs): talkative.

bled up in amusement. They all went into the front room later, because Haru's mother quaveringly called to her to fix the tea and rice cakes and open a can of sliced peaches for everybody. Rosie noticed that her mother and Mr. Hayano were talking together at the little table—they were discussing a haiku that Mr. Hayano was planning to send to the *Mainichi*, while her father was sitting at one end of the sofa looking through a copy of *Life*, the new picture magazine. Occasionally, her father would comment on a photograph, holding it toward Mrs. Hayano and speaking to her as he always did—loudly, as though he thought someone such as she must surely be at least a trifle deaf also.

The five girls had their refreshments at the kitchen table, and it was while Rosie was showing the sisters her trick of swallowing peach slices without chewing (she chased each slippery crescent down with a swig of tea) that her father brought his empty teacup and untouched saucer to the sink and said, "Come on, Rosie, we're going home now."

"Already?" asked Rosie.

"Work tomorrow," he said.

He sounded irritated, and Rosie, puzzled, gulped one last yellow slice and stood up to go, while the sisters began protesting, as was their wont.

"We have to get up at five-thirty," he told them, going into the front room quickly, so that they did not have their usual chance to hang onto his hands and plead for an extension of time.

Rosie, following, saw that her mother and Mr. Hayano were sipping tea and still talking together, while Mrs. Hayano concentrated, quivering, on raising the handleless Japanese cup to her lips with both her hands and lowering it back to her lap. Her father, saying nothing, went out the door, onto the bright porch, and down the steps. Her mother looked up and asked, "Where is he going?"

"Where is he going?" Rosie said. "He said we were going home now."

"Going home?" Her mother looked with embarrassment at Mr. Hayano and his absorbed wife and then forced a smile. "He must be tired," she said.

Haru was not giving up yet. "May Rosie stay overnight?" she asked, and Natsu, Aki, and Fuyu came to reinforce their sister's plea by helping her make a circle around Rosie's mother. Rosie, for once having no desire to stay, was relieved when her mother, apologizing to the perturbed Mr. and Mrs. Hayano for her father's abruptness at the same time, managed to shake her head no at the quartet, kindly but adamant, so that they broke their circle and let her go.

Rosie's father looked ahead into the windshield as the two joined him. "I'm sorry," her mother said. "You must be tired." Her father, stepping on the starter, said nothing. "You know how I get when it's haiku," she continued, "I forget what time it is." He only grunted.

As they rode homeward silently, Rosie, sitting between, felt a rush of hate for both—for her mother for begging, for her father for denying her mother. I wish this old Ford would crash, right now, she thought, then immediately, no, no, I wish my father would laugh, but it was too late: already the vision had passed through her mind of the green pick-up crumpled in the dark against one of the mighty eucalyptus trees they were just riding past, of the three contorted, bleeding bodies, one of them hers.

Rosie ran between two patches of tomatoes, her heart working more rambunctiously than she had ever known it to. How lucky it was that Aunt Taka and Uncle Gimpachi[9] had come tonight, though, how very lucky.

---

9. Aunt Taka (tä′ kä) . . . **Uncle Gimpachi** (gēm pä′ chē).

Otherwise she might not have really kept her half-promise to meet Jesus Carrasco. Jesus was going to be a senior in September at the same school she went to, and his parents were the ones helping with the tomatoes this year. She and Jesus, who hardly remembered seeing each other at Cleveland High where there were so many other people and two whole grades between them, had become great friends this summer—he always had a joke for her when he periodically drove the loaded pick-up up from the fields to the shed where she was usually sorting while her mother and father did the packing, and they laughed a great deal together over infinitesimal[10] repartee[11] during the afternoon break for chilled watermelon or ice cream in the shade of the shed.

What she enjoyed most was racing him to see which could finish picking a double row first. He, who could work faster, would tease her by slowing down until she thought she would surely pass him this time, then speeding up furiously to leave her several sprawling vines behind. Once he had made her screech hideously by crossing over, while her back was turned, to place atop the tomatoes in her green-stained bucket a truly monstrous, pale green worm (it had looked more like an infant snake). And it was when they had finished a contest this morning, after she had pantingly pointed a green finger at the immature tomatoes evident in the lugs[12] at the end of his row and he had returned the accusation (with justice), that he had startlingly brought up the matter of their possibly meeting outside the range of both their parents' dubious eyes.

"What for?" she had asked.
"I've got a secret I want to tell you," he said.
"Tell me now," she demanded.
"It won't be ready till tonight," he said.
She laughed. "Tell me tomorrow then."
"It'll be gone tomorrow," he threatened.
"Well, for seven hakes,[13] what is it?" she had

asked, more than twice, and when he had suggested that the packing shed would be an appropriate place to find out, she had cautiously answered maybe. She had not been certain she was going to keep the appointment until the arrival of mother's sister and her husband. Their coming seemed a sort of signal of permission, of grace, and she had definitely made up her mind to lie and leave as she was bowing them welcome.

So as soon as everyone appeared settled back for the evening, she announced loudly that she was going to the privy outside, "I'm going to the *benjo!*" and slipped out the door. And now that she was actually on her way, her heart pumped in such an undisciplined way that she could hear it with her ears. It's because I'm running, she told herself, slowing to a walk. The shed was up ahead, one more patch away, in the middle of the fields. Its bulk, looming in the dimness, took on a sinisterness that was funny when Rosie reminded herself that it was only a wooden frame with a canvas roof and three canvas walls that made a slapping noise on breezy days.

Jesus was sitting on the narrow plank that was the sorting platform and she went around to the other side and jumped backwards to seat herself on the rim of a packing stand. "Well, tell me," she said without greeting, thinking her voice sounded reassuringly familiar.
"I saw you coming out the door," Jesus said. "I heard you running part of the way, too."
"Uh-huh," Rosie said. "Now tell me the secret."
"I was afraid you wouldn't come," he said.

---

10. infinitesimal (in′ fin i tes′ i məl): too small to be measured; infinitely small.
11. repartee (rep′ ər tē′): quick, witty conversation.
12. lugs: shallow boxes in which fruit is shipped.
13. seven hakes: a play on the phrase "heaven's sake."

Rosie delved around on the chicken-wire bottom of the stall for number two tomatoes, ripe, which she was sitting beside, and came up with a left-over that felt edible. She bit into it and began sucking out the pulp and seeds. "I'm here," she pointed out.

"Rosie, are you sorry you came?"

"Sorry? What for?" she said. "You said you were going to tell me something."

"I will, I will," Jesus said, but his voice contained disappointment, and Rosie fleetingly felt the older of the two, realizing a brand-new power which vanished without category under her recognition.

"I have to go back in a minute," she said. "My aunt and uncle are here from Wintersburg. I told them I was going to the privy."

Jesus laughed. "You funny thing," he said. "You slay me!"

"Just because you have a bathroom *inside*," Rosie said. "Come on, tell me."

Chuckling, Jesus came around to lean on the stand facing her. They still could not see each other very clearly, but Rosie noticed that Jesus became very sober again as he took the hollow tomato from her hand and dropped it back into the stall. When he took hold of her empty hand, she could find no words to protest; her vocabulary had become distressingly constricted and she thought desperately that all that remained intact now was yes and no and oh, and even these few sounds would not easily out. Thus, kissed by Jesus, Rosie fell for the first time entirely victim to a helplessness delectable beyond speech. But the terrible, beautiful sensation lasted no more than a second, and the reality of Jesus' lips and tongue and teeth and hands made her pull away with such strength that she nearly tumbled.

Rosie stopped running as she approached the lights from the windows of home. How long since she had left? She could not guess, but gasping yet, she went to the privy in back and locked herself in. Her own breathing deafened her in the dark, close space, and she sat and waited until she could hear at last the nightly calling of the frogs and crickets. Even then, all she could think to say was oh, my, and the pressure of Jesus' face against her face would not leave.

No one had missed her in the parlor, however, and Rosie walked in and through quickly, announcing that she was next going to take a bath. "Your father's in the bathhouse," her mother said, and Rosie, in her room, recalled that she had not seen him when she entered. There had been only Aunt Taka and Uncle Gimpachi with her mother at the table, drinking tea. She got her robe and straw sandals and crossed the parlor again to go outside. Her mother was telling them about the haiku competition in the *Mainichi* and the poem she had entered.

Rosie met her father coming out of the bathhouse. "Are you through, Father?" she asked. "I was going to ask you to scrub my back."

"Scrub your own back," he said shortly, going toward the main house.

"What have I done now?" she yelled after him. She suddenly felt like doing a lot of yelling. But he did not answer, and she went into the bathhouse. Turning on the dangling light, she removed her denims and T-shirt and threw them in the big carton for dirty clothes standing next to the washing machine. Her other things she took with her into the bath compartment to wash after her bath. After she had scooped a basin of hot water from the square wooden tub, she sat on the gray cement of the floor and soaped herself at exaggerated leisure, singing "Red Sails in the Sunset" at the top of her voice and using da-da-da where she suspected her words. Then, standing up, still singing, for she was possessed by the notion that any attempt now to analyze would result in spoilage and she believed that the larger her

he did not seem to hear and she said again, "Mother says she'll be back in a minute."

"All right, all right," he nodded, and they worked again in silence. But suddenly, her father uttered an incredible noise, exactly like the cork of a bottle popping, and the next Rosie knew, he was stalking angrily toward the house, almost running in fact, and she chased after him crying, "Father! Father! What are you going to do?"

He stopped long enough to order her back to the shed. "Never mind!" he shouted. "Get on with the sorting!"

And from the place in the fields where she stood, frightened and <u>vacillating</u>,[20] Rosie saw her father enter the house. Soon Mr. Kuroda came out alone, putting on his coat. Mr. Kuroda got into his car and backed out down the driveway onto the highway. Next her father emerged, also alone, something in his arms (it was the picture, she realized), and, going over to the bathhouse woodpile, he threw the picture on the ground and picked up the axe. Smashing the picture, glass and all (she heard the explosion faintly), he reached over for the kerosene that was used to encourage the bath fire and poured it over the wreckage. I am dreaming, Rosie said to herself, I am dreaming, but her father, having made sure that his act of cremation was irrevocable, was even then returning to the fields.

Rosie ran past him and toward the house. What had become of her mother? She burst into the parlor and found her mother at the back window watching the dying fire. They watched together until there remained only a feeble smoke under the blazing sun. Her mother was very calm.

"Do you know why I married your father?" she said without turning.

"No," said Rosie. It was the most frightening question she had ever been called upon to answer. Don't tell me now, she wanted to say, tell me tomorrow, tell me next week, don't tell me today. But she knew she would be told now, that the telling would combine with the other violence of the hot afternoon to level her life, her world to the very ground.

It was like a story out of the magazines illustrated in sepia,[21] which she had consumed so greedily for a period until the information had somehow reached her that those wretchedly unhappy autobiographies, offered to her as the testimonials of living men and women, were largely inventions: Her mother, at nineteen, had come to America and married her father as an alternative to suicide.

At eighteen she had been in love with the first son of one of the well-to-do families in her village. The two had met whenever and wherever they could, secretly, because it would not have done for his family to see him favor her —her father had no money; he was a drunkard and a gambler besides. She had learned she was with child; an excellent match had already been arranged for her lover. Despised by her family, she had given premature birth to a stillborn son, who would be seventeen now. Her family did not turn her out, but she could no longer project herself in any direction without refreshing in them the memory of her <u>indiscretion</u>.[22] She wrote to Aunt Taka, her favorite sister in America, threatening to kill herself if Aunt Taka would not send for her. Aunt Taka hastily arranged a marriage with a young man of whom she knew, but lately arrived from Japan, a young man of simple mind, it was said, but of kindly heart. The young man was never told why his unseen betrothed was so eager to hasten the day of meeting.

---

20. **vacillating** (vas′ ə lāt′ iŋ): wavering in opinion.
21. **sepia:** a dark reddish-brown color.
22. **indiscretion** (in′ di skresh′ ən): an act showing lack of good judgment.

The story was told perfectly, with neither groping for words nor untoward passion. It was as though her mother had memorized it by heart, reciting it to herself so many times over that its nagging vileness had long since gone.

"I had a brother then?" Rosie asked, for this was what seemed to matter now; she would think about the other later, she assured herself, pushing back the illumination which threatened all that darkness that had hitherto been merely mysterious or even glamorous. "A half-brother?"

"Yes."

"I would have liked a brother," she said.

Suddenly, her mother knelt on the floor and took her by the wrists. "Rosie," she said urgently, "promise me you will never marry!" Shocked more by the request than the revelation, Rosie stared at her mother's face. Jesus, Jesus, she called silently, not certain whether she was invoking the help of the son of the Carrascos or of God, until there returned sweetly the memory of Jesus' hand, how it had touched her and where. Still her mother waited for an answer, holding her wrists so tightly that her hands were going numb. She tried to pull free. Promise, her mother whispered fiercely, promise. Yes, yes, I promise, Rosie said. But for an instant she turned away, and her mother, hearing the familiar glib[23] agreement, released her. Oh, you, you, you, her eyes and twisted mouth said, you fool. Rosie, covering her face, began at last to cry, and the embrace and consoling hand came much later than she expected.

---

23. glib (glib): spoken in a smooth, careless manner, often in a way that is not convincing.

Thinking About the Story

A PERSONAL RESPONSE

sharing impressions

1. Which character were you most thinking of as you finished reading? Briefly record your thoughts about this character in your journal.

constructing interpretations

2. Do you think Mrs. Hayashi is justified in pressuring Rosie to promise not to marry? Give reasons for your answer.

Think about
- the nature of her marriage to Rosie's father
- what she wants for Rosie
- Rosie's immediate reaction to the demand

3. In your opinion, why does Rosie's father react as he does to Mrs. Hayashi's writing?

Think about
- the difference between the way Mrs. Hayashi and Mrs. Hayano act as wives
- what kind of wife Mr. Hayashi might prefer to have
- the pleasure Mrs. Hayashi takes in writing and discussing *haiku*

- the intensity of the farm work and the need for her labor
- the elegance of the prize Mrs. Hayashi wins and of the man who brings it
- the description of Mr. Hayashi as a man "of simple mind . . . but of kindly heart"

4. Is there anything Mrs. Hayashi can do to resolve the conflict between her husband's needs and her own desires? Explain your answer.

5. What incidents most clearly reveal to you how Rosie is affected by the conflict between her parents? Cite details from the story.

A CREATIVE RESPONSE

6. Do you think Rosie is more likely to follow her mother's advice not to marry, to model her behavior on her mother's, or to follow her own way?

Think about
- connections between Mrs. Hayashi's illicit romance in Japan and Rosie's budding romance with Jesus Carrasco
- the conflict between the way Rosie and her mother view Japanese culture and American culture
- similarities and differences between Rosie's personality and her mother's
- whether life in the United States will offer Rosie different opportunities from those her mother had

A CRITICAL RESPONSE

7. Between 1885 and 1924 many young Japanese men came to America seeking a new life. Some later returned to Japan to marry, while others, like Mr. Hayashi, found wives by exchanging photographs with Japanese women looking for husbands in America. What aspects of the Hayashi marriage do you think are directly related to these cultural circumstances, and what aspects could be present in any marriage? Cite examples from the story to support your answer.

8. According to one critic, Mrs. Hayashi's impassioned kneeling and clasping of Rosie at the end of the story is ironically similar to that of an ardent lover proposing marriage. Explain whether you agree or disagree with this critical interpretation, citing details from the story for support.

Analyzing the Writer's Craft

PLOT AND THEME

What do you think Yamamoto wants to communicate about Rosie and her adolescent awakening?

Building a Literary Vocabulary. Plot refers to the actions and events in a literary work. A short story sometimes has two or more plots that operate simultaneously. Each plot may suggest a theme, or central idea; all the plots and themes are somehow related. In "Seventeen Syllables" the development of Rosie's relationship with Jesus forms one plot line. In this part of the story, Yamamoto explores the conflicting emotions that often surround such a relationship. The second plot line involves Mrs. Hayashi's *haiku* writing and the conflicts she and her family experience because of it.

Application: Examining Plot and Theme. Working with a partner, create two time lines, one above the other. Indicate events related to Rosie's romance with Jesus on the top line and events connected with Mrs. Hayashi's *haiku* writing on the bottom one. Circle points on the time lines where the two plots overlap at crucial times. Then write a thematic statement that presents the central idea communicated by the two plots considered together. Share your time line and thematic statement with the class.

Connecting Reading and Writing

1. Write a **haiku** to share with a poetry reading group. Use the details about *haiku* presented in the story as a guide to writing your poem.

Option: Find examples of *haiku* to share with your poetry group and write **annotations** to accompany the poems.

2. Imagine that you are Rosie. In a **diary entry**, describe your feelings about your mother's forcing you to promise not to marry.

Option: Write a **note** that you might pass to your closest friend explaining what has happened in your family and asking for advice on what to do next.

3. Write the next **scene** for this story, in which Mr. and Mrs. Hayashi visit a close friend and advisor in an attempt to resolve their conflict.

Option: Write **journal note**s that the friend and advisor might write after the Hayashis' visit.

4. Read more about the picture brides who came to America to marry men they had never met. Share your findings with the class in the form of an **oral presentation**.

Option: Write a brief **dramatic scene** to communicate the thoughts and emotions of several picture brides when they meet their future husbands for the first time.

from Kaffir Boy

MARK MATHABANE

A biography of Mathabane appears on page 426.

$\mathcal{A}$pproaching the Selection

In _Kaffir Boy,_ Mark Mathabane (mä tä bä′ ne) describes what it was like to be a black growing up in Johannesburg, South Africa in the 1960's. The South African government had established its policy of apartheid, which legalizes segregation and discrimination against blacks, forcing them to live in overcrowded, disease-ridden townships and severely limiting the opportunities for meaningful work and a better life. The word _kaffir_ (ka′ fər), a term used to refer to blacks, means "infi-del" in Arabic, reflecting this racist attitude. In this excerpt from his autobiography, Mathabane tells about the day on which he made an important decision.

$\mathcal{B}$uilding Vocabulary

These essential words are footnoted within the selection.

coteries (kōt′ ər ēz): Workless men and women were beginning to assemble in their usual **coteries.** (page 225)

austere (ô stir′), **inscrutable** (in skr$\overline{oo}$t′ ə bəl): His **austere,** shiny face, **inscrutable** and imposing, reminded me of my father. (page 226)

mores (mōr′ ēz): Many tribal women questioned her sanity in daring to question well-established **mores.** (page 229)

$\mathcal{C}$onnecting Writing and Reading

Imagine yourself ten to fifteen years from now. Where will you live? What kind of job will you have? How important do you think your education will be in helping you create the kind of life that you want? Jot down your ideas in your journal. As you read, compare your thoughts about the value of education with the different characters' views on the value of education.

"Education will open doors where none seem to exist."

WHEN MY mother began dropping hints that I would soon be going to school, I vowed never to go, because school was a waste of time. She laughed and said, "We'll see. You don't know what you're talking about." My philosophy on school was that of a gang of ten-, eleven- and twelve-year-olds whom I so revered that their every word seemed that of an oracle.

These boys had long left their homes and were now living in various neighborhood junkyards, making it on their own. They slept in abandoned cars, smoked glue and benzene, ate pilchards[1] and brown bread, sneaked into the white world to caddy and, if unsuccessful, came back to the township to steal beer and soda bottles from shebeens,[2] or goods from the Indian traders on First Avenue. Their lifestyle was exciting, adventurous and full of surprises; and I was attracted to it. My mother told me that they were no-gooders, that they would amount to nothing, that I should not associate with them, but I paid no heed. What does she know? I used to tell myself. One thing she did not know was that the gang's way of life had captivated me wholly, particularly their philosophy on school: they hated it and considered an education a waste of time.

They, like myself, had grown up in an environment where the value of an education was never emphasized; where the first thing a child learned was not how to read and write and spell but how to fight and steal and rebel; where the money to send children to school was grossly lacking, for survival was first priority. I kept my membership in the gang, knowing that for as long as I was under its influence, I would never go to school.

One day my mother woke me up at four in the morning.

"Are they here? I didn't hear any noises," I asked in the usual way.

"No," my mother said. "I want you to get into that washtub over there."

"What!" I balked, upon hearing the word *washtub*. I feared taking baths like one feared the plague. Throughout seven years of hectic living the number of baths I had taken could be counted on one hand with several fingers missing. I simply had no natural inclination for water; cleanliness was a trait I still had to acquire. Besides, we had only one bathtub in the house, and it constantly sprung a leak.

"I said get into that tub!" My mother shook a finger in my face.

Reluctantly, I obeyed, yet wondered why all of a sudden I had to take a bath. My mother, armed with a scropbrush and a piece of Lifebuoy soap, purged me of years and years of grime till I ached and bled. As I howled, feeling pain shoot through my limbs as the thistles of the brush encountered stubborn calluses, there was a loud knock at the door.

Instantly my mother leaped away from the tub and headed, on tiptoe, toward the bedroom. Fear seized me as I, too, thought of the police. I sat frozen in the bathtub, not knowing what to do.

"Open up, Mujaji[3] (my mother's maiden name)," Granny's voice came shrilling through the door. "It's me."

My mother heaved a sigh of relief; her tense limbs relaxed. She turned and headed to the

---

1. **pilchards** (pil' chərdz): small, oily fishes.
2. **shebeens** (shi bēnz'): establishments where liquor is sold without a license.
3. **Mujaji** (mᴏᴏ jä' jē).

kitchen door, unlatched it and in came Granny and Aunt Bushy.

"You scared me half to death," my mother said to Granny. "I had forgotten all about your coming."

"Are you ready?" Granny asked my mother.

"Yes—just about," my mother said, beckoning me to get out of the washtub.

She handed me a piece of cloth to dry myself. As I dried myself, questions raced through my mind: What's going on? What's Granny doing at our house this ungodly hour of the morning? And why did she ask my mother, "Are you ready?" While I stood debating, my mother went into the bedroom and came out with a stained white shirt and a pair of faded black shorts.

"Here," she said, handing me the togs, "put these on."

"Why?" I asked.

"Put them on I said!"

I put the shirt on; it was grossly loosefitting. It reached all the way down to my ankles. Then I saw the reason why: it was my father's shirt!

"But this is Papa's shirt," I complained. "It don't fit me."

"Put it on," my mother insisted. "I'll make it fit."

"The pants don't fit me either," I said. "Whose are they anyway?"

"Put them on," my mother said. "I'll make them fit."

Moments later I had the garments on; I looked ridiculous. My mother started working on the pants and shirt to make them fit. She folded the shirt in so many intricate ways and stashed it inside the pants, they too having been folded several times at the waist. She then choked the pants at the waist with a piece of sisal rope to hold them up. She then lavishly smeared my face, arms and legs with a mixture of pig's fat and vaseline. "This will

insulate you from the cold," she said. My skin gleamed like the morning star and I felt as hot as the center of the sun and I smelled God knows like what. After embalming me, she headed to the bedroom.

"Where are we going, Gran'ma?" I said, hoping that she would tell me what my mother refused to tell me. I still had no idea I was about to be taken to school.

"Didn't your mother tell you?" Granny said with a smile. "You're going to start school."

"What!" I gasped, leaping from the chair where I was sitting as if it were made of hot lead. "I am not going to school!" I blurted out and raced toward the kitchen door.

My mother had just reappeared from the bedroom and guessing what I was up to, she yelled, "Someone get the door!"

Aunt Bushy immediately barred the door. I turned and headed for the window. As I leaped for the windowsill, my mother lunged at me and brought me down. I tussled, "Let go of me! I don't want to go to school! Let me go!" but my mother held fast onto me.

"It's no use now," she said, grinning triumphantly as she pinned me down. Turning her head in Granny's direction, she shouted, "Granny! Get a rope quickly!"

Granny grabbed a piece of rope nearby and came to my mother's aid. I bit and clawed every hand that grabbed me and howled protestations against going to school; however, I was no match for the two determined matriarchs. In a jiffy they had me bound, hands and feet.

"What's the matter with him?" Granny, bewildered, asked my mother. "Why did he suddenly turn into an imp when I told him you're taking him to school?"

"You shouldn't have told him that he's being taken to school," my mother said. "He doesn't want to go there. That's why I requested you come today, to help me take him there. Those boys in the streets have been a bad influence on him."

As the two matriarchs hauled me through the door, they told Aunt Bushy not to go to school but stay behind and mind the house and the children.

The sun was beginning to rise from beyond the veld when Granny and my mother dragged me to school. The streets were beginning to fill with their everyday traffic: old men and women—wizened, bent and ragged—were beginning their rambling; workless men and women were beginning to assemble in their usual coteries[4] and head for shebeens in the backyards, where they discussed how they escaped the morning pass raids and contemplated the conditions of life amidst intense beer drinking and vacant, uneasy laughter; young boys and girls, some as young as myself, were beginning their aimless wanderings along the narrow, dusty streets in search of food, carrying bawling infants piggyback.

As we went along some of the streets, boys and girls who shared the same fears about school as I were making their feelings known in a variety of ways. They were howling their protests and trying to escape. A few managed to break loose and make a mad dash for freedom, only to be recaptured in no time, admonished or whipped, or both, and ordered to march again.

As we made a turn into Sixteenth Avenue, the street leading to the tribal school I was being taken to, a short, chubby black woman came along from the opposite direction. She had a scuttle overflowing with coal on her doek-covered (cloth-covered) head. An infant, bawling deafeningly, was loosely swathed with a piece of sheepskin onto her back. Following closely behind the woman and picking up pieces of coal as they fell from the scuttle and placing them in a small plastic bag was a half-naked, potbellied and thumb-sucking boy of about four. The woman stopped abreast. For some reason we stopped too.

"I wish I had done the same to my oldest son," the strange woman said in a regretful voice, gazing at me. I was confounded by her stopping and offering her unsolicited opinion.

"I wish I had done that to my oldest son," she repeated, and suddenly burst into tears; amidst sobs, she continued, "before . . . the street claimed him . . . and . . . turned him into a tsotsi."[5]

Granny and my mother offered consolatory remarks to the strange woman.

"But it's too late now," the strange woman continued, tears now streaming freely down her puffy cheeks. She made no attempt to dry them. "It's too late now," she said for the second time; "he's beyond any help. I can't help him even if I wanted to. Uswile[6] (He is dead)."

"How did he die?" my mother asked in a sympathetic voice.

"He shunned school and, instead, grew up to live by the knife. And the same knife he lived by ended his life. That's why whenever I see a boy child refuse to go to school, I stop and tell the story of my dear little mbitsini[7] (heartbreak)."

Having said that, the strange woman left as mysteriously as she had arrived.

"Did you hear what that woman said!" my mother screamed into my ears. "Do you want the same to happen to you!"

I dropped my eyes. I was confused.

"Poor woman," Granny said ruefully. "She must have truly loved her son."

Finally, we reached the school and I was ushered into the principal's office, a tiny cubicle facing a row of privies[8] and a patch of yellowed grass.

---

4. coteries (kōt′ ər ēz): close circles of friends with common interests or backgrounds; cliques.
5. tsotsi (tsô′ tsē): a thug armed with a knife or other weapon.
6. Uswile (ᴏos wē′ le).
7. mbitsini (mbē tsē′ nē).
8. privies: outhouses.

"So this is the rascal we'd been talking about," the principal, a tall, wiry man, foppishly dressed in a black pin-striped suit, said to my mother as we entered. His austere,[9] shiny face, inscrutable[10] and imposing, reminded me of my father. He was sitting behind a brown table upon which stood piles of dust and cobweb-covered books and papers. In one upper pocket of his jacket was arrayed a variety of pens and pencils; in the other nestled a lily-white handkerchief whose presence was more decorative than utilitarian. Alongside him stood a disproportionately portly black woman, fashionably dressed in a black skirt and a white blouse. She had but one pen, and this she held in her hand. The room was hot and stuffy and buzzing with flies.

"Yes, Principal," my mother answered, "this is he."

"I see he's living up to his notoriety," remarked the principal, noticing that I had been bound. "Did he give you too much trouble?"

"Trouble, Principal," my mother sighed. "He was like an imp."

"He's just like the rest of them, Principal," Granny sighed. "Once they get out into the streets, they become wild. They take to the many vices of the streets like an infant takes to its mother's milk. They begin to think that there's no other life but the one shown them by the *tsotsis*. They come to hate school and forget about the future."

"Well," the principal said, "We'll soon remedy all that. Untie him."

"He'll run away," my mother cried.

"I don't think he's that foolish to attempt that with all of us here."

"He *is* that foolish, Principal," my mother said as she and Granny began untying me. "He's tried it before. Getting him here was an ordeal in itself."

The principal rose from his seat, took two steps to the door and closed it. As the door swung closed, I spotted a row of canes of different lengths and thicknesses hanging behind it. The principal, seeing me staring at the canes, grinned and said, in a manner suggesting that he had wanted me to see them, "As long as you behave, I won't have to use any of those on you."

Use those canes on me? I gasped. I stared at my mother—she smiled; at Granny—she smiled too. That made me abandon any inkling of escaping.

"So they finally gave you the birth certificate and the papers," the principal addressed my mother as he returned to his chair.

"Yes, Principal," my mother said, "they finally did. But what a battle it was. It took me nearly a year to get all them papers together." She took out of her handbag a neatly wrapped package and handed it to the principal. "They've been running us around for so long that there were times when I thought he would never attend school, Principal," she said.

"That's pretty much standard procedure, Mrs. Mathabane," the principal said, unwrapping the package. "But you now have the papers and that's what's important.

"As long as we have the papers," he continued, minutely perusing the contents of the package, "we won't be breaking the law in admitting your son to this school, for we'll be in full compliance with the requirements set by the authorities in Pretoria."[11]

"Sometimes I don't understand the laws from Pitori,"[12] Granny said. "They did the same to me with my Piet[13] and Bushy. Why, Principal, should our children not be allowed to learn because of some piece of paper?"

"The piece of paper you're referring to, Mrs.

---

9. austere (ô stir′): having a severe or stern manner.
10. inscrutable (in skrōōt′ ə bəl): that cannot be easily understood; completely mysterious.
11. Pretoria (pre tôr′ ē ə): capital of South Africa.
12. Pitori (pi tō′ rē): another name for Pretoria.
13. Piet (pēt).

Mabaso[14] (Granny's maiden name)," the principal said to Granny, "is as important to our children as a pass is to us adults. We all hate passes; therefore, it's only natural we should hate the regulations our children are subjected to. But as we have to live with passes, so our children have to live with the regulations, Mrs. Mabaso. I hope you understand, that is the law of the country. We would have admitted your grandson a long time ago, as you well know, had it not been for the papers. I hope you understand."

"I understand, Principal," Granny said, "but I don't understand," she added paradoxically.

One of the papers caught the principal's eye and he turned to my mother and asked, "Is your husband a Shangaan,[15] Mrs. Mathabane?"

"No, he's not, Principal," my mother said. "Is there anything wrong? He's Venda[16] and I'm Shangaan."

The principal reflected for a moment or so and then said, concernedly, "No, there's nothing seriously wrong. Nothing that we can't take care of. You see, Mrs. Mathabane, technically, the fact that your child's father is a Venda makes him ineligible to attend this tribal school because it is only for children whose parents are of the Shangaan tribe. May I ask what language the children speak at home?"

"Both languages," my mother said worriedly, "Venda and Shangaan. Is there anything wrong?"

The principal coughed, clearing his throat, then said, "I mean which language do they speak more?"

"It depends, Principal," my mother said, swallowing hard. "When their father is around, he wants them to speak only Venda. And when he's not, they speak Shangaan. And when they are out at play, they speak Zulu and Sisotho."[17]

"Well," the principal said, heaving a sigh of relief. "In that case, I think an exception can be made. The reason for such an exception is that there's currently no school for Vendas in Alexandra. And should the authorities come asking why we took in your son, we can tell them that. Anyway, your child is half-half."

Everyone broke into a nervous laugh, except me. I was bewildered by the whole thing. I looked at my mother, and she seemed greatly relieved as she watched the principal register me; a broad smile broke across her face. It was as if some enormously heavy burden had finally been lifted from her shoulders and her conscience.

"Bring him back two weeks from today," the principal said as he saw us to the door. "There're so many children registering today that classes won't begin until two weeks hence. Also, the school needs repair and cleaning up after the holidays. If he refuses to come, simply notify us, and we'll send a couple of big boys to come fetch him, and he'll be very sorry if it ever comes to that."

As we left the principal's office and headed home, my mind was still against going to school. I was thinking of running away from home and joining my friends in the junkyard.

I didn't want to go to school for three reasons: I was reluctant to surrender my freedom and independence over to what I heard every school-going child call "tyrannous discipline." I had heard many bad things about life in tribal school—from daily beatings by teachers and mistresses who worked you like a mule to long school hours—and the sight of those canes in the principal's office gave ample credence to rumors that school was nothing but a torture chamber. And there was my allegiance to the gang.

But the thought of the strange woman's

---

14. **Mabaso:** (mä bä′ sô).

15. **Shangaan** (shäŋ gän′).

16. **Venda** (ven′ dä).

17. **Zulu and Sisotho** (zōō′ lōō, si sōō′ tōō).

lamentations over her dead son presented a somewhat strong case for going to school: I didn't want to end up dead in the streets. A more compelling argument for going to school, however, was the vivid recollection of all that humiliation and pain my mother had gone through to get me the papers and the birth certificate so I could enroll in school. What should I do? I was torn between two worlds.

But later that evening something happened to force me to go to school.

I was returning home from playing soccer when a neighbor accosted me by the gate and told me that there had been a bloody fight at my home.

"Your mother and father have been at it again," the neighbor, a woman, said.

"And your mother left."

I was stunned.

"Was she hurt badly?"

"A little bit," the woman said. "But she'll be all right. We took her to your grandma's place."

I became hot with anger.

"Is anyone in the house?" I stammered, trying to control my rage.

"Yes, your father is. But I don't think you should go near the house. He's raving mad. He's armed with a meat cleaver. He's chased out your brother and sisters, also. And some of the neighbors who tried to intervene—he's threatened to carve them to pieces. I have never seen him this mad before."

I brushed aside the woman's warnings and went. Shattered windows convinced me that there had indeed been a skirmish of some sort. Several pieces of broken bricks, evidently broken after being thrown at the door, were lying about the door. I tried opening the door; it was locked from the inside. I knocked. No one answered. I knocked again. Still no one answered, until, as I turned to leave:

"Who's out there?" my father's voice came growling from inside.

"It's me, Johannes," I said.

"Go away, you bastard!" he bellowed. "I don't want you or that mother of yours setting foot in this house. Go away before I come out there and kill you!"

"Let me in!" I cried. "Dammit, let me in! I want my things!"

"What things? Go away, you black swine!"

I went to the broken window and screamed obscenities at my father, daring him to come out, hoping that if he as much as ever stuck his black face out, I would pelt him with the half-a-loaf brick in my hand. He didn't come out. He continued launching a tirade of obscenities at my mother and her mother. He was drunk, but I wondered where he had gotten the money to buy beer, because it was still the middle of the week and he was dead broke. He had lost his entire wage for the past week in dice and had had to borrow bus fare.

"I'll kill you someday for all you're doing to my mother," I threatened him, overwhelmed with rage. Several nosey neighbors were beginning to congregate by open windows and doors. Not wanting to make a spectacle of myself, which was something many of our neighbors seemed to always expect from our family, I backtracked away from the door and vanished into the dark street. I ran, without stopping, all the way to the other end of the township where Granny lived. There I found my mother, her face swollen and bruised and her eyes puffed up to the point where she could scarcely see.

"What happened, Mama?" I asked, fighting to hold back the tears at the sight of her disfigured face.

"Nothing, child, nothing," she mumbled, almost apologetically, between swollen lips. "Your papa simply lost his temper, that's all."

"But why did he beat you up like this, Mama?" Tears came down my face. "He's never beaten you like this before."

My mother appeared reluctant to answer

me. She looked searchingly at Granny, who was pounding millet with pestle and mortar and mixing it with sorghum and nuts for an African delicacy. Granny said, "Tell him, child, tell him. He's got a right to know. Anyway, he's the cause of it all."

"Your father and I fought because I took you to school this morning," my mother began. "He had told me not to, and when I told him that I had, he became very upset. He was drunk. We started arguing, and one thing led to another."

"Why doesn't he want me to go to school?"

"He says he doesn't have money to waste paying for you to get what he calls a useless white man's education," my mother replied. "But I told him that if he won't pay for your schooling, I would try and look for a job and pay, but he didn't want to hear that, also. 'There are better things for you to work for,' he said. 'Besides, I don't want you to work. How would I look to other men if you, a woman I owned, were to start working?' When I asked him why shouldn't I take you to school, seeing that you were now of age, he replied that he doesn't believe in schools. I told him that school would keep you off the streets and out of trouble, but still he was belligerent."

"Is that why he beat you up?"

"Yes, he said I disobeyed his orders."

"He's right, child," Granny interjected. "He paid *lobola*[18] (bride price) for you. And your father ate it all up before he left me."

To which my mother replied, "But I desperately want to leave this beast of a man. But with his *lobola* gone I can't do it. That worthless thing you call your husband shouldn't have sold Jackson's scrawny cattle and left you penniless."

"Don't talk like that about your father, child," Granny said. "Despite all, he's still your father, you know. Anyway, he asked for *lobola* only because he had to get back what he spent raising you. And you know it would have been

taboo for him to let you or any of your sisters go without asking for *lobola*."

"You and Papa seemed to forget that my sisters and I have minds of our own," my mother said. "We didn't need you to tell us whom to marry, and why, and how. If it hadn't been for your interference, I could have married that schoolteacher."

Granny did not reply; she knew well not to. When it came to the act of "selling" women as marriage partners, my mother was vehemently opposed to it. Not only was she opposed to this one aspect of tribal culture, but to others as well, particularly those involving relations between men and women and the upbringing of children. But my mother's sharply differing opinion was an exception rather than the rule among tribal women. Most times, many tribal women questioned her sanity in daring to question well-established <u>mores</u>.[19] But my mother did not seem to care; she would always scoff at her opponents and call them fools in letting their husbands enslave them completely.

Though I disliked school, largely because I knew nothing about what actually went on there, and the little I knew had painted a dreadful picture, the fact that a father would not want his son to go to school, especially a father who didn't go to school, seemed hard to understand.

"Why do you want me to go to school, Mama?" I asked, hoping that she might, somehow, clear up some of the confusion that was building in my mind.

"I want you to have a future, child," my mother said. "And, contrary to what your father says, school is the only means to a future. I don't want you growing up to be like your father."

---

18. *lobola* (lô bō′ lä).

19. mores (mōr′ ēz): folkways that seem favorable to the welfare of a society and are followed by most people; often become incorporated into law.

The latter statement hit me like a bolt of lightning. It just about shattered every defense mechanism and every pretext I had against going to school.

"Your father didn't go to school," she continued, dabbing her puffed eyes to reduce the swelling with a piece of cloth dipped in warm water. "That's why he's doing some of the bad things he's doing. Things like drinking, gambling and neglecting his family. He didn't learn how to read and write; therefore, he can't find a decent job. Lack of any education has narrowly focused his life. He sees nothing beyond himself. He still thinks in the old, tribal way and still believes that things should be as they were back in the old days when he was growing up as a tribal boy in Louis Trichardt.[20] Though he's my husband, and your father, he doesn't see any of that."

"Why didn't he go to school, Mama?"

"He refused to go to school because his father led him to believe that an education was a tool through which white people were going to take things away from him, like they did black people in the old days. And that a white man's education was worthless insofar as black people were concerned because it prepared them for jobs they can't have. But I know it isn't totally so, child, because times have changed somewhat. Though our lot isn't any better today, an education will get you a decent job. If you can read and write you'll be better off than those of us who can't. Take my situation: I can't find a job because I don't have papers, and I can't get papers because white people mainly want to register people who can read and write. But I want things to be different for you, child. For you and your brother and sisters. I want you to go to school because I believe that an education is the key you need to open up a new world and a new life for yourself, a world and life different from that of either your father's or mine. It is the only key that can do that, and only those who

seek it earnestly and perseveringly will get anywhere in the white man's world. Education will open doors where none seem to exist. It'll make people talk to you, listen to you and help you, people who otherwise wouldn't bother. It will make you soar, like a bird lifting up into the endless blue sky, and leave poverty, hunger, and suffering behind. It'll teach you to learn to embrace what's good and shun what's bad and evil. Above all, it'll make you a somebody in this world. It'll make you grow up to be a good and proud person. That's why I want you to go to school, child, so that education can do all that, and more, for you."

A long, awkward silence followed, during which I reflected upon the significance of my mother's lengthy speech. I looked at my mother; she looked at me.

Finally, I asked, "How come you know so much about school, Mama? You didn't go to school, did you?"

"No, child," my mother replied. "Just like your father, I never went to school." For the second time that evening, a mere statement of fact had a thunderous impact on me. All the confusion I had about school seemed to leave my mind, like darkness giving way to light. And what had previously been a dark, yawning void in my mind was suddenly transformed into a beacon of light that began to grow larger and larger, until it had swallowed up, blotted out, all the blackness. That beacon of light seemed to reveal things and facts, which, though they must have always existed in me, I hadn't been aware of up until now.

"But unlike your father," my mother went on, "I've always wanted to go to school, but couldn't because my father, under the sway of tribal traditions, thought it unnecessary to educate females. That's why I so much want you to go, child, for if you do, I know that

---

20. **Louis Trichardt** (tri′ chärt): town in northern South Africa.

someday I too would come to go, old as I would be then. Promise me, therefore, that no matter what, you'll go back to school. And I, in turn, promise that I'll do everything in my power to keep you there."

With tears streaming down my cheeks and falling upon my mother's bosom, I promised her that I would go to school "forever." That night, at seven and a half years of my life, the battle lines in the family were drawn. My mother on the one side, illiterate but determined to have me drink, for better or for worse, from the well of knowledge. On the other side, my father, he too illiterate, yet determined to have me drink from the well of ignorance. Scarcely aware of the magnitude of the decision I was making or, rather, the decision which was being emotionally thrust upon me, I chose to fight on my mother's side, and thus my destiny was forever altered.

Classroom, Rooigrond, 1984, WENDY SCHWEGMANN. From *South Africa: The Cordoned Heart,* edited by Omar Badsha.

$\mathcal{T}$hinking About the Selection

A PERSONAL RESPONSE

sharing
impressions

1. What feelings do you have after reading this account? Jot down your impressions in your journal.

constructing
interpretations

2. What do you think is the greatest challenge that the narrator's mother faces in getting her son an education?

Think about

- regulations that discourage blacks from registering at school
- her husband's brutal opposition to her plans for her son
- the tribal traditions about the status of a married woman
- the influence of the gang on her son's attitude toward school

3. Do you agree with the narrator's mother that "education will open doors where none seem to exist"?

Think about

- what an education might do for the narrator
- what you wrote in your journal about the value of education
- any possible situations in which education would not "open doors"

A CREATIVE RESPONSE

4. How might this excerpt be different if the father shared the mother's views on the value of an education?

A CRITICAL RESPONSE

5. What do you think is the most important message that Mathabane wants to share in this selection?

Think about

- Mathabane's views about the junkyard and the school
- descriptions of the people in the township
- why Mathabane's father acts the way he does

6. What do you think a crusader against apartheid might especially value in this excerpt? Go back to the selection and find details to support your opinion.

Analyzing the Writer's Craft

DIALOGUE

Think about what Mathabane gains by presenting the exact words spoken by the characters to each other.

Building a Literary Vocabulary. Dialogue is written conversation between two or more characters. The use of dialogue brings characters to life and gives the reader insights into their qualities, or personality traits. For example, consider the dialogue between the strange woman and the narrator's mother. This conversation between a mother who has lost her son and a mother fighting heroically to keep hers dramatizes the regret and sorrow of the one and the sympathy and determination of the other.

Application: Interpreting Dialogue. Get together with two classmates. Identify an episode in which dialogue is used, such as the scene with the narrator and his mother and grandmother at the end of the excerpt. First identify the characters' qualities that are reflected in the dialogue. Then each of you should choose one of the characters and as a group prepare a dramatic reading to convey those qualities.

Connecting Reading and Writing

1. Imagine that you are young Mark Mathabane and that a gang member accosts you after you have started attending school. Write a **monologue** in which you defend the value of an education.

Option: Create the **script** for a public announcement on South African television in which Mark Mathabane as an adult implores young South African blacks to go to school.

2. In the preface to *Kaffir Boy,* Mark Mathabane wrote that his purpose in writing about his experiences was to make the rest of the world "understand why apartheid cannot be reformed: it has to be abolished." Research what others have said about the effects of apartheid. In an **expository** **essay** for your classmates, summarize what you learned about apartheid from your research and from reading the excerpt from *Kaffir Boy.*

Option: Write **notes** for a panel discussion on apartheid, summarizing what you have learned.

3. Read or reread Alice Walker's poem "Women" (page 49), noting how Walker's images of women compare with Mathabane's portrayal of his mother in the excerpt from *Kaffir Boy.* Discuss the two works in a **letter** to a friend who you think would enjoy reading them.

Option: Using "Women" as a model, write a **poem** about Mathabane's mother.

Hiccups

LÉON DAMAS

A biography of Damas appears on page 421.

Approaching the Poem

One of the most important human relationships is that between parent and child. In "Hiccups" by Léon Damas (le ôn′ dà mà′), the speaker tells about his relationship with his mother when he was a child. In the poem, Damas uses words of his mother's that still live in his memory. Léon Damas sought to affirm black values in his poetry. He grew up in French Guiana, a former French colony in South America populated mostly by blacks and Creoles of mixed black and white ancestry. Damas, a Creole, was sensitive to the rejection of blackness and African heritage he perceived in the dominant French culture of his country.

Connecting Writing and Reading

What qualities do you think characterize a good relationship between a parent and child? In your journal complete the following sentences with several possibilities:

A good parent always _____.
A good parent never _____.
A good parent sometimes _____.

Discuss your sentences with your classmates and try to draw some generalizations about what makes a good parent. As you read, compare your ideas with those expressed by the speaker about a relationship between a parent and child.

I gulp down seven drinks of water
several times a day
and all in vain
instinctively
5   like the criminal to the crime
my childhood returns
in a rousing fit of hiccups

Talk about calamity
talk about disasters
10   I'll tell you

My mother wanted her son to have good manners at the table:
                keep your hands on the table
                we don't cut bread
                we break it
15   we don't gobble it down
                the bread your father sweats for
                our daily bread

                eat the bones carefully and neatly
                a stomach has to have good manners too
20   and a well-bred stomach never
                burps
                a fork is not a tooth-pick
                don't pick your nose
                in front of the whole world
25   and sit up straight
                a well-bred nose
                doesn't sweep the plate

And then
and then
30   and then in the name of the Father
                        and the Son
                        and the Holy Ghost
at the end of every meal

And then and then
35   talk about calamity
talk about disasters
I'll tell you

My mother wanted her son to have the very best marks
      if you don't know your history
40   you won't go to mass
      tomorrow
      in your Sunday suit

This child will disgrace our family name
This child will be our . . . in the name of God
45   be quiet
      have I or have I not
      told you to speak French
      the French of France
      the French that Frenchmen speak
50   French French

Talk about calamity
talk about disasters
I'll tell you

My mother wanted her son to be a mama's boy:
55   you didn't say good evening to our neighbor
      what—dirty shoes again
      and don't let me catch you any more
      playing in the street or on the grass or in the park
      underneath the War Memorial
60   playing
      or picking a fight with what's-his-name
      what's-his-name who isn't even baptized

Talk about calamity
talk about disasters
65 I'll tell you

My mother wanted her son to be
      very *do*
      very *re*
      very *mi*
70   very *fa*
      very *sol*
      very *la*
      very *ti*
      very *do-re-mi*
75   *fa-sol-la-ti-*
          do

I see you haven't been to your vi-o-lin lesson
        a banjo
        did you say a banjo
80   what do you mean
        a banjo
        you really mean
        a banjo
        no indeed young man
85   you know there won't be any
            ban-or
              jo
                or
              gui-or
90   tar
                    in our house
They are not for *colored* people
Leave them to the *black* folks!

Thinking About the Poem

A PERSONAL RESPONSE

sharing impressions

1. In your journal, jot down words and phrases that describe your feelings about the speaker's mother.

constructing interpretations

2. What is your opinion of the relationship between the parent and child in this poem?

> ### Think about
> - the musical instruments each one prefers
> - the values of the speaker and the values of the mother
> - the ideas you wrote in your journal before reading

3. Do you think the speaker is justified in using the words *calamity* and *disasters* to refer to his childhood?

> ***Think about***
> - the reprimands of the mother
> - the speaker's use of the simile "like the criminal to the crime" to describe his recollection of childhood
> - why the speaker refers to himself as "her son" instead of "me"

A CREATIVE RESPONSE

4. If the speaker had grown up to be exactly what his mother wanted, what do you think he might have gained and lost?

A CRITICAL RESPONSE

5. The poet Léopold Sédar Senghor said that the poems of Léon Damas are "charged with an emotion concealed by humor." To what extent does this evaluation apply to the poem "Hiccups"? Support your answer by citing lines from the poem.

Connecting Reading and Writing

1. Imagine that the mother in the poem "Hiccups" had asked you how she might improve her relationship with her son. Express your views in an imagined **question/answer column** for a magazine about parenting.

Option: Write a **letter** to the mother, advising her about her relationship with her son.

2. Read or reread Langston Hughes's poem "Mother to Son" (page 43). Then write an **essay** for your classmates comparing what the two mothers seem to value.

Option: Imagine that the children of the two mothers are discussing their mothers' reactions to a real-life situation, such as their receiving a low grade on a test or quitting an after-school job. Create the **dialogue** that the two children might have in which they compare their mothers' values.

3. Read three or four other poems by Damas, such as "They Came That Night," "The Black Man's Lament," "Their Thing," and "Sleepless Night." Then write a **memo** to your teacher recommending which poem might be studied along with "Hiccups."

Option: Explore Damas's major issues in **annotations** to be given to your classmates to review as they prepare to listen to an oral interpretation of these poems.

from Arctic Dreams

BARRY LOPEZ

A biography of Lopez appears on page 426.

_A_pproaching the Selection

Barry Lopez is a contemporary writer known for accounts of his extensive world travels. These accounts often focus on the relationship between humankind and the natural environment. In the preface to _Arctic Dreams_, which follows, Lopez's eloquent description and poetic style create a vivid picture of the arctic wilderness—and raise questions about its future.

_B_uilding Vocabulary

These essential words are footnoted within the selection.

fecundity (fek ən' di tē): I would bow slightly . . . toward the birds and the evidence of life in their nests—because of their **fecundity.** (page 240)

benign (bi nīn'): I had never known how **benign** sunlight could be. (page 241)

gargantuan (gär gan' chŏŏ ən), **implacable** (im plā' kə bəl): Humboldt Glacier . . . calves icebergs into Kane Basin with **gargantuan** and **implacable** force. (page 242)

pervasive (pər vā' siv), **austerity** (ô ster' ə tē): Sharply pitched arctic mountain ranges . . . complete a **pervasive** suggestion of **austerity.** (page 242)

adumbration (ad' um brā' shən): It is a region, like the desert, rich with metaphor, with **adumbration.** (page 245)

_C_onnecting Writing and Reading

In your journal list three words that describe one of your favorite places in nature. Then briefly explain how you might feel if that place were being threatened by something beyond your control. As you read, compare your feelings about your favorite place with Lopez's feelings about the arctic wilderness and the threats to this natural environment.

from Arctic Dreams

BEYOND A REGARD for the landscape itself, this book finds its origin in two moments.

One summer evening I was camped in the western Brooks Range of Alaska with a friend. From the ridge where we had pitched our tent we looked out over tens of square miles of rolling tundra[1] along the southern edge of the calving grounds of the Western Arctic caribou herd. During those days we observed not only caribou and wolves, which we'd come to study, but wolverine and red fox, ground squirrels, delicate-legged whimbrels and aggressive jaegers, all in the unfoldings of their obscure lives. One night we watched in awe as a young grizzly bear tried repeatedly to force its way past a yearling wolf standing guard alone before a den of young pups. The bear eventually gave up and went on its way. We watched snowy owls and rough-legged hawks hunt and caribou drift like smoke through the valley.

On the evening I am thinking about—it was breezy there on Ilingnorak Ridge, and cold; but the late-night sun, small as a kite in the northern sky, poured forth an energy that burned against my cheekbones—it was on that evening that I went for a walk for the first time among the tundra birds. They all build their nests on the ground, so their vulnerability is extreme. I gazed down at a single horned lark no bigger than my fist. She stared back resolute as iron. As I approached, golden plovers abandoned their nests in hysterical ploys, artfully feigning a broken wing to distract me from the woven grass cups that couched their pale, darkly speckled eggs. Their eggs glowed with a soft, pure light, like the window light in a Vermeer[2] painting. I marveled at this intense

and concentrated beauty on the vast table of the plain. I walked on to find Lapland longspurs as still on their nests as stones, their dark eyes gleaming. At the nest of two snowy owls I stopped. These are more formidable animals than plovers. I stood motionless. The wild glare in their eyes receded. One owl settled back slowly over its three eggs, with an aura of primitive alertness. The other watched me, and immediately sought a bond with my eyes if I started to move.

I took to bowing on these evening walks. I would bow slightly with my hands in my pockets, toward the birds and the evidence of life in their nests—because of their fecundity,[3] unexpected in this remote region, and because of the serene arctic light that came down over the land like breath, like breathing.

I remember the wild, dedicated lives of the birds that night and also the abandon with which a small herd of caribou crossed the Kokolik River to the northwest, the incident of only a few moments. They pranced through like wild mares, kicking up sheets of water across the evening sun and shaking it off on the far side like huge dogs, a bloom of spray that glittered in the air around them like grains of mica.[4]

I remember the press of light against my face. The explosive skitter of calves among grazing caribou. And the warm intensity of the

---

1. **tundra** (tun′ drə): the vast, nearly level treeless plain of the Arctic.
2. **Vermeer** (vər mir′): Jan Vermeer (1632–1675), a Dutch painter famous for his treatment of light.
3. **fecundity** (fek ən′ di tē): fertility; productivity.
4. **mica** (mī′ kä): a mineral that crystallizes in thin, translucent layers.

eggs beneath these resolute birds. Until then, perhaps because the sun was shining in the very middle of the night, so out of tune with my own customary perception, I had never known how benign[5] sunlight could be. How forgiving. How run through with compassion in a land that bore so eloquently the evidence of centuries of winter.

During those summer days on Ilingnorak Ridge there was no dark night. Darkness never came. The birds were born. They flourished, and then flew south in the wake of the caribou.

The second incident is more fleeting. It occurred one night when I was being driven past a graveyard in Kalamazoo, Michigan. Among the gravestones was one marking the burial place of Edward Israel, a shy young man who sailed north in 1881 with Lieutenant Adolphus Greely. Greely and his men established a base camp on Ellesmere Island, 450 miles from the North Pole, and explored the surrounding territory in the spring of 1882. A planned relief expedition failed to reach them that summer, and also failed again the next year. Desperate, Greely's party of twenty-five retreated south, hopeful of being met by a rescue party in 1884. They wintered at Cape Sabine, Ellesmere Island, where sixteen of them died of starvation and scurvy,[6] another committed suicide, and one man was executed for stealing food. Israel, the expedition's astronomer, died on May 27, 1884, three weeks before the others were rescued. The survivors remembered him as the most congenial person among them.

I remember looking out the back window of the car that evening and seeing Israel's grave in the falling light. What had this man hoped to find? What sort of place did he think lay out there before him on that bright June morning in 1881 when the *Proteus* slipped its moorings at Saint John's, Newfoundland?

No one is able to say, of course. He was drawn on by the fixations of his own imagination, as were John Davis and William Baffin

before him and as Robert Peary and Vilhjalmur Stefansson[7] would be after him. Perhaps he intended to make his mark as a scientist, to set his teeth in that high arctic landscape and come home like Darwin[8] to a sedate and contemplative life, in the farmlands of southern Michigan. Perhaps he merely hungered after the unusual. We can only imagine that he desired something, the fulfillment of some personal and private dream, to which he pinned his life.

Israel was buried with great public feeling and patriotic rhetoric. His gravestone reads

IN LIFE A TRUE CHILD OF GOD
IN DEATH A HERO

These two incidents came back to me often in the four or five years that I traveled in the Arctic. The one, timeless and full of light, reminded me of sublime innocence, of the innate beauty of undisturbed relationships. The other, a dream gone awry, reminded me of the long human struggle, mental and physical, to come to terms with the Far North. As I traveled, I came to believe that people's desires and aspirations were as much a part of the land as the wind, solitary animals, and the bright fields of stone and tundra. And, too, the land itself existed quite apart from these.

The physical landscape is baffling in its ability to transcend whatever we would make of it.

---

5. **benign** (bi nīn'): favorable; beneficial; kindly.
6. **scurvy** (skʉr' vē): a disease resulting from lack of vitamin C and characterized by weakness and anemia.
7. **John Davis . . . Vilhjalmur Stefansson:** John Davis and William Baffin were Arctic explorers who sought the Northwest Passage to Asia. Robert Peary was the first explorer to reach the North Pole. Vilhjalmur Stefansson lived among Eskimos and used their means of survival in his Arctic explorations.
8. **Darwin:** Charles Darwin (1809–1882) was the English naturalist who developed the theory of evolution and who, after extensive travel and study, returned to England to write.

It is as subtle in its expression as turns of the mind, and larger than our grasp; and yet it is still knowable. The mind, full of curiosity and analysis, disassembles a landscape and then reassembles the pieces —the nod of a flower, the color of the night sky, the murmur of an animal—trying to fathom its geography. At the same time the mind is trying to find its place within the land, to discover a way to dispel its own sense of estrangement.

The particular section of the Arctic I became concerned with extends from Bering Strait in the west to Davis Strait[9] in the east. It includes great, unrelieved stretches of snow and ice that in summer become plains of open water and an ocean that is the tundra, a tawny island beneath the sky. But there are, too, surprising and riveting sights: Wilberforce Falls on the Hood River suddenly tumbles 160 feet into a wild canyon in the midst of the Canadian tundra, and its roar can be heard for miles. Humboldt Glacier, a towering, 50-mile-long sea margin of the Greenland ice sheet, calves[10] icebergs into Kane Basin with gargantuan[11] and implacable[12] force. The badlands of east-central Melville Island, an eroded country of desert oranges, of muted yellows and reds, reminds a traveler of canyons and arroyos in southern Utah. And there are places more exotic, like the Ruggles River, which flows out of Lake Hazen on Ellesmere Island in winter and runs 2,000 feet through the Stygian[13] darkness, wreathed in frost smoke, before it disappears underneath its own ice. South of Cape Bathurst and west of the Horton River in the Northwest Territories, bituminous shale fires that have been burning underground for hundreds of years make those coastal hills seem like a vast, smoldering heap of industrial slag. South of the central Kobuk River, one-hundred-foot dunes rise above hundreds of square miles of shifting sand. In East Greenland lies an arctic oasis called Queen Louisa Land, a valley of wild grasses and summer wildflowers surrounded by the walls of the Greenland ice cap.

The Arctic, overall, has the classic lines of a desert landscape: spare, balanced, extended, and quiet. In the Queen Elizabeth Islands the well-drained tundra plains and low-lying bogs more familiar in the south give way to expanses of weathered rock and gravel, and the illusion of a desert is even more complete. On Baffin and Ellesmere islands and in northern Alaska, sharply pitched arctic mountain ranges, which retain their remoteness even as you stand within them, complete a pervasive[14] suggestion of austerity.[15] The apparent monotony of the land is relieved, however, by weather systems moving through and by the activities of animals, particularly of birds and caribou. And because so much of the country stands revealed, and because sunlight passing through the dustless air renders its edges with such unusual sharpness, animals linger before the eye. And their presence is vivid.

Like other landscapes that initially appear barren, arctic tundra can open suddenly, like the corolla of a flower, when any intimacy with it is sought. One begins to notice spots of brilliant red, orange, and green, for example, among the monotonic browns of a tundra tussock. A wolf spider lunges at a glistening beetle. A shred of musk-ox wool lies inert in the

---

9. Bering Strait . . . Davis Strait: The Bering Strait separates Alaska from Siberia, U.S.S.R. The Davis Strait separates Greenland from Baffin Island, Canada.
10. calves: releases, as in giving birth to.
11. gargantuan (gär gan′ chōō ən): huge; monumental.
12. implacable (im plā′ kə bəl): relentless.
13. Stygian (stij′ ē ən): like the river Styx, which flowed around Hades, the world of the dead in Greek mythology.
14. pervasive (pər vā′ siv): tending to spread throughout.
15. austerity (ô ster′ ə tē): the quality or condition of being forbidding or very plain and severe.

lavender blooms of a saxifrage. When Alwin Pederson, a Danish naturalist, first arrived on the northeast coast of Greenland, he wrote, "I must admit to strange feelings at the sight of this godforsaken desert of stone." Before he left, however, he was writing of musk oxen grazing in lush grass that grew higher than the animals' heads in Jameson Land, and of the stark beauty of nunataks, the ice-free spires of rock that pierce the Pleistocene[16] stillness of the Greenland ice cap. I, like Pederson, when stooping to pick up the gracile rib bone of an arctic hare, would catch sudden and unexpected sight of the silken cocoon of an arctic caterpillar.

The wealth of biological detail on the tundra dispels any feeling that the land is empty; and its likeness to a stage suggests impending events. On a summer walk, the wind-washed air proves depthlessly clear. Time and again you come upon the isolated and succinct evidence of life—animal tracks, the undigested remains of a ptarmigan in an owl's casting, a patch of barren-ground willow nibbled nearly leafless by arctic hares. You are afforded the companionship of birds, which follow after you. (They know you are an animal; sooner or later you will turn up something to eat.) Sandpipers scatter before you, screaming *tuituek*, an Eskimo name for them. Coming awkwardly down a scree slope of frost-riven limestone you make a glass-tinkling clatter—and at a distance a tundra grizzly rises on its hind legs to study you; the dish-shaped paws of its front legs deathly still, the stance so human it is unnerving.

Along creek washouts, in the western Arctic especially, you might stumble upon a mammoth tusk. Or in the eastern Arctic find undisturbed the ring of stones used by a hunter 1500 years ago to hold down the edge of his skin tent. These old Dorset[17] camps, located along the coasts where arctic people have been traveling for four millennia, are poignant with their suggestion of the timeless determination of mankind. On rare occasions a traveler might come upon the more imposing stone foundations of a large house abandoned by Thule-culture[18] people in the twelfth century. (The cold, dry arctic air might have preserved, even down to its odor, the remains of a ringed seal killed and eaten by them 800 years ago.) More often, one comes upon the remains of a twentieth-century camp, artifacts far less engaging than a scrap of worked caribou bone, or carved wood, or skewered hide at a Dorset or Thule site. But these artifacts disintegrate just as slowly—red tins of Prince Albert brand crimp-cut tobacco, cans of Pet evaporated milk and Log Cabin maple syrup. In the most recent camps one finds used flashlight batteries in clusters like animal droppings and a bewildering variety of spent rifle and shotgun ammunition.

You raise your eyes from these remains, from whatever century, to look away. The land as far as you can see is rung with a harmonious authority, the enduring force of its natural history, of which these camps are so much a part. But the most recent evidence is vaguely disturbing. It does not derive in any clear way from the land. Its claim to being part of the natural history of the region seems, somehow, false.

It is hard to travel in the Arctic today and not be struck by the evidence of recent change. What is found at modern campsites along the coast points to the sudden arrival of a foreign technology—new tools and a new way of life

---

16. **Pleistocene** (plīs′ tō sēn′): a geologic period characterized by the spreading and retreating of continental ice sheets and the appearance of modern man.

17. **Dorset:** a prehistoric Arctic culture of nomadic hunters.

18. **Thule-culture** (thoo′ lē): a prehistoric whaling culture that followed the Dorset culture and preceded the modern Eskimo.

for the local people. The initial adjustments to this were fairly simple; the rate of change, however, has continued to accelerate. Now the adjustments required are bewildering. And the new tools bring with them ever more complicated sets of beliefs. The native culture, from Saint Lawrence Island to Greenland, is today in a state of rapid economic reorganization and of internally disruptive social readjustment. In a recent article about the residents of Nunivak Island, for example, a scientist wrote that the dietary shift from wild to store-bought foods (with the many nutritional and social complications involved) is proceeding so quickly it is impossible to pin down. "By the time this paper appears in print," he wrote, "much of the information in it will be of historical value only."

Industrial changes have also come to the Arctic, following the discovery of oil at Prudhoe Bay, Alaska, in 1968: the 800-mile-long trans-Alaska pipeline itself, with its recent Kuparuk extension; base camps for oil exploration on Canada's Melville Island and Tuktoyaktuk Peninsula; huge lead-zinc mining operations on northern Baffin and Little Cornwallis islands; hundreds of miles of new roads; and increased ship, air, and truck traffic. The region's normally violent and unpredictable weather, its extreme cold and long periods of darkness, the great distance to supply depots, and the problem of stabilizing permanent structures over permafrost (which melts and shifts in erratic ways) have made the cost of these operations astronomical—indeed, in Canada they could not even be contemplated without massive assistance from the federal government.

Seen as widely separated dots and lines on a map, these recent, radical changes do not appear to amount to very much. But their rippling effect in the settlements and villages of the North—their economic, psychological, and social impact—is acute. And their success, though marginal and in some instances artificial, encourages additional schemes for devel-

opment. Of special concern to local residents is a growing concentration of power in the hands of people with enormous economic resources but a poorly developed geographic sense of the region. A man from Tuktoyaktuk, a village near the mouth of the Mackenzie River, told me a pointed story. In the 1950's he traveled regularly up and down the coast by dogsled. When a distant early warning (DEW) line radar station went up along his accustomed route, he decided to stop to see what it was. The military men welcomed him not as a resident of the region but as a figure of arctic fable. They enthusiastically fed his dogs a stack of raw steaks. Each time the man came, they pounded him on the back and fed his dogs piles of steak. Their largess seemed so odd and his rapport with them so unrealistic he stopped coming. For months afterward, however, he had tremendous difficulty controlling the dogs anytime they passed near the place.

Passing through the villages, even traveling across the uninhabited land, one cannot miss the evidence of upheaval, nor avoid being wrenched by it. The depression it engenders, because so much of it seems a heedless imposition on the land and on the people, a rude invasion, can lead one to despair. I brooded, like any traveler, over these things; but the presence of the land, the sheer weight of it before the senses, more often drew me away from the contemporary issues. What, I wondered, had compelled me to bow to a horned lark? How do people imagine the landscapes they find themselves in? How does the land shape the imaginations of the people who dwell in it? How does desire itself, the desire to comprehend, shape knowledge? These questions seemed to me to go deeper than the topical issues, to underlie any consideration of them.

In pursuit of answers I traveled with people of differing dispositions. With Eskimos hunting narwhals off northern Baffin Island and walruses in the Bering Sea. With marine ecologists on hundreds of miles of coastal and near-shore surveys. With landscape painters in the Canadian Archipelago.[19] In the company of roughnecks, drilling for oil on the winter ice in high winds at −30° F; and with the cosmopolitan crew of a freighter, sailing up the west coast of Greenland and into the Northwest Passage. They each assessed the land differently—the apparent emptiness of the tundra, which ran out like a shimmering mirage in the Northern Ocean; the blue-black vault of the winter sky, a cold beauty alive with scintillating stars; a herd of musk oxen pivoting together on a hilltop to make a defensive stand, their long guard hairs swirling around them like a single, huge wave of dark water; a vein of lead-zinc ore glinting like tiny mirrors in a damp, Mesozoic[20] wall beneath the surface of Little Cornwallis Island; the moaning and wailing in the winter sea ice as the ocean's crust warped and shattered in the crystalline air. All of it, all that the land is and evokes, its actual meaning as well as its metaphorical reverberation, was and is understood differently.

These different views make a human future in that northern landscape a matter of conjecture, and it is here that one encounters dreams, projections of hope. The individual's dream, whether it be so private a wish as that the joyful determination of nesting arctic birds might infuse a distant friend weary of life, or a magnanimous wish that a piece of scientific information wrested from the landscape might serve one's community—in individual dreams is the hope that one's own life will not have been lived for nothing. The very much larger dream, that of a people, is a story we have been carrying with us for millennia. It is a narrative of determination and hope that follows a question: What will we do as the wisdom of our past bears down on our future? It is a story of ageless conversation, not only conversation among ourselves about what we mean and wish to do, but a conversation held with the land— our contemplation and wonder at a prairie thunderstorm, or before the jagged line of a young mountain, or at the sudden rise of ducks from an isolated lake. We have been telling ourselves the story of what *we* represent in the land for 40,000 years. At the heart of this story, I think, is a simple, abiding belief: it is possible to live wisely on the land, and to live well. And in behaving respectfully toward all that the land contains, it is possible to imagine a stifling ignorance falling away from us.

Crossing the tree line to the Far North, one leaves behind the boreal owl clutching its frozen prey to its chest feathers to thaw it. Ahead lies an open, wild landscape, pointed off on the maps with arresting and anomalous names: Brother John Glacier and Cape White Handkerchief. Navy Board Inlet, Teddy Bear Island, and the Zebra Cliffs. Dexterity Fiord, Saint Patrick Canyon, Starvation Cove. Eskimos hunt the ringed seal, still, in the broad bays of the Sons of Clergy and Royal Astronomical Society islands.

This is a land where airplanes track icebergs the size of Cleveland and polar bears fly down out of the stars. It is a region, like the desert, rich with metaphor, with adumbration.[21] In a simple bow from the waist before the nest of the horned lark, you are able to stake your life, again, in what you dream.

---

19. archipelago (är′ kə pel′ ə gō): a chain of many islands.
20. Mesozoic (mes′ ō zō′ ik): the geological period characterized by the development and extinction of dinosaurs and the appearance of flowering plants, grasses, and birds.
21. adumbration (ad′ um brā′ shən): vague foreshadowing or sketchy suggestion of things to come.

Eskimo at the Seal Hole, date unknown, HENRY NAPARTUK.

Thinking About the Selection

A PERSONAL RESPONSE

sharing impressions

1. What impressions of the arctic wilderness do you have after reading Lopez's account? Briefly describe your impressions in your journal.

constructing interpretations

2. What parts of Lopez's account did you find especially striking or interesting? Cite several descriptions or incidents.

3. Do you think that Lopez's hope for the future of the arctic wilderness—his belief that "it is possible to live wisely on the land"—is justified?

> **Think about**
> - his belief in the dreams of individuals that "one's own life will not have been lived for nothing"
> - the people he talks to as the basis for his hope
> - the rapid changes that are threats to the arctic wilderness
> - the magnitude and diversity of the Arctic

- the vulnerability of some animals, such as the nesting birds mentioned at the beginning
- your own views about the future of the arctic wilderness

4. How might Lopez's feelings about the arctic wilderness differ from the feelings of other people who have gone there?

Think about

- what his "bow from the waist" suggests about his feelings
- the feelings of Edward Israel and other explorers who risked their lives
- the feelings of the local residents
- the feelings of people who go for oil exploration, for mining, and for military purposes

A CREATIVE RESPONSE

5. *Arctic Dreams* was written before the tanker *Exxon Valdez* spilled 11 million gallons of oil in Prince William Sound and ruined one thousand miles of Alaskan coastline. How do you think this oil spill—the worst in U.S. history—affected Lopez's hope for the future of the arctic wilderness?

A CRITICAL RESPONSE

6. In the final paragraph of the selection, Lopez remarks that the Arctic is a region "rich with metaphor." Which of Lopez's metaphors conveyed impressions of the Arctic most powerfully for you? Cite specific passages to support your opinion.

7. Issues of conservation and environmental protection have assumed international importance since the 1970's. How well do you think Barry Lopez presents the environmental issues confronting the arctic wilderness? Support your response with details from the selection.

Analyzing the Writer's Craft

Think about the descriptions of the Arctic.

Building a Literary Vocabulary. Description is writing that helps a reader to picture scenes, events, and characters. Effective description enables a reader to see, hear, smell, taste, or feel the subject that is described. Imagery, figures of speech, and precise use of language as well as carefully selected detail create powerful description. In portraying the splendors of the Arctic,

Lopez uses highly poetic descriptions, such as: "I remember the press of light against my face."

Application: Examining Description. Working with a partner, choose one or two examples of description that you found particularly interesting or moving. Then write some generalizations about how Lopez's descriptions make you feel about the object or scene being described. Share your generalizations with another pair of students.

Connecting Reading and Writing

1. Imagine that you are an archaelogist who accompanied Lopez on his travels in the Arctic. Write a **catalog** for the arctic artifacts that you found and examined. Your catalog should include specific artifacts mentioned in the selection as well as some from your imagination.

Option: Write a **grant proposal** to the National Archaeological Foundation in which you describe your plans for an archaeological expedition to the Arctic, using a description of the artifacts you expect to find to support your case.

2. Environmental causes need full public support today. Write a **persuasive speech** on the benefits of safeguarding the balance between the needs of animals and the needs of humans in the Arctic.

Option: Develop **publicity slogans**—such as "Save the Whales," "Ban the Bomb," or "Only You Can Prevent Forest Fires"—for safeguarding the Arctic.

3. Imagine that *Arctic Dreams* is being made into a movie, and that as musical director, you have the job of choosing music that will reflect the mood established in the preface. Write an **annotation** for the piece that you choose, providing the name of the piece, its composer, and the reason why you think that piece is appropriate for the opening scene of the film.

Option: Use details from the preface to create a **poster** advertising the movie.

4. Write a **descriptive essay,** similar to Lopez's account of the Arctic, about your favorite place in nature for a Sierra Club writing contest. Use notes from your prereading journal entry.

Option: Draw, sketch, or find photographs to depict twelve scenes from nature that you find beautiful or interesting. Write **captions** to accompany the images for your own nature calendar.

certain way; and his help is simply to be enabled to move from one conundrum[2] to the next—one is tempted to say that he moves from one disaster to the next. When one begins looking for influences one finds them by the score. I haven't thought much about my own, not enough anyway; I hazard[3] that the King James Bible, the rhetoric[4] of the store-front church, something ironic and violent and perpetually understated in Negro speech—and something of Dickens' love for bravura[5]—have something to do with me today; but I wouldn't stake my life on it. Likewise, innumerable people have helped me in many ways; but finally, I suppose, the most difficult (and most rewarding) thing in my life has been the fact that I was born a Negro and was forced, therefore, to effect some kind of truce with this reality. (Truce, by the way, is the best one can hope for.)

One of the difficulties about being a Negro writer (and this is not special pleading, since I don't mean to suggest that he has it worse than anybody else) is that the Negro problem is written about so widely. The bookshelves groan under the weight of information, and everyone therefore considers himself informed. And this information, furthermore, operates usually (generally, popularly) to reinforce traditional attitudes. Of traditional attitudes there are only two—For or Against—and I, personally, find it difficult to say which attitude has caused me the most pain. I am speaking as a writer; from a social point of view I am perfectly aware that the change from ill will to goodwill, however motivated, however imperfect, however expressed, is better than no change at all.

But it is part of the business of the writer—as I see it—to examine attitudes, to go beneath the surface, to tap the source. From this point of view the Negro problem is nearly inaccessible. It is not only written about so widely; it is written about so badly. It is quite possible to say that the price a Negro pays for becoming articulate is to find himself, at length, with nothing to be articulate about. ("You taught me language," says Caliban to Prospero, "and my profit on't is I know how to curse.")[6] Consider: the tremendous social activity that this problem generates imposes on whites and Negroes alike the necessity of looking forward, of working to bring about a better day. This is fine, it keeps the waters troubled; it is all, indeed, that has made possible the Negro's progress. Nevertheless, social affairs are not generally speaking the writer's prime concern, whether they ought to be or not; it is absolutely necessary that he establish between himself and these affairs a distance which will allow, at least, for clarity, so that before he can look forward in any meaningful sense, he must first be allowed to take a long look back. In the context of the Negro problem neither whites nor blacks, for excellent reasons of their own, have the faintest desire to look back; but I think that the past is all that makes the present coherent, and further, that the past will remain horrible for exactly as long as we refuse to assess it honestly.

I know, in any case, that the most crucial time in my own development came when I was forced to recognize that I was a kind of bastard of the West; when I followed the line of my past I did not find myself in Europe but in Africa. And this meant that in some subtle way, in a really profound way, I brought to

---

2. conundrum (kə nun′ drəm): puzzling question or problem.

3. hazard: say at the risk of being incorrect.

4. rhetoric (ret′ ər ik): the art of using words effectively in speaking or writing.

5. bravura (brə vyoor′ ə): bold attempts or displays of daring.

6. ("You taught . . . curse."): Caliban is a deformed, brutish creature enslaved and taught to speak by the magician Prospero in William Shakespeare's play *The Tempest*. This quotation is from Act One, Scene 2, lines 364–365.

Man, 1959, CHARLES WHITE. Heritage Gallery, Los Angeles.

Shakespeare, Bach, Rembrandt, to the stones of Paris, to the cathedral at Chartres, and to the Empire State Building, a special attitude. These were not really my creations, they did not contain my history; I might search in them in vain forever for any reflection of myself. I was an interloper;[7] this was not my heritage. At the same time I had no other heritage which I could possibly hope to use—I had certainly been unfitted for the jungle or the tribe. I would have to appropriate these white centuries, I would have to make them mine—I would have to accept my special attitude, my special place in this scheme—otherwise I would have no place in *any* scheme. What was the most difficult was the fact that I was forced to admit something I had always hidden from myself, which the American Negro has had to hide from himself as the price of his public progress; that I hated and feared white people. This did not mean that I loved black people; on the contrary, I despised them, possibly because they failed to produce Rembrandt. In effect, I hated and feared the world. And this meant, not only that I thus gave the world an altogether murderous power over me, but also that in such a self-destroying limbo I could never hope to write.

One writes out of one thing only—one's own experience. Everything depends on how relentlessly one forces from this experience the last drop, sweet or bitter, it can possibly give. This is the only real concern of the artist, to re-create out of the disorder of life that order which is art. The difficulty then, for me, of being a Negro writer was the fact that I was, in effect, prohibited from examining my own experience too closely by the tremendous demands and the very real dangers of my social situation.

I don't think the dilemma outlined above is uncommon. I do think, since writers work in the disastrously explicit medium of language, that it goes a little way toward explaining why, out of the enormous resources of Negro speech and life, and despite the example of Negro music, prose written by Negroes has been generally speaking so pallid and so harsh. I have not written about being a Negro at such length because I expect that to be my only subject, but only because it was the gate I had to unlock before I could hope to write about anything else. I don't think that the Negro problem in America can be even discussed coherently without bearing in mind its context; its context being the history, traditions, customs, the moral assumptions and preoccupations of the country; in short, the general social fabric. Appearances to the contrary, no one in America escapes its effects and everyone in America bears some responsibility for it. I believe this the more firmly because it is the overwhelming tendency to speak of this problem as though it were a thing apart. But in the work of Faulkner, in the general attitude and certain specific passages in Robert Penn Warren, and, most significantly, in the advent of Ralph Ellison, one sees the beginnings—at least—of a more genuinely penetrating search. Mr. Ellison, by the way, is the first Negro novelist I have ever read to utilize in language, and brilliantly, some of the ambiguity and irony of Negro life.

About my interests: I don't know if I have any, unless the morbid desire to own a sixteen-millimeter camera and make experimental movies can be so classified. Otherwise, I love to eat and drink—it's my melancholy conviction that I've scarcely ever had enough to eat (this is because it's *impossible* to eat enough if you're worried about the next meal)—and I love to argue with people who do not disagree with me too profoundly, and I love to laugh. I do *not* like bohemia, or bohemians,[8] I do not like people whose principal aim is pleasure, and I do not like people who are *earnest* about

---

7. interloper (in′ tər lō′ pər): intruder.

8. bohemians (bō hē′ mē ənz): artists or writers who adopt a mode of life in protest against or in defiance of the common conventions of society.

anything. I don't like people who like me because I'm a Negro; neither do I like people who find in the same accident grounds for contempt. I love America more than any other country in the world, and, exactly for this reason, I insist on the right to criticize her perpetually. I think all theories are suspect, that the finest principles may have to be modified, or may even be pulverized by the demands of life, and that one must find, therefore, one's own moral center and move through the world hoping that this center will guide one aright. I consider that I have many responsibilities, but none greater than this: to last, as Hemingway says, and get my work done.

I want to be an honest man and a good writer.

Thinking About the Essay

A PERSONAL RESPONSE

sharing impressions

1. What thoughts about writing and writers do you have after reading this selection? Jot them down in your journal.

constructing interpretations

2. What impression have you formed of James Baldwin as a person from your reading of these autobiographical notes?

3. Explain whether you agree with Baldwin's ideas about being a writer.
   Think about
   • how your prereading journal notes about becoming a writer compare with the course Baldwin follows
   • Baldwin's belief that "it is part of the business of the writer . . . to examine attitudes, to go beneath the surface, to tap the source"
   • why he says "social affairs are not generally speaking the writer's prime concern"
   • how he believes the writer must use his or her own experience
   • what he says about the work of William Faulkner, Robert Penn Warren, and Ralph Ellison

A CREATIVE RESPONSE

4. How might this essay be different if Baldwin had lived in a predominantly African-American society?

A CRITICAL RESPONSE

5. How do you think the paradox that a writer "could be helped in a certain way only because he was hurt in a certain way" relates to Baldwin's process of becoming a writer? Use specific details from the essay to support your answer.

6. To what extent do Baldwin's concerns apply to all writers? Explain your answer, citing examples of both general concerns and concerns that apply only to minority writers.

*A*nalyzing the Writer's Craft

CONFLICT

What are some of the outside forces that make it difficult for Baldwin to become a writer?

Building a Literary Vocabulary. Conflict is a struggle between opposing forces. An external conflict involves a character pitted against an outside force—nature, society, a physical obstacle, or another character. One of the earliest external conflicts Baldwin faces is with his father, who wants him to be a preacher, not a writer. Baldwin also has internal conflicts—conflicts between opposing tendencies within himself. One such internal conflict concerns his recognition on the one hand that he is an interloper who does not share the European heritage and his realization on the other hand that he must nevertheless appropriate it in order to have any heritage at all.

Application: Understanding Conflict. With a partner, go back through the selection and list all of the conflicts that Baldwin faced as he emerged as a writer. Identify each conflict as external or internal. Then illustrate his conflicts on a diagram similar to the one that follows. When you have finished, exchange diagrams with another pair of students and discuss any differences in the conflicts shown.

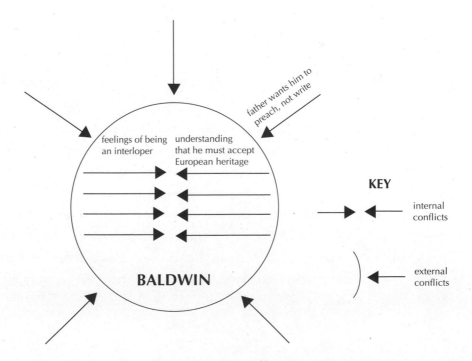

Connecting Reading and Writing

1. Write a **sermon,** addressed to your community, on the theme "Take a long look back." Use quotations from Baldwin and incidents from his life to support your points.

Option: Write an **editorial,** to be published in a major newspaper such as *The New York Times,* urging the nation to examine its past. Incorporate some of Baldwin's ideas in your editorial.

2. Think about an incident in which you, like Baldwin, wanted to achieve a goal but had to resolve both internal and external conflicts to do so. Describe that incident in an **autobiographical sketch** to be shared with your friends.

Option: Create an **outline** for a speech to be given to your classmates describing your goal and the conflicts you faced.

3. Norman Mailer, an American writer born just one year before Baldwin, said of him, "Not one of us hasn't learned something about the art of the essay from him." Write a **letter** to Mailer in which you describe what you have learned about essay writing from reading this selection.

Option: Create a **report card** grading Baldwin as an essay writer on such categories as structure, development of ideas, supporting detail, and use of language.

4. Expanding upon your answer to question 2, analyze James Baldwin's character for an **introduction** to a collection of his essays.

Option: Analyze his character in a **personality profile** to be published in a magazine about celebrities.

INSIGHT

from **Life in His Language**

Toni Morrison, widely acclaimed for her novel Beloved, *eulogized James Baldwin at his funeral service, held at the Cathedral of St. John the Divine in New York City on December 8, 1987. The following paragraph is part of this eulogy.*

You gave me a language to dwell in, a gift so perfect it seems my own invention. I have been thinking your spoken and written thoughts for so long I believed they were mine. I have been seeing the world through your eyes for so long, I believed that clear clear view was my own. Even now, even here, I need you to tell me what I am feeling and how to articulate it. So I have pored again through the 6,895 pages of your published work to acknowledge the debt and thank you for the credit. No one possessed or inhabited language for me the way you did. You made American English honest—genuinely international.

from American Hunger

RICHARD WRIGHT

A biography of Wright appears on page 431.

Approaching the Selection

Richard Wright surmounted the barriers of poverty and racial bias to become one of the most powerful African-American writers of the twentieth century. After a desolate childhood in his grandmother's household, Wright left the South and moved North. Arriving in Chicago at the age of nineteen, he worked at odd jobs—including being a dishwasher in a café—to earn a living while trying to establish himself as a writer. Wright eventually moved in with his aunt. When he was joined by his mother and brother, the apartment became unbearably crowded. *American Hunger* is the story of Wright's life in Chicago. In this excerpt he describes the various hungers that haunt him in his new surroundings.

M Y FIRST GLIMPSE of the flat black stretches of Chicago depressed and dismayed me, mocked all my fantasies. Chicago seemed an unreal city whose mythical houses were built of slabs of black coal wreathed in palls of gray smoke, houses whose foundations were sinking slowly into the dank prairie. Flashes of steam showed intermittently on the wise horizon, gleaming translucently in the winter sun. The din of the city entered my consciousness, entered to remain for years to come. The year was 1927.

What would happen to me here? Would I survive? My expectations were modest. I wanted only a job. Hunger had long been my daily companion. Diversion and recreation, with the exception of reading, were unknown. In all my life—though surrounded by many people—I had not had a single satisfying, sustained relationship with another human being and, not having had any, I did not miss it. I made no demands whatever upon others. . . .

I worked at the café all spring and in June I was called for temporary duty in the post office. My confidence soared; if I obtained an appointment as a regular clerk, I could spend at least five hours a day writing.

I reported at the post office and was sworn in as a temporary clerk. I earned seventy cents an hour and I went to bed each night now with a full stomach for the first time in my life. When I worked nights, I wrote during the day; when I worked days, I wrote during the night.

But the happiness of having a job did not keep another worry from rising to plague me. Before I could receive a permanent appointment I would have to take a physical examination. The weight requirement was one hundred and twenty-five pounds and I—with my long years of semistarvation—barely tipped the scales at a hundred and ten. Frantically I turned all of my spare money into food and ate. But my skin and flesh would not respond to the food. Perhaps I was not eating the right diet? Perhaps my chronic anxiety kept my weight down? I drank milk, ate steak, but it did not give me an extra ounce of flesh. I visited a doctor who told me that there was nothing wrong with me except malnutrition, that I must eat and sleep long hours. I did and my weight remained the same. I knew now that my job was temporary and that when the time came for my appointment, I would have to resume my job hunting again.

At night I read Stein's *Three Lives*, Crane's *The Red Badge of Courage*, and Dostoevski's *The Possessed*, all of which revealed new realms of feeling. But the most important discoveries came when I veered from fiction proper into the field of psychology and sociology. I ran through volumes that bore upon the causes of my conduct and the conduct of my people. I studied tables of figures relating population density to insanity, relating housing to disease, relating school and recreational opportunities to crime, relating various forms of neurotic behavior to environment, relating racial insecurities to the conflicts between whites and blacks. . . .

I still had no friends, casual or intimate, and felt the need for none. I had developed a self-sufficiency that kept me distant from others, emotionally and psychologically. Occasionally I went to house-rent parties, parties given by working-class families to raise money to pay the landlord, the admission to which was a quarter or a half dollar. At these affairs I drank home-brewed beer, ate spaghetti and chitterlings,[1] laughed and talked with black, Southern-born girls who worked as domestic

---

1. **chitterlings:** the small intestines of hogs, sometimes filled with highly seasoned chopped meat and then fried or boiled.

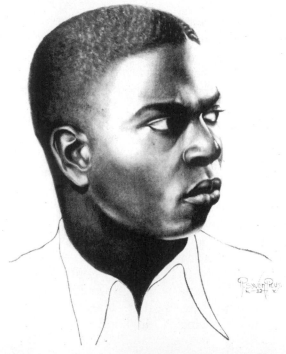

Portrait of a Singer,
1932, ROBERT SAVON PIOUS.
Hampton University Museum.

servants in white middle-class homes. But with none of them did my relations rest upon my deepest feelings. I discussed what I read with no one, and to none did I confide. Emotionally, I was withdrawn from the objective world; my desires floated loosely within the walls of my consciousness, contained and controlled.

As a protective mechanism, I developed a terse, cynical[2] mode of speech that rebuffed those who sought to get too close to me. Conversation was my way of avoiding expression; my words were reserved for those times when I sat down alone to write. My face was always a deadpan or a mask of general friendliness; no word or event could jar me into a gesture of enthusiasm or despair. A slowly, hesitantly spoken "Yeah" was my general verbal reaction to almost everything I heard. "That's pretty good," said with a slow nod of the head, was my approval. "Aw, naw," muttered with a cold smile, was my rejection. Even though I reacted deeply, my true feelings raced along underground, hidden.

I did not act in this fashion deliberately; I did not prefer this kind of relationship with people. I wanted a life in which there was a constant oneness of feeling with others, in which the basic emotions of life were shared, in which common memory formed a common past, in which collective hope reflected a national future. But I knew that no such thing was possible in my environment. The only ways in which I felt that my feelings could go outward without fear of rude rebuff or searing reprisal[3] was in writing or reading, and to me they were ways of living . . . .

Repeatedly I took stabs at writing, but the results were so poor that I would tear up the sheets. I was striving for a level of expression that matched those of the novels I read. But I always somehow failed to get onto the page what I thought and felt. Failing at sustained narrative, I compromised by playing with single sentences and phrases. Under the influence of Stein's *Three Lives,* I spent hours and days pounding out disconnected sentences for the sheer love of words.

I would write:

"The soft melting hunk of butter trickled in gold down the stringy grooves of the split yam."

Or:

"The child's clumsy fingers fumbled in sleep, feeling vainly for the wish of its dream."

"The old man huddled in the dark doorway, his bony face lit by the burning yellow in the windows of distant skyscrapers."

My purpose was to capture a physical state or movement that carried a strong subjective impression, an accomplishment which seemed supremely worth struggling for. If I could fasten the mind of the reader upon words so firmly that he would forget words and be conscious only of his response, I felt that I would be in sight of knowing how to write narrative. I strove to master words, to make them disappear, to make them important by making them new, to make them melt into a rising spiral of emotional stimuli, each greater than the other, each feeding and reinforcing the other, and all ending in an emotional climax that would drench the reader with a sense of a new world. That was the single aim of my living.

Autumn came and I was called for my physical examination for the position of regular postal clerk. I had not told my mother or brother or aunt that I knew I would fail. On the morning of the examination I drank two quarts of buttermilk, ate six bananas, but it did not hoist the red arrow of the government scales to the required mark of one hundred and

---

2. **cynical** (sinʹ i kəl): doubting the sincerity of people's motives and actions.
3. **reprisal** (ri prīʹ zəl): the doing of injury in return for injury received; retaliation.

twenty-five pounds. I went home and sat disconsolately in my back room, hating myself, wondering where I could find another job. I had almost got my hands upon a decent job and had lost it, had let it slip through my fingers. Waves of self-doubt rose to haunt me. Was I always to hang on the fringes of life? What I wanted was truly modest, and yet my past, my diet, my hunger, had snatched it from before my eyes. But these self-doubts did not last long; I dulled the sense of loss through reading, reading, writing, and more writing. . . .

I asked for my job back at the café and the boss lady allowed me to return; again I served breakfast, washed dishes, carted trays of food up into the apartments. Another postal examination was scheduled for spring, and to that end I made eating an obsession. I ate when I did not want to eat, drank milk when it sickened me. Slowly my starved body responded to food and overcame the lean years of Mississippi, Arkansas, and Tennessee, counteracting the flesh-sapping anxiety of fear-filled days.

I read Proust's *A Remembrance of Things Past,* admiring the lucid, subtle but strong prose, stupefied by its dazzling magic, awed by the vast, delicate, intricate, and psychological structure of the Frenchman's epic of death and decadence. But it crushed me with hopelessness, for I wanted to write of the people in my environment with an equal thoroughness, and the burning example before my eyes made me feel that I never could.

My ability to endure tension had now grown amazingly. From the accidental pain of Southern years, from anxiety that I had sought to avoid, from fear that had been too painful to bear, I had learned to like my unintermit-

tent burden of feeling, had become habituated to acting with all of my being, had learned to seek those areas of life, those situations, where I knew that events would complement my own inner mood. I was conscious of what was happening to me; I knew that my attitude of watchful wonder had usurped all other feelings, had become the meaning of my life, an integral part of my personality; that I was striving to live and measure all things by it. Having no claims upon others, I bent the way the wind blew, rendering unto my environment that which was my environment's, and rendering unto myself that which I felt was mine.

It was a dangerous way to live, far more dangerous than violating laws or ethical codes of conduct; but the danger was for me and me alone. Had I not been conscious of what I was doing, I could have easily lost my way in the fogbound regions of compelling fantasy. Even so, I floundered, staggered; but somehow I always groped my way back to that path where I felt a tinge of warmth from an unseen light.

Hungry for insight into my own life and the lives about me, knowing my fiercely indrawn nature, I sought to fulfill more than my share of all obligations and responsibilities, as though offering libations of forgiveness to my environment. Indeed, the more my emotions claimed my attention, the sharper—as though in ultimate self-defense—became my desire to measure accurately the reality of the objective world so that I might more than meet its demands. At twenty years of age the mold of my life was set, was hardening into a pattern, a pattern that was neither good nor evil, neither right nor wrong.

Reviewing Concepts

THE CLASH OF CULTURES: CONFRONTING OPPOSING VALUES

*making
connections*

The writers in this unit present a variety of situations in which the opposing values of two cultures generate conflicts. In the excerpt from *Kaffir Boy,* for example, Mark Mathabane describes how the opposing values of his father and mother resulted in an inner conflict for him: The traditional way of life held onto by his father clashes with his mother's desire to see her son educated so that he can overcome ignorance and make his way in the world. Mathabane decides to attend the tribal school, thus siding with his mother's values.

Think back over the cultural conflicts presented by the writers in this unit. Then make a chart like the one that follows. For each selection, identify one character who is in conflict and the opposing values that create the conflict. Then describe how the character handles the conflict. An example from *Kaffir Boy* is provided for you.

Characters in conflict	Opposing values	Handling of conflict
Mark Mathabane from *Kaffir Boy*	traditional way of life held onto by Mathabane's father and his mother's desire to see her son educated so that he can overcome ignorance and make his way in the world	Mathabane decides to attend the tribal school, thus siding with his mother's values.

*describing
connections*

Review the information on your chart. Then choose the character you admire the most and the character you admire the least for his or her handling of a cultural conflict. Write an **essay** supporting your choices and share your writing with your classmates.

Flower Vendor, EMILIO AMERO.
Galeria San Fronteras, Austin, Texas.

Engaging the Imagination

> "*Something should remind us once more that the great things in this universe are things that we never see.*"
>
> MARTIN LUTHER KING, JR.

Engaging the Imagination

Have you ever thought about why so many people enjoy stories and movies about monsters, ghosts, alien creatures, and extraordinary events? Ordinarily, life includes such mundane activities as washing the car, taking out the garbage, and doing homework. The life of the imagination, however, extends beyond the ordinary, familiar world. Through imagination, people can push back the limits of experience, exploring what might be or what might have been. They can go farther on the wings of imagination than on the feet of realism.

The first three works in this unit can be classified as fantasy, or imaginative literature that consciously disregards the restraints of reality. Fantasy presents a challenge to readers, who are asked to accept, without question, impossible occurrences. In a fantasy, the narrative is often ambiguous, leaving readers unsure of what happens at the end or even of what is happening throughout. When the imagination is engaged, however, readers readily take up the challenge.

The other works in this unit treat realistic subjects in highly imaginative ways. Poets Frank Marshall Davis, Wendy Rose, Diana Chang, Leslie Marmon Silko, and Pablo Neruda go beyond mere realistic representation, taking a fresh and original look at their subjects. In "The Form of the Sword," prose writer Jorge Luis Borges enshrouds realistic events in a dreamlike atmosphere.

As you read the following selections, savor the sometimes bizarre, often striking, experiences described by the writers. Re-create these experiences in your own imagination, and transcend the limits of the mundane world around you.

$\mathcal{L}$*iterary Vocabulary*

INTRODUCED IN THIS UNIT

Style: Magical Realism. Style is the particular way that a piece of literature is written. Style refers not so much to what is said but to how it is said. Magical realism is a style of writing that often includes exaggeration, unusual humor, magical and bizarre events, dreams that come true, and superstitions that prove warranted. Magical realism differs from pure fantasy in combining fantastic elements with realistic elements such as recognizable characters, believable dialogue, a true-to-life setting, a matter-of-fact tone, and a plot that sometimes contains historical events.

Mood. Mood is the feeling, or atmosphere, that a writer creates for the reader. Setting, figurative language, and imagery (words and phrases that re-create experiences by appealing to any of the five senses) contribute to the mood of a work, as do the sound and rhythm of the language used. For example, in Léon Damas's poem "Hiccups," the repeated lines "Talk about calamity / talk about disasters" help to create a mood of grim humor.

Personification. Personification is a figure of speech in which human qualities are attributed to an object, animal, or idea. In several poems in the Native American tradition, the speakers address natural objects using terms of endearment, such as *mother* or *father*. This technique suggests a close relationship between the speaker and nature.

REVIEWED IN THIS UNIT

Diction

A Very Old Man with Enormous Wings

GABRIEL GARCÍA MÁRQUEZ

Translated from the Spanish

A biography of García Márquez appears on page 422.

*A*pproaching the Story

Nobel Prize winner Gabriel García Márquez is a native of Colombia, a country in South America that borders on both the Pacific Ocean and the Caribbean Sea. His novels and stories contain supernatural elements and fantastic events that are accepted by the characters as plausible. García Márquez frequently draws upon the myths and superstitions of the townspeople whom he knew as a child.

*B*uilding Vocabulary

These essential words are footnoted within the story.

terrestrial (tə res′ trē əl): His main feathers had been mistreated by **terrestrial** winds. (page 268)

hermetic (hər met′ ik): He awoke with a start, ranting in his **hermetic** language. (page 269)

cataclysm (kat′ ə kliz′ əm), **repose** (ri pōz′): His passivity was . . . that of a **cataclysm** in **repose.** (page 269)

providential (präv′ ə den′ shəl), **tribulations** (trib′ yōo lā′ shənz): Those meager letters might have come and gone until the end of time if a **providential** event had not put an end to the priest's **tribulations.** (page 269)

*C*onnecting Writing and Reading

In your journal, name something that you feel is beyond your understanding. This might be a school subject, a work of art, or a concept, such as nature. Describe the feelings you have when you are confronted by this thing. Keep these feelings in mind as you read this story about people who are confronted with something beyond their understanding.

ON THE THIRD day of rain they had killed so many crabs inside the house that Pelayo[1] had to cross his drenched courtyard and throw them into the sea because the newborn child had a temperature all night and they thought it was due to the stench. The world had been sad since Tuesday. Sea and sky were a single ash-gray thing, and the sands of the beach, which on March nights glimmered like powdered light, had become a stew of mud and rotten shellfish. The light was so weak at noon that when Pelayo was coming back to the house after throwing away the crabs, it was hard for him to see what it was that was moving and groaning in the rear of the courtyard. He had to go very close to see that it was an old man, a very old man, lying face down in the mud, who, in spite of his tremendous efforts, couldn't get up, impeded by his enormous wings.

Frightened by that nightmare, Pelayo ran to get Elisenda,[2] his wife, who was putting compresses on the sick child, and he took her to the rear of the courtyard. They both looked at the fallen body with mute stupor. He was dressed like a ragpicker. There were only a few faded hairs left on his bald skull and very few teeth in his mouth, and his pitiful condition of a drenched great-grandfather had taken away any sense of grandeur he might have had. His huge buzzard wings, dirty and half-plucked, were forever entangled in the mud. They looked at him so long and so closely that Pelayo and Elisenda very soon overcame their surprise and in the end found him familiar. Then they dared speak to him, and he answered in an incomprehensible dialect with a strong sailor's voice. That was how they skipped over the inconvenience of the wings and quite intelligently concluded that he was a lonely castaway from some foreign ship wrecked by the storm. And yet, they called in a neighbor woman who knew everything about life and death to see him, and all she needed was one look to show them their mistake.

"He's an angel," she told them. "He must have been coming for the child, but the poor fellow is so old that the rain knocked him down."

On the following day everyone knew that a flesh-and-blood angel was held captive in Pelayo's house. Against the judgment of the wise neighbor woman, for whom angels in those times were the fugitive survivors of a celestial conspiracy, they did not have the heart to club him to death. Pelayo watched over him all afternoon from the kitchen, armed with his bailiff's club, and before going to bed he dragged him out of the mud and locked him up with the hens in the wire chicken coop. In the middle of the night, when the rain stopped, Pelayo and Elisenda were still killing crabs. A short time afterward the child woke up without a fever and with a desire to eat. Then they felt magnanimous and decided to put the angel on a raft with fresh water and provisions for three days and leave him to his fate on the high seas. But when they went out into the courtyard with the first light of dawn, they found the whole neighborhood in front of the chicken coop having fun with the angel, without the slightest reverence, tossing him things to eat through the openings in the wire as if he weren't a supernatural creature but a circus animal.

Father Gonzaga[3] arrived before seven o'clock, alarmed at the strange news. By that time onlookers less frivolous than those at dawn had already arrived, and they were making all kinds of conjectures concerning the captive's future. The simplest among them thought that he should be named mayor of the world. Others of sterner mind felt that he

---

1. **Pelayo** (pe lä′ yô).
2. **Elisenda** (e lē sen′ dä).
3. **Gonzaga** (gôn sä′ gä).

should be promoted to the rank of five-star general in order to win all wars. Some visionaries hoped that he could be put to stud in order to implant on earth a race of winged wise men who could take charge of the universe. But Father Gonzaga, before becoming a priest, had been a robust woodcutter. Standing by the wire, he reviewed his catechism[4] in an instant and asked them to open the door so that he could take a close look at that pitiful man, who looked more like a huge decrepit hen among the fascinated chickens. He was lying in a corner drying his open wings in the sunlight among the fruit peels and breakfast leftovers that the early risers had thrown him. Alien to the impertinences of the world, he only lifted his antiquarian eyes and murmured something in his dialect when Father Gonzaga went into the chicken coop and said good morning to him in Latin. The parish priest had his first suspicion of an imposter when he saw that he did not understand the language of God or know how to greet His ministers. Then he noticed that, seen close up, he was much too human: he had an unbearable smell of the outdoors, the back side of his wings was strewn with parasites and his main feathers had been mistreated by terrestrial[5] winds, and nothing about him measured up to the proud dignity of angels. Then he came out of the chicken coop and in a brief sermon warned the curious against the risks of being ingenuous. He reminded them that the devil had the bad habit of making use of carnival tricks in order to confuse the unwary. He argued that if wings were not the essential element in determining the difference between a hawk and an airplane, they were even less so in the recognition of angels. Nevertheless, he promised to write a letter to his bishop so that the latter would write to his primate so that the latter would write to the Supreme Pontiff[6] in order to get the final verdict from the highest courts.

His prudence fell on sterile hearts. The news of the captive angel spread with such rapidity that after a few hours the courtyard had the bustle of a marketplace and they had to call in troops with fixed bayonets to disperse the mob that was about to knock the house down. Elisenda, her spine all twisted from sweeping up so much marketplace trash, then got the idea of fencing in the yard and charging five cents admission to see the angel.

The curious came from far away. A traveling carnival arrived with a flying acrobat who buzzed over the crowd several times, but no one paid any attention to him because his wings were not those of an angel but, rather, those of a sidereal bat. The most unfortunate invalids on earth came in search of health: a poor woman who since childhood had been counting her heartbeats and had run out of numbers; a Portuguese man who couldn't sleep because the noise of the stars disturbed him; a sleepwalker who got up at night to undo the things he had done while awake; and many others with less serious ailments. In the midst of that shipwreck disorder that made the earth tremble, Pelayo and Elisenda were happy with fatigue, for in less than a week they had crammed their rooms with money, and the line of pilgrims waiting their turn to enter still reached beyond the horizon.

The angel was the only one who took no part in his own act. He spent his time trying to get comfortable in his borrowed nest, befuddled by the hellish heat of the oil lamps and sacramental candles that had been placed along the wire. At first they tried to make him eat some mothballs, which, according to the wisdom of the wise neighbor woman, were the food prescribed for angels. But he turned them down, just as he turned down the papal

---

4. catechism (kat′ ə kiz′ əm): a set of questions and answers for teaching the principles of Christianity.
5. terrestrial (tə res′ trē əl): of this world; earthly.
6. Supreme Pontiff: the Pope.

lunches that the penitents brought him, and they never found out whether it was because he was an angel or because he was an old man that in the end he ate nothing but eggplant mush. His only supernatural virtue seemed to be patience, especially during the first days when the hens pecked at him, searching for the stellar parasites that proliferated in his wings, and the cripples pulled out feathers to touch their defective parts with, and even the most merciful threw stones at him, trying to get him to rise so they could see him standing. The only time they succeeded in arousing him was when they burned his side with an iron for branding steers, for he had been motionless for so many hours that they thought he was dead. He awoke with a start, ranting in his hermetic[7] language and with tears in his eyes, and he flapped his wings a couple of times, which brought on a whirlwind of chicken dung and lunar dust and a gale of panic that did not seem to be of this world. Although many thought that his reaction had been one not of rage but of pain, from then on they were careful not to annoy him, because the majority understood that his passivity was not that of a hero taking his ease but that of a cataclysm[8] in repose.[9]

Father Gonzaga held back the crowd's frivolity with formulas of maidservant inspiration[10] while awaiting the arrival of a final judgment on the nature of the captive. But the mail from Rome showed no sense of urgency. They spent their time finding out if the prisoner had a navel, if his dialect had any connection with Aramaic,[11] how many times he could fit on the head of a pin, or whether he wasn't just a Norwegian with wings. Those meager letters might have come and gone until the end of time if a providential[12] event had not put an end to the priest's tribulations.[13]

It so happened that during those days, among so many other carnival attractions, there arrived in town the traveling show of the woman who had been changed into a spider for having disobeyed her parents. The admission to see her was not only less than the admission to see the angel, but people were permitted to ask her all manner of questions about her absurd state and to examine her up and down so that no one would ever doubt the truth of her horror. She was a frightful tarantula the size of a ram and with the head of a sad maiden. What was most heart-rending, however, was not her outlandish shape but the sincere affliction with which she recounted the details of her misfortune. While still practically a child, she had sneaked out of her parents' house to go to a dance, and while she was coming back through the woods, after having danced all night without permission, a fearful thunderclap rent the sky in two, and through the crack came the lightning bolt of brimstone that changed her into a spider. Her only nourishment came from the meatballs that charitable souls chose to toss into her mouth. A spectacle like that, full of so much human truth and with such a fearful lesson, was bound to defeat, without even trying, that of a haughty angel who scarcely deigned to look at mortals. Besides, the few miracles attributed to the angel showed a certain mental disorder, like the blind man who didn't recover his sight but grew three new teeth, or the paralytic who

---

7. **hermetic** (hər met′ ik): hard to understand; obscure.

8. **cataclysm** (kat′ ə kliz′ əm): any great upheaval that causes sudden and violent changes.

9. **repose** (ri pōz′): rest.

10. **formulas of maidservant inspiration:** superstitions.

11. **Aramaic** (ar′ ə mā′ ik): ancient Semitic language; one of its dialects was spoken by Jesus and his disciples.

12. **providential** (präv′ ə den′ shəl): as if decreed by God.

13. **tribulations** (trib′ yo͞o lā′ shənz): things that cause suffering or distress.

didn't get to walk but almost won the lottery, and the leper whose sores sprouted sunflowers. Those consolation miracles, which were more like mocking fun, had already ruined the angel's reputation when the woman who had been changed into a spider finally crushed him completely. That was how Father Gonzaga was cured forever of his insomnia and Pelayo's courtyard went back to being as empty as during the time it had rained for three days and crabs walked through the bedrooms.

The owners of the house had no reason to lament. With the money they saved, they built a two-story mansion with balconies and gardens and high netting so that crabs wouldn't get in during the winter, and with iron bars on the windows so that angels wouldn't get in. Pelayo also set up a rabbit warren close to town and gave up his job as bailiff for good, and Elisenda bought some satin pumps with high heels and many dresses of iridescent silk, the kind worn on Sunday by the most desirable women in those times. The chicken coop was the only thing that didn't receive any attention. If they washed it down with creolin and burned tears of myrrh inside it every so often, it was not in homage to the angel but to drive away the dung-heap stench that still hung everywhere like a ghost and was turning the new house into an old one. At first, when the child learned to walk, they were careful that he not get too close to the chicken coop. But then they began to lose their fears and got used to the smell, and before the child got his second teeth he'd gone inside the chicken coop to play, where the wires were falling apart. The angel was no less standoffish with him than with other mortals, but he tolerated the most ingenious infamies with the patience of a dog who had no illusions. They both came down with chickenpox at the same time. The doctor who took care of the child couldn't resist the temptation to listen to the angel's heart, and he found so much whistling in the heart and so many sounds in his kidneys that it seemed impossible for him to be alive. What surprised him most, however, was the logic of his wings. They seemed so natural on that completely human organism that he couldn't understand why other men didn't have them too.

When the child began school, it had been some time since the sun and rain had caused the collapse of the chicken coop. The angel went dragging himself about here and there like a stray dying man. They would drive him out of the bedroom with a broom and a moment later find him in the kitchen. He seemed to be in so many places at the same time that they grew to think that he'd been duplicated, that he was reproducing himself all through the house, and the exasperated and unhinged Elisenda shouted that it was awful living in that hell full of angels. He could scarcely eat, and his antiquarian eyes had also become so foggy that he went about bumping into posts. All he had left were the bare cannulae[14] of his last feathers. Pelayo threw a blanket over him and extended him the charity of letting him sleep in the shed, and only then did they notice that he had a temperature at night and was delirious with the tongue twisters of an old Norwegian. That was one of the few times they became alarmed, for they thought he was going to die, and not even the wise neighbor woman had been able to tell them what to do with dead angels.

And yet he not only survived his worst winter, but seemed improved with the first sunny days. He remained motionless for several days in the farthest corner of the courtyard, where no one would see him, and at the beginning of December some large, stiff feathers began to grow on his wings, the feathers of a scarecrow, which looked more like another misfortune of decrepitude. But he must have known the rea-

---

14. cannulae (kan′ yo͞o lē′): hollow tubes.

son for those changes, for he was quite careful that no one should notice them, that no one should hear the sea chanteys[15] that he sometimes sang under the stars. One morning Elisenda was cutting some bunches of onions for lunch when a wind that seemed to come from the high seas blew into the kitchen. Then she went to the window and caught the angel in his first attempts at flight. They were so clumsy that his fingernails opened a furrow in the vegetable patch and he was on the point of knocking the shed down with the ungainly flapping that slipped on the light and couldn't get a grip on the air. But he did manage to gain altitude. Elisenda let out a sigh of relief, for herself and for him, when she saw him pass over the last houses, holding himself up in some way with the risky flapping of a senile venture. She kept watching him even when she was through cutting the onions, and she kept on watching until it was no longer possible for her to see him, because then he was no longer an annoyance in her life but an imaginary dot on the horizon of the sea.

---

15. sea chanteys (shan′ tēz): songs formerly sung by sailors as they worked.

Thinking About the Story

A PERSONAL RESPONSE

sharing impressions

1. What would you say to the writer of this story if you could meet him? Respond in your journal.

constructing interpretations

2. What is your theory about who the winged man is and why he came to be in the town?

Think about
- the initial beliefs that Pelayo, Elisenda, the neighbor woman, and Father Gonzaga hold about who he is
- ways in which he does or does not fit common conceptions about angels
- the miracles attributed to him
- conditions in Pelayo and Elisenda's household both when he comes and when he leaves

3. What ideas do you get from this story about the ways human beings respond to things beyond their understanding?

> ***Think about***
> - how the winged man is treated by the crowds that come to see him
> - the kinds of evidence that Father Gonzaga and the Church look for to determine whether the winged man is an angel
> - why the crowds desert the winged man in favor of the spider woman

4. How accurate is the view of human beings presented in this story?

> ***Think about***
> - your own reactions to things that are beyond your understanding
> - how the townspeople's behavior compares to crowd behavior you have witnessed at zoos, carnivals, or other spectacles

A CREATIVE RESPONSE

5. Where do you think the winged man is going as he flies away?

A CRITICAL RESPONSE

6. What, in your opinion, is gained by using a third-person omniscient point of view in this story?

> ***Think about***
> - third-person omniscient point of view as the narrative technique in which the narrator stands outside the action and sees into the minds of more than one character
> - what the story would be like if told from a single character's point of view

7. What words would you use to describe the tone of this story?

> ***Think about***
> - tone as a writer's attitude toward his or her subject
> - verbal or situational ironies that you detect in this story

8. Think about the society depicted in this story. How would you compare this society with contemporary American society? Support your ideas with details from the story and examples from everyday life.

Analyzing the Writer's Craft

STYLE: MAGICAL REALISM

How realistic does this story seem to you?

Building a Literary Vocabulary. Style is the particular way in which a piece of literature is written. Style refers not so much to what is said but to how it is said. García Márquez writes in a style called magical realism, which often includes exaggeration, unusual humor, magical and bizarre events, dreams that come true, and superstitions that prove warranted. Magical realism differs from pure fantasy in combining fantastic elements with realistic elements such as recognizable characters, believable dialogue, a true-to-life setting, a matter-of-fact tone, and a plot that sometimes contains historical events. The central event in this story, the discovery of a winged man, is, of course, fantastic. Yet the man is described in realistic detail—he is old, bald, and toothless; his wings harbor parasites; his feathers are missing or in disarray.

Application: Imitating Style. Identify more of the details that make the winged man seem realistic. Then consider what the writer might have done had he wanted to make the spider woman seem as plausible as the winged man. Try to maintain the style of García Márquez as you add a new paragraph to the story, describing the spider woman in more realistic detail. Volunteers should read their paragraphs aloud, and the class as a whole might vote on the most convincing addition.

Connecting Reading and Writing

1. Write an **eyewitness account** that a reporter might submit to a local newspaper, describing the unusual events that occur in this story.

Option: Create a series of sensational **headlines** that a tabloid might use in conveying the main events of the story.

2. Retell this story from the viewpoint of the winged man in **notes** that he might have made on hidden scraps of paper.

Option: Write a **human interest story** that the winged man might submit to a weekly magazine after arriving at his destination.

3. In an interview with a reporter, García Márquez once said, "The truth is that there's not a single line in all my work that does not have a basis in reality." Respond to this statement in a **letter** to the writer, basing your comments on this story.

Option: Discuss the writer's statement in a **review** of the story intended for a radio program.

4. Write a **sequel** to this story telling what happens when the old man arrives in your community. Imitate the magical realism used by García Márquez.

Option: Extend this story in a **dramatic scene** that can be performed for the class.

The Youngest Doll

ROSARIO FERRÉ

A biography of Ferré appears on page 422.

Approaching the Story

"The Youngest Doll" by Rosario Ferré (rô sä′ rē ô̄ fer rä′) is set in Puerto Rico at the beginning of the twentieth century, a period of great change. The island had been controlled by powerful families who owned the sugar cane, coffee, and tobacco plantations on which the economy was based. The wealth and influence of these families declined after the Spanish-American War in 1898, when the island was surrendered to the United States. The economy, dominated by foreign investors, became more industrialized, and a class of newly rich businessmen and professionals arose.

This short story portrays members of the old aristocracy and the rising wealthy classes. Like the previous story, this story challenges the reader's expectations with strange turns of events.

Building Vocabulary

These essential words are footnoted within the story.

furtively (fur′ tiv lē): They would sit around her and **furtively** lift the starched ruffle of her skirt. (page 275)

ostentatious (äs′ tən tā′ shəs): He would always show up wearing . . . an **ostentatious** tiepin of extravagantly poor taste. (page 277)

exorbitant (eg zor′ bi tənt): The whole town . . . didn't mind paying **exorbitant** fees. (page 278)

Connecting Writing and Reading

In your journal jot down what comes to mind when you hear the term "living doll." What would be the gender, appearance, and personality of someone described by this label? Would you want to be described this way? As you read, be aware of how the term "living doll" changes and takes on new meanings in your mind.

ARLY IN THE morning the maiden aunt took her rocking chair out onto the porch facing the cane fields, as she always did whenever she woke up with the urge to make a doll. As a young woman, she had often bathed in the river, but one day when the heavy rains had fed the dragontail current, she had a soft feeling of melting snow in the marrow of her bones. With her head nestled among the black rocks' reverberations, she could hear the slamming of salty foam on the beach rolled up with the sound of waves, and she suddenly thought that her hair had poured out to sea at last. At that very moment, she felt a sharp bite in her calf. Screaming, she was pulled out of the water and, writhing in pain, was taken home on a stretcher.

The doctor who examined her assured her it was nothing, that she had probably been bitten by an angry river prawn.[1] But days passed and the scab wouldn't heal. A month later the doctor concluded that the prawn had worked its way into the soft flesh of her calf and had nestled there to grow. He prescribed a mustard plaster so that the heat would force it out. The aunt spent a whole week with her leg covered with mustard from thigh to ankle, but when the treatment was over, they found that the ulcer had grown even larger and that it was covered with a slimy, stonelike substance that couldn't be removed without endangering the whole leg. She then resigned herself to living with the prawn permanently curled up in her calf.

She had been very beautiful, but the prawn hidden under the long, gauzy folds of her skirt stripped her of all vanity. She locked herself up in her house, refusing to see any suitors. At first she devoted herself entirely to bringing up her sister's children, dragging her enormous leg around the house quite nimbly. In those days, the family was nearly ruined; they lived surrounded by a past that was breaking up around them with the same impassive musicality with which the dining room chandelier crumbled on the frayed linen cloth of the dining room table. Her nieces adored her. She would comb their hair, bathe and feed them, and when she read them stories, they would sit around her and furtively[2] lift the starched ruffle of her skirt so as to sniff the aroma of ripe sweetsop[3] that oozed from her leg when it was at rest.

As the girls grew up, the aunt devoted herself to making dolls for them to play with. At first they were just plain dolls, with cotton stuffing from the gourd tree and stray buttons sewn on for eyes. As time passed, though, she began to refine her craft, gaining the respect and admiration of the whole family. The birth of a doll was always cause for a ritual celebration, which explains why it never occurred to the aunt to sell them for profit, even when the girls had grown up and the family was beginning to fall into need. The aunt had continued to increase the size of the dolls so that their height and other measurements conformed to those of each of the girls. There were nine of them, and the aunt made one doll for each per year, so it became necessary to set aside a room for the dolls alone. When the eldest turned eighteen, there were one hundred and twenty-six dolls of all ages in the room. Opening the door gave the impression of entering a dovecote or the ballroom in the Czarina's[4] palace or a warehouse in which someone had spread out a row of tobacco leaves to dry. But the aunt did not enter the room for any of these pleasures. Instead, she would unlatch the door and gently pick up each doll, murmuring a lullaby as

---

1. **prawn** (prôn): a shellfish similar to a large shrimp.
2. **furtively** (fur′ tiv lē): sneakily; not openly.
3. **sweetsop**: a sweet, pungent-smelling, quickly ripening tropical fruit common in Puerto Rico.
4. **Czarina** (zä rē′ nə): the wife of a czar, the emperor of Russia.

she rocked it: "This is how you were when you were a year old, this is you at two, and like this at three," measuring out each year of their lives against the hollow they left in her arms.

The day the eldest had turned ten, the aunt sat down in her rocking chair facing the cane fields and never got up again. She would rock away entire days on the porch, watching the patterns of rain shift in the cane fields, coming out of her stupor only when the doctor paid a visit or whenever she awoke with the desire to make a doll. Then she would call out so that everyone in the house would come and help her. On that day, one could see the hired help making repeated trips to town like cheerful Inca messengers, bringing wax, porcelain clay, lace, needles, spools of thread of every color. While these preparations were taking place, the aunt would call the niece she had dreamt about the night before into her room and take her measurements. Then she would make a wax mask of the child's face, covering it with plaster on both sides, like a living face wrapped in two dead ones. She would draw out an endless flaxen thread of melted wax through a pinpoint on its chin. The porcelain of the hands and face was always translucent; it had an ivory tint to it that formed a great contrast with the curdled whiteness of the bisque faces. For the body, the aunt would send out to the garden for twenty glossy gourds. She would hold them in one hand, and with an expert twist of her knife, would slice them up against the railing of the balcony, so that the sun and breeze would dry out the cottony *guano*[5] brains. After a few days, she would scrape off the dried fluff with a teaspoon and, with infinite patience, feed it into the doll's mouth.

The only items the aunt would agree to use that were not made by her were the glass eyeballs. They were mailed to her from Europe in all colors, but the aunt considered them useless until she had left them submerged at the bottom of the stream for a few days, so that they could learn to recognize the slightest stirring of the prawns' antennae. Only then would she carefully rinse them in ammonia water and place them, glossy as gems and nestled in a bed of cotton, at the bottom of one of her Dutch cookie tins. The dolls were always dressed in the same way, even though the girls were growing up. She would dress the younger ones in Swiss embroidery and the older ones in silk *guipure*,[6] and on each of their heads she would tie the same bow, wide and white and trembling like the breast of a dove.

The girls began to marry and leave home. On their wedding day, the aunt would give each of them their last doll, kissing them on the forehead and telling them with a smile, "Here is your Easter Sunday." She would reassure the grooms by explaining to them that the doll was merely a sentimental ornament, of the kind that people used to place on the lid of grand pianos in the old days. From the porch, the aunt would watch the girls walk down the staircase for the last time. They would carry a modest checkered cardboard suitcase in one hand, the other hand slipped around the waist of the exuberant doll made in their image and likeness, still wearing the same old-fashioned kid slippers and gloves, and with Valenciennes[7] bloomers barely showing under their snowy, embroidered skirts. But the hands and faces of these new dolls looked less transparent than those of the old: they had the consistency of skim milk. This difference concealed a more subtle one: the wedding doll was never stuffed with cotton but filled with honey.

All the older girls had married and only the youngest was left at home when the doctor paid his monthly visit to the aunt, bringing

---

5. *guano* (gwä′ nō): relating to a type of palm tree.

6. *guipure* (gē pyꝏr′): a kind of lace.

7. Valenciennes (və len′ sē enz′): a kind of lace originating in the French city of Valenciennes.

along his son, who had just returned from studying medicine up north. The young man lifted the starched ruffle of the aunt's skirt and looked intently at the huge, swollen ulcer which oozed a perfumed sperm from the tip of its greenish scales. He pulled out his stethoscope and listened to her carefully. The aunt thought he was listening for the breathing of the prawn to see if it was still alive, and she fondly lifted his hand and placed it on the spot where he could feel the constant movement of the creature's antennae. The young man released the ruffle and looked fixedly at his father. "You could have cured this from the start," he told him. "That's true," his father answered, "but I just wanted you to come and see the prawn that has been paying for your education these twenty years."

From then on it was the young doctor who visited the old aunt every month. His interest in the youngest was evident from the start, so the aunt was able to begin her last doll in plenty of time. He would always show up wearing a pair of brightly polished shoes, a starched collar, and an ostentatious[8] tiepin of extravagantly poor taste. After examining the aunt, he would sit in the parlor, lean his paper silhouette against the oval frame of the chair and, each time, hand the youngest an identical bouquet of purple forget-me-nots. She would offer him ginger cookies, taking the bouquet squeamishly with the tips of her fingers, as if she were handling a sea urchin turned inside out. She made up her mind to marry him because she was intrigued by his sleepy profile and also because she was deathly curious to see what the dolphin flesh was like.

On her wedding day, as she was about to leave the house, the youngest was surprised to find that the doll her aunt had given her as a wedding present was warm. As she slipped her arm around its waist, she looked at it curiously, but she quickly forgot about it, so amazed was she at the excellence of its craft. The doll's face and hands were made of the most delicate Mikado porcelain. In the doll's half-open and slightly sad smile she recognized her full set of baby teeth. There was also another notable detail: the aunt had embedded her diamond eardrops inside the doll's pupils.

The young doctor took her off to live in town, in a square house that made one think of a cement block. Each day he made her sit out on the balcony, so that passersby would be sure to see that he had married into high society. Motionless inside her cubicle of heat, the youngest began to suspect that it wasn't only her husband's silhouette that was made of paper, but his soul as well. Her suspicions were soon confirmed. One day, he pried out the doll's eyes with the tip of his scalpel and pawned them for a fancy gold pocket watch with a long embossed chain. From then on the doll remained seated on the lid of the grand piano, but with her gaze modestly lowered.

A few months later, the doctor noticed the doll was missing from her usual place and asked the youngest what she'd done with it. A sisterhood of pious ladies had offered him a healthy sum for the porcelain hands and face, which they thought would be perfect for the image of the Veronica in the next Lenten procession.[9]

The youngest answered that the ants had at last discovered the doll was filled with honey and, streaming over the piano, had devoured it in a single night. "Since its hands and face were of Mikado porcelain," she said, "they must have thought they were made of sugar and at this very moment they are most likely

---

8. ostentatious (äs′ tən tā′ shəs): showy; flashy.

9. The Veronica in the next Lenten procession: The Veronica is the image of Jesus' face said in legend to have appeared on the veil or handkerchief used by Saint Veronica to wipe the bleeding face of Jesus. A Lenten procession is a ceremony held during Lent, the period of forty weekdays from Ash Wednesday to Easter held holy by Christian churches.

wearing down their teeth, gnawing furiously at its fingers and eyelids in some underground burrow." That night the doctor dug up all the ground around the house, to no avail.

As the years passed, the doctor became a millionaire. He had slowly acquired the whole town as his clientele, people who didn't mind paying exorbitant[10] fees in order to see a genuine member of the extinct sugar cane aristocracy up close. The youngest went on sitting in her rocking chair on the balcony, motionless in her muslin and lace, and always with lowered eyelids. Whenever her husband's patients, draped with necklaces and feathers and carrying elaborate canes, would seat themselves beside her, shaking their self-satisfied rolls of flesh with a jingling of coins, they would notice a strange scent that would involuntarily remind them of a slowly oozing sweetsop. They would then feel an uncomfortable urge to rub their hands together as though they were paws.

There was only one thing missing from the doctor's otherwise perfect happiness. He noticed that although he was aging, the youngest still kept that same firm, porcelained skin she had had when he would call on her at the big house on the plantation. One night he decided to go into her bedroom to watch her as she slept. He noticed that her chest wasn't moving. He gently placed his stethoscope over her heart and heard a distant swish of water. Then the doll lifted her eyelids, and out of the empty sockets of her eyes came the frenzied antennae of all those prawns.

---

10. **exorbitant** (eg zorʹ bi tənt): going beyond what is usual; excessive.

Thinking About the Story

A PERSONAL RESPONSE

sharing impressions

1. What questions do you have after reading this story? Note them in your journal.

constructing interpretations

2. How do you explain what the young doctor observes when he enters his wife's bedroom?

3. Does the term "living doll" have different associations for you now that you have read this story?

Think about
- how the term describes the dolls that the maiden aunt makes
- how the term describes the women in the story, particularly the youngest niece
- how positively or negatively you now view the term

4. Speculate about what the aunt hopes to accomplish by making dolls.
    Think about
- what she does when she is not making dolls
- how closely the dolls resemble her nieces
- why she submerges the dolls' eyeballs in the stream
- what she means by telling her nieces, "Here is your Easter Sunday" as she gives them their wedding dolls

5. Which character is most evil and which is most victimized?
    Think about
- the admission the old doctor makes to his son
- the reasons why the young doctor and the youngest niece marry
- the young doctor's treatment of his wife and the doll
- the degree of control the aunt has over her own fate and her youngest niece's fate

A CREATIVE RESPONSE

6. If the aunt had not belonged to an aristocratic family, would the prawn bite have affected her life in the same way?

A CRITICAL RESPONSE

7. How do you think the writer views Puerto Rican society at the turn of the century?
    Think about
- the values of the old doctor, the young doctor, and the young doctor's clientele
- the values and position of the sugar cane aristocracy
- the lives led by the women in the story
- the possible symbolism of the prawn, the hidden ulcer, and the scent of oozing sweetsop

8. What common stylistic elements do you see in "The Youngest Doll" and "A Very Old Man with Enormous Wings"?

Analyzing the Writer's Craft

MOOD

Think about the feeling you get as you read: "the aroma of ripe sweetsop that oozed from her leg."

Building a Literary Vocabulary. Mood is the feeling, or atmosphere, that the writer creates for the reader. One element that contributes strongly to mood is imagery, words and phrases that re-create experiences by appealing to any of the five senses. A literary work may evoke more than one mood, as the descriptions "bittersweet love story" and "tragicomedy" would suggest. In "The Youngest Doll" the image of ripe, oozing sweetsop creates a mood of both richness and decay.

Application: Defining Mood. At the top of a sheet of paper, write two words that describe two different moods you find in "The Youngest Doll." Below these labels list images from the story that help create these two moods. The images may be in different passages or in the same passage. Compare your findings with those of your classmates to see how many moods are evoked by the story and to reinforce your understanding of the relationship between mood and imagery.

Connecting Reading and Writing

1. Suppose a friend turns to you after reading this story and says, "I just don't get it." In an **informal note** to him or her, explain what you think happens in the story.

Option: Write your own **story** relating events from the viewpoint of the aunt, the youngest niece, or the doll itself.

2. Imagine that the doll has been acquired by a prestigious auction house and is being offered for sale. Write **catalog copy** describing the doll.

Option: Advertise the doll in a **TV commercial** for a home shopping network.

3. In an **essay** for your literature class, analyze the writer's comparison of women to dolls in this story

and comment on whether such a comparison is still valid among high school students today.

Option: Present your ideas in a **pamphlet** for distribution at a political rally.

4. Compare "The Youngest Doll" to another story by Rosario Ferré, such as "The Gift" in her collection *Sweet Diamond Dust* or "The Poisoned Tale" in *Short Stories by Latin American Women: The Magic and The Real.* Make some generalizations about Ferré's style and major themes and prepare a **list of questions** to ask her in a radio interview about her writing.

Option: Describe Ferré's style and themes in a brief **profile** intended for a reference book on Latin American writers.

What I Have Been Doing Lately

JAMAICA KINCAID

A biography of Kincaid appears on page 425.

*A*pproaching the Story

Jamaica Kincaid is a Caribbean-born writer now living in the United States. This story is an experimental work in which the characters are not named, events are left unexplained, and reality is uncertain.

*C*onnecting Writing and Reading

Recall some of the more unusual aspects of the two previous stories in this unit. In your journal jot down words and phrases that come to mind. As you read, compare your impressions of the other stories with the bizarre and surprising aspects of this story.

What I Have Been Doing Lately

HAT I HAVE been doing lately: I was lying in bed and the doorbell rang. I ran downstairs. Quick. I opened the door. There was no one there. I stepped outside. Either it was drizzling or there was a lot of dust in the air and the dust was damp. I stuck out my tongue and the drizzle or the damp dust tasted like government school ink. I looked north. I looked south. I decided to start walking north. While walking north, I noticed that I was barefoot. While walking north, I looked up and saw the planet Venus. I said, "It must be almost morning." I saw a monkey in a tree. The tree had no leaves. I said, "Ah, a monkey. Just look at that. A monkey." I walked for I don't know how long before I came up to a big body of water. I wanted to get across it but I couldn't swim. I wanted to get across it but it would take me years to build a boat. I wanted to get across it but it would take me I didn't know how long to build a bridge. Years passed and then one day, feeling like it, I got into my boat and rowed across. When I got to the other side, it was noon and my shadow was small and fell beneath me. I set out on a path that stretched out straight ahead. I passed a house, and a dog was sitting on the verandah, but it looked the other way when it saw me coming. I passed a boy tossing a ball in the air but the boy looked the other way when he saw me coming. I walked and I walked but I couldn't tell if I walked a long time because my feet didn't feel as if they would drop off. I turned around to see what I had left behind me but nothing was familiar. Instead of the straight path, I saw hills. Instead of the boy

with his ball, I saw tall flowering trees. I looked up and the sky was without clouds and seemed near, as if it were the ceiling in my house and, if I stood on a chair, I could touch it with the tips of my fingers. I turned around and looked ahead of me again. A deep hole had opened up before me. I looked in. The hole was deep and dark and I couldn't see the bottom. I thought, What's down there? so on purpose I fell in. I fell and I fell, over and over, as if I were an old suitcase. On the sides of the deep hole I could see things written, but perhaps it was in a foreign language because I couldn't read them. Still I fell, for I don't know how long. As I fell I began to see that I didn't like the way falling made me feel. Falling made me feel sick and I missed all the people I had loved. I said, "I don't want to fall anymore," and I reversed myself. I was standing again on the edge of the deep hole. I looked at the deep hole and I said, "You can close up now," and it did. I walked some more without knowing distance. I only knew that I passed through days and nights, I only knew that I passed through rain and shine, light and darkness. I was never thirsty and I felt no pain. Looking at the horizon, I made a joke for myself: I said, "The earth has thin lips," and I laughed.

Looking at the horizon again, I saw a lone figure coming toward me, but I wasn't frightened because I was sure it was my mother. As I got closer to the figure, I could see that it wasn't my mother, but still I wasn't frightened because I could see that it was a woman.

When this woman got closer to me, she looked at me hard and then she threw up her hands. She must have seen me somewhere before because she said, "It's you. Just look at

that. It's you. And just what have you been doing lately?"

I could have said, "I have been praying not to grow any taller."

I could have said, "I have been listening carefully to my mother's words, so as to make a good imitation of a dutiful daughter."

I could have said, "A pack of dogs, tired from chasing each other all over town, slept in the moonlight."

Instead, I said, "What I have been doing lately: I was lying in bed on my back, my hands drawn up, my fingers interlaced lightly at the nape of my neck. Someone rang the doorbell. I went downstairs and opened the door but there was no one there. I stepped outside. Either it was drizzling or there was a lot of dust in the air and the dust was damp. I stuck out my tongue and the drizzle or the damp dust tasted like government school ink. I looked north and I looked south. I started walking north. While walking north, I wanted to move fast, so I removed the shoes from my feet. While walking north, I looked up and saw the planet Venus, and I said, 'If the sun went out, it would be eight minutes before I would know it.' I saw a monkey sitting in a tree that had no leaves and I said, 'A monkey. Just look at that. A monkey. I picked up a stone and I threw it at the monkey.' The monkey, seeing the stone, quickly moved out of its way. Three times I threw a stone at the monkey and three times it moved away. The fourth time I threw the stone, the monkey caught it and threw it back at me. The stone struck me on my forehead over my right eye, making a deep gash. The gash healed immediately but now the skin on my forehead felt false to me. I walked for I

don't know how long before I came to a big body of water. I wanted to get across, so when the boat came I paid my fare. When I got to the other side, I saw a lot of people sitting on the beach and they were having a picnic. They were the most beautiful people I had ever seen. Everything about them was black and shiny. Their skin was black and shiny. Their shoes were black and shiny. Their hair was black and shiny. The clothes they wore were black and shiny. I could hear them laughing and chatting and I said, 'I would like to be with these people,' so I started to walk toward them; but when I got up close to them I saw that they weren't at a picnic and they weren't beautiful and they weren't chatting and laughing. All around me was black mud and the people all looked as if they had been made up out of the black mud. I looked up and saw that the sky seemed far away and nothing I could stand on would make me able to touch it with my fingertips. I thought, If only I could get out of this, so I started to walk. I must have walked for a long time because my feet hurt and felt as if they would drop off. I thought, If only just around the bend I would see my house and inside my house I would find my bed, freshly made at that, and in the kitchen I would find my mother or anyone else that I loved making me a custard. I thought, If only it was a Sunday and I was sitting in a church and I had just heard someone sing a psalm. I felt very sad so I sat down. I felt so sad that I rested my head on my own knees and smoothed my own head. I felt so sad I couldn't imagine feeling any other way again. I said, 'I don't like this. I don't want to do this anymore.' And I went back to lying in bed, just before the doorbell rang."

Thinking About the Story

A PERSONAL RESPONSE

sharing impressions

1. What are you left wondering about at the end of this story? Record your thoughts in your journal.

constructing interpretations

2. What is your understanding of the story's ending?
Think about
- what the narrator does not want to do anymore
- how she is able to return to bed
- who rings the doorbell

3. Speculate about the narrator of this story.
Think about
- her bizarre and surprising depiction of events
- her age, personality, and past experiences
- her relationship with her mother

4. How do you explain the differences in the narrator's two accounts of what she has been doing lately?
Think about
- whom she is speaking to as she gives each account
- the three answers she says she could have given, but did not give, to the question "And just what have you been doing lately?"
- whether she is describing the same journey in each account

A CREATIVE RESPONSE

5. How might the story continue?

A CRITICAL RESPONSE

6. What is the overall mood of the story? Explain.

7. Based on this story and the previous two stories in this unit, create a new definition of plot.
Think about
- the traditional definition of plot as a series of interrelated events that progress because of a conflict, or struggle between opposing forces
- the traditional structure of a plot, consisting of the exposition, rising action, climax, and falling action

8. Jamaica Kincaid immigrated to the United States from a tiny Caribbean island when she was seventeen. In what ways might her story reflect the experience of a new immigrant?

9. Do you find this story as inventive as others in this unit? Decide which story is based on the most intriguing idea.

Analyzing the Writer's Craft

STYLE: DICTION

What seems unusual about the narrator's manner of speaking?

Building a Literary Vocabulary. As you may remember, style refers to the particular way that a piece of literature is written. A significant component of style is diction, or a writer's choice of words. Diction encompasses both vocabulary (individual words) and syntax (the order or arrangement of words). Diction can be described in terms such as formal or informal, technical or common, abstract or concrete. In "What I Have Been Doing Lately" the narrator's diction is simple, even childish: "I ran downstairs. Quick. I opened the door. There was no one there." She uses short words and repeats certain constructions—"I looked," "I saw," "I walked." Contrast her diction with the more complex, formal diction of the narrator in "The Youngest Doll": "they lived surrounded by a past that was breaking up around them with the same impassive musicality with which the dining room chandelier crumbled on the frayed linen cloth of the dining room table."

Application: Analyzing Diction. Divide into groups of three or four. Write a short paragraph using diction characteristic of the narrator in "What I Have Been Doing Lately." Then write another paragraph using vocabulary and syntax that are uncharacteristic of the narrator. Exchange your paragraphs with those of another group and identify which paragraphs could have come from Kincaid's narrator. Defend your choice, pointing out specific qualities of the narrator's diction.

Connecting Reading and Writing

1. Drawing on your answer to question 5, write another **episode** in the same style and read it to classmates.

Option: Make your episode a **monologue** to be performed with appropriate props and gestures.

2. The structure of a work of literature is the way in which its parts are put together. Make a **graphic representation** of the structure of this story. The representation could be a diagram, a geometric shape, or some other figure. Explain how the story corresponds to your drawing.

Option: Analyze the story's structure in an **expository essay** for another student.

from **A Small Place**

Jamaica Kincaid

In a small place, people cultivate small events. The small event is isolated, blown up, turned over and over, and then absorbed into the everyday, so that at any moment it can and will roll off the inhabitants of the small place's tongues. For the people in a small place, every event is a domestic event; the people in a small place cannot see themselves in a larger picture, they cannot see that they might be part of a chain of something, anything. The people in a small place see the event in the distance heading directly towards them and they say, "I see the thing and it is heading towards me." The people in a small place then experience the event as if it were sitting on top of their heads, their shoulders, and it weighs them down, this enormous burden that is the event, so that they cannot breathe properly and they cannot think properly and they say, "This thing that was only coming towards me is now on top of me," and they live like that, until eventually they absorb the event and it becomes a part of them, a part of who and what they really are, and they are complete in that way until another event comes along and the process begins again.

Tenement Room: Chicago FRANK MARSHALL DAVIS

Loo-Wit WENDY ROSE

Biographies of Davis and Rose appear on pages 421 and 429.

Approaching the Poems

In these poems an indoor scene and an outdoor scene are presented in ways that transform them. The first poem describes a room in a tenement, a run-down apartment building in a slum area. The second poem describes the 1980 eruption of Mount Saint Helens, a volcano in Washington State that had been inactive since 1857. The blasts killed fifty-seven people and caused hundreds of millions of dollars worth of damage. Mount Saint Helens is known as Loo-wit ("lady of fire") by the Cowlitz, a Native American people who live in southwestern Washington.

Building Vocabulary

These essential words are defined alongside the poems.

destitution (des′ tə tōo′ shən), **gaudy** (gôd′ ē): Dirt and **destitution** / Lounge here in **gaudy** tatters ("Tenement Room: Chicago," lines 6–7)

buttes (byōots): cold **buttes** / promise nothing ("Loo-Wit," line 12)

Connecting Writing and Reading

In your journal, copy the following chart and fill it in with the names of several objects, animals, or ideas that you think of as having human qualities. In the second column list the human qualities you attribute to each thing. An example is given.

Object, animal, or idea	Human qualities
1. book	companionship, intelligence
2.	
3.	

As you read, notice that the speakers in these poems also attribute human qualities to nonhuman things.

Tenement Room: Chicago

Bruised and battered
By the dark silent hammers of night,
The day creeps
Slowly
5   From the tired room.

Dirt and destitution[1]
Lounge here in gaudy[2] tatters
Through the bright hours,
Forever shouting
10   Its bony nakedness—
A crippled table, gray from greasy water;
Two drooping chairs, spiritless as wounded soldiers shoved
    into a prison hole;
A cringing bed, age-weary;
Corseted with wire, squats a flabby stove;
15   In this corner slumps a punished trunk;
Through the lone window, broken-paned, light and
    weather spill on the dust-defeated and splintered floor.
Only night muffles
These visual cries
Of the despairing room.

20   The dusk
Lays a soothing hand
On its whimpering poverty;
Even the solitary gas jet
Eases its quivering runners
25   Of chromium[3] light
Along quiet surfaces
As
Exhausted
The room sleeps dreamlessly. . . .

1. **destitution** (des′ tə too′ shən): miserable poverty.

2. **gaudy** (gôd′ ē): bright and showy but lacking in good taste.

3. **chromium** (krō′ mē əm): of or like a particular bright metal.

Thinking About the Poem

A PERSONAL RESPONSE

sharing impressions

1. What overall feeling did you get from this poem? Describe this feeling in your journal.

constructing interpretations

2. In this poem, objects and times of day are given human qualities. What image of the room do you form as a result?

> ***Think about***
> - the qualities attributed to the furnishings of the room
> - the sense in which the room "cries" (line 18) and "sleeps" (line 29)

3. How might the speaker describe in only one sentence what he or she sees?

> ***Think about***
> - the condition of the room
> - how night and day affect the room

A CREATIVE RESPONSE

4. Who do you think lives in the room?

A CRITICAL RESPONSE

5. Could the poet have made you feel as you do about the room without giving it human qualities? Explain.

6. This poem was written more than fifty years ago. Does it seem dated to you? Why or why not?

Loo-Wit

The way they do
this old woman
no longer cares
what others think
5   but spits her black tobacco
any which way
stretching full length
from her bumpy bed.
Finally up
10   she sprinkles ashes
on the snow,
cold buttes[1]
promise nothing
but the walk
15   of winter.
Centuries of cedar
have bound her
to earth,
huckleberry ropes
20   lay prickly
on her neck.
Around her
machinery growls,
snarls and ploughs
25   great patches
of her skin.
She crouches
in the north,
her trembling
30   the source
of dawn.
Light appears
with the shudder
of her slopes,
35   the movement
of her arm.
Blackberries unravel,
stones dislodge;
it's not as if
40   they weren't warned.

1. **buttes** (byo͞ots): steep, isolated hills.

She was sleeping
but she heard the boot scrape,
the creaking floor,
felt the pull of the blanket
45 from her thin shoulder.
With one free hand
she finds her weapons
and raises them high;
clearing the twigs from her throat
50 she sings, she sings,
shaking the sky
like a blanket about her
Loo-wit sings and sings and sings!

*T*hinking *About the Poem*

A PERSONAL RESPONSE

sharing
impressions

1. What are some of your thoughts about Loo-wit? Write them down in your journal.

constructing
interpretations

2. What human qualities do you see in Loo-wit?

3. How might a reader who does not know what the word *Loo-wit* refers to figure out that Loo-wit is a volcanic mountain and not an actual woman?

> ***Think about***
> • images corresponding to the surface features of a mountain
> • images corresponding to the eruptions, earthquakes, and noise associated with a volcano

4. What reason for the volcanic eruption seems to be suggested by the poem?

> ***Think about***
> • who "they" are in line 40
> • what the machinery does in lines 22–26
> • the picture created by lines 41–48

5. If the poet had used the word *screams* instead of *sings* in lines 50 and 53, what would have been the effect?

A CRITICAL RESPONSE

6. The poet Wendy Rose describes herself as "a woman who judges." What do you think she is judging in this poem?

7. Rose is of Hopi and Miwok ancestry. Her poems are said to reflect Native American beliefs that natural objects possess souls. What details in the poem might be used to support this belief?

Analyzing the Writer's Craft

PERSONIFICATION

Think about how, in this poem and the previous poem, objects are described as though they were human beings.

Building a Literary Vocabulary. In your reading and discussion of "Loo-Wit" and "Tenement Room: Chicago," you have observed many examples of personification. Personification is a figure of speech in which human qualities are attributed to an object, animal, or idea. In "Loo-Wit" a volcano is personified when it is described as an old woman who spits tobacco and does not care what others think. In "Tenement Room: Chicago" a room is personified when it is described as "tired," "despairing," and "exhausted."

Application: Understanding Personification. To better understand the use of personification, get together with a partner and plan a dramatic presentation of "Loo-Wit," or form a group with four or five other students and plan a dramatic presentation of "Tenement Room: Chicago." In either case, one person should read the poem aloud as the other or others pantomime the human qualities and actions being described. After the presentations, decide as a class what the main message of each poem is and how personification helps to convey this message.

Rhythms   DIANA CHANG

Prayer to the Pacific   LESLIE MARMON SILKO

Biographies of Chang and Silko appear on pages 420 and 429.

Approaching the Poems

The free verse poems that follow are observations on nature and the natural rhythms that touch human lives. Diana Chang's "Rhythms" focuses on the motion in the natural world that a casual observer often fails to note. "Prayer to the Pacific" reflects Leslie Marmon Silko's Native American heritage in the portrayal of the close relationship between humans and nature.

Connecting Writing and Reading

Think about the phrase "rhythms of nature." What movements, sounds, or events in nature might be considered rhythmic? In your journal create a cluster diagram similar to the one below. List words, phrases, ideas, and feelings that come to mind when you think of the rhythms of nature. As you read, see whether your ideas about the rhythms of nature are reflected in the poems.

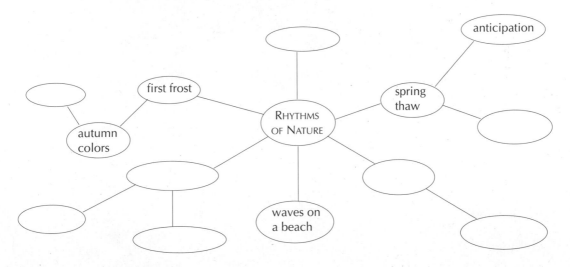

Rhythms

The landscape comes apart
in birds

A horse
detaches himself

5 from a fence
A criminal of love

breaks away
The child drops out of a tree

A ship uncouples
10 from the street

The canal, unhinged,
proceeds

Cars are pieces of the world
tearing away

15 But the crows
collect

in heaps
And stone

and sky
20 poised with being

grow steep
before

they faint
into the wind

25 and things
fly

again

Prayer to the Pacific

1

I traveled to the ocean
     distant
          from my southwest land of sandrock
         to the moving blue water
   Big as the myth of origin.

2

Pale
pale water in the yellow-white light of
         sun floating west
            to China
       where ocean herself was born
Clouds that blow across the sand are wet.

3

Squat in the wet sand and speak to Ocean:
   I return to you turquoise the red coral you sent us,
       sister spirit of Earth.
Four round stones in my pocket I carry back the ocean
     to suck and to taste.

4

Thirty thousand years ago
        Indians came riding across the ocean
        carried by giant sea turtles.
Waves were high that day
    great sea turtles waded slowly out
      from the gray sundown sea.
Grandfather Turtle rolled in the sand four times
     and disappeared
       swimming into the sun.

5

And so from that time
    immemorial,
      as the old people say,
rainclouds drift from the west
      gift from the ocean.

6
Green leaves in the wind
Wet earth on my feet
        swallowing raindrops
            clear from China.

*T*hinking About the Poems

A PERSONAL RESPONSE

sharing impressions

1. Which of these poems made the stronger impression on you? Briefly record your impressions in your journal.

constructing interpretations

2. In your own words, explain why the speaker in "Prayer to the Pacific" travels to the Pacific Ocean.
Think about
- the ocean as the source of rain in lines 29–30
- why the speaker returns the turquoise and coral back to the ocean in stanza 3
- why the poem is called a prayer
- the Indian origin myth referred to in stanza 1 and described in stanza 4
- the connection that the speaker sees between China, the Pacific, and her southwest homeland in stanzas 2 and 6

3. What do the rhythms described in Diana Chang's poem suggest to you about life?
Think about
- the things that come apart in the poem
- the things that come together
- which rhythms are part of nature and which are not
- why the poem concludes with the rhythm of stone and sky in lines 18–27

4. Which poem comes closer to your own concept of the rhythms of nature? Explain your answer, using references to your prereading diagram and to lines in the poems.

A CREATIVE RESPONSE

5. If the poets had chosen to use traditional rhyme and meter, how might your response to these poems be different?

6. "It's stories that make up this community," Leslie Marmon Silko remarked about Laguna Pueblo, New Mexico, where she was raised. What story do you think she is telling in this poem?

7. Diana Chang's poems have been described as "lyrical and concise, perhaps even too condensed." Citing details from "Rhythms," explain whether you agree or disagree with this opinion.

Connecting Reading and Writing

1. Keeping the style of Chang or Silko in mind, write your own **free-verse poem** about the rhythms of nature to be published in a school poetry anthology.

Option: Write a **sonnet** that expresses your feelings about the rhythms of nature for the same anthology.

2. Imagine that the poems "Tenement Room: Chicago," "Loo-Wit," "Rhythms," and "Prayer to the Pacific" are being gathered into a collection for students to use next year. Write **instructions** to an art researcher about the kinds of illustrations that should be used with the poems.

Option: Write an **introduction** for the poetry collection giving suggestions to students about how to approach the reading of these poems.

3. Create some kind of visual presentation of images from "Rhythms" or "Prayer to the Pacific,"

such as a painting, drawing, or photo collection. Write **notes** explaining the connection between the poem and the visual presentation.

Option: Write a **proposal** to your school's art department for collaboration on an art/poetry project. Use images from the two poems as examples of elements of the poems that could be illustrated.

4. Read more poetry by Silko. Choose two or three poems and compare them with "Prayer to the Pacific" in a **review** of Silko's poetry for a literary magazine. Focus on subject, structure, images, and ideas.

Option: Compare the poems on a **chart** to use as a visual aid for an oral presentation on Silko's poetry.

The Form of the Sword

JORGE LUIS BORGES

A biography of Borges appears on page 419.

Approaching the Story

Jorge Luis Borges (hôr′ hə lōō ēs′ bôr′ hes) is an Argentine writer whose stories often portray high-action adventure in dreamlike settings. The story you are about to read is a frame story. In the "frame" the narrator describes his encounter with an English landowner who has been the subject of curious speculation on the part of his South American neighbors. The Englishman, whose own story forms the central part of "The Form of the Sword," recalls an incident that occurred in Ireland during the civil war some years before.

HIS FACE WAS crossed with a rancorous scar: a nearly perfect ashen arc which sank into his temple on one side and his cheek on the other. His real name is of no importance: in Tacuarembo[1] everyone knew him as the Englishman of La Colorada.[2] The great landowner of these parts, Cardoso,[3] had not been interested in selling; I have heard that the Englishman had recourse to an unexpected argument: he told him the secret history of the scar. The Englishman had come from the frontier, from Rio Grande del Sur;[4] there were those who said he had been a smuggler in Brazil. His fields were overgrown with underbrush; the wells were bitter; to remedy these faults, the Englishman worked alongside his *peones*.[5] They say he was strict to the point of cruelty but scrupulously fair. They also say he was a drinking man: a couple of times a year he would lock himself up in a room in the tower, and two or three days later he would emerge as if from a bout of insanity or from the battlefield, pale, tremulous, abashed—and as authoritarian as ever. I remember his glacial eyes, his energetic thinness, his gray mustache. He had scant dealings with anyone; true, his Spanish was rudimentary, contaminated with Brazilian. Apart from an occasional commercial letter or pamphlet, he received no correspondence.

The last time I made a trip through the northern provinces, a flash flood in the Caraguatá arroyo[6] forced me to spend the night at La Colorada. I was only there a few minutes when I felt that my presence was inopportune. I tried getting into the good

1. **Tacuarembo** (tä kwä *rem*′ bô).
2. **La Colorada** (lä kô lô *rä*′ dä).
3. **Cardoso** (kär dô′ sô).
4. **Rio Grande del Sur** (*rē*′ ô grän′ dä del sōōr).
5. ***peones*** (pē ô′ nes) *Spanish*: peasants.
6. **Caraguatá arroyo** (kä *rä* gwä tä′ ə rơi′ ō): an arroyo is a narrow ravine.

graces of the Englishman; I resorted to the least acute of all the passions: patriotism. I said that a country with the spirit of England was invincible. My interlocutor[7] agreed, but he added with a smile that he was not English. He was Irish, from Dungarvan. Having said this, he stopped himself, as if he had revealed a secret.

After supper, we went out to look at the sky. It had cleared, but behind the ridge of the mountains, the south, fissured and shot through with lightning flashes, was brewing up another storm. Back in the deserted dining room, the waiter who had served us supper brought out a bottle of rum. We drank steadily, in silence.

I do not know what hour of the night it might have been when I realized that I was drunk; I do not know what inspiration or exultation or tedium made me mention the scar. The Englishman's face changed color. For a few seconds, I thought he was going to ask me to leave. Finally he said, in a normal voice, "I'll tell you the story of my wound on one condition: that you do not minimize the opprobrium[8] it calls forth, that you not belittle a single infamous circumstance."

I agreed. And this, then, is the story he recounted, in a mixture of English, Spanish, and Portuguese:

About 1922, in a city in Connaught,[9] I was one of many men conspiring for Irish independence. Of my comrades, some survived to engage in peaceful pursuits; others, paradoxically, fight in the desert and at sea under the English colors; another, the man of greatest worth, died in the courtyard of a barracks, at dawn, before a firing squad of soldiers drowsy with sleep; still others (not the most unfortunate ones) met their fate in the anonymous and nearly secret battles of the civil war. We were Republicans, Catholics; we were, I suspect, romantics. For us, Ireland was not only

the utopian[10] future and the intolerable present; it was a bitter and loving mythology, it was the circular towers and red bogs, it was the repudiation of Parnell[11] and the enormous epics which sing of the theft of bulls who in a former incarnation were heroes and in others were fish and mountains. . . . On one evening I shall never forget, we were joined by a comrade from Munster: a certain John Vincent Moon.

He was scarcely twenty years old. He was thin and soft at the same time. He gave one the uncomfortable impression of being invertebrate. He had studied, with fervor and vanity, every page of some communist manual or other; dialectic materialism[12] served him as a means to end any and all discussion. The reasons that one man may have to abominate another, or love him, are infinite: Moon reduced universal history to a sordid economic conflict. He asserted that the revolution is predestined to triumph. I told him that only lost causes can interest a gentleman. . . . By then it was nighttime. We continued our disagreements along the corridor, down the stairs, into the vague streets. The judgments emitted by Moon impressed me less than their unattractive and apodictic[13] tone. The new comrade did not argue: he passed judgment with obvious disdain and a certain fury.

As we came to the outlying houses, a sud-

---

7. interlocutor (in' tər läk' yo͞o tər): one who takes part in a conversation; talker; interpreter.

8. opprobrium (ə prō' brē əm): scorn or contempt, especially involving condemnation.

9. Connaught (kä' nôt).

10. utopian (yo͞o tō' pē ən): based on ideas of perfection in social and political organization.

11. Parnell: Charles Stewart Parnell, advocate of home rule for Ireland.

12. dialectic materialism (dī ə lek' tik): philosophy developed by Karl Marx.

13. apodictic (ap' ə dik' tik): involving or expressing necessary truth; absolutely certain.

den exchange of gunfire caught us by surprise. (Just before or after, we skirted the blank wall of a factory or barracks.) We took refuge along a dirt road; a soldier, looming gigantic in the glare, rushed out of a burning cabin. He shrieked at us and ordered us to halt. I pressed on; my comrade did not follow me. I turned back; John Vincent Moon was frozen in his tracks, fascinated and eternalized, as it were, by terror. I rushed to his side, brought down the soldier with a single blow, shook and pounded Vincent Moon, berated him, and ordered him to follow me. I was forced to yank him by his arm; a passionate fear paralyzed him. We fled through a night suddenly shot through with blazes. A burst of rifle fire sought us out; a bullet grazed Moon's right shoulder; while we ran among the pines, he broke into feeble sobbing.

During that autumn of 1922, I had taken refuge in a country house belonging to General Berkeley. This officer (whom I had never seen) was carrying out some administrative assignment in Bengal. His house, though it was less than a hundred years old, was dark and deteriorated and abounded in perplexing corridors and vain antechambers. A museum and an enormous library usurped the ground floor: controversial and incompatible books which, somehow, make up the history of the nineteenth century; scimitars from Nishapur,[14] in whose arrested circular arcs the wind and violence of battle seem to last. We entered (I seem to remember) through the back part of the house. Moon, his lips dry and quivering, muttered that the events of the evening had been very interesting. I dressed his wound and brought him a cup of tea. (His "wound," I saw, was superficial.) Suddenly he stammered perplexedly, "But you took a considerable chance."

I told him not to worry. (The routine of the civil war had impelled me to act as I had acted. Besides, the capture of a single one of our men could have compromised our cause.)

The following day Moon had recovered his aplomb.[15] He accepted a cigarette and severely cross-questioned me concerning "the economic resources of our revolutionary party." His questions were quite lucid. I told him (in all truth) that the situation was serious. Shattering volleys of rifle fire reverberated in the south. I told Moon that our comrades expected us. My trench coat and revolver were in my room; when I returned, I found Moon stretched on the sofa, his eyes shut. He thought he had fever; he spoke of a painful shoulder spasm.

I realized then that his cowardice was irreparable. I awkwardly urged him to take care of himself and took my leave. I blushed for this fearful man, as if I, and not Vincent Moon, were the coward. What one man does is something done, in some measure, by all men. For that reason, a disobedience committed in a garden contaminates the human race; for that reason, it is not unjust that the crucifixion of a single Jew suffices to save it. Perhaps Schopenhauer is right: I am all others, any man is all men, Shakespeare is in some way the wretched John Vincent Moon.

We spent nine days in the enormous house of the general. Of the agony and splendor of the battle I shall say nothing: my intention is to tell the story of this scar which affronts me. In my memory, those nine days form a single day; except for the next to the last, when our men rushed a barracks and we were able to avenge, man for man, the sixteen comrades who had been machine-gunned at Elphin. I would slip out of the house toward dawn, in the confusion of the morning twilight. I was back by dusk. My companion would be waiting for me upstairs: his wound did not allow him to come down to meet me. I can see him

---

14. **Nishapur** (ni′ shə po͞or).
15. **aplomb** (ə pläm′): poise; composure.

with some book of strategy in his hand: F. N. Maude or Clausewitz.[16] "The artillery is my preferred arm," he conceded one night. He would inquire into our plans; he liked to censure or revamp them. He was also in the habit of denouncing our "deplorable economic base." Dogmatic and somber, he would prophesy a ruinous end. *C'est une affaire flambee,*[17] he would murmur. In order to show that his being a physical coward made no difference to him, he increased his intellectual arrogance. Thus, for better or for worse, passed nine days.

On the tenth, the city definitively fell into the hands of the Black and Tans. Tall, silent horsemen patrolled the streets. The wind was filled with ashes and smoke. At an intersection in the middle of a square, I saw a corpse—less tenacious in my memory than a manikin—upon which some soldiers interminably practiced their marksmanship. . . . I had left my quarters as the sunrise hung in the sky. I returned before midday. In the library, Moon was talking to someone; by his tone of voice I realized that he was using the telephone. Then I heard my name; then that I would return at seven; then the suggestion that I be arrested as I crossed the garden. My reasonable friend was selling me reasonably. I heard him requesting certain guarantees of personal security.

At this point my story becomes confused, its thread is lost. I know I pursued the informer down the dark corridors of nightmare and the deep stairs of vertigo.[18] Moon had come to know the house very well, much better than I. Once or twice I lost him. I cornered him before the soldiers arrested me. From one of the general's mounted sets of arms I snatched down a cutlass; with the steel half-moon I sealed his face, forever, with a half-moon of blood. Borges, I have confessed this to you, a stranger. *Your* contempt will not wound me as much.

Here the narrator stopped. I noticed that his hands were trembling.

"And Moon?" I asked him.

"He was paid the Judas-money and fled to Brazil. And that afternoon, he watched some drunks in an impromptu firing squad in the town square shoot down a manikin."

I waited in vain for him to go on with his story. At length I asked him to continue.

A sob shook his body. And then, with feeble sweetness, he pointed to the white arced scar.

"You don't believe me?" he stammered. "Don't you see the mark of infamy[19] written on my face? I told you the story the way I did so that you would hear it to the end. I informed on the man who took me in: I am Vincent Moon. Despise me."

---

16. Clausewitz (klou′ zə wits).

17. *C'est une affaire flambée* (set ün à fer′ flän be′) *French*: idiom meaning "It is a lost cause."

18. vertigo (vʉr′ ti gō′): a condition in which one has the feeling of whirling, causing imbalance; a dizzy, confused state of mind.

19. infamy (in′ fə mē): disgrace, especially when it is widely known and involves well-deserved and extreme contempt; notoriety.

Ode to the Watermelon

PABLO NERUDA

Translated from the Spanish by Robert Bly

A biography of Neruda appears on page 427.

Approaching the Poem

Close your eyes and imagine heat so overpowering that the air seems to shimmer.
Thirst becomes an obsession. Now imagine how you would feel about something
that has the power to rescue you from such torment, and you may understand why
Pablo Neruda wrote a poem glorifying the watermelon. Born in Chile, Neruda is
one of the most original poets to write in the Spanish language. He called this
poem an ode, a kind of poem written, usually in a dignified style, to commemorate
a person, event, or thing—in this case, a watermelon.

The tree of intense
summer,
hard,
is all blue sky,
5   yellow sun,
fatigue in drops,
a sword
above the highways,
a scorched shoe
10   in the cities:
the brightness and the world
weigh us down,
hit us
in the eyes
15   with clouds of dust,
with sudden golden blows,
they torture
our feet
with tiny thorns,

20   with hot stones,
and the mouth
suffers
more than all the toes:
the throat
25   becomes thirsty,
the teeth,
the lips, the tongue:
we want to drink
waterfalls,
30   the dark blue night,
the South Pole,
and then
the coolest of all
the planets crosses
35   the sky,
the round, magnificent,
star-filled watermelon.

It's a fruit from the thirst-tree.
It's the green whale of the summer.
40 The dry universe
all at once
given dark stars
by this firmament of coolness
lets the swelling
45 fruit
come down:
its hemispheres open
showing a flag
green, white, red,
50 that dissolves into
wild rivers, sugar,
delight!

Jewel box of water, phlegmatic[1]
queen
55 of the fruitshops,
warehouse
of profundity,[2] moon
on earth!
You are pure,
60 rubies fall apart
in your abundance,
and we
want
to bite into you,
65 to bury our
face
in you, and
our hair, and
the soul!
70 When we're thirsty
we glimpse you
like
a mine or a mountain
of fantastic food,
75 but
among our longings and our teeth
you change
simply
into cool light

1. **phlegmatic** (fleg mat′ ik):
calm and composed.

2. **profundity** (prō fun′ də tē):
depth, especially great depth.

80 that slips in turn into
spring water
that touched us once
singing.
And that is why
85 you don't weigh us down
in the siesta hour[3]
that's like an oven,
you don't weigh us down,
you just
90 go by
and your heart, some cold ember,
turned itself into a single
drop of water.

3. siesta hour (sē es′ tə): a time period after lunch used for napping, especially in Latin America and southern Europe.

Watermelon, 1990, ZHOU PING.

Reviewing Concepts

THE POWER OF IMAGINATION: CREATING UNUSUAL PERSPECTIVES

*making
connections*

The writers in this unit stretch the imaginations of their readers, offering them unusual ways of looking at objects and experiences. The fiction writers combine fantastic and realistic elements in their works, whereas the poets transform their subjects through figurative language. For example, in the story "A Very Old Man with Enormous Wings," García Márquez presents ordinary townspeople who react to a supernatural occurrence in both expected and surprising ways. He thus gets readers to examine their assumptions about how human beings respond to extraordinary events. In the poem "Loo-Wit," Wendy Rose personifies Mount Saint Helens so that readers may view the destructive volcano in a new way—as a somewhat sympathetic figure who finally fights back after centuries of abuse by nature and humans.

To review the selections in this unit, think about the perspectives on objects and experiences that the writers share with you. For each selection you have read, identify the perspective conveyed about the subject. Organize your ideas in a chart similar to the one below.

Selection	Perspective conveyed
"A Very Old Man with Enormous Wings"	A supernatural occurrence may or may not have the expected impact on people's lives.
"Loo-Wit"	Mount Saint Helens is a somewhat sympathetic figure who finally fights back after centuries of abuse by nature and humans.

*describing
connections*

Review the information on your chart and choose three selections that you would like to explore in greater depth. Then write a **personal essay** in which you comment on whether each of the three perspectives offered by the writers did or did not change your understanding of an object or an experience. Be sure to give reasons for believing as you do.

Woodcut, LYND WARD. From *Storyteller Without Words* by Lynd Ward.
Courtesy of May McNeer Ward.

Examining Life Experiences

"*So you keep questioning and the only way to find answers is to write detailed stories that relate to your life.*"

AMY TAN

Examining Life Experiences

One of the pleasures of reading literature is that it invites you to think about life and what it means to be human. By examining the characters, situations, and messages in literary works, you gain insights about yourself and about those whose lives touch yours.

Literature has been used to convey truths about human life since earliest times. Ancient myths, epics, and legends feature heroes and heroines who provide noble images of humanity and who model the values of a society. Traditional folk tales from all parts of the world teach lessons about how to live, often by showing the consequences of human frailties. Today's writers are more likely to focus on ordinary characters in everyday situations, but they are still fulfilling the same function of illuminating human life for their readers.

The writers represented in this unit examine life experiences and suggest timeless truths—about hopes and fears, dreams and frustrations, aspirations and limitations. Fundamental questions explored by these writers include What does being an adult really mean? Why do actions often fall short of ideals? What happens when people are not allowed to pursue their dreams? What are the deepest needs of all human beings?

To examine human experience and explore crucial questions, some writers create true-to-life characters and realistic situations. Playwright Lorraine Hansberry, for example, explores the conflicts and dreams of an African-American family. Short story writers William Melvin Kelley and Eugenia Collier take the reader into the minds of first-person narrators grappling with the complex motives behind human acts.

Other writers communicate their experiences, attitudes, and messages through autobiographical accounts, such as journalist Eddy Harris's recollections of his solitary canoe trip down the Mississippi River. Poets often create speakers who represent the poets themselves at various points in their lives. Gwendolyn Brooks, Mari Evans, Nikki Giovanni, and Gary Soto, for example, speak to the reader in highly personal voices about experiences and ideas meaningful to them.

As you read the selections that follow, think about the life experiences examined by the writers. Consider whether you agree with their perceptions of life and whether your own experiences and feelings are similar to those depicted in the selections.

Literary Vocabulary

INTRODUCED IN THIS UNIT

Speaker. The speaker in a poem is the voice that talks to the reader. Through inference the reader can learn many things about the speaker in a poem, insights that in turn enhance the meaning of the poem for the reader. In "Hiccups," for example, the reader can infer that the speaker is indignant over the way his mother treated him as a child, trying to mold him according to her image of a perfect son. This inference sheds light on the meaning of the poem, namely, that a parent has no right to attempt to mold a child according to arbitrary standards of perfection.

Symbol. A symbol is a person, place, object, or activity that stands for something beyond itself. Cultural symbols are those whose meanings can be understood by people in the same culture. For example, in certain cultures, roses symbolize love. Literary symbols take on meaning within the context of a literary work. For example, in Alberto Alvaro Ríos's "The Secret Lion," the grinding ball symbolizes perfection to Sergio and the narrator.

REVIEWED IN THIS UNIT

Mood

Dialogue

Kitchenette Building

One wants a Teller in a time like this

Speech to the Young/
Speech to the Progress-Toward

Horses Graze

A biography of Brooks appears on page 419.

*A*pproaching the Poems

Reading several poems by the same poet can give you a comprehensive look at the poet's work. The four poems that follow are by Gwendolyn Brooks, the first African-American poet to win a Pulitzer Prize. Brooks lives and works in the heart of Chicago's African-American community, and much of her work focuses on the everyday lives of her neighbors. The poems are presented in chronological order; they span a period from 1945 to 1975. The kitchenette building in the first poem is a type of apartment house found in low-income urban areas. The small apartments have compact kitchens, and bathrooms are shared by the tenants on a floor. For the third poem Brooks includes a dedication to her children, Nora and Henry III.

*B*uilding Vocabulary

These essential words are defined alongside the poems.

aria (ä' rē ə): Flutter, or sing an **aria** down these rooms ("Kitchenette Building," line 7)

majestic, (mə jes' tik), **oblivion** (ə bliv' ē ən): bowed / in **majestic oblivion** ("Horses Graze," lines 10–11)

affirmation (af' ər mā' shən): with wonderful gentleness, in **affirmation,** ("Horses Graze," line 21)

Think of yourself in the following situations:

- You see a lost dog wandering the streets
- You are suspected of a wrong-doing, such as shoplifting or loitering
- You read about a new law that you believe is unjust
- You see a homeless person picking through garbage cans

When you are faced with injustice, ignorance, or other problems in life, what do you do? Do you react with resignation, confusion, or protest? Do you try to remain above it all? In your journal, describe the reaction you have most often. As you read each of these poems by Gwendolyn Brooks, compare your own way of reacting with the way each speaker reacts to life.

Kitchenette Building

We are things of dry hours and the involuntary plan,
Grayed in, and gray. "Dream" makes a giddy sound, not strong
Like "rent," "feeding a wife," "satisfying a man."

But could a dream send up through onion fumes
5 Its white and violet, fight with fried potatoes
And yesterday's garbage ripening in the hall,
Flutter, or sing an <u>aria</u>[1] down these rooms

Even if we were willing to let it in,
Had time to warm it, keep it very clean,
10 Anticipate a message, let it begin?

We wonder. But not well! not for a minute!
Since Number Five is out of the bathroom now,
We think of lukewarm water, hope to get in it.

1. **aria** (ä′ rē ə): a song or melody for a solo voice in an opera.

Thinking About the Poem

A PERSONAL RESPONSE

sharing impressions

1. What state of mind does this poem put you in? Comment in your journal.

constructing interpretations

2. What words and phrases would you use to describe the kind of life lived by the tenants of the kitchenette building?

Think about

- what the phrases "dry hours," "involuntary plan," and "grayed in, and gray" suggest
- the concerns named in line 3 and lines 12–13

3. How would you restate what the speaker is saying about the survival of a dream in this building?

Think about

- how the description of the dream contrasts with the descriptions of the building and the tenants' concerns
- what the dream requires of the tenants
- what interrupts the thoughts about the dream

A CREATIVE RESPONSE

4. What kinds of dreams do you think the tenants might have?

A CRITICAL RESPONSE

5. Does the message about life communicated by this poem apply only to the poor? Explain your views.

6. Read the poem aloud. Would you say that it sounds more like natural speech or more like formal poetry? Support your answer.

One wants a Teller in a time like this

One wants a Teller in a time like this.

One's not a man, one's not a woman grown,
To bear enormous business all alone.

One cannot walk this winding street with pride,
5   Straight-shouldered, tranquil-eyed,
Knowing one knows for sure the way back home.
One wonders if one has a home.

One is not certain if or why or how.
One wants a Teller now:—

10   *Put on your rubbers and you won't catch cold.*
Here's hell, there's heaven. Go to Sunday School.
Be patient, time brings all good things—(and cool
Strong balm to calm the burning at the brain?)—
Behold,
15   *Love's true, and triumphs; and God's actual.*

ᵀhinking About the Poem

A PERSONAL RESPONSE

sharing impressions

1. What questions do you have after reading this poem? Write them down in your journal.

constructing interpretations

2. Why might a person want to hear the things the Teller says in the last stanza?

3. How do you interpret "a time like this"?

Think about

- "time" as a stage of life, such as adolescence or middle age
- "time" as a particular historical period
- "time" as any moment in life that troubles a person
- details from the poem that support any of these interpretations

A CREATIVE RESPONSE

4. What would have been the effect if Brooks had used the pronoun *I* or *you* instead of *one?*

5. What qualities would you look for in your own Teller?

A CRITICAL RESPONSE

6. Brooks has said that "you can get the essence of a novel into a short poem." In your opinion, does her idea hold true for this poem? Explain.

 nalyzing the Writer's Craft

SPEAKER

Think back to "Kitchenette Building." What impression do you have of the speaker?

Building a Literary Vocabulary. As you know, the speaker in a poem is the voice that talks to the reader. Through inference the reader can learn many things about the speaker in a poem, insights that in turn enhance the meaning of the poem for the reader. In "Kitchenette Building," for example, the speaker uses the pronoun *we.* The reader can infer, therefore, that the speaker is one of the tenants in the kitchenette building. From such phrases as "dry hours" and "grayed in," the reader can infer that the speaker is disillusioned with his or her surroundings and possibly also with life itself. The speaker's attitude of futility is reinforced as he or she asks if a dream is possible in a place filled with the mundane realities of life: onion fumes, fried potatoes, garbage, and the inconvenience of a shared bathroom.

Application: Analyzing Speaker. Reread "One wants a Teller" and list all the information you can infer about the speaker in the poem. Then get together with several other students and discuss your lists, citing examples to support the inferences you have made. As you read the two remaining poems by Brooks, analyze the information provided about the speakers.

Speech to the Young / Speech to the Progress-Toward

(Among them Nora and Henry III)

Say to them,
say to the down-keepers,
the sun-slappers,
the self-soilers,
5   the harmony-hushers,
"Even if you are not ready for day
it cannot always be night."
You will be right.
For that is the hard home-run.

10   Live not for battles won.
Live not for the-end-of-the-song.
Live in the along.

Youth Leading the Blind, 1966, CYRIL FABIO.

Thinking About the Poem

A PERSONAL RESPONSE

sharing impressions

1. What thoughts are you left with after reading this poem? Write about them in your journal.

constructing interpretations

2. Why do you think the speaker is delivering this "speech"?
   Think about
   • who the speaker is addressing
   • who the "down-keepers, / the sun-slappers, / the self-soilers, / the harmony-hushers" might be (lines 2–5)
   • what is meant by "Live in the along" (line 12)

A CREATIVE RESPONSE

3. If the speaker had been born into wealth, how might the message about life be different?

A CRITICAL RESPONSE

4. Speculate about why Brooks chose to use alliteration and repetition in this poem.
   Think about
   • alliteration as the repetition of initial consonant sounds
   • alliterative phrases in lines 2–5
   • repetition of the word *say* in lines 1–2 and the word *live* in lines 10–12
   • how the alliterative phrases and repetition affect you as a reader

5. Based on your own experience, how easy do you think it will be for the "young" and "progress-toward" to follow the speaker's advice? Explain.

Horses Graze

Cows graze.
Horses graze.
They
eat
5 eat
eat.
Their graceful heads
are bowed
bowed
10 bowed
in majestic[1] oblivion.[2]
They are nobly oblivious
to your follies,
your inflation,
15 the knocks and nettles of administration.
They
eat
eat
eat.
20 And at the crest of their brute satisfaction,
with wonderful gentleness, in affirmation,[3]
they lift their clean calm eyes and they lie down
and love the world.
They speak with their companions.
25 They do not wish that they were otherwhere.
Perhaps they know that creature feet may press
only a few earth inches at a time,
that earth is anywhere earth,
that an eye may see,
30 wherever it may be,
the Immediate arc, alone, of life, of love.
In Sweden,
China,
Afrika,
35 in India or Maine
the animals are sane;
they know and know and know
there's ground below
and sky
40 up high.

1. majestic (mə jes′ tik): very
grand or dignified.
2. oblivion (ə bliv′ ē ən):
lack of awareness; disregard.

3. affirmation (af′ ər mā′
sʰən): positive declaration.

*T*hinking About the Poem

A PERSONAL RESPONSE

sharing impressions

1. What is your response to this poem? Describe your response in your journal.

constructing interpretations

2. Explain in your own words what the speaker is saying in this poem.

Think about
- what the speaker appreciates about horses
- the speaker's reference to "your follies, / your inflation" (lines 13–14)
- what the speaker seems to be implying about human life

3. Do you agree with the speaker's ideas about human life? Explain.

A CREATIVE RESPONSE

4. If Brooks had expressed these same ideas in an essay rather than in a poem, how might the impact of the ideas be different?

A CRITICAL RESPONSE

5. To what situations in human life might the message of this poem be applied? Explain your response.

6. Based on your reading of the four poems by Brooks, how would you characterize her attitude toward life?

*C*onnecting Reading and Writing

1. Write a **poem** modeled after "Speech to the Young / Speech to the Progress-Toward" or "Horses Graze" in which you present a message about life.

Option: Create several **aphorisms** for young people that present your message about life.

2. Prepare a **report card** for Brooks in which you evaluate each of her four poems on the basis of theme, imagery, word choice, and overall effectiveness.

Option: Write a **memo** to your school librarian, suggesting that one of the four poems be included in a poetry reading to take place after school for

interested students. Incorporate an evaluation of the poems you are suggesting.

3. Research the lifetime contributions that Brooks has made to literature and to the cause of introducing young people to poetry. Based on your findings, write a **letter** to the Nobel Prize Foundation recommending that Brooks be nominated to receive the Nobel Prize in literature.

Option: Prepare an **introductory speech** to be delivered at a dinner held in Brooks's honor. Be sure to mention her outstanding achievements.

A Raisin in the Sun

LORRAINE HANSBERRY

A biography of Hansberry appears on page 423.

Approaching the Play

A Raisin in the Sun premiered on Broadway on March 11, 1959. Two months later it became the first work by an African American to receive the New York Drama Critics Circle award for best play. It was a landmark drama; James Baldwin wrote that "never before, in the entire history of the American theater, had so much of the truth of black people's lives been seen on the stage." The play reflects society in the 1950's, before fair-housing and equal-employment laws were enforced, before pride in African heritage became widespread, before the terms "black" and "African American" came into use, and before most African nations had gained independence from European rulers. The play's title comes from a Langston Hughes poem, "Harlem," which asks what happens to a dream that is deferred, or put off. A portion of this poem serves as the epigraph of the play.

Building Vocabulary

These essential words are footnoted within the play.

indictment (in dīt′ mənt): *And always in his voice there is a quality of indictment.* (page 322)

vindicated (vin′ də kāt′ əd): *The boy finally turns . . . knowing . . . he is vindicated.* (page 324)

assimilationism (ə sim′ ə lā′ shən iz′ əm): **Assimilationism** is so popular in your country. (page 339)

resignation (rez′ ig nā′ shən): *She waits a long time, and then with resignation starts to put away her things.* (page 353)

retrogression (re′ trə gresh′ ən): And then quiet again. **Retrogression** even. (page 375)

Connecting Writing and Reading

In your journal describe a dream you have for the future. What might make you abandon this dream, and how would you be affected? Keep these ideas in mind as you read about the characters and their dreams.

A Raisin in the Sun

What happens to a dream deferred?
Does it dry up
Like a raisin in the sun?
Or fester like a sore—
And then run?
Does it stink like rotten meat?
Or crust and sugar over—
Like a syrupy sweet?

Maybe it just sags
Like a heavy load.

Or does it explode?

—Langston Hughes

CHARACTERS

Ruth Younger
Travis Younger
Walter Lee Younger
Beneatha Younger
Lena Younger
Joseph Asagai
George Murchison
Karl Lindner
Bobo
Moving Men

Time. *Sometime between World War II and the present.*

Place. *Chicago's South Side.*

The Younger living room would be a comfortable and well-ordered room if it were not for a number of indestructible contradictions to this state of being. Its furnishings are typical and undistinguished, and their primary feature now is that they have clearly had to accommodate the living of too many people for too many years—and they are tired. Still, we can see that at some time, a time probably no longer remembered by the family (except perhaps for Mama), the furnishings of this room were actually selected with care and love and even hope—and brought to this apartment and arranged with taste and pride.

That was a long time ago. Now the once-loved pattern of the couch upholstery has to fight to show itself from under acres of crocheted doilies and couch covers that have themselves finally come to be more important than the upholstery. And here a table or chair has been moved to disguise the worn places in the carpet; but the carpet has fought back by showing its weariness, with depressing uniformity, elsewhere on its surface.

Weariness has, in fact, won in this room. Everything has been polished, washed, sat on, used, scrubbed too often. All pretenses but living itself have long since vanished from the very atmosphere of this room.

Moreover, a section of this room, for it is not really a room unto itself, though the landlord's lease would make it seem so, slopes backward to provide a small kitchen area, where the family prepares the meals that are eaten in the living room proper, which must also serve as dining room. The single window that has been provided for these "two" rooms is located in this kitchen area. The sole natural light the family may enjoy in the course of a day is only that which fights its way through this little window.

At left, a door leads to a bedroom that is shared by Mama and her daughter, Beneatha. At right, opposite, is a second room (which in the beginning of the life of this apartment was probably a breakfast room) that serves as a bedroom for Walter and his wife, Ruth.

ACT ONE

SCENE 1. *Friday morning.*

It is morning dark in the living room. Travis is asleep on the make-down bed at center. An alarm clock sounds from within the bedroom at right, and presently Ruth enters from that room and closes the door behind her. She crosses sleepily toward the window. As she passes her sleeping son she reaches down and shakes him a little. At the window she raises the shade and a dusky South Side morning light comes in feebly. She fills a pot with water and puts it on to boil. She calls to

the boy, between yawns, in a slightly muffled voice.

Ruth is about thirty. We can see that she was a pretty girl, even exceptionally so, but now it is apparent that life has been little that she expected, and disappointment has already begun to hang in her face. In a few years, before thirty-five even, she will be known among her people as a "settled woman."

She crosses to her son and gives him a good, final, rousing shake.

Ruth. Come on now, boy, it's seven-thirty! (*Her son sits up at last, in a stupor of sleepiness.*) I say hurry up, Travis! You ain't the only person in the world got to use a bathroom! (*The child, a sturdy, handsome little boy of ten or eleven, drags himself out of the bed and almost blindly takes his towels and "today's clothes" from drawers and a closet and goes out to the bathroom, which is in an outside hall and which is shared by another family or families on the same floor. Ruth crosses to the bedroom door at right and opens it and calls in to her husband.*) Walter Lee! . . . It's after seven-thirty! Lemme see you do some waking up in there now! (*She waits.*) You better get up from there, man! It's after seven-thirty I tell you. (*She waits again.*) All right, you just go ahead and lay there and the next thing you know Travis be finished and Mr. Johnson'll be in there and you'll be fussing and cussing round here like a mad man! And be late too! (*She waits, at the end of patience.*) Walter Lee—it's time for you to get up!

(*She waits another second and then starts to go into the bedroom but is apparently satisfied that her husband has begun to get up. She stops, pulls the door to, and returns to the kitchen area. She wipes her face with a moist cloth and runs her fingers through her sleep-disheveled hair in a vain effort and ties an apron around her housecoat. The bedroom door at right opens and her husband stands in the doorway in his pajamas, which are rumpled and mismated. He is a lean, intense young man in his middle thirties, inclined to quick nervous movements and erratic speech habits—and always in his voice there is a quality of* <u>indictment</u>.[1])

Walter. Is he out yet?

Ruth. What do you mean *out?* He ain't hardly got in there good yet.

Walter (*wandering in, still more oriented to sleep than to a new day*). Well, what was you doing all that yelling for if I can't even get in there yet? (*stopping and thinking*) Check coming today?

Ruth. They *said* Saturday and this is just Friday and I hopes to God you ain't going to get up here first thing this morning and start talking to me 'bout no money—'cause I 'bout don't want to hear it.

Walter. Something the matter with you this morning?

Ruth. No—I'm just sleepy as the devil. What kind of eggs you want?

Walter. Not scrambled. (Ruth *starts to scramble eggs.*) Paper come? (Ruth *points impatiently to the rolled up* Tribune *on the table, and he gets it and spreads it out and vaguely reads the front page.*) Set off another bomb yesterday.

Ruth (*maximum indifference*). Did they?

Walter (*looking up*). What's the matter with you?

Ruth. Ain't nothing the matter with me. And don't keep asking me that this morning.

Walter. Ain't nobody bothering you. (*reading the news of the day absently again*). Say Colonel McCormick[2] is sick.

Ruth (*affecting tea-party interest*). Is he now? Poor thing.

Walter (*sighing and looking at his watch*). Oh, me. (*He waits.*) Now what is that boy doing in the bathroom all this time? He just going to have to start getting up earlier. I can't be being late to work on account of him fooling around in there.

Ruth (*turning on him*). Oh, no, he ain't going to be getting up no earlier no such thing! It ain't his fault that he can't get to bed no earlier nights 'cause he got a bunch of crazy good-for-nothing clowns sitting up running their mouths in what is supposed to be his bedroom after ten o'clock at night. . . .

Walter. That's what you mad about, ain't it? The things I want to talk about with my friends just couldn't be important in your mind, could they?

(*He rises and finds a cigarette in her handbag on the table and crosses to the little window and looks out, smoking and deeply enjoying this first one.*)

Ruth (*almost matter-of-factly, a complaint too automatic to deserve emphasis*). Why you always got to smoke before you eat in the morning?

Walter (*at the window*). Just look at 'em down there. . . . Running and racing to work. . . . (*He turns and faces his wife and watches her a moment at the stove, and then, suddenly.*) You look young this morning, baby.

Ruth (*indifferently*). Yeah?

Walter. Just for a second—stirring them eggs. It's gone now—just for a second it

---

1. **indictment** (in dīt′ mənt): accusation; blame.
2. **Colonel McCormick:** the publisher of the *Chicago Tribune* newspaper.

was—you looked real young again. (*then, drily*) It's gone now—you look like yourself again.

Ruth. Man, if you don't shut up and leave me alone.

Walter (*looking out to the street again*). First thing a man ought to learn in life is not to make love to no colored woman first thing in the morning. You all some evil people at eight o'clock in the morning.

(Travis *appears in the hall doorway, almost fully dressed and quite wide awake now, his towels and pajamas across his shoulders. He opens the door and signals for his father to make the bathroom in a hurry.*)

Travis (*watching the bathroom*). Daddy, come on!

(Walter *gets his bathroom utensils and flies out to the bathroom.*)

Ruth. Sit down and have your breakfast, Travis.

Travis. Mama, this is Friday. (*gleefully*) Check coming tomorrow, huh?

Ruth. You get your mind off money and eat your breakfast.

Travis (*eating*). This is the morning we supposed to bring the fifty cents to school.

Ruth. Well, I ain't got no fifty cents this morning.

Travis. Teacher say we have to.

Ruth. I don't care what teacher say. I ain't got it. Eat your breakfast, Travis.

Travis. I *am* eating.

Ruth. Hush up now and just eat!

(*The boy gives her an exasperated look for her lack of understanding, and eats grudgingly.*)

Travis. You think Grandmama would have it?

Ruth. No! And I want you to stop asking your grandmother for money, you hear me?

Travis (*outraged*). Gaaaleee! I don't ask her, she just gimme it sometimes!

Ruth. Travis Willard Younger—I got too much on me this morning to be—

Travis. Maybe Daddy—

Ruth. *Travis!*

(*The boy hushes abruptly. They are both quiet and tense for several seconds.*)

Travis (*presently*). Could I maybe go carry some groceries in front of the supermarket for a little while after school then?

Ruth. Just hush, I said. (Travis *jabs his spoon into his cereal bowl viciously, and rests his head in anger upon his fists.*) If you through eating, you can get over there and make up your bed.

(*The boy obeys stiffly and crosses the room, almost mechanically, to the bed and more or less carefully folds the covering. He carries the bedding into his mother's room and returns with his books and cap.*)

Travis (*sulking and standing apart from her unnaturally*). I'm gone.

Ruth (*looking up from the stove to inspect him automatically*). Come here. (*He crosses to her and she studies his head.*) If you don't take this comb and fix this here head, you better! (Travis *puts down his books with a great sigh of oppression, and crosses to the mirror. His mother mutters under her breath about his "slubbornness."*) 'Bout to march out of here with that head looking just like chickens slept in it! I just don't know where you get your slubborn ways. . . . And get your jacket, too. Looks chilly out this morning.

Travis (*with conspicuously brushed hair and jacket*). I'm gone.

Ruth. Get carfare and milk money—(*waving one finger*)—and not a single penny for no caps, you hear me?

Travis (*with sullen politeness*). Yes'm.

(*He turns in outrage to leave. His mother watches after him as in his frustration he approaches the door almost comically. When she speaks to him, her voice has become a very gentle tease.*)

Ruth (*mocking; as she thinks he would say it*). Oh, Mama makes me so mad sometimes, I don't know what to do! (*She waits and continues to his back as he stands stock-still in front of the door.*) I wouldn't kiss that woman goodbye for nothing in this world this morning! (*The boy finally turns around and rolls his eyes at her, knowing the mood has changed and he is <u>vindicated</u>;[3] he does not, however, move toward her yet.*) Not for nothing in this world! (*She finally laughs aloud at him and holds out her arms to him, and we see that it is a way between them, very old and practiced. He crosses to her and allows her to embrace him warmly but keeps his face fixed with masculine rigidity. She holds him back from her presently and looks at him and runs her fingers over the features of his face. With utter gentleness—*) Now— whose little old angry man are you?

Travis (*The masculinity and gruffness start to fade at last.*). Aw gaalee—Mama. . . .

Ruth (*mimicking*). Aw—gaaaaalleeeee, Mama! (*She pushes him, with rough playfulness and finality, toward the door.*) Get on out of here or you going to be late.

Travis (*in the face of love, new aggressive-*

ness). Mama, could I please go carry groceries?

Ruth. Honey, it's starting to get so cold evenings.

Walter (*coming in from the bathroom and drawing a make-believe gun from a make-believe holster and shooting at his son*). What is it he wants to do?

Ruth. Go carry groceries after school at the supermarket.

Walter. Well, let him go . . .

Travis (*quickly, to the ally*). I have to—she won't gimme the fifty cents. . . .

Walter (*to his wife only*). Why not?

Ruth (*simply and with flavor*). 'Cause we don't have it.

Walter (*to Ruth only*). What you tell the boy things like that for? (*reaching down into his pants with a rather important gesture*). Here, son—

(*He hands the boy the coin, but his eyes are directed to his wife's. Travis takes the money happily.*)

Travis. Thanks, Daddy.

(*He starts out. Ruth watches both of them with murder in her eyes. Walter stands and stares back at her with defiance, and suddenly reaches into his pocket again on an afterthought.*)

Walter (*without even looking at his son, still staring hard at his wife*). In fact, here's another fifty cents. . . . Buy yourself some fruit today—or take a taxicab to school or something!

Travis. Whoopee—

---

3. **vindicated** (vin′ də kāt′ əd): cleared from criticism or guilt.

(*He leaps up and clasps his father around the middle with his legs, and they face each other in mutual appreciation; slowly Walter Lee peeks around the boy to catch the violent rays from his wife's eyes and draws his head back as if shot.*)

Walter. You better get down now—and get to school, man.

Travis (*at the door*). OK. Goodbye.

(*He exits.*)

Walter (*after him, pointing with pride*). That's my boy. (*She looks at him in disgust and turns back to her work.*) You know what I was thinking 'bout in the bathroom this morning?

Ruth. No.

Walter. How come you always try to be so pleasant!

Ruth. What is there to be pleasant 'bout!

Walter. You want to know what I was thinking 'bout in the bathroom or not!

Ruth. I know what you thinking 'bout.

Walter (*ignoring her*). 'Bout what me and Willy Harris was talking about last night.

Ruth (*immediately—a refrain*). Willy Harris is a good-for-nothing loudmouth.

Walter. Anybody who talks to me has got to be a good-for-nothing loudmouth, ain't he? And what you know about who is just a good-for-nothing loudmouth? Charlie Atkins was a "good-for-nothing loudmouth" too, wasn't he! When he wanted me to go in the dry-cleaning business with him. And now—he's grossing a hundred thousand dollars a year! You still call *him* a loudmouth!

Ruth (*bitterly*). Oh, Walter Lee. . . .

(*She folds her head on her arms over the table.*)

Walter (*rising and coming to her and standing over her*). You tired, ain't you? Tired of everything. Me, the boy, the way we live—this beat-up hole—everything. Ain't you? (*She doesn't look up, doesn't answer.*) So tired—moaning and groaning all the time, but you wouldn't do nothing to help, would you? You couldn't be on my side that long for nothing, could you?

Ruth. Walter, please leave me alone.

Walter. A man needs for a woman to back him up. . . .

Ruth. Walter—

Walter. Mama would listen to you. You know she listen to you more than she do me and Bennie. She think more of you. All you have to do is just sit down with her when you drinking your coffee one morning and talking 'bout things like you do and—(*He sits beside her and demonstrates graphically what he thinks her methods and tone should be.*)—you just sip your coffee, see, and say easy like that you been thinking 'bout that deal Walter Lee is so interested in, 'bout the store and all, and sip some more coffee, like what you saying ain't really all that important to you—And the next thing you know, she be listening good and asking you questions and when I come home—I can tell her the details. This ain't no fly-by-night proposition, baby. I mean we figured it out, me and Willy and Bobo.

Ruth (*with a frown*). Bobo?

Walter. Yeah. You see, this little liquor store we got in mind cost seventy-five thousand, and we figured the initial investment on the place be 'bout thirty thousand, see. That be ten thousand each. Course, there's a couple of hundred you got to pay so's you don't spend your life just waiting for them clowns to let your license get approved—

Ruth. You mean graft?

Walter (*frowning, impatiently*). Don't call it that. See there, that just goes to show you what women understand about the world. Baby, don't *nothing* happen for you in this world 'less you pay *somebody* off!

Ruth. Walter, leave me alone! (*She raises her head and stares at him vigorously—then says, more quietly.*) Eat your eggs, they gonna be cold.

Walter (*straightening up from her and looking off*). That's it. There you are. Man say to his woman: I got me a dream. His woman say: Eat your eggs. (*sadly, but gaining in power*) Man say: I got to take hold of this here world, baby! And a woman will say: Eat your eggs and go to work. (*passionately now*) Man say: I got to change my life, I'm choking to death, baby! And his woman say—(*in utter anguish as he brings his fists down on his thighs*)—Your eggs is getting cold!

Ruth (*softly*). Walter, that ain't none of our money.

Walter (*not listening at all or even looking at her*). This morning I was lookin' in the mirror and thinking about it. . . . I'm thirty-five years old; I been married eleven years and I got a boy who sleeps in the living room—(*very, very quietly*)—and all I got to give him is stories about how rich white people live. . . .

Ruth. Eat your eggs, Walter.

Walter. *Damn my eggs . . . damn all the eggs that ever was!*

Ruth. Then go to work.

Walter (*looking up at her*). See—I'm trying to talk to you 'bout myself—(*shaking his head with the repetition*)—and all you can say is eat them eggs and go to work.

Ruth (*wearily*). Honey, you never say nothing new. I listen to you every day, every night and every morning, and you never say nothing new. (*shrugging*) So you would rather *be* Mr. Arnold than be his chauffeur. So—I would *rather* be living in Buckingham Palace.

Walter. That is just what is wrong with the colored women in this world. . . . Don't understand about building their men up and making 'em feel like they somebody. Like they can do something.

Ruth (*drily, but to hurt*). There *are* colored men who do things.

Walter. No thanks to the colored woman.

Ruth. Well, being a colored woman, I guess I can't help myself none.

(*She rises and gets the ironing board and sets it up and attacks a huge pile of rough-dried clothes, sprinkling them in preparation for the ironing and then rolling them into tight fat balls.*)

Walter (*mumbling*). We one group of men tied to a race of women with small minds.

(*His sister Beneatha enters. She is about twenty, as slim and intense as her brother. She is not as pretty as her sister-in-law, but her lean, almost intellectual face has a handsomeness of its own. She wears a bright-red flannel nightie, and her thick hair stands wildly about her head. Her speech is a mixture of many things; it is different from the rest of the family's insofar as education has permeated her sense of English—and perhaps the Midwest rather than the South has finally—at last—won out in her inflection; but not altogether, because over all of it is a soft slurring and transformed use of vowels that is the decided influence of the South Side. She passes through the room without looking at either* Ruth *or* Walter *and goes to the outside door and looks, a little blindly, out to the bathroom. She sees that it has been lost to the Johnsons. She closes the door with a sleepy vengeance and crosses to the table and sits down a little defeated.*)

Beneatha. I am going to start timing those people.

Walter. You should get up earlier.

Beneatha (*Her face in her hands. She is still fighting the urge to go back to bed.*). Really—would you suggest dawn? Where's the paper?

Walter (*pushing the paper across the table to her as he studies her almost clinically, as though he has never seen her before*). You a horrible-looking chick at this hour.

Beneatha (*drily*). Good morning, everybody.

Walter (*senselessly*). How is school coming?

Beneatha (*in the same spirit*). Lovely. Lovely. And you know, biology is the greatest. (*looking up at him*) I dissected something that looked just like you yesterday.

Walter. I just wondered if you've made up your mind and everything.

Beneatha (*gaining in sharpness and impatience*). And what did I answer yesterday morning—and the day before that?

Ruth (*from the ironing board, like someone disinterested and old*). Don't be so nasty, Bennie.

Beneatha (*still to her brother*). And the day before that and the day before that!

Walter (*defensively*). I'm interested in you.

Something wrong with that? Ain't many girls who decide—

Walter *and* **Beneatha** (*in unison*).—"to be a doctor." (*silence*)

Walter. Have we figured out yet just exactly how much medical school is going to cost?

Ruth. Walter Lee, why don't you leave that girl alone and get out of here to work?

Beneatha (*exits to the bathroom and bangs on the door*). Come on out of there, please!

(*She comes back into the room.*)

Walter (*looking at his sister intently*). You know the check is coming tomorrow.

Beneatha (*turning on him with a sharpness all her own*). That money belongs to Mama, Walter, and it's for her to decide how she wants to use it. I don't care if she wants to buy a house or a rocket ship or just nail it up somewhere and look at it. It's hers. Not ours—*hers.*

Walter (*bitterly*). Now ain't that fine! You just got your mother's interest at heart, ain't you, girl? You such a nice girl—but if Mama got that money she can always take a few thousand and help you through school too—can't she?

Beneatha. I have never asked anyone around here to do anything for me!

Walter. No! And the line between asking and just accepting when the time comes is big and wide—ain't it!

Beneatha (*with fury*). What do you want from me, Brother—that I quit school or just drop dead, which!

Walter. I don't want nothing but for you to stop acting holy 'round here. Me and Ruth done made some sacrifices for you—why can't you do something for the family?

Ruth. Walter, don't be dragging me in it.

Walter. You are in it—don't you get up and go work in somebody's kitchen for the last three years to help put clothes on her back?

Ruth. Oh, Walter—that's not fair. . . .

Walter. It ain't that nobody expects you to get on your knees and say thank you, Brother; thank you, Ruth; thank you, Mama—and thank you, Travis, for wearing the same pair of shoes for two semesters—

Beneatha (*dropping to her knees*). Well—I *do*—all right?—thank everybody . . . and forgive me for ever wanting to be anything at all . . . forgive me, forgive me!

Ruth. Please stop it! Your mama'll hear you.

Walter. Who the hell told you you had to be a doctor? If you so crazy 'bout messing 'round with sick people—then go be a nurse like other women—or just get married and be quiet. . . .

Beneatha. Well—you finally got it said. . . . It took you three years but you finally got it said. Walter, give up; leave me alone—it's Mama's money.

Walter. *He was my father, too!*

Beneatha. So what? He was mine, too—and Travis' grandfather—but the insurance money belongs to Mama. Picking on me is not going to make her give it to you to invest in any liquor stores—(*underbreath, dropping into a chair*)—and I for one say, God bless Mama for that!

Walter (*to Ruth*). See—did you hear? Did you hear!

Ruth. Honey, please go to work.

Walter. Nobody in this house is ever going to understand me.

Beneatha. Because you're a nut.

Walter. Who's a nut?

Beneatha. You—you are a nut. Thee is mad, boy.

Walter (*looking at his wife and his sister from the door, very sadly*). The world's most backward race of people, and that's a fact.

Beneatha (*turning slowly in her chair*). And then there are all those prophets who would lead us out of the wilderness— (Walter *slams out of the house*)—into the swamps!

Ruth. Bennie, why you always gotta be pickin' on your brother? Can't you be a little sweeter sometimes? (*Door opens. Walter walks in.*)

Walter (*to Ruth*). I need some money for carfare.

Ruth (*looks at him, then warms; teasing, but tenderly*). Fifty cents? (*She goes to her bag and gets money.*) Here, take a taxi.

(Walter *exits.* Mama *enters. She is a woman in her early sixties, full-bodied and strong. She is one of those women of a certain grace and beauty who wear it so unobtrusively that it takes a while to notice. Her dark-brown face is surrounded by the total whiteness of her hair, and being a woman who has adjusted to many things in life and overcome many more, her face is full of strength. She has, we can see, wit and faith of a kind that keep her eyes lit and full of interest and expectancy. She is, in a word, a beautiful woman. Her bearing is perhaps most like the noble bearing of the women of the Hereros[4] of Southwest Africa— rather as if she imagines that as she walks she still bears a basket or a vessel upon her head. Her speech, on the other hand, is as careless*

---

4. **Hereros** (he′ rə′ rōz).

as her carriage is precise—she is inclined to slur everything—but her voice is perhaps not so much quiet as simply soft.)

Mama. Who that 'round here slamming doors at this hour?

(She crosses through the room, goes to the window, opens it, and brings in a feeble little plant growing doggedly in a small pot on the window sill. She feels the dirt and puts it back out.)

Ruth. That was Walter Lee. He and Bennie was at it again.

Mama. My children and they tempers. Lord, if this little old plant don't get more sun than it's been getting it ain't never going to see spring again. *(She turns from the window.)* What's the matter with you this morning, Ruth? You looks right peaked. You aiming to iron all them things? Leave some for me. I'll get to 'em this afternoon. Bennie honey, it's too drafty for you to be sitting 'round half-dressed. Where's your robe?

Beneatha. In the cleaners.

Mama. Well, go get mine and put it on.

Beneatha. I'm not cold, Mama, honest.

Mama. I know—but you so thin. . . .

Beneatha *(irritably)*. Mama, I'm not cold.

Mama *(seeing the make-down bed as* Travis *has left it)*. Lord have mercy, look at that poor bed. Bless his heart—he tries, don't he?

(She moves to the bed Travis *has sloppily made up.)*

Ruth. No—he don't half try at all 'cause he knows you going to come along behind him and fix everything. That's just how come he don't know how to do nothing right now—you done spoiled that boy so.

Mama. Well—he's a little boy. Ain't sup-posed to know 'bout housekeeping. My baby, that's what he is. What you fix for his breakfast this morning?

Ruth *(angrily)*. I feed my son, Lena!

Mama. I ain't meddling—*(underbreath; busybodyish)* I just noticed all last week he had cold cereal, and when it starts getting this chilly in the fall a child ought to have some hot grits or something when he goes out in the cold—

Ruth *(furious)*. I gave him hot oats—is that all right!

Mama. I ain't meddling. *(pause)* Put lots of nice butter on it? (Ruth *shoots her an angry look and does not reply.)* He likes lots of butter.

Ruth *(exasperated)*. Lena—

Mama. (To Beneatha. Mama *is inclined to wander conversationally sometimes.)* What was you and your brother fussing 'bout this morning?

Beneatha. It's not important, Mama.

(She gets up and goes to look out at the bathroom, which is apparently free, and she picks up her towels and rushes out.)

Mama. What was they fighting about?

Ruth. Now you know as well as I do.

Mama. *(shaking her head)*. Brother still worrying hisself sick about that money?

Ruth. You know he is.

Mama. You had breakfast?

Ruth. Some coffee.

Mama. Girl, you better start eating and looking after yourself better. You almost thin as Travis.

Ruth. Lena—

Mama. Un-hunh?

Ruth. What are you going to do with it?

Mama. Now don't you start, child. It's too early in the morning to start talking about money. It ain't Christian.

Ruth. It's just that he got his heart set on that store—

Mama. You mean that liquor store that Willy Harris want him to invest in?

Ruth. Yes—

Mama. We ain't no business people, Ruth. We just plain working folks.

Ruth. Ain't nobody business people till they go into business. Walter Lee say colored people ain't never going to start getting ahead till they start gambling on some different kinds of things in the world—investments and things.

Mama. What done got into you, girl? Walter Lee done finally sold you on investing.

Ruth. No. Mama, something is happening between Walter and me. I don't know what it is—but he needs something—something I can't give him any more. He needs this chance, Lena.

Mama (*frowning deeply*). But liquor, honey—

Ruth. Well—like Walter say—I spec people going to always be drinking themselves some liquor.

Mama. Well—whether they drinks it or not ain't none of my business. But whether I go into business selling it to 'em *is*, and I don't want that on my ledger this late in life. (*stopping suddenly and studying her daughter-in-law*) Ruth Younger, what's the matter with you today? You look like you could fall over right there.

Ruth. I'm tired.

Mama. Then you better stay home from work today.

Ruth. I can't stay home. She'd be calling up the agency and screaming at them, "My girl didn't come in today—send me somebody! My girl didn't come in!" Oh, she just have a fit. . . .

Mama. Well, let her have it. I'll just call her up and say you got the flu—

Ruth (*laughing*). Why the flu?

Mama. 'Cause it sounds respectable to 'em. Something white people get, too. They know 'bout the flu. Otherwise they think you been cut up or something when you tell 'em you sick.

Ruth. I got to go in. We need the money.

Mama. Somebody would of thought my children done all but starved to death the way they talk about money here late. Child, we got a great big old check coming tomorrow.

Ruth (*sincerely, but also self-righteously*). Now that's your money. It ain't got nothing to do with me. We all feel like that—Walter and Bennie and me—even Travis.

Mama (*thoughtfully, and suddenly very far away*). Ten thousand dollars—

Ruth. Sure is wonderful.

Mama. Ten thousand dollars.

Ruth. You know what you should do, Miss Lena? You should take yourself a trip somewhere. To Europe or South America or someplace—

Mama (*throwing up her hands at the thought*). Oh, child!

Ruth. I'm serious. Just pack up and leave!

Go on away and enjoy yourself some. Forget about the family and have yourself a ball for once in your life—

Mama (*drily*). You sound like I'm just about ready to die. Who'd go with me? What I look like wandering 'round Europe by myself?

Ruth. Shoot—these here rich white women do it all the time. They don't think nothing of packing up they suitcases and piling on one of them big steamships and—swoosh!—they gone, child.

Mama. Something always told me I wasn't no rich white woman.

Ruth. Well—what are you going to do with it, then?

Mama. I ain't rightly decided. (*Thinking. She speaks now with emphasis.*) Some of it got to be put away for Beneatha and her schoolin'—and ain't nothing going to touch that part of it. Nothing. (*She waits several seconds, trying to make up her mind about something, and looks at* Ruth *a little tentatively before going on.*) Been thinking that we maybe could meet the notes on a little old two-story somewhere, with a yard where Travis could play in the summertime, if we use part of the insurance for a down payment and everybody kind of pitch in. I could maybe take on a little day work again, few days a week—

Ruth (*studying her mother-in-law furtively and concentrating on her ironing, anxious to encourage without seeming to*). Well, Lord knows, we've put enough rent into this here rat trap to pay for four houses by now. . . .

Mama (*looking up at the words "rat trap" and then looking around and leaning back and sighing—in a suddenly reflective mood—*). "Rat trap"—yes, that's all it is. (*smiling*) I remember just as well the day me and Big Walter moved in here. Hadn't been married but two weeks and wasn't planning on living here no more than a year. (*She shakes her head at the dissolved dream.*) We was going to set away, little by little, don't you know, and buy a little place out in Morgan Park.[5] We had even picked out the house. (*chuckling a little*) Looks right dumpy today. But Lord, child, you should know all the dreams I had 'bout buying that house and fixing it up and making me a little garden in the back—(*She waits and stops smiling.*) And didn't none of it happen.

(*dropping her hands in a futile gesture*)

Ruth (*keeps her head down, ironing*). Yes, life can be a barrel of disappointments, sometimes.

Mama. Honey, Big Walter would come in here some nights back then and slump down on that couch there and just look at the rug, and look at me and look at the rug and then back at me—and I'd know he was down then . . . really down. (*After a second very long and thoughtful pause; she is seeing back to times that only she can see.*) And then, Lord, when I lost that baby—little Claude—I almost thought I was going to lose Big Walter too. Oh, that man grieved hisself! He was one man to love his children.

Ruth. Ain't nothin' can tear at you like losin' your baby.

Mama. I guess that's how come that man finally worked hisself to death like he done. Like he was fighting his own war with this here world that took his baby from him.

Ruth. He sure was a fine man, all right. I always liked Mr. Younger.

---

5. **Morgan Park:** an area on the South Side of Chicago.

Mama. Crazy 'bout his children! God knows there was plenty wrong with Walter Younger—hardheaded, mean, kind of wild with women—plenty wrong with him. But he sure loved his children. Always wanted them to have something—be something. That's where Brother gets all these notions, I reckon. Big Walter used to say, he'd get right wet in the eyes sometimes, lean his head back with the water standing in his eyes and say, "Seem like God didn't see fit to give the black man nothing but dreams—but He did give us children to make those dreams seem worthwhile." (*She smiles.*) He could talk like that, don't you know.

Ruth. Yes, he sure could. He was a good man, Mr. Younger.

Mama. Yes, a fine man—just couldn't never catch up with his dreams, that's all.

(Beneatha *comes in, brushing her hair and looking up to the ceiling, where the sound of a vacuum cleaner has started up.*)

Beneatha. What could be so dirty on that woman's rugs that she has to vacuum them every single day?

Ruth. I wish certain young women 'round here who I could name would take inspiration about certain rugs in a certain apartment I could also mention.

Beneatha (*shrugging*). How much cleaning can a house need?

Mama. Bennie!

Ruth. Just listen to her—just listen!

Beneatha. Oh, God!

Mama. If you use the Lord's name just one more time—

Beneatha (*a bit of a whine*). Oh, Mama—

Ruth. Fresh—just fresh as salt, this girl!

Beneatha (*drily*). Well—if the salt loses its savor—

Mama. Now that will do. I just ain't going to have you 'round here reciting the scriptures in vain—you hear me?

Beneatha. How did I manage to get on everybody's wrong side by just walking into a room?

Ruth. If you weren't so fresh—

Beneatha. Ruth, I'm twenty years old.

Mama. What time you be home from school today?

Beneatha. Kind of late. (*with enthusiasm*) Madeline is going to start my guitar lessons today.

(Mama *and* Ruth *look up with the same expression.*)

Mama. Your *what* kind of lessons?

Beneatha. Guitar.

Ruth. Oh, Father!

Mama. How come you done take it in your mind to learn to play the guitar?

Beneatha. I just want to, that's all.

Mama (*smiling*). Lord, child, don't you know what to do with yourself? How long it going to be before you get tired of this now—like you got tired of that little play-acting group you joined last year? (*looking at* Ruth) And what was it the year before that?

Ruth. The horseback-riding club for which she bought that fifty-five-dollar riding habit that's been hanging in the closet ever since!

Mama (*to* Beneatha). Why you got to flit so from one thing to another, baby?

Beneatha (*sharply*). I just want to learn to

play the guitar. Is there anything wrong with that?

Mama. Ain't nobody trying to stop you. I just wonders sometimes why you has to flit so from one thing to another all the time. You ain't never done nothing with all that camera equipment you brought home—

Beneatha. I don't flit! I—I experiment with different forms of expression—

Ruth. Like riding a horse?

Beneatha. —People have to express themselves one way or another.

Mama. What is it you want to express?

Beneatha (*angrily*). Me! (Mama *and* Ruth *look at each other and burst into raucous laughter.*) Don't worry—I don't expect you to understand.

Mama (*to change the subject*). Who you going out with tomorrow night?

Beneatha (*with displeasure*). George Murchison again.

Mama (*pleased*). Oh—you getting a little sweet on him?

Ruth. You ask me, this child ain't sweet on nobody but herself—(*underbreath*) Express herself!

(*They laugh.*)

Beneatha. Oh—I like George all right, Mama. I mean I like him enough to go out with him and stuff, but—

Ruth (*for devilment*). What does *and stuff* mean?

Beneatha. Mind your own business.

Mama. Stop picking at her now, Ruth. (*a thoughtful pause, and then a suspicious sudden look at her daughter as she turns in her chair for emphasis*) What *does* it mean?

Beneatha (*wearily*). Oh, I just mean I couldn't ever really be serious about George. He's—he's so shallow.

Ruth. Shallow—what do you mean he's shallow? He's *Rich!*

Mama. Hush, Ruth.

Beneatha. I know he's rich. He knows he's rich, too.

Ruth. Well, what other qualities a man got to have to satisfy you, little girl?

Beneatha. You wouldn't even begin to understand. Anybody who married Walter could not possibly understand.

Mama (*outraged*). What kind of way is that to talk about your brother?

Beneatha. Brother is a flip—let's face it.

Mama (*to* Ruth, *helplessly*). What's a flip?

Ruth (*glad to add kindling*). She's saying he's crazy.

Beneatha. Not crazy. Brother isn't really crazy yet—he—he's an elaborate neurotic.

Mama. Hush your mouth!

Beneatha. As for George. Well. George looks good—he's got a beautiful car and he takes me to nice places and, as my sister-in-law says, he is probably the richest boy I will ever get to know and I even like him sometimes—but if the Youngers are sitting around waiting to see if their little Bennie is going to tie up the family with the Murchisons, they are wasting their time.

Ruth. You mean you wouldn't marry George Murchison if he asked you someday? That pretty, rich thing? Honey, I knew you was odd—

Beneatha. No I would not marry him if all I felt for him was what I feel now. Besides, George's family wouldn't really like it.

Mama. Why not?

Beneatha. Oh, Mama—The Murchisons are honest-to-God-real-*live*-rich colored people, and the only people in the world who are more snobbish than rich white people are rich colored people. I thought everybody knew that. I've met Mrs. Murchison. She's a scene!

Mama. You must not dislike people 'cause they well off, honey.

Beneatha. Why not? It makes just as much sense as disliking people 'cause they are poor, and lots of people do that.

Ruth (*a wisdom-of-the-ages manner. To* Mama). Well, she'll get over some of this—

Beneatha. Get over it? What are you talking about, Ruth? Listen, I'm going to be a doctor. I'm not worried about who I'm going to marry yet—if I ever get married.

Mama *and* **Ruth.** *If!*

Mama. Now, Bennie—

Beneatha. Oh I probably will . . . but first I'm going to be a doctor and George, for one, still thinks that's pretty funny. I couldn't be bothered with that. I'm going to be a doctor and everybody around here better understand that!

Mama (*kindly*). 'Course you going to be a doctor, honey, God willing.

Beneatha (*drily*). God hasn't got a thing to do with it.

Mama. Beneatha—that just wasn't necessary.

Beneatha. Well—neither is God. I get sick of hearing about God.

Mama. Beneatha!

Beneatha. I mean it! I'm just tired of hearing about God all the time. What has He got to do with anything? Does he pay tuition?

Mama. You 'bout to get your fresh little jaw slapped!

Ruth. That's just what she needs, all right!

Beneatha. Why? Why can't I say what I want to around here, like everybody else?

Mama. It don't sound nice for a young girl to say things like that—you wasn't brought up that way. Me and your father went to trouble to get you and Brother to church every Sunday.

Beneatha. Mama, you don't understand. It's all a matter of ideas, and God is just one idea I don't accept. It's not important. I am not going out and be immoral or commit crimes because I don't believe in God. I don't even think about it. It's just that I get tired of Him getting credit for all the things the human race achieves through its own stubborn effort. There simply is no God—there is only man and it is he who makes miracles.

(Mama *absorbs this speech, studies her daughter and rises slowly and crosses to* Beneatha *and slaps her powerfully across the face. After, there is only silence and the daughter drops her eyes from her mother's face, and* Mama *is very tall before her.*)

Mama. Now—you say after me, in my mother's house there is still God. (*There is a long pause and* Beneatha *stares at the floor wordlessly.* Mama *repeats the phrase with precision and cool emotion.*) In my mother's house there is still God.

Beneatha. In my mother's house there is still God.

(*a long pause*)

Mama. (*Walking away from* Beneatha, *too disturbed for triumphant posture. Stopping and turning back to her daughter.*). There are some ideas we ain't going to have in this house. Not long as I am at the head of this family.

Beneatha. Yes, ma'am.

(Mama *walks out of the room.*)

Ruth (*almost gently, with profound understanding*). You think you a woman, Bennie —but you still a little girl. What you did was childish—so you got treated like a child.

Beneatha. I see. (*quietly*) I also see that everybody thinks it's all right for Mama to be a tyrant. But all the tyranny in the world will never put a God in the heavens!

(*She picks up her books and goes out.*)

Ruth (*goes to* Mama's *door*). She said she was sorry.

Mama (*coming out, going to her plant*). They frightens me, Ruth. My children.

Ruth. You got good children, Lena. They just a little off sometimes—but they're good.

Mama. No—there's something come down between me and them that don't let us understand each other, and I don't know what it is. One done almost lost his mind thinking 'bout money all the time and the other done commence to talk about things I can't seem to understand in no form or fashion. What is it that's changing, Ruth?

Ruth (*soothingly, older than her years*). Now . . . you take it all too seriously. You just got strong-willed children and it takes a strong woman like you to keep 'em in hand.

Mama (*looking at her plant and sprinkling a little water on it*). They spirited all right, my children. Got to admit they got spirit—

Bennie and Walter. Like this little old plant that ain't never had enough sunshine or nothing—and look at it. . . .

(*She has her back to* Ruth, *who has had to stop ironing and lean against something and put the back of her hand to her forehead.*)

Ruth (*trying to keep* Mama *from noticing*). You . . . sure . . . loves that little old thing, don't you? . . .

Mama. Well, I always wanted me a garden like I used to see sometimes at the back of the houses down home. This plant is close as I ever got to having one. (*She looks out the window as she replaces the plant.*) Lord, ain't nothing as dreary as the view from this window on a dreary day, is there? Why ain't you singing this morning, Ruth? Sing that "No Ways Tired." That song always lifts me up so—(*She turns at last to see that* Ruth *has slipped quietly into a chair, in a state of semi-consciousness.*) Ruth! Ruth honey—what's the matter with you . . . Ruth!

SCENE 2

It is the following morning, a Saturday morning, and house cleaning is in progress at the Youngers'. Furniture has been shoved hither and yon, and Mama is giving the kitchen-area walls a washing down. Beneatha, in dungarees, with a handkerchief tied around her face, is spraying insecticide into the cracks in the walls. As they work, the radio is on and a South Side disk-jockey program is inappropriately filling the house with a rather exotic saxophone blues. Travis, the sole idle one, is leaning on his arms, looking out of the window.

Travis. Grandmama, that stuff Bennie is using smells awful. Can I go downstairs, please?

Mama. Did you get all them chores done already? I ain't seen you doing much.

Travis. Yes'm—finished early. Where did Mama go this morning?

Mama (*looking at* Beneatha). She had to go on a little errand.

Travis. Where?

Mama. To tend to her business.

Travis. Can I go outside then?

Mama. Oh, I guess so. You better stay right in front of the house, though . . . and keep a good lookout for the postman.

Travis. Yes'm. (*He starts out and decides to give his* Aunt Beneatha *a good swat on the legs as he passes her.*) Leave them poor little old cockroaches alone, they ain't bothering you none.

(*He runs as she swings the spray gun at him both viciously and playfully.* Walter *enters from the bedroom and goes to the phone.*)

Mama. Look out there, girl, before you be spilling some of that stuff on that child!

Travis (*teasing*). That's right—look out now!

(*He exits.*)

Beneatha (*drily*). I can't imagine that it would hurt him—it has never hurt the roaches.

Mama. Well, little boys' hides ain't as tough as South Side roaches.

Walter (*into phone*). Hello—let me talk to Willy Harris.

Mama. You better get over there behind the bureau. I seen one marching out of there like Napoleon yesterday.

Walter. Hello, Willy? It ain't come yet. It'll be here in a few minutes. Did the lawyer give you the papers?

Beneatha. There's only one way to get rid of them, Mama—

Mama. How?

Beneatha. Set fire to the building.

Walter. Good. Good. I'll be right over.

Beneatha. Where did Ruth go, Walter?

Walter. I don't know.

(*He exits abruptly.*)

Beneatha. Mama, where did Ruth go?

Mama (*looking at her with meaning*). To the doctor, I think.

Beneatha. The doctor? What's the matter? (*They exchange glances.*) You don't think—

Mama (*with her sense of drama*). Now I ain't saying what I think. But I ain't never been wrong 'bout a woman neither.

(*The phone rings.*)

Beneatha (*at the phone*). Hay-lo. . . . (*pause, and a moment of recognition*) Well—when did you get back! . . . And how was it? . . . Of course I've missed you—in my way. . . . This morning? No . . . house cleaning and all that and Mama hates it if I let people come over when the house is like this. . . . You *have?* Well, that's different. . . . What is it—Oh, what the hell, come on over. . . . Right, see you then.

(*She hangs up.*)

Mama (*who has listened vigorously, as is her habit*). Who is that you inviting over here with the house looking like this? You ain't got the pride you was born with!

Beneatha. Asagai doesn't care how houses look, Mama—he's an intellectual.

Mama. *Who?*

Beneatha. Asagai—Joseph Asagai. He's an African boy I met on campus. He's been studying in Canada all summer.

Mama. What's his name?

Beneatha. Asagai, Joseph. As-sah-guy. . . . He's from Nigeria.

Mama. Oh, that's the little country that was founded by slaves way back. . . .

Beneatha. No, Mama—that's Liberia.

Mama. I don't think I never met no African before.

Beneatha. Well, do me a favor and don't ask him a whole lot of ignorant questions about Africans. I mean, do they wear clothes and all that—

Mama. Well, now I guess if you think we so ignorant 'round here maybe you shouldn't bring your friends here—

Beneatha. It's just that people ask such crazy things. All anyone seems to know about when it comes to Africa is Tarzan—

Mama (*indignantly*). Why should I know anything about Africa?

Beneatha. Why do you give money at church for the missionary work?

Mama. Well, that's to help save people.

Beneatha. You mean save them from *heathenism*—

Mama (*innocently*). Yes.

Beneatha. I'm afraid they need more salvation from the British and the French.

(Ruth *comes in forlornly and pulls off her coat with dejection. They both turn to look at her.*)

Ruth (*distractedly*). Well I guess from all the happy faces—everybody knows.

Beneatha. You pregnant?

Mama. Lord have mercy, I sure hope it's a little old girl. Travis ought to have a sister.

(Beneatha *and* Ruth *give her a hopeless look for this grandmotherly enthusiasm.*)

Beneatha. How far along are you?

Ruth. Two months.

Beneatha. Did you mean to? I mean did you plan it or was it an accident?

Mama. What do you know about planning or not planning?

Beneatha. Oh, Mama.

Ruth (*wearily*). She's twenty years old, Lena.

Beneatha. Did you plan it, Ruth?

Mama. Mind your own business.

Beneatha. It is my business—where is he going to live, on the *roof*? (*There is silence following the remark as the three women react to the sense of it.*) Gee—I didn't mean it like that, Ruth, honest. Gee, I don't feel like that at all. I—I think it is wonderful.

Ruth (*dully*). Wonderful.

Beneatha. Yes—really.

Mama (*looking at* Ruth, *worried*). Doctor say everything going to be all right?

Ruth (*far away*). Yes—she says everything is going to be fine. . . .

Mama (*immediately suspicious*). "She"— What doctor you went to?

(Ruth *folds over, near hysteria.*)

Mama (*worriedly hovering over* Ruth). Ruth

honey—what's the matter with you—you sick?

(Ruth *has her fists clenched on her thighs and is fighting hard to suppress a scream that seems to be rising in her.*)

Beneatha. What's the matter with her, Mama?

Mama (*working her fingers in Ruth's shoulder to relax her*). She be all right. Women gets right depressed sometimes when they get her way. (*speaking softly, expertly, rapidly*) Now you just relax. That's right. . . . just lean back, don't think 'bout nothing at all . . . nothing at all—

Ruth. I'm all right. . . .

(*The glassy-eyed look melts and then she collapses into a fit of heavy sobbing. The bell rings.*)

Beneatha. Oh—that must be Asagai.

Mama (*to Ruth*). Come on now, honey. You need to lie down and rest awhile . . . then have some nice hot food.

(*They exit, Ruth's weight on her mother-in-law. Beneatha, herself profoundly disturbed, opens the door to admit a rather dramatic-looking young man with a large package.*)

Asagai. Hello, Alaiyo—[6]

Beneatha (*holding the door open and regarding him with pleasure*). Hello. . . . (*long pause*) Well—come in. And please excuse everything. My mother was very upset about my letting anyone come here with the place like this.

Asagai (*coming into the room*). You look disturbed too. . . . Is something wrong?

Beneatha (*still at door, absently*). Yes . . . we've all got acute ghetto-itus. (*She smiles*

and comes toward him, finding a cigarette and sitting.) So—sit down! How was Canada?

Asagai (*a sophisticate*). Canadian.

Beneatha (*looking at him*). I'm very glad you are back.

Asagai (*looking at her in turn*). Are you really?

Beneatha. Yes—very.

Asagai. Why—you were quite glad when I went away. What happened?

Beneatha. You went away.

Asagai. Ahhhhhhh.

Beneatha. Before—you wanted to be so serious before there was time.

Asagai. How much time must there be before one knows what one feels?

Beneatha (*stalling this particular conversation. Her hands pressed together, in a deliberately childish gesture.*). What did you bring me?

Asagai (*handing her the package*). Open it and see.

Beneatha (*eagerly opening the package and drawing out some records and the colorful robes of a Nigerian woman*). Oh, Asagai! You got them for me! . . . How beautiful . . . and the records too! (*She lifts out the robes and runs to the mirror with them and holds the drapery up in front of herself.*)

Asagai (*coming to her at the mirror*). I shall have to teach you how to drape it properly. (*He flings the material about her for the moment and stands back to look at her.*) Ah—Oh-pay-gay-day, oh-gbah-mu-shay.

---

6. **Alaiyo** (ə lī′ yo).

(*a Yoruba*[7] *exclamation of admiration*) You wear it well . . . very well . . . mutilated hair and all.

Beneatha (*turning suddenly*). My hair—what's wrong with my hair?

Asagai (*shrugging*). Were you born with it like that?

Beneatha (*reaching up to touch it*). No . . . of course not.

(*She looks back to the mirror, disturbed.*)

Asagai (*smiling*). How then?

Beneatha. You know perfectly well how . . . as crinkly as yours . . . that's how.

Asagai. And is it ugly to you that way?

Beneatha (*quickly*). Oh, no—not ugly. . . . (*more slowly, apologetically*) But it's so hard to manage when it's, well—raw.

Asagai. And so to accommodate that—you mutilate it every week?

Beneatha. It's not mutilation!

Asagai (*laughing aloud at her seriousness*). Oh . . . please! I am only teasing you because you are so very serious about these things. (*He stands back from her and folds his arms across his chest as he watches her pulling at her hair and frowning in the mirror.*) Do you remember the first time you met me at school? . . . (*He laughs.*) You came up to me and you said—and I thought you were the most serious little thing I had ever seen—you said: (*He imitates her.*) "Mr. Asagai—I want very much to talk with you. About Africa. You see, Mr. Asagai, I am looking for my *identity.*"

(*He laughs.*)

Beneatha (*turning to him, not laughing*). Yes—

(*Her face is quizzical, profoundly disturbed.*)

Asagai (*still teasing, and reaching out and taking her face in his hands and turning her profile to him*). Well . . . it is true that this is not so much a profile of a Hollywood queen as perhaps a queen of the Nile—(*a mock dismissal of the importance of the question*) But what does it matter? Assimilationism[8] is so popular in your country.

Beneatha (*wheeling, passionately, sharply*). I am not an assimilationist!

Asagai (*The protest hangs in the room for a moment and Asagai studies her, his laughter fading.*). Such a serious one. (*There is a pause.*) So—you like the robes? You must take excellent care of them—they are from my sister's personal wardrobe.

Beneatha (*with incredulity*). You—you sent all the way home—for me?

Asagai (*with charm*). For you—I would do much more. . . . Well, that is what I came for. I must go.

Beneatha. Will you call me Monday?

Asagai. Yes . . . We have a great deal to talk about. I mean about identity and time and all that.

Beneatha. Time?

Asagai. Yes. About how much time one needs to know what one feels.

Beneatha. You never understood that there is more than one kind of feeling which can exist between a man and a woman—or, at least, there should be.

---

7. Yoruba (yō′ rōō bə): an African tribal people who live in southwestern Nigeria and parts of Benin and Togo.

8. assimilationism (ə sim′ ə lā′ sʰən iz′ əm): the policy of completely absorbing minority groups into the main culture.

Asagai (*shaking his head negatively but gently*). No. Between a man and a woman there need be only one kind of feeling. I have that for you. . . . Now even . . . right at this moment. . . .

Beneatha. I know—and by itself—it won't do. I can find that anywhere.

Asagai. For a woman it should be enough.

Beneatha. I know—because that's what it says in all the novels that men write. But it isn't. Go ahead and laugh—but I'm not interested in being someone's little episode in America or—(*with feminine vengeance*)—one of them! (*Asagai has burst into laughter again.*) That's funny as hell, huh!

Asagai. It's just that every American girl I have known has said that to me. White—black—in this you are all the same. And the same speech, too!

Beneatha (*angrily*). Yuk, yuk, yuk!

Asagai. It's how you can be sure that the world's most liberated women are not liberated at all. You all talk about it too much!

(*Mama enters and is immediately all social charm because of the presence of a guest.*)

Beneatha. Oh—Mama—this is Mr. Asagai.

Mama. How do you do?

Asagai (*total politeness to an elder*). How do you do, Mrs. Younger. Please forgive me for coming at such an outrageous hour on a Saturday.

Mama. Well, you are quite welcome. I just hope you understand that our house don't always look like this. (*chatterish*) You must come again. I would love to hear about—(*not sure of the name*)—your country. I

think it's so sad the way our American Negroes don't know nothing about Africa 'cept Tarzan and all that. And all that money they pour into these churches when they ought to be helping you people over there drive out them French and Englishmen done take away your land.

(*The mother flashes a slightly superior look at her daughter upon completion of the recitation.*)

Asagai (*taken aback by this sudden and acutely unrelated expression of sympathy*). Yes . . . yes . . .

Mama (*smiling at him suddenly and relaxing and looking him over*). How many miles is it from here to where you come from?

Asagai. Many thousands.

Mama (*looking at him as she would* Walter). I bet you don't half look after yourself, being away from your mama, either. I spec you better come 'round here from time to time and get yourself some decent home-cooked meals. . . .

Asagai (*moved*). Thank you. Thank you very much. (*They are all quiet, then—*) Well . . . I must go. I will call you Monday, Alaiyo.

Mama. What's that he call you?

Asagai. Oh—"Alaiyo." I hope you don't mind. It is what you would call a nickname, I think. It is a Yoruba word. I am a Yoruba.

Mama (*looking at* Beneatha). I—I thought he was from—

Asagai (*understanding*). Nigeria is my country. Yoruba is my tribal origin—

Beneatha. You didn't tell us what Alaiyo means . . . for all I know, you might be calling me Little Idiot or something. . . .

Asagai. Well . . . let me see . . . I do not know how just to explain it. . . . The sense of a thing can be so different when it changes languages.

Beneatha. You're evading.

Asagai. No—really, it is difficult. . . . (*thinking*) It means . . . it means One for Whom Bread—Food—Is Not Enough. (*He looks at her.*) Is that all right?

Beneatha (*understanding, softly*). Thank you.

Mama (*looking from one to the other and not understanding any of it*). Well . . . that's nice. . . . You must come see us again— Mr.—

Asagai. Ah-sah-guy. . . .

Mama. Yes . . . Do come again.

Asagai. Goodbye.

(*He exits.*)

Mama (*after him*). Lord, that's a pretty thing just went out here! (*insinuatingly, to her daughter*) Yes, I guess I see why we done commence to get so interested in Africa 'round here. Missionaries, my aunt Jenny!

(*She exits.*)

Beneatha. Oh, Mama! . . .

(*She picks up the Nigerian dress and holds it up to her in front of the mirror again. She sets the headdress on haphazardly and then notices her hair again and clutches at it and then replaces the headdress and frowns at herself. Then she starts to wriggle in front of the mirror as she thinks a Nigerian woman might. Travis enters and regards her.*)

Travis. You cracking up?

Beneatha. Shut up.

(*She pulls the headdress off and looks at her-self in the mirror and clutches at her hair again and squinches her eyes as if trying to imagine something. Then, suddenly, she gets her raincoat and kerchief and hurriedly prepares for going out.*)

Mama (*coming back into the room*). She's resting now. Travis, baby, run next door and ask Miss Johnson to please let me have a little kitchen cleanser. This here can is empty as Jacob's kettle.

Travis. I just came in.

Mama. Do as you're told. (*He exits and she looks at her daughter.*) Where you going?

Beneatha (*halting at the door*). To become a queen of the Nile!

(*She exits in a breathless blaze of glory. Ruth appears in the bedroom doorway.*)

Mama. Who told you to get up?

Ruth. Ain't nothing wrong with me to be lying in no bed for. Where did Bennie go?

Mama (*drumming her fingers*). Far as I could make out—to Egypt. (*Ruth just looks at her.*) What time is it getting to?

Ruth. Ten-twenty. And the mailman going to ring that bell this morning just like he done every morning for the last umpteen years.

(*Travis comes in with the cleanser can.*)

Travis. She say to tell you that she don't have much.

Mama (*angrily*). Lord, some people I could name sure is tightfisted! (*directing her grandson*) Mark two cans of cleanser down on the list there. If she that hard up for kitchen cleanser, I sure don't want to forget to get her none!

Ruth. Lena—maybe the woman is just short on cleanser—

Mama (*not listening*). —Much baking powder as she done borrowed from me all these years, she could of done gone into the baking business!

(*The bell sounds suddenly and sharply, and all three are stunned—serious and silent—midspeech. In spite of all the other conversations and distractions of the morning, this is what they have been waiting for, even Travis, who looks helplessly from his mother to his grandmother. Ruth is the first to come to life again.*)

Ruth (*to Travis*). *Get down them steps, boy!*

(*Travis snaps to life and flies out to get the mail.*)

Mama (*her eyes wide, her hand to her breast*). You mean it done really come?

Ruth (*excited*). Oh, Miss Lena!

Mama (*collecting herself*). Well . . . I don't know what we all so excited about 'round here for. We known it was coming for months.

Ruth. That's a whole lot different from having it come and being able to hold it in your hands . . . a piece of paper worth ten thousand dollars. . . . (*Travis bursts back into the room. He holds the envelope high above his head, like a little dancer; his face is radiant and he is breathless. He moves to his grandmother with sudden slow ceremony and puts the envelope in her hands. She accepts it, and then merely holds it and looks at it.*) Come on! Open it. . . . Lord have mercy. I wish Walter Lee was here!

Travis. Open it, Grandmama!

Mama (*staring at it*). Now you all be quiet. It's just a check.

Ruth. Open it . . .

Mama (*still staring at it*). Now don't act silly. . . . We ain't never been no people to act silly 'bout no money—

Ruth (*swiftly*). We ain't never had none before—open it!

(Mama *finally makes a good strong tear and pulls out the thin blue slice of paper and inspects it closely. The boy and his mother study it raptly over Mama's shoulders.*)

Mama. *Travis!* (*She is counting off with doubt.*) Is that the right number of zeros?

Travis. Yes'm . . . ten thousand dollars. Gaalee, Grandmama, you rich.

Mama (*She holds the check away from her, still looking at it. Slowly her face sobers into a mask of unhappiness.*). Ten thousand dollars. (*She hands it to Ruth.*) Put it away somewhere, Ruth. (*She does not look at Ruth; her eyes seem to be seeing something somewhere very far off.*) Ten thousand dollars they give you. Ten thousand dollars.

Travis (*to his mother, sincerely*). What's the matter with Grandmama—don't she want to be rich?

Ruth (*distractedly*). You go on out and play now, baby. (*Travis exits. Mama starts wiping dishes absently humming intently to herself. Ruth turns to her, with kind exasperation.*) You've gone and got yourself upset.

Mama (*not looking at her*). I spec if it wasn't for you all . . . I would just put that money away or give it to the church or something.

Ruth. Now what kind of talk is that. Mr. Younger would just be plain mad if he could hear you talking foolish like that.

Mama (*stopping and staring off*). Yes . . . he sure would. (*sighing*) We got enough to do with that money, all right. (*She halts then,* and turns and looks at her daughter-in-law hard; Ruth *avoids her eyes and Mama* wipes *her hands with finality and starts to speak firmly to* Ruth.) Where did you go today, girl?

Ruth. To the doctor.

Mama (*impatiently*). Now, Ruth . . . you know better than that. Old Doctor Jones is strange enough in his way but there ain't nothing 'bout him make somebody slip and call him "she"—like you done this morning.

Ruth. Well, that's what happened—my tongue slipped.

Mama. You went to see that woman, didn't you?

Ruth (*defensively, giving herself away*). What woman you talking about?

Mama (*angrily*). That woman who—

(Walter *enters in great excitement.*)

Walter. Did it come?

Mama (*quietly*). Can't you give people a Christian greeting before you start asking about money?

Walter (*to* Ruth). Did it come? (Ruth *unfolds the check and lays it quietly before him, watching him intently with thoughts of her own.* Walter *sits down and grasps it close and counts off the zeros.*) Ten thousand dollars—(*He turns suddenly, frantically, to his mother and draws some papers out of his breast pocket.*) Mama—look. Old Willy Harris put everything on paper—

Mama. Son—I think you ought to talk to your wife. . . . I'll go on out and leave you alone if you want—

Walter. I can talk to her later—Mama, look—

Mama. Son—

Walter. WILL SOMEBODY PLEASE LISTEN TO ME TODAY!

Mama (*quietly*). I don't 'low no yellin' in this house, Walter Lee, and you know it—(Walter *stares at them in frustration and starts to speak several times.*) And there ain't going to be no investing in no liquor stores. I don't aim to have to speak on that again.

(*a long pause*)

Walter. Oh—so you don't aim to have to speak on that again? So *you* have decided . . . (*crumpling his papers*) Well, *you* tell that to my boy tonight when you put him to sleep on the living-room couch. . . . (*turning to* Mama *and speaking directly to her*) Yeah—and tell it to my wife, Mama, tomorrow when she has to go out of here to look after somebody else's kids. And tell it to *me*, Mama, every time we need a new pair of curtains, and I have to watch *you* go out and work in somebody's kitchen. Yeah, you tell me then!

(Walter *starts out.*)

Ruth. Where you going?

Walter. I'm going out!

Ruth. Where?

Walter. Just out of the house somewhere—

Ruth (*getting her coat*). I'll come too.

Walter. I don't want you to come!

Ruth. I got something to talk to you about, Walter.

Walter. That's too bad.

Mama (*still quietly*). Walter Lee—(*She waits and he finally turns and looks at her.*) Sit down.

Walter. I'm a grown man, Mama.

Mama. Ain't nobody said you wasn't grown. But you still in my house and my presence. And as long as you are—you'll talk to your wife civil. Now sit down.

Ruth (*suddenly*). Oh, let him go on out and drink himself to death! He makes me sick to my stomach! (*She flings her coat against him.*)

Walter (*violently*). And you turn mine too, baby! (Ruth *goes into their bedroom and slams the door behind her.*) That was my greatest mistake—

Mama (*still quietly*). Walter, what is the matter with you?

Walter. Matter with me? Ain't nothing the matter with *me!*

Mama. Yes there is. Something eating you up like a crazy man. Something more than me not giving you this money. The past few years I been watching it happen to you. You get all nervous acting and kind of wild in the eyes—(Walter *jumps up impatiently at her words.*) I said sit there now, I'm talking to you!

Walter. Mama—I don't need no nagging at me today.

Mama. Seem like you getting to a place where you always tied up in some kind of knot about something. But if anybody ask you 'bout it you just yell at 'em and bust out the house and go out and drink somewheres. Walter Lee, people can't live with that. Ruth's a good, patient girl in her way—but you getting to be too much. Boy, don't make the mistake of driving that girl away from you.

Walter. Why—what she do for me?

Mama. She loves you.

Walter. Mama—I'm going out. I want to go off somewhere and be by myself for a while.

Mama. I'm sorry about your liquor store, son. It just wasn't the thing for us to do. That's what I want to tell you about—

Walter. I got to go out, Mama—

(*He rises.*)

Mama. It's dangerous, son.

Walter. What's dangerous?

Mama. When a man goes outside his home to look for peace.

Walter (*beseechingly*). Then why can't there never be no peace in this house then?

Mama. You done found it in some other house?

Walter. No—there ain't no woman! Why do women always think there's a woman somewhere when a man gets restless. (*coming to her*) Mama—Mama—I want so many things. . . .

Mama. Yes, son—

Walter. I want so many things that they are driving me kind of crazy. . . . Mama—look at me.

Mama. I'm looking at you. You a good-looking boy. You got a job, a nice wife, a fine boy and—

Walter. A job. (*He looks at her.*) Mama, a job? I open and close car doors all day long. I drive a man around in his limousine and I say "Yes, sir; no sir; very good, sir; shall I take the Drive, sir?" Mama, that ain't no kind of a job. . . . that ain't nothing at all. (*very quietly*) Mama, I don't know if I can make you understand.

Mama. Understand what, baby?

Walter (*quietly*). Sometimes it's like I can see the future stretched out in front of me—just plain as day. The future, Mama. Hanging over there at the edge of my days. Just waiting for me—a big, looming blank

Think about
- Walter's comments to Ruth about what men need from women (page 326)
- the reasons Walter and Beneatha argue
- Mama and Ruth's discussion about Travis's breakfast
- the reason Mama slaps Beneatha and the statement she makes her repeat (page 334)
- Mama's response to Walter's assertion that money is life (page 345)

5. What do you predict will happen now that Mama has the insurance check?

A CREATIVE RESPONSE

6. What might the family's situation be like if Big Walter were still alive?

7. How would the impact of this play have been different if Hansberry had not provided elaborate stage directions?
Think about
- the description of Ruth at the beginning of Scene 1 (page 321)
- the description of Mama (pages 328–329)
- the stage directions describing Ruth as she irons (page 326)
- the stage directions as Walter and Beneatha fight (pages 327–328)

A CRITICAL RESPONSE

8. The playwright, Lorraine Hansberry, was angered by false, stereotypical portrayals of African Americans in literature. How true to life do you find her characters? Support your response.

9. Two poems in this book describe Chicago settings: "Tenement Room: Chicago" by Frank Marshall Davis (page 288) and "Kitchenette Building" by Gwendolyn Brooks (page 311). In your view, how well do these poems capture the spirit of the Younger home?
Think about
- the description of the apartment in the stage directions at the beginning of the play
- the dreams and frustrations of the Youngers

ACT TWO

SCENE 1. *Later the same day.*

Ruth *is ironing again. She has the radio going. Presently* Beneatha's *bedroom door opens and* Ruth's *mouth falls and she puts down the iron in fascination.*

Ruth. What have we got on tonight!

Beneatha (*emerging grandly from the doorway so that we can see her thoroughly robed in the costume Asagai brought*). You are looking at what a well-dressed Nigerian woman wears—(*She parades for* Ruth, *her hair completely hidden by the headdress; she is coquettishly fanning herself with an ornate oriental fan, mistakenly more like Butterfly[1] than any Nigerian that ever was.*) Isn't it beautiful? (*She promenades to the radio and, with an arrogant flourish, turns off the good loud blues that is playing.*) Enough of this assimilationist junk! (*Ruth follows her with her eyes as she goes to the phonograph and puts on a record and turns and waits ceremoniously for the music to come up. Then, with a shout—*) OCOMOGOSIAY!

(*Ruth jumps. The music comes up, a lovely Nigerian melody.* Beneatha *listens, enraptured, her eyes far away—"back to the past." She begins to dance.* Ruth *is dumbfounded.*)

Ruth. What kind of dance is that?

Beneatha. A folk dance.

Ruth (*Pearl Bailey*). What kind of folks do that, honey?

Beneatha. It's from Nigeria. It's a dance of welcome.

Ruth. Who you welcoming?

Beneatha. The men back to the village.

Ruth. Where they been?

Beneatha. How should I know—out hunting or something. Anyway, they are coming back now. . . .

Ruth. Well, that's good.

Beneatha (*with the record*).

> Alundi, alundi
> Alundi alunya
> Jop pu a jeepua
> Ang gu sooooooooo
> Ai yai yae. . . .
> Ayehaye—alundi . . .

(Walter *comes in during this performance; he has obviously been drinking. He leans against the door heavily and watches his sister, at first with distaste. Then his eyes look off— "back to the past"—as he lifts both his fists to the roof, screaming.*)

Walter. YEAH . . . AND ETHIOPIA STRETCH FORTH HER HANDS AGAIN!

Ruth (*drily, looking at him*). Yes—and Africa sure is claiming her own tonight. (*She gives them both up and starts ironing again.*)

Walter (*all in a dramatic shout*). Shut up! . . . I'm digging them drums . . . them drums move me! . . . (*He makes his weaving way to his wife's face and leans in close to her.*) In my *heart of hearts*—(*He thumps his chest.*) —I am much warrior!

Ruth (*without even looking up*). In your heart of hearts you are much drunkard.

Walter (*coming away from her and starting to wander around the room, shouting*). Me

---

1. Butterfly: Madame Butterfly, the main character in *Madame Butterfly,* an opera set in Japan.

and Jomo[2].... (*Intently, in his sister's face. She has stopped dancing to watch him in this unknown mood.*) That's my man, Kenyatta. (*shouting and thumping his chest*) FLAMING SPEAR! (*He is suddenly in possession of an imaginary spear and actively spearing enemies all over the room.*) OCOMOGOSIAY.... THE LION IS WAKING.... OWIMO-WEH! (*He pulls his shirt open and leaps up on a table and gestures with his spear. The bell rings. Ruth goes to answer.*)

Beneatha (*to encourage* Walter, *thoroughly caught up with this side of him*). OCO-MOGOSIAY, FLAMING SPEAR!

Walter (*on the table, very far gone, his eyes pure glass sheets. He sees what we cannot, that he is a leader of his people, a great chief, a descendant of Chaka,[3] and that the hour to march has come*). Listen, my black brothers—

Beneatha. OCOMOGOSIAY!

Walter. —Do you hear the waters rushing against the shores of the coastlands—

Beneatha. OCOMOGOSIAY!

Walter. —Do you hear the screeching of the cocks in yonder hills beyond where the chiefs meet in council for the coming of the mighty war—

Beneatha. OCOMOGOSIAY!

Walter. —Do you hear the beating of the wings of the birds flying low over the mountains and the low places of our land—

(Ruth *opens the door.* George Murchison *enters.*)

Beneatha. OCOMOGOSIAY!

Walter. —Do you hear the singing of the women, singing the war songs of our fathers to the babies in the great houses . . . singing the sweet war songs? OH, DO YOU HEAR, MY BLACK BROTHERS!

Beneatha (*completely gone*). We hear you, Flaming Spear—

Walter. Telling us to prepare for the greatness of the time—(*to* George). Black Brother!

(*He extends his hand for the fraternal clasp.*)

George. Black Brother, hell!

Ruth (*having had enough, and embarrassed for the family*). Beneatha, you got company—what's the matter with you? Walter Lee Younger, get down off that table and stop acting like a fool. . . .

(Walter *comes down off the table suddenly and makes a quick exit to the bathroom.*)

Ruth. He's had a little to drink. . . . I don't know what her excuse is.

George (*to* Beneatha). Look honey, we're going to the theater—we're not going to be in it . . . so go change, huh?

Ruth. You expect this boy to go out with you looking like that?

Beneatha (*looking at* George). That's up to George. If he's ashamed of his heritage—

George. Oh, don't be so proud of yourself, Bennie—just because you look eccentric.

Beneatha. How can something that's natural be eccentric?

George. That's what being eccentric means—being natural. Get dressed.

Beneatha. I don't like that, George.

---

2. **Jomo:** Jomo Kenyatta (jō′ mō ken yät′ ə), African political leader and first president of Kenya, from 1964 to 1978.
3. **Chaka** (chäk′ ə): a Zulu chief, the conqueror of most of southeast Africa, who lived from 1773 to 1823.

Ruth. Why must you and your brother make an argument out of everything people say?

Beneatha. Because I hate assimilationist Negroes!

Ruth. Will somebody please tell me what assimila-whoever means!

George. Oh, it's just a college girl's way of calling people Uncle Toms[4]—but that isn't what it means at all.

Ruth. Well, what does it mean?

Beneatha (*cutting* George *off and staring at him as she replies to* Ruth). It means someone who is willing to give up his own culture and submerge himself completely in the dominant, and in this case, *oppressive* culture!

George. Oh, dear, dear, dear! Here we go! A lecture on the African past! On our Great West African Heritage! In one second we will hear all about the great Ashanti empires; the great Songhay civilizations; and the great sculpture of Bénin—and then some poetry in the Bantu[5]—and the whole monologue will end with the word *heritage!* (*nastily*) Let's face it baby, your heritage is nothing but a bunch of raggedy spirituals and some grass huts!

Beneatha. *Grass huts!* (Ruth *crosses to her and forcibly pushes her toward the bedroom.*) See there . . . you are standing there in your splendid ignorance talking about people who were the first to smelt iron on the face of the earth! (Ruth *is pushing her through the door.*) The Ashanti were performing surgical operations when the English—(Ruth *pulls the door to, with* Beneatha *on the other side, and smiles graciously at* George. Beneatha *opens the door and shouts the end of the sentence defiantly at* George.)—were still tat-

tooing themselves with blue dragons. . . . (*She goes back inside.*)

Ruth. Have a seat, George. (*They both sit.* Ruth *folds her hands rather primly on her lap, determined to demonstrate the civilization of the family.*) Warm, ain't it? I mean for September. (*pause*) Just like they always say about Chicago weather. If it's too hot or cold for you, just wait a minute and it'll change. (*She smiles happily at this cliché of clichés.*) Everybody say it's got to do with them bombs and things they keep setting off. (*pause*) Would you like a nice cold beer?

George. No, thank you. I don't care for beer. (*He looks at his watch.*) I hope she hurries up.

Ruth. What time is the show?

George. It's an eight-thirty curtain. That's just Chicago, though. In New York standard curtain time is eight-forty.

(*He is rather proud of his knowledge.*)

Ruth (*properly appreciating it*). You get to New York a lot?

George (*offhand*). Few times a year.

Ruth. Oh—that's nice. I've never been to New York.

(Walter *enters. We feel he has relieved himself, but the edge of unreality is still with him.*)

Walter. New York ain't got nothing Chicago ain't. Just a bunch of hustling

---

4. **Uncle Toms:** a contemptuous term applied to African Americans who act slavishly to gain white acceptance.

5. **Ashanti, Songhay, Bénin, Bantu** (ə shän' tē, säŋ gī', be' nēn, ban' tōō): African references; respectively, a tribe, an ancient kingdom, a city, and a language.

people all squeezed up together—being "Eastern."

(*He turns his face into a screw of pleasure.*)

George. Oh—you've been?

Walter. *Plenty* of times.

Ruth (*shocked at the lie*). Walter Lee Younger!

Walter (*staring her down*). Plenty! (*pause*) What we got to drink in this house? Why don't you offer this man some refreshment. (*to George*) They don't know how to entertain people in this house, man.

George. Thank you—I don't really care for anything.

Walter (*feeling his head; sobriety coming*). Where's Mama?

Ruth. She ain't come back yet.

Walter (*looking Murchison over from head to toe, scrutinizing his carefully casual tweed sports jacket over cashmere V-neck sweater over soft eyelet shirt and tie and soft slacks, finished off with white buckskin shoes*). Why all you college boys wear them fairyish-looking white shoes?

Ruth. Walter Lee!

(*George Murchison ignores the remark.*)

Walter (*to Ruth*). Well, they look crazy as hell—white shoes, cold as it is.

Ruth (*crushed*). You have to excuse him—

Walter. No he don't! Excuse me for what? What you always excusing me for! I'll excuse myself when I needs to be excused! (*a pause*) They look as funny as them black knee socks Beneatha wears out of here all the time.

Ruth. It's the college *style*, Walter.

Walter. Style, hell! She looks like she got burnt legs or something!

Ruth. Oh, Walter—

Walter (*an irritable mimic*). Oh, Walter! Oh, Walter! (*to Murchison*) How's your old man making out? I understand you all going to buy that big hotel on the Drive? (*he finds a beer in the refrigerator, wanders over to Murchison, sipping and wiping his lips with the back of his hand, and straddling a chair backward to talk to the other man.*) Shrewd move. Your old man is all right, man. (*tapping his head and half winking for emphasis*) I mean he knows how to operate. I mean he thinks *big*, you know what I mean, I mean for a *home*, you know? But I think he's kind of running out of ideas now. I'd like to talk to him. Listen, man, I got some plans that could turn this city upside down. I mean I think like he does. *Big*. Invest big, gamble big, hell, lose *big* if you have to, you know what I mean. It's hard to find a man on this whole South Side who understands my kind of thinking—you dig? (*He scrutinizes Murchison again, drinks his beer, squints his eyes and leans in close, confidential, man to man.*) Me and you ought to sit down and talk sometimes, man. Man, I got me some ideas. . . .

George (*with boredom*). Yeah—sometimes we'll have to do that, Walter.

Walter (*understanding the indifference, and offended*). Yeah—well, when you get the time, man. I know you a busy little boy.

Ruth. Walter, please—

Walter (*bitterly, hurt*). I know ain't nothing in this world as busy as you colored college boys with your fraternity pins and white shoes. . . .

Ruth (*covering her face with humiliation*). Oh, Walter Lee—

Walter. I see you all all the time—with the books tucked under your arms—going to your (*British A—a mimic*) "clahsses." And for what! What the hell you learning over there? Filling up your heads—(*counting off on his fingers*)—with the sociology and the psychology—but they teaching you how to be a man? How to take over and run the world? They teaching you how to run a rubber plantation or a steel mill? Naw—just to talk proper and read books and wear white shoes. . . .

George (*looking at him with distaste, a little above it all*). You're all wacked up with bitterness, man.

Walter (*intently, almost quietly, between the teeth, glaring at the boy*). And you—ain't you bitter, man? Ain't you just about had it yet? Don't you see no stars gleaming that you can't reach out and grab? You happy?—you happy? You got it made? Bitter? Man, I'm a volcano. Bitter? Here I am a giant—surrounded by ants! Ants who can't even understand what it is the giant is talking about.

Ruth (*passionately and suddenly*). Oh, Walter—ain't you with nobody!

Walter (*violently*). No! 'Cause ain't nobody with me! Not even my own mother!

Ruth. Walter, that's a terrible thing to say!

(Beneatha *enters, dressed for the evening in a cocktail dress and earrings.*)

George. Well—hey, you look great.

Beneatha. Let's go, George. See you all later.

Ruth. Have a nice time.

George. Thanks. Good night. (*to Walter, sarcastically*) Good night, Prometheus.[6]

(Beneatha *and* George *exit.*)

Walter (*to Ruth*). Who is Prometheus?

Ruth. I don't know. Don't worry about it.

Walter (*in fury, pointing after George*). See there—they get to a point where they can't insult you man to man—they got to go talk about something ain't nobody never heard of!

Ruth. How do you know it was an insult? (*to humor him*) Maybe Prometheus is a nice fellow.

Walter. Prometheus! I bet there ain't even no such thing! I bet that simple-minded clown—

Ruth. Walter—

(*She stops what she is doing and looks at him.*)

Walter (*yelling*). Don't start!

Ruth. Start what?

Walter. Your nagging! Where was I? Who was I with? How much money did I spend?

Ruth (*plaintively*). Walter Lee—why don't we just try to talk about it. . . .

Walter (*not listening*). I been out talking with people who understand me. People who care about the things I got on my mind.

Ruth (*wearily*). I guess that means people like Willy Harris.

Walter. Yes, people like Willy Harris.

Ruth (*with a sudden flash of impatience*). Why don't you all just hurry up and go into the banking business and stop talking about it!

Walter. Why? You want to know why?

---

6. **Prometheus** (prə mē′ thē əs): in Greek mythology, a Titan, or giant god, who stole fire from the gods for the benefit of humankind.

'Cause we all tied up in a race of people that don't know how to do nothing but moan, pray, and have babies!

(*The line is too bitter even for him, and he looks at her and sits down.*)

Ruth. Oh, Walter. . . . (*softly*) Honey, why can't you stop fighting me?

Walter (*without thinking*). Who's fighting you? Who even cares about you?

(*This line begins the retardation of his mood.*)

Ruth. Well—(*She waits a long time, and then with* resignation[7] *starts to put away her things.*) I guess I might as well go to bed. . . . (*more or less to herself*) I don't know where we lost it . . . but we have. . . . (*then to him*) I—I'm sorry about this new baby, Walter, I guess maybe I better go on and do what I started. . . . I guess I just didn't realize how bad things was with us. . . . I guess I just didn't really realize—(*She starts out to the bedroom and stops.*) You want some hot milk?

Walter. Hot milk?

Ruth. Yes—hot milk.

Walter. Why hot milk?

Ruth. 'Cause after all that liquor you come home with, you ought to have something hot in your stomach.

Walter. I don't want no milk.

Ruth. You want some coffee then?

Walter. No, I don't want no coffee. I don't want nothing hot to drink. (*almost plaintively*) Why you always trying to give me something to eat?

Ruth (*standing and looking at him helplessly*). What else can I give you, Walter Lee Younger?

(*She stands and looks at him and presently turns to go out again. He lifts his head and watches her going away from him in a new mood that began to emerge when he asked her "Who cares about you?"*)

Walter. It's been rough, ain't it, baby? (*She hears and stops but does not turn around, and he continues to her back.*) I guess between two people there ain't never as much understood as folks generally think there is. I mean like between me and you— (*She turns to face him.*) How we gets to the place where we scared to talk softness to each other. (*He waits, thinking hard himself.*) Why you think it got to be like that? (*He is thoughtful, almost as a child would be.*) Ruth, what is it gets into people ought to be close?

Ruth. I don't know, honey. I think about it a lot.

Walter. On account of you and me, you mean? The way things are with us. The way something done come down between us.

Ruth. There ain't so much between us, Walter. . . . Not when you come to me and try to talk to me. Try to be with me . . . a little even.

Walter (*total honesty*). Sometimes . . . sometimes . . . I don't even know how to try.

Ruth. Walter—

Walter. Yes?

Ruth (*coming to him, gently and with misgiving, but coming to him*). Honey . . . life don't have to be like this. I mean sometimes people can do things so that things are better. . . . You remember how we used to talk when Travis was born . . . about the way we were going to live . . . the kind of house . . .

---

7. **resignation** (rez′ ig nā′ shən): passive acceptance.

(*She is stroking his head.*) Well, it's all starting to slip away from us. . . .

(Mama *enters, and* Walter *jumps up and shouts at her.*)

Walter. Mama, where have you been?

Mama. My—them steps is longer than they used to be. Whew! (*She sits down and ignores him.*) How you feeling this evening, Ruth?

(Ruth *shrugs, disturbed some at having been prematurely interrupted and watching her husband knowingly.*)

Walter. Mama, where have you been all day?

Mama (*still ignoring him and leaning on the table and changing to more comfortable shoes*). Where's Travis?

Ruth. I let him out earlier and he ain't come back yet. Boy, is he going to get it!

Walter. Mama!

Mama (*as if she had heard him for the first time*). Yes, son?

Walter. Where did you go this afternoon?

Mama. I went downtown to tend to some business I had to tend to.

Walter. What kind of business?

Mama. You know better than to question me like a child, Brother.

Walter (*rising and bending over the table*). Where were you, Mama? (*bringing his fists down and shouting*) Mama, you didn't go do something with that insurance money, something crazy?

(*The front door opens slowly, interrupting him, and* Travis *peeks his head in, less than hopefully.*)

Travis (*to his mother*). Mama, I—

Ruth. "Mama I" nothing! You're going to get it, boy! Get on in that bedroom and get yourself ready!

Travis. But I—

Mama. Why don't you all never let the child explain hisself.

Ruth. Keep out of it now, Lena.

(Mama *clamps her lips together, and* Ruth *advances toward her son menacingly.*)

Ruth. A thousand times I have told you not to go off like that—

Mama (*holding out her arms to her grandson*). Well—at least let me tell him something. I want him to be the first one to hear. . . . Come here, Travis. (*The boy obeys, gladly.*) Travis—(*She takes him by the shoulder and looks into his face.*)—you know that money we got in the mail this morning?

Travis. Yes'm.

Mama. Well—what do you think your grandmama gone and done with that money?

Travis. I don't know, Grandmama.

Mama (*putting her finger on his nose for emphasis*). She went out and bought you a house! (*The explosion comes from* Walter *at the end of the revelation, and he jumps up and turns away from all of them in a fury.* Mama *continues, to* Travis.) You glad about the house? It's going to be yours when you get to be a man.

Travis. Yeah—I always wanted to live in a house.

Mama. All right, gimme some sugar then—(Travis *puts his arms around her neck as she watches her son over the boy's shoulder. Then, to* Travis, *after the embrace.*)

Now when you say your prayers tonight, you thank God and your grandfather—'cause it was him who give you the house—in his way.

Ruth (*taking the boy away from* Mama *and pushing him toward the bedroom*). Now you get out of here and get ready for your beating.

Travis. Aw, Mama—

Ruth. Get on in there—(*closing the door behind him and turning radiantly to her mother-in-law*) So you went and did it!

Mama (*quietly, looking at her son with pain*). Yes, I did.

Ruth (*raising both arms classically*). Praise God! (*Looks at Walter a moment, who says nothing. She crosses rapidly over to her husband.*) Please, honey—let me be glad . . . you be glad too. (*She has laid her hands on his shoulders, but he shakes himself free of her roughly, without turning to face her.*) Oh, Walter . . . a home . . . a home. (*She comes back to Mama.*) Well—where is it? How big is it? How much is it going to cost?

Mama. Well—

Ruth. When we moving?

Mama (*smiling at her*). First of the month.

Ruth (*throwing back her head with jubilance*). Praise God!

Mama (*tentatively, still looking at her son's back turned against her and* Ruth). It's—it's a nice house too. . . . (*She cannot help speaking directly to him. An imploring quality in her voice, her manner; makes her almost like a girl now.*) Three bedrooms—nice big one for you and Ruth. . . . Me and Beneatha still have to share our room, but Travis have one of his own—and (*with difficulty*) I figure if the—new baby—is a boy, we could get one

of them double-decker outfits. . . . And there's a yard with a little patch of dirt where I could maybe get to grow me a few flowers. . . . And a nice big basement . . .

Ruth. Walter, honey, be glad—

Mama (*still to his back, fingering things on the table*). 'Course I don't want to make it sound fancier than it is. . . . It's just a plain little old house—but it's made good and solid—and it will be *ours*. Walter Lee—it makes a difference in a man when he can walk on floors that belong to *him*. . . .

Ruth. Where is it?

Mama (*frightened at this telling*). Well—well—it's out there in Clybourne Park—

(Ruth's *radiance fades abruptly, and Walter finally turns slowly to face his mother with incredulity and hostility.*)

Ruth. Where?

Mama (*matter-of-factly*). Four o six Clybourne Street, Clybourne Park.

Ruth. Clybourne Park? Mama, there ain't no colored people living in Clybourne Park.

Mama (*almost idiotically*). Well, I guess there's going to be some now.

Walter (*bitterly*). So that's the peace and comfort you went out and bought for us today!

Mama (*raising her eyes to meet his finally*). Son—I just tried to find the nicest place for the least amount of money for my family.

Ruth (*trying to recover from the shock*). Well—well—'course I ain't one never been 'fraid of no crackers,[8] mind you—but—well—wasn't there no other houses nowhere?

---

8. **crackers:** slang for poor whites.

Mama. Them houses they put up for colored in them areas way out all seem to cost twice as much as other houses. I did the best I could.

Ruth (*struck senseless with the news, in its various degrees of goodness and trouble, she sits a moment, her fists propping her chin in thought, and then she starts to rise, bringing her fists down with vigor, the radiance spreading from cheek to cheek again.*) Well—well!—All I can say is—if this is my time in life—*my time*—to say goodbye—(*and she builds with momentum as she starts to circle the room with an exuberant, almost tearfully happy release*)—to these cracking walls!—(*She pounds the walls.*)—and these marching roaches!—(*She wipes at an imaginary army of marching roaches.*)—and this cramped little closet which ain't now or never was no kitchen . . . then I say it loud and good, Hallelujah! and goodbye misery . . . . I don't never want to see your ugly face again. (*She laughs joyously, having practically destroyed the apartment, and flings her arms up and lets them come down happily, slowly, reflectively, over her abdomen, aware for the first time perhaps that the life therein pulses with happiness and not despair.*) Lena?

Mama (*moved, watching her happiness*). Yes, honey?

Ruth (*looking off*). Is there—is there a whole lot of sunlight?

Mama (*understanding*). Yes, child, there's a whole lot of sunlight.

(*long pause*)

Ruth (*collecting herself and going to the door of the room* Travis *is in*). Well—I guess I better see 'bout Travis. (*to Mama*) Lord, I sure don't feel like whipping nobody today!

(*She exits.*)

Mama (*The mother and son are left alone now and the mother waits a long time, considering deeply, before she speaks*). Son—you—you understand what I done, don't you? (Walter *is silent and sullen.*) I—I just seen my family falling apart today . . . just falling to pieces in front of my eyes. . . . We couldn't of gone on like we was today. We was going backward 'stead of forwards—talking 'bout killing babies and wishing each other was dead. . . . When it gets like that in life—you just got to do something different, push on out and do something bigger. . . . (*She waits.*) I wish you say something, son . . . . I wish you'd say how deep inside you you think I done the right thing—

Walter (*crossing slowly to his bedroom and finally turning there and speaking measuredly*). What you need me to say you done right for? *You* the head of this family. You run our lives like you want to. It was your money and you did what you wanted with it. So what you need for me to say it was all right for? (*bitterly, to hurt her as deeply as he knows is possible*) So you butchered up a dream of mine—you—who always talking 'bout your children's dreams. . . .

Mama. Walter Lee—

(*He just closes the door behind him. Mama sits alone, thinking heavily.*)

SCENE 2

Friday night. A few weeks later. Packing crates mark the intention of the family to move. Beneatha and George come in, presumably from an evening out again.

George. OK. . . . OK, whatever you say. . . . (*They both sit on the couch. He tries to kiss her. She moves away.*) Look, we've had a nice evening; let's not spoil it, huh? . . .

(*He again turns her head and tries to nuzzle in and she turns away from him, not with distaste but with momentary lack of interest; in a mood to pursue what they were talking about.*)

Beneatha. I'm *trying* to talk to you.

George. We always talk.

Beneatha. Yes—and I love to talk.

George (*exasperated; rising*). I know it and I don't mind it sometimes. . . . I want you to cut it out, see—The moody stuff, I mean. I don't like it. You're a nice-looking girl . . . all over. That's all you need, honey, forget the atmosphere. Guys aren't going to go for the atmosphere—they're going to go for what they see. Be glad for that. Drop the Garbo[9] routine. It doesn't go with you. As for myself, I want a nice—(*groping*)—simple—(*thoughtfully*)—sophisticated girl . . . not a poet—OK?

(*She rebuffs him again and he starts to leave.*)

Beneatha. Why are you angry?

George. Because this is stupid! I don't go out with you to discuss the nature of "quiet desperation" or to hear all about your thoughts—because the world will go on thinking what it thinks regardless—

Beneatha. Then why read books? Why go to school?

George (*with artificial patience, counting on his fingers*). It's simple. You read books—to learn facts—to get grades—to pass the course—to get a degree. That's all—it has nothing to do with thoughts.

(*a long pause*)

Beneatha. I see. (*a longer pause as she looks at him*) Good night, George.

(*George looks at her a little oddly, and starts to exit. He meets Mama coming in.*)

George. Oh—hello, Mrs. Younger.

Mama. Hello, George, how you feeling?

George. Fine—fine, how are you?

Mama. Oh, a little tired. You know them steps can get you after a day's work. You all have a nice time tonight?

George. Yes—a fine time. Well, good night.

Mama. Good night. (*He exits. Mama closes the door behind her.*) Hello, honey. What you sitting like that for?

Beneatha. I'm just sitting.

Mama. Didn't you have a nice time?

Beneatha. No.

Mama. No? What's the matter?

Beneatha. Mama, George is a fool—honest. (*She rises.*)

Mama (*Hustling around unloading the packages she has entered with. She stops.*). Is he, baby?

Beneatha. Yes.

(*Beneatha makes up Travis's bed as she talks.*)

Mama. You sure?

Beneatha. Yes.

Mama. Well—I guess you better not waste your time with no fools.

(Beneatha *looks up at her mother, watching her put groceries in the refrigerator. Finally she gathers up her things and starts into the*

---

9. **Garbo:** Greta Garbo, a movie actress known for her aura of introspection and mystery.

bedroom. At the door she stops and looks back at her mother.)

Beneatha. Mama—

Mama. Yes, baby—

Beneatha. Thank you.

Mama. For what?

Beneatha. For understanding me this time.

(*She exits quickly and the mother stands, smiling a little, looking at the place where* Beneatha *just stood.* Ruth *enters.*)

Ruth. Now don't you fool with any of this stuff, Lena—

Mama. Oh, I just thought I'd sort a few things out.

(*The phone rings.* Ruth *answers.*)

Ruth (*at the phone*). Hello—Just a minute. (*goes to the door*) Walter, it's Mrs. Arnold. (*Waits. Goes back to the phone. Tense.*) Hello. Yes, this is his wife speaking. . . . He's lying down now. Yes . . . well, he'll be in tomorrow. He's been very sick. Yes—I know we should have called, but we were so sure he'd be able to come in today. Yes—yes, I'm very sorry. Yes . . . Thank you very much. (*She hangs up.* Walter *is standing in the doorway of the bedroom behind her.*) That was Mrs. Arnold.

Walter (*indifferently*). Was it?

Ruth. She said if you don't come in tomorrow that they are getting a new man. . . .

Walter. Ain't that sad—ain't that crying sad.

Ruth. She said Mr. Arnold has had to take a cab for three days. . . . Walter, you ain't been to work for three days! (*This is a revelation to her.*) Where you been, Walter Lee Younger? (Walter *looks at her and starts to laugh.*) You're going to lose your job.

Walter. That's right.

Ruth. Oh, Walter, and with your mother working like a dog every day—

Walter. That's sad too—Everything is sad.

Mama. What you been doing for these three days, son?

Walter. Mama—you don't know all the things a man what got leisure can find to do in this city. . . . What's this—Friday night? Well—Wednesday I borrowed Willy Harris' car and I went for a drive . . . just me and myself and I drove and drove . . . Way out . . . way out past South Chicago, and I parked the car and I sat and looked at the steel mills all day long. I just sat in the car and looked at them big black chimneys for hours. Then I drove back and I went to the Green Hat. (*pause*) And Thursday—Thursday I borrowed the car again and I got in it and I pointed it the other way and I drove the other way—for hours—way, way up to Wisconsin, and I looked at the farms. I just drove and looked at the farms. Then I drove back and went to the Green Hat. (*pause*) And today—today I didn't get the car. Today I just walked. All over the South Side. And I looked at the Negroes and they looked at me and finally I just sat down on the curb at Thirty-ninth and South Parkway and I just sat there and watched the Negroes go by. And then I went to the Green Hat. You all sad? You all depressed? And you know where I am going right now—

(Ruth *goes out quietly.*)

Mama. Oh, Big Walter, is this the harvest of our days?

Walter. You know what I like about the Green Hat? (*He turns the radio on and a* *steamy, deep blues pours into the room.*) I like this little cat they got there who blows a sax. . . . He blows. He talks to me. He ain't but 'bout five feet tall and he's got a conked head[10] and his eyes is always closed and he's all music—

Mama (*rising and getting some papers out of her handbag*). Walter—

Walter. And there's this other guy who plays the piano . . . and they got a sound. I mean they can work on some music. . . . They got the best little combo in the world at the Green Hat. . . . You can sit there and drink and listen to the three men play, and you realize that don't nothing matter worth a damn, but just being there—

Mama. I've helped do it to you, haven't I, son? Walter, I've been wrong.

Walter. Naw—you ain't never been wrong about nothing, Mama.

Mama. Listen to me now. I say I been wrong, son. That I been doing to you what the rest of the world been doing to you. (*She stops and he looks up slowly at her and she meets his eyes pleadingly.*) Walter—what you ain't never understood is that I ain't got nothing, don't own nothing, ain't never really wanted nothing that wasn't for you. There ain't nothing as precious to me. . . . There ain't nothing worth holding on to, money, dreams, nothing else—if it means— if it means it's going to destroy my boy. (*She puts her papers in front of him and he watches her without speaking or moving.*) I paid the man thirty-five hundred dollars down on the house. That leaves sixty-five hundred dollars. Monday morning I want you to take this money and take three thousand dollars and put it in a savings account for Beneatha's medical schooling. The rest you put into a checking account—with your name on it. And from now on any penny

that come out of it or that go in it is for you to look after. For you to decide. (*She drops her hands a little helplessly.*) It ain't much, but it's all I got in the world, and I'm putting it in your hands. I'm telling you to be the head of this family from now on like you supposed to be.

Walter (*stares at the money*). You trust me like that, Mama?

Mama. I ain't never stop trusting you. Like I ain't never stop loving you.

(*She goes out, and* Walter *sits looking at the money on the table as the music continues in its idiom, pulsing in the room. Finally, in a decisive gesture, he gets up, and, in mingled joy and desperation, picks up the money. At the same moment,* Travis *enters for bed.*)

Travis. What's the matter, Daddy? You drunk?

Walter (*sweetly, more sweetly than we have ever known him*). No, Daddy ain't drunk. Daddy ain't going to never be drunk again. . . .

Travis. Well, good night, Daddy.

(*The* Father *has come from behind the couch and leans over, embracing his son.*)

Walter. Son, I feel like talking to you tonight.

Travis. About what?

Walter. Oh, about a lot of things. About you and what kind of man you going to be when you grow up. . . . Son—son, what do you want to be when you grow up?

Travis. A bus driver.

Walter (*laughing a little*). A what? Man, that ain't nothing to want to be!

Travis. Why not?

---

10. **conked head:** artificially straightened hair.

Walter. 'Cause, man—it ain't big enough— you know what I mean.

Travis. I don't know then. I can't make up my mind. Sometimes Mama asks me that too. And sometimes when I tell her I just want to be like you—she says she don't want me to be like that and sometimes she says she does. . . .

Walter (*gathering him up in his arms*). You know what, Travis? In seven years you going to be seventeen years old. And things is going to be very different with us in seven years, Travis. . . . One day when you are seventeen I'll come home—home from my office downtown somewhere—

Travis. You don't work in no office, Daddy.

Walter. No—but after tonight. After what your daddy gonna do tonight, there's going to be offices—a whole lot of offices. . . .

Travis. What you gonna do tonight, Daddy?

Walter. You wouldn't understand yet, son, but your daddy's gonna make a transaction . . . a business transaction that's going to change our lives. . . . That's how come one day when you 'bout seventeen years old I'll come home and I'll be pretty tired, you know what I mean, after a day of conferences and secretaries getting things wrong the way they do . . . 'cause an executive's life is hell, man—(*The more he talks the farther away he gets.*) And I'll pull the car up on the driveway . . . just a plain black Chrysler, I think, with whitewalls—no—black tires. More elegant. Rich people don't have to be flashy . . . though I'll have to get something a little sportier for Ruth—maybe a Cadillac convertible to do her shopping in. . . . And I'll come up the steps to the house and the gardener will be clipping away at the hedges and he'll say, "Good evening, Mr. Younger."

And I'll say, "Hello, Jefferson, how are you this evening?" And I'll go inside and Ruth will be coming downstairs and meet me at the door and we'll kiss each other and she'll take my arm and we'll go up to your room to see you sitting there on the floor with catalogs of all the great schools in America around you. . . . All the great schools of the world! And—and I'll say, all right son—it's your seventeenth birthday, what is it you've decided? . . . Just tell me where you want to go to school and you'll *go*. Just tell me, what it is you want to be—and you'll *be* it. . . . . Whatever you want to be—Yessir! (*He holds his arms open for* Travis.) You just name it son . . . (Travis *leaps into them.*) and I hand you the world!

(Walter's *voice has risen in pitch and hysterical promise and on the last line he lifts Travis high.*)

SCENE 3

Saturday, moving day, one week later. Before the curtain rises, Ruth's *voice, a strident, dramatic church alto, cuts through the silence.*

It is, in the darkness, a triumphant surge, a penetrating statement of expectation: "Oh, Lord, I don't feel no ways tired! Children, oh, glory hallelujah!"

As the curtain rises we see that Ruth *is alone in the living room, finishing up the family's packing. It is moving day. She is nailing crates and tying cartons. Beneatha enters, carrying a guitar case, and watches her exuberant sister-in-law.*

Ruth. Hey!

Beneatha (*putting away the case*). Hi.

Ruth (*pointing at a package*). Honey—look in that package there and see what I found on sale this morning at the South Center. (Ruth *gets up and moves to the package and draws out some curtains.*) Lookahere— hand-turned hems!

Beneatha. How do you know the window size out there?

Ruth (*who hadn't thought of that*). Oh— Well, they bound to fit something in the whole house. Anyway, they was too good a bargain to pass up. (Ruth *slaps her head, suddenly remembering something.*) Oh, Bennie—I meant to put a special note on that carton over there. That's your mama's good china, and she wants 'em to be very careful with it.

Beneatha. I'll do it.

(Beneatha *finds a piece of paper and starts to draw large letters on it.*)

Ruth. You know what I'm going to do soon as I get in that new house?

Beneatha. What?

Ruth. Honey—I'm going to run me a tub of water up to here. . . . (*with her fingers practically up to her nostrils*) And I'm going to get in it—and I am going to sit . . . and sit . . . and sit in that hot water and the first person who knocks to tell me to hurry up and come out—

Beneatha. Gets shot at sunrise.

Ruth (*laughing happily*). You said it, sister! (*noticing how large Beneatha is absent-mindedly making the note*) Honey, they ain't going to read that from no airplane.

Beneatha (*laughing herself*). I guess I always think things have more emphasis if they are big, somehow.

Ruth (*looking up at her and smiling*). You and your brother seem to have that as a phi-losophy of life. Lord, that man—done changed so 'round here. You know—you know what we did last night? Me and Walter Lee?

Beneatha. What?

Ruth (*smiling to herself*). We went to the movies. (*looking at* Beneatha *to see if she understands*) We went to the movies. You know the last time me and Walter went to the movies together?

Beneatha. No.

Ruth. Me neither. That's how long it been. (*smiling again*) But we went last night. The picture wasn't much good, but that didn't seem to matter. We went—and we held hands.

Beneatha. Oh, Lord!

Ruth. We held hands—and you know what?

Beneatha. What?

Ruth. When we come out of the show it was late and dark and all the stores and things was closed up . . . and it was kind of chilly and there wasn't many people on the streets . . . and we was still holding hands, me and Walter.

Beneatha. You're killing me.

(Walter *enters with a large package. His happiness is deep within him; he cannot keep still with his new-found exuberance. He is singing and wiggling and snapping his fingers. He puts his package in a corner and puts a phonograph record, which he has brought in with him, on the record player. As the music comes up, he dances over to* Ruth *and tries to get her to dance with him. She gives in at last to his raunchiness and in a fit of giggling allows herself to be drawn into his mood* and together they deliberately burlesque an old social dance of their youth.)

Beneatha (*regarding them a long time as they dance, then drawing in her breath for a deeply exaggerated comment which she does not particularly mean*). Talk about old-dddddddd-fashionedddddddd—Negroes!

Walter (*stopping momentarily*). What kind of Negroes?

(*He says this in fun. He is not angry with her today, nor with anyone. He starts to dance with his wife again.*)

Beneatha. Old-fashioned.

Walter (*as he dances with* Ruth). You know, when these New Negroes have their convention—(*pointing at his sister*)—that is going to be the chairman of the Committee on Unending Agitation. (*He goes on dancing, then stops.*) Race, race, race! . . . Girl, I do believe you are the first person in the history of the entire human race to successfully brainwash yourself. (Beneatha *breaks up and he goes on dancing. He stops again, enjoying his tease.*) Damn, even the N double A C P takes a holiday sometimes! (Beneatha *and* Ruth *laugh. He dances with* Ruth *some more and starts to laugh and stops and pantomimes someone over an operating table.*) I can just see that chick someday looking down at some poor cat on an operating table before she starts to slice him, saying . . . (*pulling his sleeves back maliciously*) "By the way, what are your views on civil rights down there? . . ."

(*He laughs at her again and starts to dance happily. The bell sounds.*)

Beneatha. Sticks and stones may break my bones but . . . words will never hurt me!

(Beneatha *goes to the door and opens it as* Walter *and* Ruth *go on with the clowning.* Beneatha *is somewhat surprised to see a* quiet-looking middle-aged white man in a business suit holding his hat and a briefcase in his hand and consulting a small piece of paper.)

Man. Uh—how do you do, miss. I am looking for a Mrs.—(*He looks at the slip of paper.*) Mrs. Lena Younger?

Beneatha (*smoothing her hair with slight embarrassment*). Oh—yes, that's my mother. Excuse me. (*She closes the door and turns to quiet the other two.*) Ruth! Brother! Somebody's here. (*Then she opens the door. The man casts a curious quick glance at all of them.*) Uh—come in please.

Man (*coming in*). Thank you.

Beneatha. My mother isn't here just now. Is it business?

Man. Yes . . . well, of a sort.

Walter (*freely, the Man of the House*). Have a seat. I'm Mrs. Younger's son. I look after most of her business matters.

(Ruth *and* Beneatha *exchange amused glances.*)

Man (*regarding* Walter *and sitting*). Well— My name is Karl Lindner. . . .

Walter (*stretching out his hand*). Walter Younger. This is my wife—(Ruth *nods politely.*)—and my sister.

Lindner. How do you do.

Walter (*amiably, as he sits himself easily on a chair, leaning with interest forward on his knees and looking expectantly into the newcomer's face*). What can we do for you, Mr. Lindner!

Lindner (*some minor shuffling of the hat and briefcase on his knees*). Well—I am a representative of the Clybourne Park Improvement Association—

Walter (*pointing*). Why don't you sit your things on the floor?

Lindner. Oh—yes. Thank you. (*He slides the briefcase and hat under the chair.*) And as I was saying—I am from the Clybourne Park Improvement Association, and we have had it brought to our attention at the last meeting that you people—or at least your mother—has bought a piece of residential property at—(*He digs for the slip of paper again.*)—four o six Clybourne Street. . . .

Walter. That's right. Care for something to drink? Ruth, get Mr. Lindner a beer.

Lindner (*upset for some reason*). Oh—no, really. I mean thank you very much, but no thank you.

Ruth (*innocently*). Some coffee?

Lindner. Thank you, nothing at all.

(Beneatha *is watching the man carefully.*)

Lindner. Well, I don't know how much you folks know about our organization. (*He is a gentle man, thoughtful and somewhat labored in his manner.*) It is one of these community organizations set up to look after—oh, you know, things like block upkeep and special projects, and we also have what we call our New Neighbors Orientation Committee. . . .

Beneatha (*drily*). Yes—and what do they do?

Lindner (*turning a little to her and then returning the main force to* Walter). Well— it's what you might call a sort of welcoming committee, I guess. I mean they, we, I'm the chairman of the committee—go around and see the new people who move into the neighborhood and sort of give them the lowdown on the way we do things out in Clybourne Park.

Beneatha (*with appreciation of the two meanings, which escape* Ruth *and* Walter). Un-huh.

Lindner. And we also have the category of what the association calls—(*He looks elsewhere.*)—uh—special community problems. . . .

Beneatha. Yes—and what are some of those?

Walter. Girl, let the man talk.

Lindner (*with understated relief*). Thank you. I would sort of like to explain this thing in my own way. I mean I want to explain it to you in a certain way.

Walter. Go ahead.

Lindner. Yes. Well, I'm going to try to get right to the point. I'm sure we'll all appreciate that in the long run.

Beneatha. Yes.

Walter. Be still now!

Lindner. Well—

Ruth (*still innocently*). Would you like another chair—you don't look comfortable.

Lindner (*more frustrated than annoyed*). No, thank you very much. Please. Well—to get right to the point—I—(*a great breath and he is off at last*) I am sure you people must have heard of some of the incidents that have happened in various parts of the city when colored people have moved into certain areas—(Beneatha *exhales heavily and starts tossing a piece of fruit up and down in the air.*) Well—because we have what I think is going to be a unique type of organization in American community life—not only do we deplore that kind of thing—but we are trying to do something about it. (Beneatha *stops tossing and turns* *with a new and quizzical interest in the man.*) We feel—(*gaining confidence in his mission because of the interest in the faces of the people he is talking to*)—we feel that most of the trouble in this world, when you come right down to it—(*He hits his knee for emphasis.*)—most of the trouble exists because people just don't sit down and talk to each other.

Ruth (*nodding as she might in church, pleased with the remark*). You can say that again, mister.

Lindner (*more encouraged by such affirmation*). That we don't try hard enough in this world to understand the other fellow's problem. The other guy's point of view.

Ruth. Now that's right.

(Beneatha *and* Walter *merely watch and listen with genuine interest.*)

Lindner. Yes—that's the way we feel out in Clybourne Park. And that's why I was elected to come here this afternoon and talk to you people. Friendly like, you know, the way people should talk to each other and see if we couldn't find some way to work this thing out. As I say, the whole business is a matter of *caring* about the other fellow. Anybody can see that you are a nice family of folks, hard-working and honest, I'm sure. (Beneatha *frowns slightly, quizzically, her head tilted regarding him.*) Today everybody knows what it means to be on the outside of *something.* And of course, there is always somebody who is out to take advantage of people who don't always understand.

Walter. What do you mean?

Lindner. Well—you see our community is made up of people who've worked hard as the dickens for years to build up that little community. They're not rich and fancy people; just hard-working, honest people who

don't really have much but those little homes and a dream of the kind of community they want to raise their children in. Now, I don't say we are perfect, and there is a lot wrong in some of the things they want. But you've got to admit that a man, right or wrong, has the right to want to have the neighborhood he lives in a certain kind of way. And at the moment the overwhelming majority of our people out there feel that people get along better, take more of a common interest in the life of the community, when they share a common background. I want you to believe me when I tell you that race prejudice simply doesn't enter into it. It is a matter of the people of Clybourne Park believing, rightly or wrongly, as I say, that for the happiness of all concerned that our Negro families are happier when they live in their *own* communities.

Beneatha (*with a grand and bitter gesture*). This, friends, is the Welcoming Committee!

Walter (*dumbfounded, looking at* Lindner). Is this what you came marching all the way over here to tell us?

Lindner. Well, now, we've been having a fine conversation. I hope you'll hear me all the way through.

Walter (*tightly*). Go ahead, man.

Lindner. You see—in the face of all things I have said, we are prepared to make your family a very generous offer. . . .

Beneatha. Thirty pieces[11] and not a coin less!

Walter. Yeah?

---

11. **thirty pieces:** a reference to the thirty pieces of silver for which Judas betrayed Jesus. Beneatha means that it would be self-betrayal for the Youngers to accept the offer.

Lindner (*putting on his glasses and drawing a form out of the briefcase*). Our association is prepared, through the collective effort of our people, to buy the house from you at a financial gain to your family.

Ruth. Lord have mercy, ain't this the living gall!

Walter. All right, you through?

Lindner. Well, I want to give you the exact terms of the financial arrangement—

Walter. We don't want to hear no exact terms of no arrangements. I want to know if you got any more to tell us 'bout getting together?

Lindner (*taking off his glasses*). Well—I don't suppose that you feel . . .

Walter. Never mind how I feel—you got any more to say 'bout how people ought to sit down and talk to each other? . . . Get out of my house, man.

(*He turns his back and walks to the door.*)

Lindner (*looking around at the hostile faces and reaching and assembling his hat and briefcase*). Well—I don't understand why you people are reacting this way. What do you think you are going to gain by moving into a neighborhood where you just aren't wanted and where some elements—well—people can get awful worked up when they feel that their whole way of life and everything they've ever worked for is threatened.

Walter. Get out.

Lindner (*at the door, holding a small card*). Well—I'm sorry it went like this.

Walter. Get out.

Lindner (*almost sadly regarding* Walter). You just can't force people to change their hearts, son.

(*He turns and puts his card on a table and exits.* Walter *pushes the door to with stinging hatred, and stands looking at it.* Ruth *just sits and* Beneatha *just stands. They say nothing.* Mama *and* Travis *enter.*)

Mama. Well—all this packing got done since I left out of here this morning. I testify before God that my children got all the energy of the dead. What time the moving men due?

Beneatha. Four o' clock. You had a caller, Mama.

(*She is smiling, teasingly.*)

Mama. Sure enough—who?

Beneatha (*her arms folded saucily*). The Welcoming Committee.

(Walter *and* Ruth *giggle.*)

Mama (*innocently*). Who?

Beneatha. The Welcoming Committee. They said they're sure going to be glad to see you when you get there.

Walter (*devilishly*). Yeah, they said they can't hardly wait to see your face.

(*laughter*)

Mama (*sensing their facetiousness*). What's the matter with you all?

Walter. Ain't nothing the matter with us. We just telling you 'bout this gentleman who came to see you this afternoon. From the Clybourne Park Improvement Association.

Mama. What he want?

Ruth (*in the same mood as* Beneatha *and* Walter). To welcome you, honey.

Walter. He said that they can't hardly wait. He said the one thing they don't have that they just *dying* to have out there is a fine family of colored people! (*to Ruth and Beneatha*) Ain't that right!

Ruth and **Beneatha** (*mockingly*). Yeah! He left his card in case—

(*They indicate the card, and Mama picks it up and throws it on the floor—understanding and looking off as she draws her chair up to the table on which she has put her plant and some sticks and some cord.*)

Mama. Father, give us strength. (*knowingly and without fun*) Did he threaten us?

Beneatha. Oh—Mama—they don't do it like that any more. He talked Brotherhood. He said everybody ought to learn how to sit down and hate each other with good Christian fellowship.

(*She and Walter shake hands to ridicule the remark.*)

Mama (*sadly*). Lord, protect us. . . .

Ruth. You should hear the money those folks raised to buy the house from us. All we paid and then some.

Beneatha. What they think we going to do—eat 'em?

Ruth. No, honey, marry 'em.

Mama (*shaking her head*). Lord, Lord, Lord. . . .

Ruth. Well—that's the way the crackers crumble. Joke.

Beneatha (*laughingly noticing what her mother is doing*). Mama, what are you doing?

Mama. Fixing my plant so it won't get hurt none on the way.

Beneatha. Mama, you going to take *that* to the new house?

Mama. Un-huh—

Beneatha. That raggedy-looking old thing?

Mama (*stopping and looking at her*). It expresses *me*.

Ruth (*with delight, to Beneatha*). So there, Miss Thing!

(*Walter comes to Mama suddenly and bends down behind her and squeezes her in his arms with all his strength. She is overwhelmed by the suddenness of it, and, though delighted, her manner is like that of Ruth with Travis.*)

Mama. Look out now, boy. You make me mess up my thing here!

Walter (*His face lit, he slips down on his knees beside her, his arms still about her.*). Mama . . . you know what it means to climb up in the chariot?

Mama (*gruffly, very happy*). Get on away from me now. . . .

Ruth (*near the gift-wrapped package, trying to catch Walter's eye*). Psst—

Walter. What the old song say, Mama. . . .

Ruth. Walter—Now?

(*She is pointing at the package.*)

Walter (*speaking the lines, sweetly, playfully, in his mother's face*).
I got wings . . . you got wings . . .
All God's Children got wings . . .

Mama. Boy—get out of my face and do some work. . . .

Walter.
When I get to heaven gonna put on my
     wings,
Gonna fly all over God's heaven . . .

Beneatha (*teasingly, from across the room*).

Everybody talking 'bout heaven ain't going there.

Walter (to Ruth, *who is carrying the box across to them*). I don't know, you think we ought to give her that . . . Seems to me she ain't been very appreciative around here.

Mama (*eyeing the box, which is obviously a gift*). What is that?

Walter (*taking it from* Ruth *and putting it on the table in front of* Mama). Well—what you all think? Should we give it to her?

Ruth. Oh—she was pretty good today.

Mama. I'll good you—

(*She turns her eyes to the box again.*)

Beneatha. Open it, Mama.

(*She stands up, looks at it, and looks at all of them, and then presses her hands together and does not open the package.*)

Walter (*sweetly*). Open it, Mama. It's for you. (Mama *looks in his eyes. It is the first present in her life without its being Christmas. Slowly she opens her package and lifts out, one by one, a brand-new sparkling set of gardening tools.* Walter *continues, prodding.*) Ruth made up the note—read it. . . .

Mama (*picking up the card and adjusting her glasses*). "To our own Mrs. Miniver"[12]— Love from Brother, Ruth, and Beneatha." Ain't that lovely. . . .

Travis (*tugging at his father's sleeve*). Daddy, can I give her mine now?

Walter. All right, son. (Travis *flies to get his gift.*) Travis didn't want to go in with the rest of us, Mama. He got his own. (*somewhat amused*) We don't know what it is. . . .

Travis (*racing back in the room with a large hatbox and putting it in front of his grandmother*). Here!

Mama. Lord have mercy, baby. You done gone and bought your grandmother a hat?

Travis (*very proud*). Open it!

(*She does and lifts out an elaborate, but very elaborate, wide gardening hat, and all the adults break up at the sight of it.*)

Ruth. Travis, honey, what is that?

Travis (*who thinks it is beautiful and appropriate*). It's a gardening hat! Like the ladies always have on in the magazines when they work in their gardens.

Beneatha (*giggling fiercely*). Travis—we were trying to make Mama Mrs. Miniver— not Scarlett O'Hara![13]

Mama (*indignantly*). What's the matter with you all! This here is a beautiful hat! (*absurdly*) I always wanted me one just like it!

(*She pops it on her head to prove it to her grandson, and the hat is ludicrous and considerably oversized.*)

Ruth. Hot dog! Go, Mama!

Walter (*doubled over with laughter*). I'm sorry, Mama—but you look like you ready to go out and chop you some cotton sure enough!

(*They all laugh except* Mama, *out of deference to* Travis's *feelings.*)

Mama (*gathering the boy up to her*). Bless your heart—this is the prettiest hat I ever owned—(Walter, Ruth, *and* Beneatha *chime in—noisily, festively and insincerely congratulating* Travis *on his gift.*) What are we all

---

12. **Mrs. Miniver:** the noble, brave heroine of a 1942 motion picture, *Mrs. Miniver,* who tended her garden in wartime despite bombs falling nearby.

13. **Scarlett O'Hara:** a Georgia belle, the heroine of the novel *Gone with the Wind.*

standing around here for? We ain't finished packin' yet. Bennie, you ain't packed one book.

(*The bell rings.*)

Beneatha. That couldn't be the movers . . . it's not hardly two good yet—

(Beneatha *goes into her room.* Mama *starts for door.*)

Walter (*turning, stiffening*). Wait—wait—I'll get it.

(*He stands and looks at the door.*)

Mama. You expecting company, son?

Walter (*just looking at the door*). Yeah—yeah. . . .

(Mama *looks at* Ruth, *and they exchange innocent and unfrightened glances.*)

Mama (*not understanding*). Well, let them in, son.

Beneatha (*from her room*). We need some more string.

Mama. Travis—you run to the hardware and get me some string cord.

(Mama *goes out and* Walter *turns and looks at* Ruth. Travis *goes to a dish for money.*)

Ruth. Why don't you answer the door, man?

Walter (*suddenly bounding across the floor to her*). 'Cause sometimes it hard to let the future begin! (*stooping down in her face*)
>   I got wings! You got wings!
>   All God's children got wings!

(*He crosses to the door and throws it open. Standing there is a very slight little man in a not too prosperous business suit and with haunted frightened eyes and a hat pulled down tightly, brim up, around his forehead.* Travis *passes between the men and exits.*

Walter *leans deep in the man's face, still in his jubilance.*)
>   When I get to heaven gonna put on my
>   wings,
>   Gonna fly all over God's heaven. . . .
(*The little man just stares at him.*) Heaven—(*Suddenly he stops and looks past the little man into the empty hallway.*) Where's Willy, man?

Bobo. He ain't with me.

Walter (*not disturbed*). Oh—come on in. You know my wife.

Bobo (*dumbly, taking off his hat*). Yes—h'you, Miss Ruth.

Ruth (*quietly, a mood apart from her husband already, seeing* Bobo). Hello, Bobo.

Walter. You right on time today. . . . Right on time. That's the way! (*He slaps* Bobo *on his back.*) Sit down . . . lemme hear.

(Ruth *stands stiffly and quietly in back of them, as though somehow she senses death, her eyes fixed on her husband.*)

Bobo (*his frightened eyes on the floor, his hat in his hands*). Could I please get a drink of water, before I tell you about it, Walter Lee?

(Walter *does not take his eyes off the man.* Ruth *goes blindly to the tap and gets a glass of water and brings it to* Bobo).

Walter. There ain't nothing wrong, is there?

Bobo. Lemme tell you—

Walter. Man—didn't nothing go wrong?

Bobo. Lemme tell you—Walter Lee.

(*Looking at* Ruth *and talking to her more than to* Walter) You know how it was. I got to tell you how it was. I mean first I got to tell you how it was all the way. . . . I mean about the money I put in, Walter Lee. . . .

Walter (*with taut agitation now*). What about the money you put in?

Bobo. Well—it wasn't much as we told you—me and Willy—(*He stops.*) I'm sorry, Walter. I got a bad feeling about it. I got a real bad feeling about it. . . .

Walter. Man, what you telling me about all this for? . . . Tell me what happened in Springfield. . . .

Bobo. Springfield.

Ruth (*like a dead woman*). What was supposed to happen in Springfield?

Bobo (*to her*). This deal that me and Walter went into with Willy—Me and Willy was going to go down to Springfield and spread some money 'round so's we wouldn't have to wait so long for the liquor license. . . . That's what we were going to do. Everybody said that was the way you had to do, you understand, Miss Ruth?

Walter. Man—what happened down there?

Bobo (*a pitiful man, near tears*). I'm trying to tell you, Walter.

Walter (*screaming at him suddenly*). THEN TELL ME. . . . WHAT'S THE MATTER WITH YOU?

Bobo. Man . . . I didn't go to no Springfield, yesterday.

Walter (*halted, life hanging in the moment*). Why not?

Bobo (*the long way, the hard way to tell*). 'Cause I didn't have no reasons to. . . .

Walter. Man, what are you talking about!

Bobo. I'm talking about the fact that when I got to the train station yesterday morn-

ing—eight o'clock like we planned. . . . Man—*Willy didn't never show up.*

Walter. Why . . . where was he . . . where is he?

Bobo. That's what I'm trying to tell you. . . . I don't know. . . . I waited six hours. . . . I called his house . . . and I waited . . . six hours. . . . I waited in that train station six hours. . . . (*breaking into tears*) That was all the extra money I had in the world. . . . (*looking up at* Walter *with the tears running down his face*) Man, *Willy is gone.*

Walter. Gone, what you mean Willy is gone? Gone where? You mean he went by himself. You mean he went off to Springfield by himself—to take care of getting the license—(*turns and looks anxiously at* Ruth) You mean maybe didn't want too many people in on the business down there? (*Looks to* Ruth *again, as before.*) You know Willy got his own ways. (*Looks back to* Bobo.) Maybe you was late yesterday and he just went down there without you. Maybe—maybe—he's been callin' you at home tryin' to tell you what happened or something. Maybe—maybe—he just got sick. He's somewhere—he's got to be somewhere. We just got to find him—me and you got to find him. (*Grabs* Bobo *senselessly by the collar and starts to shake him*) We got to!

Bobo (*in sudden angry, frightened agony*). What's the matter with you, Walter? *When a cat take off with your money he don't leave you no maps!*

Walter (*turning madly as though he is looking for* Willy *in the very room*). Willy! . . . Willy . . . don't do it. . . . Please don't do it. . . . Man, not with that money. . . . Oh, God. . . . Don't let it be true. . . . (*He is wandering around, crying out for* Willy *and looking for him or perhaps for help from God.*) Man . . .

I trusted you. . . . Man, I put my life in your hands. . . . (*He starts to crumple down on the floor as* Ruth *just covers her face in horror.* Mama *opens the door and comes into the room, with* Beneatha *behind her.*) Man. . . . (*He starts to pound the floor with his fists, sobbing wildly.*) That money is made out of my father's flesh. . . .

Bobo (*standing over him helplessly*). I'm sorry, Walter. . . . (*Only Walter's sobs reply.* Bobo *puts on his hat.*) I had my life staked on this deal, too. . . .

(*He exits.*)

Mama (*to* Walter). Son—(*She goes to him—bends down to him, talks to his bent head.*) Son . . . Is it gone? Son, I gave you sixty-five hundred dollars. Is it gone? All of it? Beneatha's money too?

Walter (*lifting his head slowly*). Mama . . . I never . . . went to the bank at all. . . .

Mama (*not wanting to believe him*). You mean . . . your sister's school money . . . you used that too . . . Walter? . . .

Walter. Yessss! . . . All of it. . . . It's all gone. . . .

(*There is total silence.* Ruth *stands with her face covered with her hands;* Beneatha *leans forlornly against a wall, fingering a piece of red ribbon from the mother's gift.* Mama *stops and looks at her son without recognition and then, quite without thinking about it, starts to beat him senselessly in the face.* Beneatha *goes to them and stops it.*)

Beneatha. Mama!

(Mama *stops and looks at both of her children and rises slowly and wanders vaguely, aimlessly away from them.*)

Mama. I seen . . . him . . . night after night . . . come in . . . and look at that rug . . . and then look at me . . . the red showing in his eyes . . . the veins moving in his head . . . I seen him grow thin and old before he was forty . . . working and working and working like somebody's old horse . . . killing himself . . . and you—you give it all away in a day . . .

Beneatha. Mama—

Mama. Oh, God . . . (*She looks up to Him.*) Look down here—and show me the strength.

Beneatha. Mama—

Mama (*folding over*). Strength . . .

Beneatha (*plaintively*). Mama . . .

Mama. Strength!

Thinking About Act Two

A PERSONAL RESPONSE

sharing impressions

1. How do you feel about what Walter has done? Write your reaction in your journal.

constructing interpretations

2. In your view, which family member has been hurt most by Willy's theft of the money?

Think about
- Walter's dreams of how his family's life will be in seven years (page 360)
- Walter's pleas to the absent Willy (pages 369–370)
- Mama's actions and words when she learns that the money is gone
- Ruth's hopes for her husband and for the future
- Beneatha's dreams and how they may be affected
- Travis's future

3. How would you judge the decisions Mama makes in Act Two?

Think about
- the immediate consequences of her buying the house in Clybourne Park and possible consequences in the future
- the consequences of her giving the remainder of the money to Walter
- the reasons she makes both decisions

4. How do you account for the changes in the relationships between family members that are seen in Act Two? Give examples to support your answer.

A CREATIVE RESPONSE

5. Predict what will happen to the family members and their dreams now that the money is gone.

6. If Mama had not given the money to Walter, what do you think would have happened?

A CRITICAL RESPONSE

7. In your opinion, do the references to Africa strengthen or weaken the play?

Think about
- what Africa represents to Beneatha, Walter, George, and Asagai
- how events in Africa relate to the struggles of the Younger family
- how your interest in the play was affected by these references

8. Consider the character of Mr. Lindner. How widespread do you think his attitude is today? Give examples to support your answer.

*A*nalyzing the Writer's Craft

MOOD AND DRAMA

How does your feeling at the end of Act Two compare with the feeling you had at the beginning of the act?

Building a Literary Vocabulary. As you may recall, mood is the feeling, or atmosphere, that the writer creates for the reader. In general terms, mood can be described as light or dark. More specifically, mood can be described in such terms as joyous, despairing, apprehensive, or disturbed. In drama, mood is created mostly through dialogue and action that reveal the characters' emotional states. For example, at the beginning of Act Two, the mood is light. Beneatha and Walter's rapturous celebration of their African past and Ruth's

humorously skeptical comments create a hopeful atmosphere. With the entrance of George Murchison, however, the mood grows darker. As George and Walter bait each other and Walter grows bitter, the mood becomes tense.

Application: Analyzing Mood in Drama. On a diagram like the one below, chart the pattern of mood created in Act Two, noting the events that cause the mood to grow lighter or darker. Compare your diagram with the diagrams of classmates, and discuss the events that cause a shift in mood. Speculate about why Hansberry structured Act Two as she did.

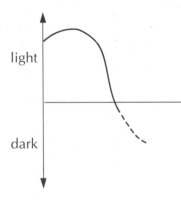

ACT THREE

An hour later.

There is a sullen light of gloom in the living room, gray light, not unlike that which began the first scene of Act One. At left we can see Walter within his room, alone with himself. He is stretched out on the bed, his shirt out and open, his arms under his head. He does not smoke, he does not cry out, he merely lies there, looking up at the ceiling, much as if he were alone in the world.

In the living room Beneatha sits at the table, still surrounded by the now almost ominous packing crates. She sits looking off. We feel that this is a mood struck perhaps an hour before, and it lingers now, full of the empty sound of profound disappointment. We see on a line from her brother's bedroom the sameness of their attitudes. Presently the bell rings and Beneatha rises without ambition or interest in answering. It is Asagai, smiling broadly, striding into the room with energy and happy expectation and conversation.

Asagai. I came over. . . . I had some free time. I thought I might help with the packing. Ah, I like the look of packing crates! A household in preparation for a journey! It depresses some people . . . but for me . . . it is another feeling. Something full of the flow of life, do you understand? Movement, progress. . . . It makes me think of Africa.

Beneatha. Africa!

Asagai. What kind of a mood is this? Have I told you how deeply you move me?

Beneatha. He gave away the money, Asagai. . . .

Asagai. Who gave away what money?

Beneatha. The insurance money. My brother gave it away.

Asagai. Gave it away?

Beneatha. He made an investment! With a man even Travis wouldn't have trusted.

Asagai. And it's gone?

Beneatha. Gone!

Asagai. I'm very sorry. . . . And you, now?

Beneatha. Me? . . . Me? . . . Me, I'm nothing. . . . Me. When I was very small . . . we used to take our sleds out in the wintertime and the only hills we had were the ice-covered stone steps of some houses down the street. And we used to fill them in with snow and make them smooth and slide down them all day . . . and it was very dangerous you know . . . far too steep . . . and sure enough one day a kid named Rufus came down too fast and hit the sidewalk . . . and we saw his face just split open right there in front of us. . . . And I remember standing there looking at his bloody open face thinking that was the end of Rufus. But the ambulance came and they took him to the hospital and they fixed the broken bones and they sewed it all up . . . and the next time I saw Rufus he just had a little line down the middle of his face. . . . I never got over that. . . .

(Walter sits up, listening on the bed. Throughout this scene it is important that we feel his reaction at all times, that he visibly respond to the words of his sister and Asagai.)

Asagai. What?

Beneatha. That that was what one person could do for another, fix him up—sew up the problem, make him all right again. That was the most marvelous thing in the world. . . . I wanted to do that. I always thought it was the one concrete thing in the world that a human being could do. Fix up the sick, you know—and make them whole again. This was truly being God. . . .

Asagai. You wanted to be God?

Beneatha. No—I wanted to cure. It used to be so important to me. I wanted to cure. It used to matter. I used to care. I mean about people and how their bodies hurt. . . .

Asagai. And you've stopped caring?

Beneatha. Yes—I think so.

Asagai. Why?

(Walter *rises, goes to the door of his room and is about to open it, then stops and stands listening, leaning on the door jamb.*)

Beneatha. Because it doesn't seem deep enough, close enough to what ails mankind—I mean this thing of sewing up bodies or administering drugs. Don't you understand? It was a child's reaction to the world. I thought that doctors had the secret to all the hurts. . . . That's the way a child sees things—or an idealist.

Asagai. Children see things very well sometimes—and idealists even better.

Beneatha. I know that's what you think. Because you are still where I left off—you still care. This is what you see for the world, for Africa. You with the dreams of the future will patch up all Africa—you are going to cure the Great Sore of colonialism with Independence—

Asagai. Yes!

Beneatha. Yes—and you think that one word is the penicillin of the human spirit: "Independence!" But then what?

Asagai. That will be the problem for another time. First we must get there.

Beneatha. And where does it end?

Asagai. End? Who even spoke of an end? To life? To living?

Beneatha. An end to misery!

Asagai (*smiling*). You sound like a French intellectual.

Beneatha. No! I sound like a human being who just had her future taken right out of her hands! While I was sleeping in my bed in there, things were happening in this world that directly concerned me—and nobody asked me, consulted me—they just went out and did things—and changed my life. Don't you see there isn't any real progress, Asagai, there is only one large circle that we march in, around and around, each of us with our own little picture—in front of us—our own little mirage that we think is the future.

Asagai. That is the mistake.

Beneatha. What?

Asagai. What you just said—about the circle. It isn't a circle—it is simply a long line—as in geometry, you know, one that reaches into infinity. And because we cannot see the end—we also cannot see how it changes. And it is very odd, but those who see the changes are called "idealists"—and those who cannot, or refuse to think, they are the "realists." It is very strange, and amusing too, I think.

Beneatha. You—you are almost religious.

Asagai. Yes . . . I think I have the religion of doing what is necessary in the world—and of worshipping man—because he is so marvelous, you see.

Beneatha. Man is foul! And the human race deserves its misery!

Asagai. You see: *you* have become the religious one in the old sense. Already, and after such a small defeat, you are worshiping despair.

Beneatha. From now, I worship the truth—and the truth is that people are puny, small and selfish. . . .

Asagai. Truth? Why is it that you despairing ones always think that only you have the truth? I never thought to see *you* like that. You! Your brother made a stupid, childish mistake—and you are grateful to him. So that now you can give up the ailing human race on account of it. You talk about what good is struggle; what good is anything? Where are we all going? And why are we bothering?

Beneatha. *And you cannot answer it!* All your talk and dreams about Africa and Independence. Independence and then what? What about all the crooks and petty thieves and just plain idiots who will come into power to steal and plunder the same as before—only now they will be black and do it in the name of the new Independence— You cannot answer that.

Asagai (*shouting over her*). *I live the answer!* (*pause*) In my village at home it is the exceptional man who can even read a newspaper . . . or who ever *sees* a book at all. I will go home and much of what I will have to say will seem strange to the people of my village. . . . But I will teach and work and things will happen, slowly and swiftly. At times it will seem that nothing changes at all . . . and then again . . . the sudden dramatic events that make history leap into the future. And then quiet again. Retrogression[1] even. Guns, murder, revolution. And I even will have moments when I wonder if the quiet was not better than all that death and hatred. But I will look about my village at the illiteracy and disease and ignorance, and I will not wonder long. And perhaps . . . perhaps I will be a great man. . . . I mean perhaps I will hold on to the substance of truth and find my way always with the right course . . . and perhaps for it I will be butchered in my bed some night by the servants of empire. . . .

Beneatha. *The martyr!*

Asagai. . . . or perhaps I shall live to be a very old man, respected and esteemed in my new nation. . . . And perhaps I shall hold office, and this is what I'm trying to tell you, Alaiyo; perhaps the things I believe now for my country will be wrong and outmoded, and I will not understand and do terrible things to have things my way or merely to keep my power. Don't you see that there will be young men and women, not British soldiers then, but my own black countrymen . . . to step out of the shadows some evening and slit my then useless throat? Don't you see they have always been there . . . that they always will be. And that such a thing as my own death will be an advance? They who might kill me even . . . actually replenish me!

Beneatha. Oh, Asagai, I know all that.

Asagai. Good! Then stop moaning and groaning and tell me what you plan to do.

Beneatha. Do?

Asagai. I have a bit of a suggestion.

Beneatha. What?

Asagai (*rather quietly for him*). That when it is all over—that you come home with me—

Beneatha (*slapping herself on the forehead with exasperation born of misunderstanding*). Oh—Asagai—at this moment you decide to be romantic!

Asagai (*quickly understanding the misunderstanding*). My dear, young creature of the New World—I do not mean across the

---

1. retrogression (re′ trə gresh′ ən): a moving backward, especially into a worse condition.

city—I mean across the ocean; home—to Africa.

Beneatha (*slowly understanding and turning to him with murmured amazement*). To—to Nigeria?

Asagai. Yes! . . . (*smiling and lifting his arms playfully*) Three hundred years later the African Prince rose up out of the seas and swept the maiden back across the middle passage over which her ancestors had come—

Beneatha (*unable to play*). Nigeria?

Asagai. Nigeria. Home. (*coming to her with genuine romantic flippancy*) I will show you our mountains and our stars; and give you cool drinks from gourds and teach you the old songs and the ways of our people—and, in time, we will pretend that—(*very softly*)—you have only been away for a day—

(*She turns her back to him, thinking. He swings her around and takes her full in his arms in a long embrace which proceeds to passion.*)

Beneatha (*pulling away*). You're getting me all mixed up—

Asagai. Why?

Beneatha. Too many things—too many things have happened today. I must sit down and think. I don't know what I feel about anything right this minute.

(*She promptly sits down and props her chin on her fist.*)

Asagai (*charmed*). All right, I shall leave you. No—don't get up. (*touching her, gently, sweetly*) Just sit awhile and think. . . . Never be afraid to sit awhile and think. (*He goes to door and looks at her.*) How often I have looked at you and said, "Ah—so this is what the New World hath finally wrought. . . ."

(*He exits. Beneatha sits on alone. Presently Walter enters from his room and starts to rummage through things, feverishly looking for something. She looks up and turns in her seat.*)

Beneatha (*hissingly*). Yes—just look at what the New World hath wrought! . . . Just look! (*She gestures with bitter disgust.*) There he is! Monsieur le petit bourgeois noir[2]—himself! There he is—Symbol of a Rising Class! Entrepreneur! Titan of the System! (*Walter ignores her completely and continues frantically and destructively looking for something and hurling things to the floor and tearing things out of their place in his search. Beneatha ignores the eccentricity of his actions and goes on with the monologue of insult.*) Did you dream of yachts on Lake Michigan, Brother? Did you see yourself on that Great Day sitting down at the Conference Table, surrounded by all the mighty bald-headed men in America? All halted, waiting, breathless, waiting for your pronouncements on industry? Waiting for you—Chairman of the Board? (*Walter finds what he is looking for—a small piece of white paper—and pushes it in his pocket and puts on his coat and rushes out without ever having looked at her. She shouts after him.*) I look at you and I see the final triumph of stupidity in the world!

(*The door slams and she returns to just sitting again. Ruth comes quickly out of Mama's room.*)

Ruth. Who was that?

Beneatha. Your husband.

Ruth. Where did he go?

---

2. ***Monsieur le petit bourgeois noir*** (mə syö′ lə pə tē′ bōōr zhwä′ nwär) *French:* Mr. Lower-Middle-Class Black.

Beneatha. Who knows—maybe he has an appointment at U.S. Steel.

Ruth (*anxiously, with frightened eyes*). You didn't say nothing bad to him, did you?

Beneatha. Bad? Say anything bad to him? No—I told him he was a sweet boy and full of dreams and everything is strictly peachy keen as the ofay[3] kids say!

(Mama *enters from her bedroom. She is lost, vague, trying to catch hold, to make some sense of her former command of the world, but it still eludes her. A sense of waste overwhelms her gait; a measure of apology rides on her shoulders. She goes to her plant, which has remained on the table, looks at it, picks it up and takes it to the window sill and sets it outside, and she stands and looks at it a long moment. Then she closes the window, straightens her body with effort and turns around to her children.*)

Mama. Well—ain't it a mess in here, though? (*a false cheerfulness, a beginning of something*) I guess we all better stop moping around and get some work done. All this unpacking and everything we got to do. (Ruth *raises her head slowly in response to the sense of the line; and Beneatha in similar manner turns very slowly to look at her mother.*) One of you all better call the moving people and tell 'em not to come.

Ruth. Tell 'em not to come?

Mama. Of course, baby. Ain't no need in 'em coming all the way here and having to go back. They charges for that too. (*She sits down, fingers to her brow, thinking.*) Lord, ever since I was a little girl, I always remembers people saying, "Lena—Lena Eggleston, you aims too high all the time. You needs to slow down and see life a little more like it is. Just slow down some." That's what they always used to say down home—"Lord, that

Lena Eggleston is a high-minded thing. She'll get her due one day!"

Ruth. No, Lena. . . .

Mama. Me and Big Walter just didn't never learn right.

Ruth. Lena, no! We gotta go. Bennie—tell her. . . . (*She rises and crosses to* Beneatha *with her arms outstretched.* Beneatha *doesn't respond.*) Tell her we can still move . . . the notes ain't but a hundred and twenty-five a month. We got four grown people in this house—we can work. . . .

Mama (*to herself*). Just aimed too high all the time—

Ruth (*turning and going to* Mama *fast—the words pouring out with urgency and desperation*). Lena—I'll work. . . . I'll work twenty hours a day in all the kitchens in Chicago. . . . I'll strap my baby on my back if I have to and scrub all the floors in America and wash all the sheets in America if I have to—but we got to move. . . . We got to get out of here. . . .

(Mama *reaches out absently and pats* Ruth's *hand.*)

Mama. No—I sees things differently now. Been thinking 'bout some of the things we could do to fix this place up some. I seen a second-hand bureau over on Maxwell Street just the other day that could fit right there. (*She points to where the new furniture might go.* Ruth *wanders away from her.*) Would need some new handles on it and then a little varnish and then it look like something brand-new. And—we can put up them new curtains in the kitchen. . . . Why this place be looking fine. Cheer us all up so that we forget trouble ever came. . . . (*to* Ruth) And

---

3. ofay: slang term for a white person.

you could get some nice screens to put up in your room round the baby's bassinet. . . . (*She looks at both of them, pleadingly.*) Sometimes you just got to know when to give up some things . . . and hold on to what you got.

(Walter *enters from the outside, looking spent and leaning against the door, his coat hanging from him.*)

Mama. Where you been, son?

Walter (*breathing hard*). Made a call.

Mama. To who, son?

Walter. To The Man.

Mama. What man, baby?

Walter. The Man, Mama. Don't you know who The Man is?

Ruth. Walter Lee?

Walter. *The Man.* Like the guys in the streets say—The Man. Captain Boss—Mistuh Charley. . . . Old Captain Please Mr. Bossman. . . .

Beneatha (*suddenly*). Lindner!

Walter. That's right! That's good. I told him to come right over.

Beneatha (*fiercely, understanding*). For what? What do you want to see him for!

From the 1961 movie *Raisin in the Sun,*
starring Sidney Poitier, Ruby Dee, Claudia McNeil, and Diana Sands.
Photofest, New York.

Walter (*looking at his sister*). We going to do business with him.

Mama. What you talking 'bout, son?

Walter. Talking 'bout life, Mama. You all always telling me to see life like it is. Well—I laid in there on my back today . . . and I figured it out. Life just like it is. Who gets and who don't get. (*He sits down with his coat on and laughs.*) Mama, you know it's all divided up. Life is. Sure enough. Between the takers and the "tooken." (*He laughs.*) I've figured it out finally. (*He looks around at them.*) Yeah. Some of us always getting "tooken." (*He laughs.*) People like Willy Harris, they don't never get "tooken." And you know why the rest of us do? 'Cause we all mixed up. Mixed up bad. We get to looking 'round for the right and the wrong; and we worry about it and cry about it and stay up nights trying to figure out 'bout the wrong and the right of things all the time. . . . And all the time, man, them takers is out there operating, just taking and taking. Willy Harris? Shoot—Willy Harris don't even count. He don't even count in the big scheme of things. But I'll say one thing for old Willy Harris . . . he's taught me something. He's taught me to keep my eye on what counts in this world. Yeah—(*shouting out a little*) Thanks, Willy!

Ruth. What did you call that man for, Walter Lee?

Walter. Called him to tell him to come on over to the show. Gonna put on a show for the man. Just what he wants to see. You see, Mama, the man came here today and he told us that them people out there where you want us to move—well they so upset they willing to pay us not to move out there. (*He laughs again.*) And—and oh, Mama—you would of been proud of the way me and Ruth and Bennie acted. We told him to get

out. . . . Lord have mercy! We told the man to get out. Oh, we was some proud folks this afternoon, yeah. (*He lights a cigarette.*) We were still full of that old-time stuff. . . .

Ruth (*coming toward him slowly*). You talking 'bout taking them people's money to keep us from moving in that house?

Walter. I ain't just talking 'bout it, baby—I'm telling you that's what's going to happen.

Beneatha. Oh, God! Where is the bottom! Where is the real honest-to-God bottom so he can't go any farther!

Walter. See—that's the old stuff. You and that boy that was here today. You all want everybody to carry a flag and a spear and sing some marching songs, huh? You wanna spend your life looking into things and trying to find the right and the wrong part, huh? Yeah. You know what's going to happen to that boy someday—he'll find himself sitting in a dungeon, locked in forever—and the takers will have the key! Forget it, baby! There ain't no causes—there ain't nothing but taking in this world, and he who takes most is smartest—and it don't make a bit of difference *how*.

Mama. You making something inside me cry, son. Some awful pain inside me.

Walter. Don't cry, Mama. Understand. That white man is going to walk in that door able to write checks for more money than we ever had. It's important to him and I'm going to help him. . . . I'm going to put on the show, Mama.

Mama. Son—I come from five generations of people who was slaves and sharecroppers—but ain't nobody in my family never let nobody pay 'em no money that was a way of telling us we wasn't fit to walk the earth.

We ain't never been that poor. (*raising her eyes and looking at him*) We ain't never been that dead inside.

Beneatha. Well—we are dead now. All the talk about dreams and sunlight that goes on in this house. All dead.

Walter. What's the matter with you all! I didn't make this world! It was give to me this way! Hell, yes, I want me some yachts someday! Yes, I want to hang some real pearls 'round my wife's neck. Ain't she supposed to wear no pearls? Somebody tell me—tell me, who decides which women is suppose to wear pearls in this world. I tell you I am a *man*—and I think my wife should wear some pearls in this world!

(*This last line hangs a good while, and* Walter *begins to move about the room. The word "Man" has penetrated his consciousness; he mumbles it to himself repeatedly between strange agitated pauses as he moves about.*)

Mama. Baby, how you going to feel on the inside?

Walter. Fine! . . . Going to feel fine . . . a man. . . .

Mama. You won't have nothing left then, Walter Lee.

Walter (*coming to her*). I'm going to feel fine, Mama. I'm going to look The Man in the eyes and say—(*He falters.*)—and say, "All right, Mr. Lindner—(*He falters even more.*)—that's your neighborhood out there. You got the right to keep it like you want. You got the right to have it like you want. Just write the check and—the house is yours." And, and I am going to say—(*His voice almost breaks.*) And you—you people just put the money in my hand and you won't have to live next to this bunch of stinking niggers—(*He straightens up and*

moves away from his mother, walking around the room*). Maybe—maybe I'll just get down on my black knees. . . . (*He does so;* Ruth *and* Bennie *and* Mama *watch him in frozen horror.*) Captain, Mistuh, Bossman. (*He starts crying.*) A-hee-hee-hee! (*Wringing his hands in profoundly anguished imitation.*) Yasssssuh! Great White Father, just gi' ussen de money, fo' God's sake, and we's ain't gwine come out deh and dirty up yo' white folks neighborhood. . . .

(*He breaks down completely, then gets up and goes into the bedroom.*)

Beneatha. That is not a man. That is nothing but a toothless rat. . . .

Mama. Yes—death done come in this here house. (*She is nodding, slowly, reflectively.*) Done come walking in my house. On the lips of my children. You what supposed to be my beginning again. You—what supposed to be my harvest. (*to* Beneatha) You—you mourning your brother?

Beneatha. He's no brother of mine.

Mama. What you say?

Beneatha. I said that that individual in that room is no brother of mine.

Mama. That's what I thought you said. You feeling like you better than he is today? (Beneatha *does not answer.*) Yes? What you tell him a minute ago? That he wasn't a man? Yes? You give him up for me? You done wrote his epitaph too—like the rest of the world? Well, who give you the privilege?

Beneatha. Be on my side for once! You saw what he just did, Mama! You saw him—down on his knees. Wasn't it you who taught me—to despise any man who would do that. Do what he's going to do.

Mama. Yes—I taught you that. Me and your daddy. But I thought I taught you something else too. . . . I thought I taught you to love him.

Beneatha. Love him? There is nothing left to love.

Mama. There is always something left to love. And if you ain't learned that, you ain't learned nothing. (*looking at her*) Have you cried for that boy today? I don't mean for yourself and for the family 'cause we lost the money. I mean for him; what he been through and what it done to him. Child, when do you think is the time to love somebody the most; when they done good and made things easy for everybody? Well then, you ain't through learning—because that ain't the time at all. It's when he's at his lowest and can't believe in hisself 'cause the world done whipped him so. When you starts measuring somebody, measure him right, child, measure him right. Make sure you done taken into account what hills and valleys he come through before he got to wherever he is.

(Travis *bursts into the room at the end of the speech, leaving the door open.*)

Travis. Grandmama—the moving men are downstairs! The truck just pulled up.

Mama (*turning and looking at him*). Are they, baby? They downstairs?

(*She sighs and sits.* Lindner *appears in the doorway. He peers in and knocks lightly, to gain attention, and comes in. All turn to look at him.*)

Lindner (*hat and briefcase in hand*). Uh—hello. . . .

(Ruth *crosses mechanically to the bedroom door and opens it and lets it swing open freely and slowly as the lights come up on Walter within, still in his coat, sitting at the far corner of the room. He looks up and out through the room to Lindner.*)

Ruth. He's here.

(*A long minute passes and Walter slowly gets up.*)

Lindner (*coming to the table with efficiency, putting his briefcase on the table and starting to unfold papers and unscrew fountain pens*). Well, I certainly was glad to hear from you people. (Walter *has begun the trek out of the room, slowly and awkwardly, rather like a small boy, passing the back of his sleeve across his mouth from time to time.*) Life can really be so much simpler than people let it be most of the time. Well—with whom do I negotiate? You, Mrs. Younger, or your son here? (Mama *sits with her hands folded on her lap and her eyes closed as Walter advances.* Travis *goes close to Lindner and looks at the papers curiously.*) Just some official papers, sonny.

Ruth. Travis, you go downstairs.

Mama (*opening her eyes and looking into* Walter's). No. Travis, you stay right here. And you make him understand what you doing, Walter Lee. You teach him good. Like Willy Harris taught you. You show where our five generations done come to. Go ahead, son—

Walter (*looks down into his boy's eyes.* Travis *grins at him merrily, and Walter draws him beside him with his arm lightly around his shoulders.*). Well, Mr. Lindner. (Beneatha *turns away.*) We called you— (*There is a profound, simple groping quality in his speech.*)—because, well, me and my family (*He looks around and shifts from one foot to the other.*) Well—we are very plain people . . . .

Lindner. Yes—

Walter. I mean—I have worked as a chauffeur most of my life—and my wife here, she does domestic work in people's kitchens. So does my mother. I mean—we are plain people. . . .

Lindner. Yes, Mr. Younger—

Walter (*really like a small boy, looking down at his shoes and then up at the man*). And—us—well, my father, well, he was a laborer most of his life.

Lindner (*absolutely confused*). Uh, yes—

Walter (*looking down at his toes once again*). My father almost beat a man to death once because this man called him a bad name or something, you know what I mean?

Lindner. No, I'm afraid I don't.

Walter (*finally straightening up*). Well, what I mean is that we come from people who had a lot of pride. I mean—we are very proud people. And that's my sister over there and she's going to be a doctor—and we are very proud—

Lindner. Well—I am sure that is very nice, but—

Walter (*starting to cry and facing the man eye to eye*). What I am telling you is that we called you over here to tell you that we are very proud and that this is—this is my son, who makes the sixth generation of our family in this country, and that we have all thought about your offer and we have decided to move into our house because my father—my father—he earned it. (Mama *has her eyes closed and is rocking back and forth as though she were in church, with her head nodding the amen yes.*) We don't want to make no trouble for nobody or fight no causes—but we will try to be good neighbors. That's all we got to say. (*He looks the man absolutely in the eyes.*) We don't want your money.

(*He turns and walks away from the man.*)

Lindner (*looking around at all of them*).

I take it then that you have decided to occupy.

Beneatha. That's what the man said.

Lindner (*to Mama in her reverie*). Then I would like to appeal to you, Mrs. Younger. You are older and wiser and understand things better I am sure. . . .

Mama (*rising*). I am afraid you don't understand. My son said we was going to move and there ain't nothing left for me to say. (*shaking her head with double meaning*) You know how these young folks is nowadays, mister. Can't do a thing with 'em. Goodbye.

Lindner (*folding up his materials*). Well—if you are that final about it. . . . There is nothing left for me to say. (*He finishes. He is almost ignored by the family, who are concentrating on Walter Lee. At the door* Lindner *halts and looks around.*) I sure hope you people know what you're doing.

(*He shakes his head and exits.*)

Ruth (*looking around and coming to life*). Well, for God's sake—if the moving men are here—LET'S GET THE HELL OUT OF HERE!

Mama (*into action*). Ain't it the truth! Look at all this here mess. Ruth, put Travis's good jacket on him. . . . Walter Lee, fix your tie and tuck your shirt in; you look just like somebody's hoodlum. Lord have mercy, where is my plant? (*She flies to get it amid the general bustling of the family, who are deliberately trying to ignore the nobility of the past moment.*) You all start on down. . . . Travis child, don't go empty-handed. . . . Ruth, where did I put that box with my skillets in it? I want to be in charge of it myself. . . . I'm going to make us the biggest dinner we ever ate tonight. . . . Beneatha, what's the matter with them stockings? Pull them things up, girl. . . .

(*The family starts to file out as two moving men appear and begin to carry out the heavier pieces of furniture, bumping into the family as they move about.*)

Beneatha. Mama, Asagai—asked me to marry him today and go to Africa—

Mama (*in the middle of her getting-ready activity*). He did? You ain't old enough to marry nobody—(*Seeing the moving men lifting one of her chairs precariously.*) Darling, that ain't no bale of cotton, please handle it so we can sit in it again. I had that chair twenty-five years. . . .

(*The movers sigh with exasperation and go on with their work.*)

Beneatha (*girlishly and unreasonably trying to pursue the conversation*). To go to Africa, Mama—be a doctor in Africa. . . .

Mama (*distracted*). Yes, baby—

Walter. Africa! What he want you to go to Africa for?

Beneatha. To practice there. . . .

Walter. Girl, if you don't get all them silly ideas out your head! You better marry yourself a man with some loot. . . .

Beneatha (*angrily, precisely as in the first scene of the play*). What have you got to do with who I marry!

Walter. Plenty. Now I think George Murchison—

(*He and Beneatha go out yelling at each other vigorously; Beneatha is heard saying that she would not marry George Murchison if he were Adam and she were Eve, etc. The anger is loud and real till their voices diminish. Ruth stands at the door and turns to Mama and smiles knowingly.*)

Mama (*fixing her hat at last*). Yeah—they something all right, my children. . . .

Ruth. Yeah—they're something. Let's go, Lena.

Mama (*stalling, starting to look around at the house*). Yes—I'm coming. Ruth—

Ruth. Yes?

Mama (*quietly, woman to woman*). He finally come into his manhood today, didn't he? Kind of like a rainbow after the rain. . . .

Ruth (*biting her lip lest her own pride explode in front of* Mama). Yes, Lena.

(*Walter's voice calls for them raucously.*)

Mama (*waving* Ruth *out vaguely*). All right, honey—go on down. I be down directly.

(*Ruth hesitates, then exits. Mama stands, at last alone in the living room, her plant on the table before her as the lights start to come down. She looks around at all the walls and ceilings and suddenly, despite herself, while the children call below, a great heaving thing rises in her and she puts her fist to her mouth, takes a final desperate look, pulls her coat about her, pats her hat, and goes out. The lights dim down. The door opens and she comes back in, grabs her plant, and goes out for the last time.*)

$\mathcal{T}$*hinking About Act Three*

A PERSONAL RESPONSE

sharing impressions

1. What is your attitude toward Walter at the end of the play? Describe your feelings in your journal.

constructing interpretations

2. In your opinion, why does Walter change his mind about accepting Lindner's offer? Support your answer.

3. Judging from her play, what do you think Hansberry would see as true and false definitions of manhood?

Think about
- Walter's reference to Lindner as The Man (page 378)
- Walter's assertion, "I tell you I am a *man*—and I think my wife should wear some pearls in this world" (page 380)
- Beneatha's comment about Walter, "That is not a man" (page 380), and her later comment to Lindner, "That's what the man said" (page 382)
- Mama's statement "He finally come into his manhood today" (page 383)

4. After reading this play, what thoughts or ideas about dreams do you come away with?

Think about
- Beneatha's attack on Asagai's idealism and Asagai's response (page 375)
- your reactions to Mama and Walter when they decide to "see life like it is" (pages 377 and 379)
- the status of each character's dream at the end of the play

5. Do you believe that the play has a happy ending? Explain your answer.

Think about
- what has and has not changed for the family
- the emotional state of the family upon leaving the apartment
- the reception they are likely to get from their new neighbors

A CREATIVE RESPONSE

6. If Walter had accepted Lindner's money, how would that decision have affected him and the family?

A CRITICAL RESPONSE

7. What does Mama's plant symbolize to you? Explain your answer.

8. An epigraph is a quotation that appears at the beginning of a book or play; it often suggests the theme of the work. Reread the poem by Langston Hughes on page 320. How well do you think it works as an epigraph for this play?

9. The critic Anne Cheney writes: *"Raisin* at first seems a plea for racial tolerance or a fable of man's overcoming an insensitive society, but the simple eloquence of the characters elevates the play into a universal representation of all people's hopes, fears, and dreams." How would you relate this play to your own hopes, fears, or dreams?

Connecting Reading and Writing

1. Analyze the character of Mama or Walter for a **playbill** to be distributed at a performance of the play.

Option: Fully describe the character of Mama or Walter in **director's notes** intended for the actor or actress playing the role.

2. In a **diagram** to be explained before the class, contrast either of these pairs of minor characters: Ruth and Beneatha or George Murchison and Asagai. Identify ideas that Hansberry explores through these characters.

Option: Write a **note** to a friend explaining why you think he or she would be perfect for the role of Ruth, Beneatha, Asagai, or George Murchison.

3. Continue the story of the Younger family in a **dramatic scene** taking place one year after their

move to Clybourne Park. Assign roles and perform the scene for your class.

Option: Have one of the family members deliver a **monologue** describing how his or her life has changed or not changed in the year since the move.

4. *New York Times* critic Frank Rich writes: "Walter is not just a black victim of white racism but also a victim of a materialistic American dream that can enslave men or women of any race." Use this quotation in a **letter** to a local theater group explaining the relevance of the play today and suggesting that the group undertake a production of the play.

Option: React to Rich's interpretation of Walter in a **review** of *A Raisin in the Sun* for your own school newspaper.

A Visit to Grandmother

WILLIAM MELVIN KELLEY

A biography of Kelley appears on page 425.

Approaching the Story

Parts of the story you are about to read recall the South before the era of civil rights, at a time when African Americans were forced to attend separate schools, made to use separate public facilities, and prevented from voting. In addition, they were sometimes lynched—hanged by lawless mobs. In this story an African-American doctor, living in the North in the early 1960's, returns to the South to visit his mother, whom he has not seen in many years. The visit is described from the viewpoint of the doctor's teenage son Chig, who has accompanied him.

Building Vocabulary

These essential words are footnoted within the story.

indulgence (in dul′ jəns): He had spoken of GL with the kind of **indulgence** he would have shown a cute, but ill-behaved and potentially dangerous, five-year-old. (page 387)

engaging (en gāj′ iŋ): He stood in the doorway, smiling broadly, an **engaging,** open, friendly smile, the innocent smile of a five-year-old. (page 391)

Connecting Writing and Reading

In which of the situations described below would it be fair to give a person special consideration? In which situations would it be unfair? Copy the box below and, for each statement, mark an **X** in the appropriate column. Give reasons for your responses.

	Fair	Unfair
The person is more attractive than others.	_____	_____
The person is less attractive than others.	_____	_____
The person is less responsible than others.	_____	_____

As you read this story about a mother and two sons, consider your thoughts about when someone should be indulged.

CHIG KNEW SOMETHING was wrong the instant his father kissed her. He had always known his father to be the warmest of men, a man so kind that when people ventured timidly into his office, it took only a few words from him to make them relax, and even laugh. Doctor Charles Dunford cared about people.

But when he had bent to kiss the old lady's black face, something new and almost ugly had come into his eyes: fear, uncertainty, sadness, and perhaps even hatred.

Ten days before in New York, Chig's father had decided suddenly he wanted to go to Nashville to attend his college class reunion, twenty years out. Both Chig's brother and sister, Peter and Connie, were packing for camp and besides were too young for such an affair. But Chig was seventeen, had nothing to do that summer, and his father asked if he would like to go along. His father had given him additional reasons: "All my running buddies got their diplomas and were snapped up by them crafty young gals, and had kids within a year—now all those kids, some of them gals, are your age."

The reunion had lasted a week. As they packed for home, his father, in a far too off-hand way, had suggested they visit Chig's grandmother. "We this close. We might as well drop in on her and my brothers."

So, instead of going north, they had gone farther south, had just entered her house. And Chig had a suspicion now that the reunion had been only an excuse to drive south, that his father had been heading to this house all the time.

His father had never talked much about his family, with the exception of his brother GL, who seemed part con man, part practical joker, and part Don Juan; he had spoken of GL with the kind of indulgence[1] he would have shown a cute, but ill-behaved and potentially dangerous, five-year-old.

Chig's father had left home when he was fifteen. When asked why, he would answer, "I wanted to go to school. They didn't have a black high school at home, so I went up to Knoxville and lived with a cousin and went to school."

They had been met at the door by Aunt Rose, GL's wife, and ushered into the living room. The old lady had looked up from her seat by the window. Aunt Rose stood between the visitors.

The old lady eyed his father. "Rose, who that? Rose?" She squinted. She looked like a doll, made of black straw, the wrinkles in her face running in one direction like the head of a broom. Her hair was white and coarse and grew out straight from her head. Her eyes were brown—the whites, too, seemed light brown—and were hidden behind thick glasses, which remained somehow on a tiny nose. "That Hiram?" That was another of his father's brothers. "No, it ain't Hiram; too big for Hiram." She turned then to Chig. "Now that man, he look like Eleanor, Charles's wife, but Charles wouldn't never send my grandson to see me. I never even hear from Charles." She stopped again.

"It Charles, Mama. That who it is." Aunt Rose, between them, led them closer. "It Charles come all the way from New York to see you, and brung little Charles with him."

The old lady stared up at them. "Charles? Rose, that really Charles?" She turned away, and reached for a handkerchief in the pocket of her clean, ironed, flowered housecoat, and wiped her eyes. "God have mercy. Charles." She spread her arms up to him, and he bent down and kissed her cheek. That was when Chig saw his face, grimacing. She hugged him; Chig watched the muscles in her arms as they tightened around his father's neck. She half rose out of her chair. "How are you, son?"

---

1. **indulgence** (in dul′ jəns): a yielding; lack of strictness.

Chig could not hear his father's answer.

She let him go, and fell back into her chair, grabbing the arms. Her hands were as dark as the wood, and seemed to become part of it. "Now, who that standing there? Who that man?"

"That's one of your grandsons, Mama." His father's voice cracked. "Charles Dunford, junior. You saw him once, when he was a baby, in Chicago. He's grown now."

"I can see that, boy!" She looked at Chig squarely. "Come here, son, and kiss me once." He did. "What they call you? Charles too?"

"No, ma'am, they call me Chig."

She smiled. She had all her teeth, but they were too perfect to be her own. "That's good. Can't have two boys answering to Charles in the same house. Won't nobody at all come. So you that little boy. You don't remember me, do you. I used to take you to church in Chicago, and you'd get up and hop in time to the music. You studying to be a preacher?"

"No, ma'am. I don't think so. I might be a lawyer."

"You'll be an honest one, won't you?"

"I'll try."

"Trying ain't enough! You be honest, you hear? Promise me. You be honest like your daddy."

"All right. I promise."

"Good. Rose, where's GL at? Where's that thief? He gone again?"

"I don't know, Mama." Aunt Rose looked embarrassed. "He say he was going by the store. He'll be back."

"Well, then where's Hiram? You call up those boys, and get them over here—now! You got enough to eat? Let me go see." She started to get up. Chig reached out his hand. She shook him off. "What they tell you about me, Chig? They tell you I'm all laid up? Don't believe it. They don't know nothing about old ladies. When I want help, I'll let you know. Only time I'll need help getting anywheres is when I dies and they lift me into the ground."

She was standing now, her back and shoulders straight. She came only to Chig's chest. She squinted up at him. "You eat much? Your daddy ate like two men."

"Yes, ma'am."

"That's good. That means you ain't nervous. Your mama, she ain't nervous. I remember that. In Chicago, she'd sit down by a window all afternoon and never say nothing, just knit." She smiled. "Let me see what we got to eat."

"I'll do that, Mama." Aunt Rose spoke softly. "You haven't seen Charles in a long time. You sit and talk."

The old lady squinted at her. "You can do the cooking if you promise it ain't because you think I can't."

Aunt Rose chuckled. "I know you can do it, Mama."

"All right. I'll just sit and talk a spell." She sat again and arranged her skirt around her short legs.

Chig did most of the talking, told all about himself before she asked. His father only spoke when he was spoken to, and then, only one word at a time, as if by coming back home, he had become a small boy again, sitting in the parlor while his mother spoke with her guests.

When Uncle Hiram and Mae, his wife, came, they sat down to eat. Chig did not have to ask about Uncle GL's absence; Aunt Rose volunteered an explanation: "Can't never tell where the man is at. One Thursday morning he left here and next thing we knew, he was calling from Chicago, saying he went up to see Joe Louis fight. He'll be here though; he ain't as young and footloose as he used to be." Chig's father had mentioned driving down that GL was about five years older than he was, nearly fifty.

Uncle Hiram was somewhat smaller than Chig's father; his short-cropped kinky hair was half gray, half black. One spot, just off his forehead, was totally white. Later, Chig found out it had been that way since he was twenty. Mae (Chig could not bring himself to call her Aunt) was a good deal younger than Hiram, pretty enough so that Chig would have looked at her twice on the street. She was a honey-colored woman, with long eyelashes. She was wearing a white sheath.

At dinner, Chig and his father sat on one side, opposite Uncle Hiram and Mae; his grandmother and Aunt Rose sat at the ends. The food was good; there was a lot and Chig ate a lot. All through the meal, they talked about the family as it had been thirty years before, and particularly about the young GL. Mae and Chig asked questions; the old lady answered; Aunt Rose directed the discussion, steering the old lady onto the best stories; Chig's father laughed from time to time; Uncle Hiram ate.

"Why don't you tell them about the horse, Mama?" Aunt Rose, over Chig's weak protest, was spooning mashed potatoes onto his plate. "There now, Chig."

"I'm trying to think." The old lady was holding her fork halfway to her mouth, looking at them over her glasses. "Oh, you talking about that crazy horse GL brung home that time."

"That's right, Mama." Aunt Rose nodded and slid another slice of white meat on Chig's plate.

Mae started to giggle. "Oh, I've heard this. This is funny, Chig."

The old lady put down her fork and began. "Well, GL went out of the house one day with an old, no-good chair I wanted him to take over to the church for a bazaar, and he met up with this man who'd just brung in some horses from out West. Now, I reckon you can expect one swindler to be in every town, but you don't rightly think there'll be two; and God forbid they should ever meet—but they did, GL and his chair, this man and his horses.

Well, I wished I'd-a been there; there must-a been some mighty high-powered talking going on. That man with his horses, he told GL them horses was half-Arab, half-Indian, and GL told that man the chair was an antique he'd stole from some rich white folks. So they swapped. Well, I was a-looking out the window and seen GL dragging this animal to the house. It looked pretty gentle and its eyes was most closed and its feet was shuffling.

"'GL, where'd you get that thing?' I says.

"'I swapped him for that old chair, Mama,' he says. 'And made myself a bargain. This is even better than Papa's horse.'

"Well, I'm a-looking at this horse and noticing how he be looking more and more wide awake every minute, sort of warming up like a teakettle until, I swears to you, that horse is blowing steam out its nose.

"'Come on, Mama,' GL says, 'come on and I'll take you for a ride.' Now George, my husband, God rest his tired soul, he'd brung home this white folks' buggy which had a busted wheel and fixed it and was to take it back that day and GL says: 'Come on, Mama, we'll use this fine buggy and take us a ride.'

"'GL,' I says, 'no, we ain't. Them white folks'll burn us alive if we use their buggy. You just take that horse right on back.' You see, I was sure that boy'd come by that animal ungainly.[2]

"'Mama, I can't take him back,' GL says.

"'Why not?' I says.

"'Because I don't rightly know where that man is at,' GL says.

"'Oh,' I says. 'Well, then I reckon we stuck with it.' And I turned around to go back into the house because it was getting late, near dinner time, and I was cooking for ten.

"'Mama,' GL says to my back. 'Mama, ain't you coming for a ride with me?'

---

2. **ungainly** (un gān′ lē): a colloquial term meaning "improperly, in an immoral or illegal manner."

"'Go on, boy. You ain't getting me inside kicking range of that animal.' I was eying that beast and it was boiling hotter all the time. I reckon maybe that man had drugged it. 'That horse is wild, GL,' I says.

"'No, he ain't. He ain't. That man say he is buggy and saddle broke and as sweet as the inside of a apple.'

"My oldest girl, Essie, had-a come out on the porch and she says, 'Go on, Mama. I'll cook. You ain't been out the house in weeks.'

"'Sure, come on, Mama,' GL says. 'There ain't nothing to be fidgety about. This horse is gentle as a rose petal.' And just then that animal snorts so hard it sets up a little dust storm around its feet.

"'Yes, Mama,' Essie says, 'you can see he gentle.' Well, I looked at Essie and then at that horse because I didn't think we could be looking at the same animal. I should-a figured how Essie's eyes ain't never been so good.

"'Come on, Mama,' GL says.

"'All right,' I says. So I stood on the porch and watched GL hitching that horse up to the white folks' buggy. For a while there, the animal was pretty quiet, pawing a little, but not much. And I was feeling a little better about riding with GL behind that crazy-looking horse. I could see how GL was happy I was going with him. He was scurrying around that animal buckling buckles and strapping straps, all the time smiling, and that made me feel good.

"Then he was finished, and I must say, that horse looked mighty fine hitched to that buggy and I knew anybody what climbed up there would look pretty good too. GL came around and stood at the bottom of the steps, and took off his hat and bowed and said, 'Madam,' and reached out his hand to me and I was feeling real elegant like a fine lady. He helped me up to the seat and then got up beside me and we moved out down our alley. And I remember how black folks come out on their porches and shook their heads, saying, 'Lord now, will you look at Eva Dunford, the fine lady! Don't she look good sitting up there!' And I pretended not to hear and sat up straight and proud.

"We rode on through the center of town, up Market Street, and all the way out where Hiram is living now, which in them days was all woods, there not being even a farm in sight and that's when that horse must-a first realized he weren't at all broke or tame or maybe thought he was back out West again, and started to gallop.

"'GL,' I says, 'now you ain't joking with your mama, is you? Because if you is, I'll strap you purple if I live through this.'

"Well, GL was pulling on the reins with all his meager strength, and yelling, 'Whoa, you. Say now, whoa!' He turned to me just long enough to say, 'I ain't fooling with you, Mama. Honest!'

"I reckon that animal weren't too satisfied with the road, because it made a sharp right turn just then, down into a gulley, and struck out across a hilly meadow. 'Mama,' GL yells. 'Mama, do something!'

"I didn't know what to do, but I figured I had to do something so I stood up, hopped down onto the horse's back and pulled it to a stop. Don't ask me how I did that; I reckon it was that I was a mother and my baby asked me to do something, is all.

"Well, we walked that animal all the way home; sometimes I had to club it over the nose with my fist to make it come, but we made it, GL and me. You remember how tired we was, Charles?"

"I wasn't here at the time." Chig turned to his father and found his face completely blank, without even a trace of a smile or a laugh.

"Well, of course you was, son. That happened in . . . in . . . it was a hot summer that year and—"

"I left here in June of that year. You wrote me about it."

The old lady stared past Chig at him. They

all turned to him; Uncle Hiram looked up from his plate.

"Then you don't remember how we all laughed?"

"No, I don't, Mama. And I probably wouldn't have laughed. I don't think it was funny." They were staring into each other's eyes.

"Why not, Charles?"

"Because in the first place, the horse was gained by fraud. And in the second place, both of you might have been seriously injured or even killed." He broke off their stare and spoke to himself more than to any of them. "And if I'd done it, you would've beaten me good for it."

"Pardon?" The old lady had not heard him; only Chig had heard.

Chig's father sat up straight as if preparing to debate. "I said that if I had done it, if I had done just exactly what GL did, you would have beaten me good for it, Mama." He was looking at her again.

"Why you say that, son?" She was leaning toward him.

"Don't you know? Tell the truth. It can't hurt me now." His voice cracked, but only once. "If GL and I did something wrong, you'd beat me first and then be too tired to beat him. At dinner, he'd always get seconds and I wouldn't. You'd do things with him, like ride in that buggy; but if I wanted you to do something with me, you were always too busy." He paused and considered whether to say what he finally did say. "I cried when I left here. Nobody loved me, Mama. I cried all the way up to Knoxville. That was the last time I ever cried in my life."

"Oh, Charles." She started to get up, to come around the table to him.

He stopped her. "It's too late."

"But you don't understand."

"What don't I understand? I understood then; I understand now."

Tears now traveled down the lines in her face, but when she spoke, her voice was clear. "I thought you knew. I had ten children. I had to give all of them what they needed most." She nodded. "I paid more mind to GL. I had to. GL could-a ended up swinging if I hadn't. But you was smarter. You was more growed up than GL when you was five and he was ten, and I tried to show you that by letting you do what you wanted to do."

"That's not true, Mama. You know it. GL was light-skinned and had good hair and looked almost white and you loved him for that."

"Charles, no. No, son. I didn't love any one of you more than any other."

"That can't be true." His father was standing now, his fists clenched tight. "Admit it, Mama . . . please!" Chig looked at him, shocked; the man was actually crying.

"It may not-a been right what I done, but I ain't no liar." Chig knew she did not really understand what had happened, what he wanted of her. "I'm not lying to you, Charles."

Chig's father had gone pale. He spoke very softly. "You're about thirty years too late, Mama." He bolted from the table. Silverware and dishes rang and jumped. Chig heard him hurrying up to their room.

They sat in silence for awhile and then heard a key in the front door. A man with a new, lacquered straw hat came in. He was wearing brown-and-white two-tone shoes with very pointed toes and a white summer suit. "Say now! Man! I heard my brother was in town. Where he at? Where that rascal?"

He stood in the doorway, smiling broadly, an engaging,[3] open, friendly smile, the innocent smile of a five-year-old.

---

3. **engaging** (en gāj′ iŋ): tending to draw favorable attention; attractive.

Thinking About the Story

A PERSONAL RESPONSE

sharing impressions

1. What is your impression of Charles, GL, and their mother? Jot down some thoughts about these characters in your journal.

constructing interpretations

2. In your opinion, should GL have been indulged by his mother? Explain your answer.

> ***Think about***
> - what his family's descriptions of him, particularly in the story about the horse, reveal about his character
> - what his mother means by saying that GL "could-a ended up swinging" if she had not paid more attention to him
> - the effect that the mother's indulgence of GL has had on her son Charles
> - your views about what entitles someone to be indulged

3. Is Charles right to feel that his mother does not love him? Tell why or why not.

A CREATIVE RESPONSE

4. What could the mother have done in the past, and what can she do now, to keep Charles from feeling such resentment?

5. How might GL view Charles?

A CRITICAL RESPONSE

6. What do you think are the advantages of telling this story from Chig's viewpoint instead of Charles's?

7. To what degree does the setting shape the events of this story?

> ***Think about***
> - how the mother's actions are influenced by the time and place in which she lives
> - whether the same family tensions could have developed had she raised her children in the North or in today's South

8. In 1964 the critic Louis Rubin, Jr., wrote that this story "leaves one unsatisfied because the author has failed to bring out the rich potentialities of the situation. . . . This story isn't concerned enough with the race problem, and it also isn't sufficiently concerned with exploring the full human relationships." Tell whether you agree or disagree with these criticisms, and why.

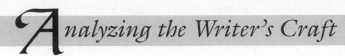

Analyzing the Writer's Craft

DIALOGUE

What do you learn about the characters in "A Visit to Grandmother" from what they say to each other?

Building a Literary Vocabulary. Dialogue is written conversation between two or more characters. Realistic, well-placed dialogue enlivens narrative prose and provides the reader with insights into characters and their personalities. William Melvin Kelley relies heavily on dialogue to tell this story. The dialogue is consistent with his African-American characters, reproducing their rural Southern and urban Northern dialects. (A dialect is the particular variety of language spoken in one place by a distinct group of people.) The dialogue is also emotionally expressive, revealing the feelings and relationships of the characters. Reread the dialogue between the mother and Aunt Rose when Charles and Chig first enter the room (page 387). Here the reader learns that the mother cannot see well and that she has been hurt by never receiving visits from her son. She is profoundly moved that they have finally come to see her. The reader also learns that Aunt Rose is a peacemaker, happy to soothe the mother's feelings.

Application: Interpreting Dialogue. Look at three other passages of dialogue in the story: the exchanges between the mother, Aunt Rose, and Chig from when the mother asks where GL is until she sits down to talk to Chig (page 388); during the horse story, the exchanges between the mother, GL, and Essie from when the mother asks GL where he got the horse until she agrees to ride (page 390); the exchange between the mother and Charles from when she finishes her story until Charles leaves the room (page 391). Several students, taking the parts of the characters, should read these exchanges aloud. The class should discuss what the dialogue reveals about the characters and the relationships between them.

Connecting Reading and Writing

1. Continue this story as a **dialogue** between Charles and his son Chig as they drive back to New York.

Option: Present Charles's view of the situation and the suggestions you would offer him in a **newspaper advice column** similar to "Dear Abby."

2. Write up **personality profiles** of GL and Charles that might appear in their high school yearbooks.

Option: Have the mother describe GL and Charles in an annual church **pamphlet** in which members and their families are profiled.

3. Interview a parent of two or more children, asking whether he or she treats all the children the same or treats them differently according to their special needs. Present this parent's experiences, and note any parallels in the story, in a **newspaper column** devoted to child rearing.

Option: As a class, combine your interview results in a **research report** for your teacher.

If There Be Sorrow

Mari Evans

If there be sorrow
let it be
for things undone
undreamed
    unrealized
        unattained

to these add one:
love withheld
  restrained

Self-portrait, 1934,
KÄTHE KOLLWITZ.
Philadelphia Museum of Art: Given
by Dr. and Mrs. William Wolgin.

Choices   NIKKI GIOVANNI

Oranges   GARY SOTO

Biographies of Giovanni and Soto appear on pages 423 and 429.

Approaching the Poems

African-American poet Nikki Giovanni and Mexican-American poet Gary Soto have much in common. Their poems are personal and autobiographical. In addition, both poets write in a simple style and use language that sounds like natural speech. Giovanni's poem "Choices" uses no punctuation or capitalization. Soto's poem is a narrative that tells about a boy's first date.

Connecting Writing and Reading

Recall some choices you have made that involved compromises. For example, consider the choices you made in any of the following situations:

- discussing with a date whether to go to a sports event, a rock concert, or a movie
- deciding who will do what for a group project involving library research
- negotiating rules and privileges, such as curfew time and the use of the family car, with a parent

In your journal briefly describe one of your choices and the compromise that it entailed. As you read the poems, note that the speakers, too, make choices that involve compromises.

Choices

if i can't do
what i want to do
then my job is to not
do what i don't want
5   to do

it's not the same thing
but it's the best i can
do

if i can't have
10   what i want   then
my job is to want
what i've got
and be satisfied
that at least there
15   is something more
to want

since i can't go
where i need
to go   then i must go
20   where the signs point
though always understanding
parallel movement
isn't lateral

when i can't express
25   what i really feel
i practice feeling
what i can express
and none of it is equal
i know
30   but that's why mankind
alone among the mammals
learns to cry

Oranges

The first time I walked
With a girl, I was twelve,
Cold, and weighted down
With two oranges in my jacket.
5 December. Frost cracking
Beneath my steps, my breath
Before me, then gone,
As I walked toward
Her house, the one whose
10 Porch light burned yellow
Night and day, in any weather.
A dog barked at me, until
She came out pulling
At her gloves, face bright
15 With rouge. I smiled,
Touched her shoulder, and led
Her down the street, across
A used car lot and a line
Of newly planted trees,
20 Until we were breathing
Before a drugstore. We
Entered, the tiny bell
Bringing a saleslady
Down a narrow aisle of goods.
25 I turned to the candies
Tiered like bleachers,
And asked what she wanted—
Light in her eyes, a smile
Starting at the corners

30 Of her mouth. I fingered
A nickel in my pocket,
And when she lifted a chocolate
That cost a dime,
I didn't say anything.
35 I took the nickel from
My pocket, then an orange,
And set them quietly on
The counter. When I looked up,
The lady's eyes met mine,
40 And held them, knowing
Very well what it was all
About.

          Outside,
A few cars hissing past,
45 Fog hanging like old
Coats between the trees.
I took my girl's hand
In mine for two blocks,
Then released it to let
50 Her unwrap the chocolate.
I peeled my orange
That was so bright against
The gray of December
That, from some distance,
55 Someone might have thought
I was making a fire in my hands.

A PERSONAL RESPONSE

sharing impressions

1. What impressions do you have of the speakers of these poems? Respond in your journal.

constructing interpretations

2. Provide several examples from your own experiences that you think demonstrate either the ideas in "Choices" or the situation in "Oranges."

Think about
- the speaker's predicaments in lines 1–2, 9–10, 17–19, and 24–25 of "Choices"
- the speaker's compromises in reacting to those predicaments
- the speaker's conclusion about mankind in the last three lines of "Choices"
- the speaker's predicament when his date selects a ten-cent chocolate in "Oranges"

3. Speculate about what the speaker in "Choices" might have said about the speaker's choice in "Oranges."

A CREATIVE RESPONSE

4. What do you think the speaker in "Oranges" might have done if the saleslady had chosen not to accept the nickel and the orange as payment for the chocolate?

5. How would the effect of "Choices" be different without the last three lines?

A CRITICAL RESPONSE

6. Why do you think both Giovanni and Soto use contrast in these poems?
Think about
- the speaker's limitations and desires in "Choices"
- details about heat and light and about cold and dark in "Oranges"

7. What effect does Giovanni create by omitting capitalization and punctuation in "Choices"? Cite lines from the poem in explaining your opinion.

Marigolds

EUGENIA COLLIER

A biography of Collier appears on page 420.

Approaching the Story

The narrator of "Marigolds" is an adult who recalls a memory from her childhood, a memory that is as much about the feelings she had as a girl of fourteen as it is about her actions. The event she remembers takes place during the Great Depression, a time of economic hardship for the entire country but especially for those who lived in the shantytowns of the rural South.

Building Vocabulary

These essential words are footnoted within the story.

futile (fyoot′ ′l), **impoverished** (im päv′ ər ishd): **Futile** waiting was the sorrowful background music of our **impoverished** little community. (page 400)

poignantly (poin′ yənt lē): As I think of those days I feel most **poignantly** the tag end of summer. (page 401)

stoicism (stō′ i siz′ əm): Her face had Indian-like features and the stern **stoicism** that one associates with Indian faces. (page 402)

perverse (pər vʉrs′): For some **perverse** reason, we children hated those marigolds. (page 402)

degradation (deg′ rə dā′ shən): The smoldering emotions of that summer swelled in me and burst—the great need for my mother . . ., the hopelessness of our poverty and **degradation**. (page 405)

contrition (kən trish′ ən): Despite my wild **contrition** she never planted marigolds again. (page 405)

Connecting Writing and Reading

Think about the kinds of things people do when they are unhappy. In your journal, briefly explain what unhappy people might do to themselves, to other people, and to things around them. Then as you read, notice how characters act when they suffer unhappiness or loss.

Marigolds

WHEN I THINK of the hometown of my youth, all that I seem to remember is dust—the brown, crumbly dust of late summer—arid, sterile dust that gets into the eyes and makes them water, gets into the throat and between the toes of bare brown feet. I don't know why I should remember only the dust. Surely there must have been lush green lawns and paved streets under leafy shade trees somewhere in town; but memory is an abstract painting—it does not present things as they are, but rather as they *feel*. And so, when I think of that time and that place, I remember only the dry September of the dirt roads and grassless yards of the shantytown where I lived. And one other thing I remember, another incongruency of memory—a brilliant splash of sunny yellow against the dust—Miss Lottie's marigolds.

Whenever the memory of those marigolds flashes across my mind, a strange nostalgia comes with it and remains long after the picture has faded. I feel again the chaotic emotions of adolescence, illusive as smoke, yet as real as the potted geranium before me now. Joy and rage and wild animal gladness and shame become tangled together in the multicolored skein of fourteen-going-on-fifteen as I recall that devastating moment when I was suddenly more woman than child, years ago in Miss Lottie's yard. I think of those marigolds at the strangest times. I remember them vividly now as I desperately pass away the time waiting for you, who will not come.

I suppose that <u>futile</u>[1] waiting was the sorrowful background music of our <u>impoverished</u>[2] little community when I was young. The Depression that gripped the nation was no new thing to us, for the black workers of rural Maryland had always been depressed. I don't know what it was that we were waiting for; certainly not for the prosperity that was "just around the corner," for those were white folks' words, which we never believed. Nor did we wait for hard work and thrift to pay off in shining success as the American Dream[3] promised, for we knew better than that, too. Perhaps we waited for a miracle, amorphous in concept but necessary if one were to have the grit to rise before dawn each day and labor in the white man's vineyard until after dark, or to wander about in the September dust offering one's sweat in return for some meager share of bread. But God was *chary* with miracles in those days, and so we waited—and waited.

We children, of course, were only vaguely aware of the extent of our poverty. Having no radios, few newspapers, and no magazines, we were somewhat unaware of the world outside our community. Nowadays we would be called "culturally deprived," and people would write books and hold conferences about us. In those days everybody we knew was just as hungry and ill-clad as we were. Poverty was the cage in which we all were trapped, and our hatred of it was still the vague, undirected restlessness of the zoo-bred flamingo who knows that nature created him to fly free.

---

1. futile (fyo͞ot′ 'l): useless; hopeless; ineffective.
2. impoverished (im päv′ ər ishd): made poor; robbed of strength or power.
3. American Dream: the American ideal of attaining success through equality of opportunity afforded all citizens.

As I think of those days I feel most poignantly[4] the tag end of summer, the bright, dry times when we began to have a sense of shortening days and the imminence of the cold.

By the time I was fourteen my brother Joey and I were the only children left at our house, the older ones having left home for early marriage or the lure of the city, and the two babies having been sent to relatives who might care for them better than we. Joey was three years younger than I, and a boy, and therefore vastly inferior. Each morning our mother and father trudged wearily down the dirt road and around the bend, she to her domestic job, he to his daily unsuccessful quest for work. After a few chores around the tumbledown shanty, Joey and I were free to run wild in the sun with other children similarly situated.

For the most part, those days are ill-defined in my memory, running together and combining like a fresh watercolor painting left out in the rain. I remember squatting in the road, drawing a picture in the dust, a picture that Joey gleefully erased with one sweep of his dirty foot. I remember fishing for minnows in a muddy creek and watching sadly as they eluded my cupped hands, while Joey laughed uproariously. And I remember, that year, a strange restlessness of body and spirit, a feeling that something old and familiar was ending, and something unknown and therefore terrifying was beginning.

One day returns to me with special clarity for some reason, perhaps because it was the beginning of the experience that in some inexplicable way marked the end of innocence. I was loafing under the great oak tree in our yard, deep in some reverie that I have now forgotten except that it involved some secret thoughts of one of the Harris boys across the yard. Joey and a bunch of kids were bored now with the old tire suspended from an oak limb, which had kept them entertained for a while.

"Hey, Lizabeth," Joey yelled. He never talked when he could yell. "Hey, Lizabeth, let's us go somewhere."

I came reluctantly from my private world. "Where at, Joey?"

The truth was that we were becoming tired of the formlessness of our summer days. The idleness whose prospect had seemed so beautiful during the busy days of spring now had degenerated to an almost desperate effort to fill up the empty midday hours.

"Let's go see can we find us some locusts on the hill," someone suggested.

Joey was scornful. "Ain't no more locusts there. Y'all got 'em all while they was still green."

The argument that followed was brief and not really worth the effort. Hunting locust trees wasn't fun any more by now.

"Tell you what," said Joey finally, his eyes sparkling. "Let's us go over to Miss Lottie's."

The idea caught on at once, for annoying Miss Lottie was always fun. I was still child enough to scamper along with the group over rickety fences and through bushes that tore our already raggedy clothes, back to where Miss Lottie lived. I think now that we must have made a tragicomic spectacle, five or six kids of different ages, each of us clad in only one garment—the girls in faded dresses that were too long or too short, the boys in patchy pants, their sweaty brown chests gleaming in the hot sun. A little cloud of dust followed our thin legs and bare feet as we tramped over the barren land.

When Miss Lottie's house came into view we stopped, ostensibly to plan our strategy but actually to reinforce our courage.

Miss Lottie's house was the most ramshackle of all our ramshackle homes. The sun and rain had long since faded its rickety frame siding

---

4. poignantly (poin' yənt lē): in a manner that sharply, keenly, or painfully affects the feelings.

from white to a sullen gray. The boards themselves seemed to remain upright not from being nailed together but rather from leaning together like a house that a child might have constructed from cards.

A brisk wind might have blown it down, and the fact that it was still standing implied a kind of enchantment that was stronger than the elements. There it stood, and as far as I know is standing yet—a gray, rotting thing with no porch, no shutters, no steps, set on a cramped lot with no grass, not even weeds—a monument to decay.

In front of the house in a squeaky rocking chair sat Miss Lottie's son, John Burke, completing the impression of decay. John Burke was what was known as "queer-headed." Black and ageless, he sat, rocking day in and day out in a mindless stupor, lulled by the monotonous squeak-squawk of the chair. A battered hat atop his shaggy head shaded him from the sun. Usually John Burke was totally unaware of everything outside his quiet dream world. But if you disturbed him, if you intruded upon his fantasies, he would become enraged, strike out at you, and curse at you in some strange enchanted language which only he could understand. We children made a game of thinking of ways to disturb John Burke and then to elude his violent retribution.

But our real fun and our real fear lay in Miss Lottie herself. Miss Lottie seemed to be at least a hundred years old. Her big frame still held traces of the tall, powerful woman she must have been in youth, although it was now bent and drawn. Her smooth skin was a dark reddish-brown, and her face had Indian-like features and the stern stoicism[5] that one associates with Indian faces.

Miss Lottie didn't like intruders either, especially children. She never left her yard, and nobody ever visited her. We never knew how she managed those necessities that depend on human interaction—how she ate, for example, or even whether she ate. When we were tiny children, we thought Miss Lottie was a witch, and we made up tales, that we half believed ourselves, about her exploits. We were far too sophisticated now, of course, to believe the witch-nonsense. But old fears have a way of clinging like cobwebs, and so when we sighted the tumbledown shack, we had to stop to reinforce our nerves.

"Look, there she," I whispered, forgetting that Miss Lottie could not possibly have heard me from that distance. "She fooling with them crazy flowers."

"Yeh, look at 'er."

Miss Lottie's marigolds were perhaps the strangest part of the picture. Certainly they did not fit in with the crumbling decay of the rest of her yard. Beyond the dusty brown yard, in front of the sorry gray house, rose suddenly and shockingly a dazzling strip of bright blossoms, clumped together in enormous mounds, warm and passionate and sun-golden. The old black witch-woman worked on them all summer, every summer, down on her creaky knees, weeding and cultivating and arranging, while the house crumbled and John Burke rocked. For some perverse[6] reason, we children hated those marigolds. They interfered with the perfect ugliness of the place; they were too beautiful; they said too much that we could not understand; they did not make sense. There was something in the vigor with which the old woman destroyed the weeds that intimidated us. It should have been a comical sight—the old woman with the man's hat on her cropped white head, leaning over the bright mounds, her big backside in the air—but it wasn't comical; it was something we could not name. We had to annoy her by whizzing a pebble into her

---

5. **stoicism** (stō′ i siz′ əm): stern control or holding in of emotion.
6. **perverse** (pər vurs′): stubbornly contrary; wrong, harmful, or against one's own interests.

flowers or by yelling a dirty word, then dancing away from her rage, reveling in our youth and mocking her age. Actually, I think it was the flowers we wanted to destroy, but nobody had the nerve to try it, not even Joey, who was usually fool enough to try anything.

"Y'all git some stones," commanded Joey now, and was met with instant giggling obedience as everyone except me began to gather pebbles from the dusty ground. "Come on, Lizabeth."

I just stood there peering through the bushes, torn between wanting to join the fun and feeling that it was all a bit silly.

"You scared, Lizabeth?"

I cursed and spat on the ground—my favorite gesture of phony bravado. "Y'all children get the stones. I'll show you how to use 'em."

I said before that we children were not consciously aware of how thick were the bars of our cage. I wonder now, though, whether we were not more aware of it than I thought. Perhaps we had some dim notion of what we were, and how little chance we had of being anything else. Otherwise, why would we have been so preoccupied with destruction? Anyway, the pebbles were collected quickly, and everybody looked at me to begin the fun.

"Come on, y'all."

We crept to the edge of the bushes that bordered the narrow road in front of Miss Lottie's place. She was working placidly kneeling over the flowers, her dark hand plunged into the golden mound. Suddenly "zing"—an expertly aimed stone cut the head off one of the blossoms.

"Who out there?" Miss Lottie's backside came down and her head came up as her sharp eyes searched the bushes. "You better git!"

We had crouched down out of sight in the bushes, where we stifled the giggles that insisted on coming. Miss Lottie gazed warily across the road for a moment, then cautiously returned to her weeding. "Zing"—Joey sent a pebble into the blooms, and another marigold was beheaded.

Miss Lottie was enraged now. She began struggling to her feet, leaning on a rickety cane and shouting, "Y'all git! Go on home!" Then the rest of the kids let loose with their pebbles, storming the flowers and laughing wildly and senselessly at Miss Lottie's impotent rage. She shook her stick at us and started shakily toward the road crying, "Git 'long! John Burke! John Burke, come help!"

Then I lost my head entirely, mad with the power of inciting such rage, and ran out of the bushes in the storm of pebbles, straight toward Miss Lottie chanting madly, "Old lady witch, fell in a ditch, picked up a penny and thought she was rich!" The children screamed with delight, dropped their pebbles and joined the crazy dance, swarming around Miss Lottie like bees and chanting, "Old lady witch!" while she screamed curses at us. The madness lasted only a moment, for John Burke, startled at last, lurched out of his chair, and we dashed for the bushes just as Miss Lottie's cane went whizzing at my head.

I did not join the merriment when the kids gathered again under the oak in our bare yard. Suddenly I was ashamed, and I did not like being ashamed. The child in me sulked and said it was all in fun, but the woman in me flinched at the thought of the malicious attack that I had led. The mood lasted all afternoon. When we ate the beans and rice that was supper that night, I did not notice my father's silence, for he was always silent these days, nor did I notice my mother's absence, for she always worked until well into evening. Joey and I had a particularly bitter argument after supper; his exuberance got on my nerves. Finally I stretched out upon the pallet in the room we shared and fell into a fitful doze.

When I awoke, somewhere in the middle of the night, my mother had returned, and I vaguely listened to the conversation that was audible through the thin walls that separated our rooms. At first I heard no words, only voices. My mother's voice was like a cool, dark room in summer—peaceful, soothing, quiet. I loved to listen to it; it made things seem all right somehow. But my father's voice cut through hers, shattering the peace.

"Twenty-two years, Maybelle, twenty-two years," he was saying, "and I got nothing for you, nothing, nothing."

"It's all right, honey, you'll get something. Everybody out of work now, you know that."

"It ain't right. Ain't no man ought to eat his woman's food year in and year out, and see his children running wild. Ain't nothing right about that."

"Honey, you took good care of us when you had it. Ain't nobody got nothing nowadays."

"I ain't talking about nobody else, I'm talking about *me*. God knows I try." My mother said something I could not hear, and my father cried out louder. "What must a man do, tell me that?"

"Look, we ain't starving. I git paid every week, and Mrs. Ellis is real nice about giving me things. She gonna let me have Mr. Ellis's old coat for you this winter—"

"Forget Mr. Ellis's coat! And forget his money! You think I want white folks' leavings? Oh, Maybelle"—and suddenly he sobbed, loudly and painfully, and cried helplessly and hopelessly in the dark night. I had never heard a man cry before. I did not know men ever cried. I covered my ears with my hands but could not cut off the sound of my father's harsh, painful, despairing sobs. My father was a strong man who would whisk a child upon his shoulders and go singing through the house. My father whittled toys for us and laughed so loud that the great oak seemed to laugh with him, and taught us how to fish and hunt rabbits. How could it be that my father was crying? But the sobs went on, unstifled, finally

quieting until I could hear my mother's voice, deep and rich, humming softly as she used to hum to a frightened child.

The world had lost its boundary lines. My mother, who was small and soft, was now the strength of the family; my father, who was the rock on which the family had been built, was sobbing like the tiniest child. Everything was suddenly out of tune, like a broken accordion. Where did I fit into this crazy picture? I do not now remember my thoughts, only a feeling of great bewilderment and fear.

Long after the sobbing and the humming had stopped, I lay on the pallet, still as stone with my hands over my ears, wishing that I could cry and be comforted. The night was silent now except for the sound of the crickets and of Joey's soft breathing. But the room was too crowded with fear to allow me to sleep, and finally, feeling the terrible aloneness of 4 A.M., I decided to awaken Joey.

"Ouch! What's the matter with you? What you want?" he demanded disagreeably when I had pinched and slapped him awake.

"Come on, wake up."

"What for? Go 'way."

I was lost for a reasonable reply. I could not say, "I'm scared, and I don't want to be alone," so I merely said, "I'm going out. If you want to come, come on."

The promise of adventure awoke him. "Going out now? Where at, Lizabeth? What you going to do?"

I was pulling my dress over my head. Until now I had not thought of going out. "Just come on," I replied tersely.

I was just out the window and halfway down the road before Joey caught up with me.

"Wait, Lizabeth, where you going?"

I was running as if the Furies[7] were after me,

---

7. **Furies** (fyoor′ ēz): in Greek and Roman mythology, female spirits with serpentine hair who punished wrongdoers.

as perhaps they were—running silently and furiously until I came to where I had half known I was headed—to Miss Lottie's yard.

The half-dawn light was more eerie than complete darkness, and in it the old house was like the ruin that my world had become—foul and crumbling, a grotesque creature. It looked haunted, but I was not afraid because I was haunted too.

"Lizabeth, you lost your mind?" panted Joey.

I had indeed lost my mind, for all the smoldering emotions of that summer swelled in me and burst—the great need for my mother who was never there, the hopelessness of our poverty and degradation,[8] the bewilderment of being neither child nor woman and yet both at once, the fear unleashed by my father's tears. And these feelings combined in one great impulse toward destruction.

"Lizabeth!"

I leaped furiously into the mounds of marigolds and pulled madly, trampling and pulling and destroying the perfect yellow blooms. The fresh smell of early morning and of dew-soaked marigolds spurred me on as I went tearing and mangling and sobbing while Joey tugged my dress or my waist crying, "Lizabeth stop, please stop!"

And then I was sitting in the ruined little garden among the uprooted and ruined flowers, crying and crying, and it was too late to undo what I had done. Joey was sitting beside me, silent and frightened, not knowing what to say. Then, "Lizabeth, look."

I opened my swollen eyes and saw in front of me a pair of large calloused feet; my gaze lifted to the swollen legs, the age-distorted body clad in a tight cotton night dress, and then the shadowed Indian face surrounded by stubby white hair. And there was no rage in the face now, now that the garden was destroyed and there was nothing any longer to be protected.

"M-miss Lottie!" I scrambled to my feet and just stood there and stared at her, and that was

the moment when childhood faded and womanhood began. The violent, crazy act was the last act of childhood. For as I gazed at the immobile face with sad, weary eyes, I gazed upon a kind of reality that is hidden to childhood. The witch was no longer a witch but only a broken old woman who had dared to create beauty in the midst of ugliness and sterility. She had been born in squalor and had lived in it all her life. Now at the end of that life she had nothing except a falling-down hut, a wrecked body, and John Burke, the mindless son of her passion. Whatever verve there was left in her, whatever was of love and beauty and joy that had not been squeezed out by life, had been there in the marigolds she had so tenderly cared for.

Of course I could not express the things that I knew about Miss Lottie as I stood there awkward and ashamed. The years have put words to the things I knew in that moment, and as I look back upon it, I know that that moment marked the end of innocence. . . . Innocence involves an unseeing acceptance of things at face value, an ignorance of the area below the surface. In that humiliating moment I looked beyond myself and into the depths of another person. This was the beginning of compassion, and one cannot have both compassion and innocence.

The years have taken me worlds away from that time and that place, from the dust and squalor of our lives and from the bright thing that I destroyed in a blind, childish striking out at God-knows-what. Miss Lottie died long ago, and many years have passed since I last saw her hut, completely barren at last, for despite my wild contrition[9] she never planted marigolds again. Yet, there are

---

8. degradation (deg′ rə dā′ shən): a state of corruption and loss of dignity and humanity.
9. contrition (kən trish′ ən): feeling of sorrow or regret for wrong doing.

times when the image of those passionate yellow mounds returns with a painful poignancy. For one does not have to be ignorant and poor to find that one's life is barren as the dusty yards of one's town. And I too have planted marigolds.

Thinking About the Story

A PERSONAL RESPONSE

sharing impressions

1. What was the strongest emotion you felt as you read this story? Write about this emotion in your journal.

constructing interpretations

2. What does Lizabeth mean when she says that she too has planted marigolds?
Think about
- her interpretation of Miss Lottie's reasons for planting marigolds
- her statement that "one does not have to be ignorant and poor to find that one's life is barren as the dusty yards of one's town"
- the "you" she addresses in the second paragraph of the story

3. Why does Lizabeth destroy the marigolds?
Think about
- why the children like to annoy Miss Lottie
- how Lizabeth describes the unhappiness in her family
- how Lizabeth describes being "fourteen-going-on-fifteen"

4. How does the destruction of the marigolds signal the end of Lizabeth's childhood and the beginning of womanhood?

5. How do different characters in the story suffer unhappiness or loss?

A CRITICAL RESPONSE

6. What does the use of flashback add to the story?
Think about
- flashback as an event that happened before the beginning of the story
- how the story might have been different if it had been told by the child Lizabeth right after it happened
- how the incident continues to affect the adult narrator

7. Analyze the sources of the tensions that lead Lizabeth to destroy the marigolds. Support your analysis with examples from the story.

Analyzing the Writer's Craft

SYMBOL

Reread the description of John Burke sitting in front of his mother's house. What does his presence tell you about Miss Lottie's life?

Building a Literary Vocabulary. A symbol is a person, place, object, or activity that stands for something beyond itself. Usually, a son or daughter represents a parent's hopes and dreams for the future. Because of John Burke's infirmities, he is unable to function outside his own dream world, and in this story he can be seen as a symbol of Miss Lottie's frustrated hopes and desires. The narrator describes him as "completing the impression of decay" associated with Miss Lottie and her house.

Application: Analyzing a Symbol. Work in a small group to make a list of what the marigolds mean to Lizabeth, both as the adult narrator and as the child she remembers. Then make a list of what the marigolds mean to Miss Lottie. Compare the lists to analyze how a single symbol can have complex meaning in a story.

Connecting Reading and Writing

1. Draw or find pictures that illustrate the story. Around the pictures create a **cluster diagram** of words associated with the pictures.

Option: Write a **proposal** to the publisher of this story explaining why your pictures would be the best illustrations.

2. Describe an incident in which you expressed your anger, either constructively or destructively. Create a **word search puzzle** of adjectives and verbs you associate with the incident, which might be used in a book of word games.

Option: Write a **script** for a skit that would portray the incident in flashback.

3. Support or challenge this quotation from the story: "One cannot have both compassion and innocence." Using specific examples from your reading and from real life, argue your opinion in a **sermon.**

Option: Argue your opinion in an **editorial**.

4. Analyze Lizabeth's character at fourteen, exploring both her positive and negative qualities. Present your analysis in a teacher's **note** to Lizabeth's parents.

Option: Create a **dialogue** between two of Lizabeth's close friends.

My City   JAMES WELDON JOHNSON

The Tropics in New York   CLAUDE McKAY

Biographies of Johnson and McKay appear on pages 425 and 427.

Approaching the Poems

New York City stirred strong feelings among the black Americans who migrated there in the early twentieth century. To some, New York was a charismatic place, representing freedom and opportunities for self-fulfillment; to others, the harsh realities of urban living, such as overcrowding, unemployment, and prejudice, frustrated the expectations that had originally prompted the migration. The following poems by James Weldon Johnson and the Jamaican-born Claude McKay reflect these different feelings about New York City.

Building Vocabulary

The following essential words are defined alongside "The Tropics in New York."

laden (lād′ ′n): Of fruit-trees **laden** by low-singing rills, (line 6)

mystical (mis′ ti kəl), **benediction** (ben′ ə dik′ shən): **mystical** blue skies / In **benediction** over nun-like hills. (lines 7–8)

Connecting Writing and Reading

What place in your school holds special meaning for you? the stadium? the auditorium? the science laboratory? the cafeteria? the library? In your journal jot down a few words that describe the feelings you associate with this particular place. As you read, keep in mind your own responses as you consider the responses to New York City presented in these poems.

My City

When I come down to sleep death's endless night,
The threshold of the unknown dark to cross,
What to me then will be the keenest loss,
When this bright world blurs on my fading sight?
5 Will it be that no more I shall see the trees
Or smell the flowers or hear the singing birds
Or watch the flashing streams or patient herds?
No, I am sure it will be none of these.

But, ah! Manhattan's sights and sounds, her smells,
10 Her crowds, her throbbing force, the thrill that comes
From being of her a part, her subtle spells,
Her shining towers, her avenues, her slums—
O God! the stark, unutterable pity,
To be dead, and never again behold my city!

New York (detail), c. 1925,
LOUIS LOZOWICK.
©The Estate of Louis Lozowick/
VAGA, New York, 1991.

The Tropics in New York

Bananas ripe and green, and ginger–root,
  Cocoa in pods and alligator pears,[1]
And tangerines and mangoes and grapefruit,
  Fit for the highest prize at parish fairs,

5 Set in the window, bringing memories
  Of fruit-trees <u>laden</u>[2] by low-singing <u>rills</u>,[3]
And dewy dawns, and <u>mystical</u>[4] blue skies
  In <u>benediction</u>[5] over nun-like hills.

My eyes grew dim, and I could no more gaze;
10 A wave of longing through my body swept,
And, hungry for the old, familiar ways,
  I turned aside and bowed my head and wept.

1. **alligator pears:** avocados.

2. **laden** (lād''ən): loaded;
burdened.

3. **rills:** brooks; creeks; small
streams.

4. **mystical** (mis' ti kəl):
having a spiritual nature.

5. **benediction** (ben' ə dik'
shən): a blessing.

Thinking About the Poems

A PERSONAL RESPONSE

sharing impressions

1. What impressions of New York City do you have after reading these poems? Respond in your journal.

constructing interpretations

2. What might account for the different responses to New York City presented in these poems?

Think about
- the implied contrast between New York City and the speaker's native land in "The Tropics in New York"
- the speaker's anticipated loss of Manhattan in "My City"
- the attitude toward nonurban environments in each poem

3. Is your concept of New York City closer to Johnson's or to McKay's?

Think about
- what you know of New York City from your reading or from watching films set in this city
- your own experiences in this city or in large cities in general
- the picture of the city created by or implied by the details in the two poems
- the speakers' responses to the city

A CREATIVE RESPONSE

4. Do you think the speaker in "The Tropics in New York" would have been so homesick if products from his native land were not available to him? Why or why not?

A CRITICAL RESPONSE

5. Which images in these poems best convey the depth of the writers' feelings? Explain your choices.

6. Read or review "From the Poets in the Kitchen" (page 32). How would you compare the responses of the immigrants in that essay with the responses of the speaker in "The Tropics in New York"?

from Mississippi Solo

EDDY HARRIS

A biography of Harris appears on page 423.

*A*pproaching the Selection

Mississippi Solo relates the experiences of writer Eddy Harris as he canoes down the Mississippi River from Lake Itasca, Minnesota, to New Orleans. In the following excerpt, Harris approaches the antebellum town of Natchez, Mississippi, on the last stretch of his journey.

*T*OO MANY MARVELOUS days in a row and you begin to get used to it, to think that's the way it's supposed to be. Too many good days, too many bad days—you need some break in the monotony of one to appreciate the other. If you only get sunshine, someone said, you end up in a desert.

I guess I'd had enough hard days to last me for a while, enough scary times to be able to appreciate the peaceful, easy, glorious days. On the way to Natchez, I had another one, and I took full advantage of it to do absolutely nothing. No singing, no thinking, no talking to myself. Just feeling. Watching the river, noticing the changes in color, seeing the way it rises and falls depending on the wind and on what lies on the river bed. Each change had something to say, and I listened to the river. The river was talking to me, changing colors from puce to brown to thick, murky green. Saying nothing. The idle chatter you get when you walk with your favorite niece or nephew going no place in particular with nothing special on your minds and the little kid just jabbers away

because it's comfortable and he feels like it. The river was like that to me. A comfortable buddy sharing a lazy day.

Nothing else mattered then. Going someplace or not. Arriving in New Orleans or shooting past and landing in Brazil. I didn't care about anything. The river kept me company and kept me satisfied. Nothing else mattered.

Then the river whispered, "Get ready. Get ready."

The day turned gray and strange. Clouds rolled overhead in wild swirls like batter in a bowl. I could see the rainstorm forming off in the distance but swirling rapidly toward me like a dark gray avalanche. I felt the river dip down and up—a shallow dale in the water. I passed from the cool moisture surrounding me and into a pocket of thin air hot and dry. It was as though a gap had opened in the clouds and the sun streamed through to boil the water and heat up this isolated patch of river a scant thirty yards long. My first thought was to shed a shirt and stay cool, but when I passed through the far curtain of the insulated air, I knew I had better do just the opposite. I drifted and donned my yellow rain suit and hood. The sky above grew serious and advanced in my direction with the speed of a hurricane. Looking for a place to land, I scanned the shore. There was no shore. Only trees. Because of the heavy rains and the high water, the shore had disappeared, and the new shoreline of solid earth had been pushed back through the trees and beyond the woods. How far beyond, I couldn't tell. I looked across to the other side of the river half a mile away. No way could I have made it over there. Halfway across and the wind would have kicked up and trapped me in the middle.

The leading edge of the storm came, and the first sprinkles passed over like army scouts. The wooded area lasted only another hundred yards or so, and I thought I could easily get there before the rains arrived. I could then turn left and find ground to pull out and wait out the storm. But the voice of the river came out and spoke to me teasingly but with a chill of seriousness down my spine. I could have ignored it, but as if reading my thoughts and not wanting me to fight it, the river grabbed the end of the canoe and turned me toward the trees. I thought I was looking for land. I wasn't. I was looking for shelter.

The urge to get into the trees came on me quite suddenly and really without thought or effort on my part. Almost an instinct.

No sooner had I ducked into the trees than the sky split open with a loud crash and a splintery crackle of lightning. I was not going to make it through the trees. The wind came in at hurricane strength. The tips of the trees bent way over and aimed toward the ground, like fishing rods hooked on a big one. Water flooded like the tide rushing upstream. The trees swooshed loudly as the leaves and branches brushed hard together. Branches fell. Rains came and poured down bucketfuls.

The trees were tall and no more than three feet around. I maneuvered the canoe as best I

could in the wind and rushing water, turned it to face upstream, and kept my back to the rain, which slanted in at a sharp angle. I reached out for the sturdiest tree I could get my arms around and I held on.

Water everywhere. The river sloshed over the side and into the canoe. I tried to keep the stern pointed right into the flow so the canoe could ride the waves, but it didn't work. The canoe was twisted about, and water poured over the side. The rain was heavier than any I had ever been in or seen before. It really was more like a tropical storm. The heavy winds, the amount of water, the warmth of the air, and the cold rain. Only my neck was exposed to the rain. When the rain hit my neck, it ran under the rain suit and very cold down my back.

The wind shifted as the storm came directly overhead. Water streamed straight down. I was drenched, and the canoe was filling up quickly. Anything in the canoe that could float was floating. If the rain continued for long or if the wind kept up strong and the rain kept spilling into the canoe, I would sink. But I was not worried, hardly more than concerned. In fact I enjoyed the feeling of the water all around me and on me, enveloping me like a cocoon, and despite the drama I felt no real threat. I was more amazed than anything, trying to analyze the voice I had heard or whatever instinct or intuition[1] it was that urged me to park in these trees. It had been something so very definite that I could feel it and yet so ethereal[2] that I could not put my finger on it. So I stopped trying and just sat there patiently waiting and hugging my tree. I was one with this river, and nothing could happen to me.

---

1. **intuition** (in' tōō ish' ən): the direct knowing or learning of something without the conscious use of reasoning.
2. **ethereal** (ē thir' ē əl): very light; airy; like the upper regions of space.

The storm slid forward, and the rain slanted in on my face. Then it moved on farther up the river to drench someone else. It was gone as suddenly as it had arisen. Only the trailing edge was left, a light rain that lasted almost until I reached Natchez.

The sky remained gray but lightened, and I paddled from my rain forest and downriver to Natchez. My little boat lumbered through the water. The canoe carried six inches of water and was heavy, and I could find no speed. But I didn't need any. I was relaxed and floating in the mist as thick as the mysteries of the river. It was evening when I reached Natchez.

Natchez, Mississippi, sits high above the river. Green trees and grassy hills rise up from the river to the city. Rising out of the hills and overhanging the river, huge white antebellum mansions guard the approach to the city like statues lining the wide corridor of some great cathedral. The homes stand beautiful and proud, reminders of gentler and nobler times.

The *Delta Queen*, another reminder, was moored at the foot of the old part of town. I went right up to get a closer look. A massive paddle wheeler that takes her voyagers back in time as she carries them up and down the river, stopping for brief glimpses of history at Natchez and St. Francisville and ancient plantations along the route. The captain told me she sails as far up as St. Paul and down to New Orleans, with trips up the Ohio River to Cincinnati. They were on their way shortly to New Orleans, and I asked for a ride.

"You don't want a ride," the captain said. "This is something you want to do all by yourself. You'll feel better if you do, and you'd hate yourself if you didn't."

No, I wouldn't. If he had said OK, I would have hopped quickly on board and ridden down with him. I had already found it, whatever this trip was for; I had done it, even if I didn't understand it yet and probably wouldn't until years from now anyway.

A few great blasts from the steam whistle and she pushed away from shore and set out, lights on the big calliope playing merry music like a circus. It was 1836 all over again. The *Queen* paddled upriver, turned around, and slowly splashed south, the staterooms all lit up and gay. You couldn't see the boat at all in the darkness, only the lights. They seemed to float along with no structure holding them together. Too soon the lights were gone round the bend and the calliope faded into the night and the crowd that had gathered at the riverfront to watch as of old began to disperse.

I bailed out my canoe using a milk carton. It took a while. I had a few passing conversations and then walked up the hill. It was drizzling again, and I must have looked lost.

This was the old town. A little park stretched off to the south—more a promenade than a park—and there were a few quaint shops for the tourists and a bar and a couple of nice-looking restaurants. Three beautiful women were getting out of a car parked along the side of the road when I passed. The three prettiest women in Mississippi. They were going to eat in one of the cute little restaurants. They were all dressed up and hurried because of the rain. They wouldn't want to get their hair and clothes messed up. I asked them quickly if they knew the time, and two of the three ignored me totally and kept walking. I felt like the invisible man. But the third woman had heard me. She looked toward her two friends. She wore a quizzical expression, and it was plain that she was looking for the translation. She must have thought I was speaking a foreign language.

"I won't bite you," I said. "I just want the time."

Then she turned, and the three of them walked purposefully on, and I stood stunned for two seconds; I said nothing else. I chuckled to myself and silently wished for them to slip and fall in the mud. When they didn't, when they had crossed the little gravel parking lot and climbed up the three wooden steps and disappeared into the warmth and dryness of the cozy little eatery, leaving me standing out in the drizzle, I hoped they would order seafood, and I hoped that each one would get a bad oyster or a tainted piece of catfish.

Two steps farther on, I passed a man sitting all alone in his pickup truck. He was killing time, watching the river, and he turned to watch me walk by. When our eyes met, I tapped my wrist and gave the international symbol for "What time is it?" I don't know why I wanted to know; I had no place I had to be and nothing I had to do apart from finding a place to pitch my tent, which I couldn't do until all the shops had closed and everyone had gone home.

Bill invited me to warm up in his truck.

"Do you need to go to the store or any-thing?" He had a great Southern accent, heavy but cultured and easily understandable.

"Well, I guess I could use some milk and a few things."

He took me on a little tour of Natchez. He was proud of this little place, I could see, and he was happy to drive me around. He even tried to arrange a place for me to sleep for the night and later pointed out the Salvation Army shelter where I could at least be dry all night long. I half expected him to invite me home, put me up in the attic, and then keep me over for Thanksgiving dinner tomorrow night, but that was asking too much. He already had relatives visiting for the holiday.

I told him I'd probably just pitch camp in the little park.

"I wouldn't build a fire or anything if I were you. The police will come down there and make you move. They might even want to lock you up for the night."

Then he fished in his wallet and pulled out a business card.

"If they do come along and throw you in jail, give me a call. You can sleep there for the night, and I can get you out in the morning. I'm the city attorney."

Actually, he was an attorney with a local practice, and he was the acting city attorney whenever the regular city attorney was away, like now.

I had the feeling he wasn't too thrilled to be going home to his wife and the visiting in-laws, that he would rather have stayed down on the levee watching the river and the *Queen* or talking to me or driving me around showing me the beautiful homes of Natchez. Hope Farm. Stanton Hall. Longwood. D'Evereux. Ellicott Hill. Propinquity. Montaigne. Mount Repose. Homes as beautiful and stately and elegant as the names. But Bill had to get on home.

He drove away, and I hung around killing time until late in the evening. When every-thing had closed and everyone had gone home—about nine o'clock, I'd guess—I pulled my canoe a few yards downriver and put up the tent. It was in a little gully at the edge of the water with the blunt face of a muddy hill behind me. Not one of my more picturesque campsites. A rickety rowboat full of junk was tied up not far away, and later on the owner of it staggered back drunk from town, climbed into the boat, and slept there. I met him in the morning and was shocked to find out who he was—shocked and pleased.

Eleven hundred miles and I don't know how many days ago, Wally at Piasa Harbor had told me about a religious zealot[3] rowing for Jesus down the river in a rickety rowboat of homemade construction. As James White talked the following morning, pieces fell into place and it hit me.

"Hey!" I shouted out of the blue. "I know you."

---

3. zealot (zel′ ət): person who shows passion and devotion for something, especially to an excessive degree.

"You do?"

"I don't know you, but I heard about you. Back near Alton they were talking about this nut who had taken his bicycle apart and built a contraption for pedaling a boat down the river."

"That's me all right."

How strange to have caught up with him after all this time! I hadn't thought of him once since I left Wally.

We had breakfast together in a fancy hotel restaurant, and they gave us a few funny looks but served us without complaint. Smiles and good-humored politeness instead.

We took our good, sweet time and sat there like millionaires chatting away the morning, talking about the two journeys. Jim had left Idaho on a bicycle pulling a little trailer that held his belongings. He had received the call directly, he said, from Jesus, who had told him to go across the country on this bicycle and spread the good word, get a feeling for this nation, and set the place right. And, I presumed, to report back.

As a man who himself had heard the voice of God, I could not brush his calling aside as fanaticism or lunacy, but I looked askance just the same. The whispers I'd heard never told me directly what to do. Not in simple English, anyway.

When Jim got to Iowa and the river, he was instructed to change his course, get a boat, and go down the river until further notice. He took to rowing down the river until his oars broke apart. He then dismantled the bicycle and set about sawing planks and hammering and putting together until finally he had constructed a paddle wheeler out of his rowboat. Now he could sit on his seat and pedal the crankset of the bicycle, and the wooden planks fashioned into paddle wheels on each side of the boat would propel him.

It was slow but a good idea, except that he got stuck in the rock dam just below Alton,

and Okie, the salvage operator I had met, had to tow him out. Then Jim had to rebuild and repair the damage.

Now, at Natchez, he actually prayed for the boat to fall apart. That would be a sign that his voyage was finished.

"I have to keep going until the voyage is done. Maybe in New Orleans, or maybe I'll have to keep going right on through to the Gulf of Mexico and South America."

"And then what?"

"I'll do whatever He tells me to do. But I'm sure sick of this river."

For a man spreading the good word, he hadn't met with much success, finding the land full of skeptics[4] and godless people not willing to listen. So it would be disaster for them all, he said. Disaster and ruin will strike all those who refused him or who mocked him or who would not turn to God, and I made it a point not to say the wrong thing.

Jim had the look of a monk. Tall and lean, disheveled gray hair and matching stubble on his chin, unconcerned about his appearance, a youthful face that lied about his age, and wild eyes. . . .

"Maybe we could travel together," he offered. "Share Thanksgiving dinner, camp together, keep each other company. It gets lonely, you know."

His boat had everything in the world in it except a television. I don't know how he managed to fit inside and sleep. But he pushed junk aside and squeezed inside and showed me how he slid the plywood platform around that made his bed.

"You could ride inside with me," he said. "We could tie your canoe off and tow it and you could rest."

I declined but did accept the offer for Thanksgiving dinner.

---

4. skeptics (skep′ tiks): those who doubt religious teachings.

"You go on ahead. I need to fill up my water bag and take down my tent. I'll catch up with you."

Before he left he pulled a pair of pliers from his junk and repaired the zippers on my tent flaps. Now I wouldn't have to worry about mosquitoes sneaking into the tent at night.

"You learn to fix just about everything out here," he said.

He took off, pedaling down the river, and I watched him go. He looked very silly. Watching him, I felt the arrogance that towboat pilots feel, the contempt for lesser boats, and still the comradery[5] of sharers of the river—rivermen all of us.

I caught up with him after an hour or so, and we built a fire on a sandbar. We boiled rice and heated a big can of beef stew, and Jim prayed over it, and we ate our Thanksgiving meal. It wasn't the finest holiday meal ever, but maybe this time I had so much to be thankful for and was really aware of it for once that this meal of all meals felt most like a Thanksgiving dinner.

---

5. comradery (käm′ rad rē): loyalty and warm, friendly feeling among companions, associates, fellow workers, etc.

*EXAMINING LIFE
EXPERIENCES*

Reviewing Concepts

THE WRITER'S MESSAGE: SHEDDING LIGHT ON HUMAN LIFE

*making
connections*

The writers in this unit present a variety of experiences and communicate many messages about human life. These messages, or themes, might concern human nature, relationships between individuals, or the individual in society. In the poem "One wants a Teller in a time like this," for example, Gwendolyn Brooks shares a theme about human nature that might be expressed in the following way: In times of trouble, human beings long for the sense of certainty experienced during childhood.

Review the selections you have read in this unit and think about the themes that they impart. Make a chart like the following and record in the appropriate column a theme from each selection. For complex selections like *A Raisin in the Sun,* you might record themes in more than one column.

Selection	Human nature	Relationships between individuals	Individual in society
"One wants a Teller . . ."	In times of trouble, human beings long for the sense of certainty experienced during childhood.		

*describing
connections*

From each column choose the theme that you consider most relevant to teenagers today. Get together with a group of classmates and discuss what makes each chosen theme relevant. Take notes on your discussion. Then write a unit **introduction** for teachers in which you recommend the three selections that treat the themes most relevant to students.

Biographies of Authors

Teresa Palomo Acosta (born 1949) attributes her interest in literature to her grandfather, Maximino Palomo. During her childhood, he would spend summer evenings on her family's front porch sharing with the neighborhood children stories of his life in Mexico and as a cowboy. After completing an undergraduate degree in ethnic studies at the University of Texas and a graduate degree in journalism at Columbia University, Acosta returned to Texas to work as a journalist and teacher. Acosta wrote "My Mother Pieced Quilts" as an assignment for a creative writing class at the University of Texas and had no intention of publishing the poem. She recalls writing it in one hour and making few revisions. Acosta believes that she wrote the poem so quickly because she had been carrying the images in her memory for years and had probably been composing the poem subconsciously for a long time. Her poems have appeared in anthologies and in collections of Chicano literature.

Maya Angelou (born 1928) has a vast array of accomplishments to her credit. Although best known for her autobiographical works, she has written poems, stage plays, screenplays, television specials, short stories, and magazine articles. She has also worked for newspapers in Egypt and Ghana. In addition, Angelou studied dance with Martha Graham, toured twenty-two countries in a production of the opera Porgy and Bess, directed and acted in off-Broadway shows, and served as a television narrator and interviewer. She has written and recorded songs and has composed musical scores for her screenplays. Angelou has also toured the country as a lecturer and visiting professor at various colleges and universities. During the 1960's she worked with Dr. Martin Luther King, Jr., as a coordinator for the Southern Christian Leadership Conference.

James Baldwin (1924–1987) became a preacher in New York's Harlem when he was only fourteen. Baldwin preached for three years but finally quit when he realized that his lack of faith was costing him his self-respect. After his stepfather's death two years later, Baldwin moved to Greenwich Village where he worked at menial jobs and wrote in the evenings. He received encouragement from the novelist Richard Wright, who helped him win a Eugene Saxton Fellowship. With the money from that award, Baldwin moved to Paris to escape the racial discrimination that made him feel like an alien in his own land. Although often poor and hungry in Paris, Baldwin was able to develop as a writer, and by 1953 he had published his first novel, *Go Tell It on the Mountain.* His reflections on the racial situation he had left behind are contained in his essay collection *Notes of a Native Son* (1955). Because of the racial tensions in the United States, Baldwin remained abroad for most of his life. He never lost his love for his country, however, and continued to address America's social problems in his fiction and essays.

© Jill Krementz

Toni Cade Bambara (born 1939) had a remarkably varied education, ranging from a school for mimes in Paris and the University of Florence in Italy to the Katherine Dunham Dance Studio and the Harlem Film Institute in New York City. In the 1970's Bambara became actively involved in social and political activities in the African-American community, activities to which she is still deeply committed. Reviewers of her fiction remark on her distinctive style, which combines poetic rhythms and imagery with street-talk slang. Bambara's first novel, *The Salt Eaters,* received the American Book Award in 1981, and her documentary film "The Bombing of Osage" has also won a number of awards.

Black Elk (1863–1950), a Sioux, had a vision at age nine in which he was given the power to help his fellow Sioux. He later interpreted his vision to mean he should help them survive the coming of white settlers, a belief that grew stronger as he witnessed the defeat of Custer's troops at the Battle of the Little Bighorn. In his twenties Black Elk joined Buffalo Bill's Wild West Show. After touring Europe with the show, he returned home in 1889 to find that a new treaty had deprived his tribe of half their land. Tensions between the Sioux and the United States Army led to the Battle of Wounded Knee in which soldiers massacred nearly three hundred unarmed men, women, and children. Black Elk did not fight in the battle but arrived in time to help people escape. For the rest of his life, he lived on the reservation, saddened that he had failed to save his people. He told the story of his life to John Neihardt, who helped him write his autobiography, *Black Elk Speaks* (1932). Reissued in 1961, the book did not gain wide popularity until the 1970's.

Arna Bontemps (1902–1973) significantly contributed to the development of African-American identity through his poetry, novels, and plays. He was born in Alexandria, Louisiana, the son of a brickmason and a teacher. While attending Pacific Union College, he heard the black social reformer Marcus Garvey speak in Los Angeles and learned about the excitement of the Harlem Renaissance. After graduating from college in 1923, Bontemps moved to Harlem, where he taught school and wrote. His first novel, *God Sends Sunday* (1931), is considered the final work of the Harlem Renaissance movement. Three years later he moved to Huntsville, Alabama, to write while teaching at Oakwood Junior College. During the next decade he wrote two novels about slave revolts, *Black Thunder* (1936) and *Drums at Dusk* (1939). He also collaborated on plays with Langston Hughes and others. After earning another degree at the University of Chicago, Bontemps worked as a librarian at Fisk University for twenty years and then returned to the University of Chicago to teach in 1965. At his death, he was the Writer-in-Residence at Fisk University.

Jorge Luis Borges (1899–1986) was an Argentine poet, short story writer, and essayist who learned to speak and read English before he learned Spanish. In 1914 his family took him to Geneva, Switzerland, where he learned French and German and earned his bachelor's degree from the College of Geneva. Next the family lived in Majorca and Spain before returning to Buenos Aires in 1921. Borges now wrote poems about the history and beauty of his native city and began trying his hand at fiction as well. In 1938 he suffered a severe head wound, resulting in blood poisoning that almost cost him his life. After this experience he began to create his best poetry and the fantastic stories for which he is known. In 1955 Borges became director of the national library and a professor of English and American literature at the University of Buenos Aires. By this time, he had become totally blind. In 1961 Borges and Samuel Beckett shared the prestigious Formentor Prize. Since then his poems and tales have been recognized as classics.

Gwendolyn Brooks (born 1917) has spent most of her life in Chicago. Although her background is middle-class, she identifies deeply with poor people and often makes them the subject of her poems and short stories. From the beginning, Brooks's poetry won praise for its simplicity and depth of feeling. *Annie Allen,* her second book, won the 1950 Pulitzer Prize. In 1969 she was named poet laureate of Illinois, and in 1985 she was appointed poetry consultant to the Library of Congress. When not writing poetry, Brooks has worked to support African-American community organizations and writing workshops.

Diana Chang (born 1934), whose birthplace was New York City, spent some of her childhood in China, where she was raised by her Eurasian mother. After World War II, she returned to the United States to complete her education. Settling in New York City, she enrolled in Barnard College, and graduated in 1955. Chang's poetry has appeared in many different magazines, quarterlies, and anthologies, and she has also written several novels. These include *The Frontiers of Love* (1956), *The Only Game in Town* (1963), and *Eye to Eye* (1974). In addition to writing, Chang is a painter whose work has been shown in solo and group exhibitions.

Lucille Clifton (born 1936) writes with love, warmth, and humor about the vitality of African-American life. Best known for her many books for children, she is also a celebrated author of adult verse, novels, and an autobiography, *Generations* (1976). Her first collection of poetry, *Good Times,* appeared in 1969, followed by *Good News About the Earth* (1972), *An Ordinary Woman* (1974), and *Two-Headed Woman* (1980). Clifton also was the co-author of *Free To Be You and Me,* a television special that won a 1974 Emmy Award. In 1979, she was named poet laureate of Maryland.

Eugenia Collier (born 1928), received what she describes as a "conventional, Western-type education" and did not begin to explore her roots—her African-American heritage—until years later. This exploration of her heritage sparked an intensive writing career in her middle age. One of her first literary efforts, "Marigolds," won the 1969 Gwendolyn Brooks Award for Fiction. Since then, Collier's fiction, poetry, and essays have been published widely. In addition, she produced a television series on African-American folklore. Collier has taught college literature since 1955; currently, she is professor of English at Coppin State College in Baltimore.

Countee Cullen (1903–1946), while he was still an undergraduate at New York University, had poems published in *The Crisis* and *Opportunity,* two major black periodicals, as well as in *Harper's, The Century,* and *Poetry.* A superb student, he won a major poetry prize and was elected to the Phi Beta Kappa national honor society. After graduating in 1925, Cullen earned a master's degree at Harvard. His first poetry collection, *Color* (1925), established his reputation as a poet. Later, in his introduction to the anthology *Caroling Dusk* (1927), Cullen stated his belief that African-American poets should draw their idiom from traditional English poetry rather than from dialect. He held to this standard in producing several additional volumes of his own verse. At the peak of his career, he married the daughter of black historian W. E. B. DuBois, but the marriage collapsed within a few months. The ensuing emotional turmoil is reflected in Cullen's *The Black Christ* (1929), written while studying in Paris on a Guggenheim fellowship. Cullen also wrote a novel and collaborated on a play with Arna Bontemps. In 1934 he took a job teaching French to junior high students, a position he held until his death.

Léon Damas (1912–1978) left his native French Guiana in South America in order to study in Paris in the early 1930's. There he met other young black French-speaking poets from the French colonies, and together they formed the literary movement known as Négritude, promoting African identity, culture, and values. Damas's first book of poetry, *Pigments* (1937), announced that movement to the world. The work has been called "a cry of pain, an anguished inventory of the personal loss of Africa." Through their writings, the poets of Négritude attempted to strengthen African consciousness and to promote traditional African values. For many years Damas represented French Guiana in the French National Assembly. He spent his last years teaching college literature in Washington, D.C.

Frank Marshall Davis (1905–1987) was an accomplished journalist and jazz radio broadcaster. In 1931 he helped found the *Atlanta Daily World,* the nation's first successful daily newspaper for African Americans. It was in his poetry, however, that Davis expressed his deepest feelings about black life and pride and against racial inequality. Although his collections *Black Man's Verse, I Am the American Negro,* and *47th Street* appeared in the 1930's and 40's, they are still strikingly powerful today. In 1948 Davis moved to Hawaii, where he opened a wholesale paper business and wrote a weekly column for the *Honolulu Record.* Years passed before the publication of his next books of poetry, *Awakenings, and Other Poems* (1978) and *Jazz Interlude* (1985).

Frederick Douglass (1817–1895) grew up in slavery in Maryland and escaped to Massachusetts disguised as a sailor when he was twenty-one. Three years later he spoke publicly for the first time about his experiences as a slave and soon afterward became one of the country's most prominent antislavery speakers. The publication of his autobiography, *Narrative of the Life of Frederick Douglass, an American Slave* (1845), resulted in widespread publicity and the possibility of recapture by his former owner. To remove himself from this dangerous situation, he embarked on a two-year speaking tour abroad. Soon after, a group of admirers purchased his freedom for seven hundred dollars. Back in America, Douglass became the first African American to publish a newspaper. He worked for the underground railroad and recruited African-American soldiers for the Union Army during the Civil War. After the war he spoke on behalf of both civil rights and women's rights. He also held several government positions, including the post of Minister to Haiti.

Paul Laurence Dunbar (1872–1906) was born in Dayton, Ohio, the son of former slaves who had escaped through the underground railroad. After high school, Dunbar took a job as an elevator operator, the only work he could find. His literary career was launched when a former teacher asked him to read his poems before a writers' group in 1892. With the help of high school friends Orville and Wilbur Wright, Dunbar published his first volume of poetry, *Oak and Ivy,* in 1893. The publication of his second volume, *Majors and Minors,* in 1895 attracted the attention of writer William Dean Howells. At Howells's suggestion, Dunbar combined the poems from both books to create *Lyrics of Lowly Life* (1896), which earned him critical acclaim. His fame turned out to be a mixed blessing, however. The book became popular because of poems in which Dunbar uses black dialect to create a sentimental, nonthreatening picture of African-American life. The public ignored his more serious lyrics, such as "We Wear the Mask." A disappointed man, Dunbar died of tuberculosis at age thirty-four, not knowing that future generations would eventually rediscover and value the poignant honesty of his best work.

Mari Evans is a widely read poet whose poems express both the dignity and the frustration of the African-American experience in contemporary society. Evans's collection of verse _I Am a Black Woman_ has won several awards, and her poems have appeared in more than two hundred anthologies and textbooks. In addition, Evans is the author of several books for younger readers, including _I Look at Me, J. D., Singing Black,_ and _Jim Flying High._ From 1968 to 1973 she wrote, produced, and directed a weekly television program called _The Black Experience._ More recently, she edited the acclaimed _Black Women Writers (1950–1980): A Critical Evaluation._

© 1989 Layle Silbert

Rosario Ferré (born 1942) comes from a traditional upper-class family in Ponce, Puerto Rico. The author of poetry, novels, and stories for children and adults, Ferré began writing in 1970 when her short story "The Youngest Doll" was published. Her first book, a collection of short stories and verse called _Pandora's Papers_ (1976), was an immediate success. One critic called it "a constant tearing apart of memory, imagination, and word—impossible to read with indifference." A painstaking writer, Ferré has said that she usually revises a story at least eighteen times before she considers it finished. Subjects common in Ferré's works include feminist concerns, ancient myths, and the life and people of her beloved Puerto Rico.

Ernesto Galarza (1905–1984) began life in the remote Mexican village of Jalcocotan. When he was a young boy, his family fled the violence of the Mexican Revolution and settled in Sacramento, California. Galarza became a U. S. citizen and eventually earned a doctorate from Columbia University. He then worked as a labor union leader, fighting for the rights of American farm workers. Galarza was also a professor, a member of the U.S. House of Representatives Committee on Education and Labor, and a consultant to the Civil Rights Commission. His books range from autobiography (_Barrio Boy_) to poetry (_Kodachromes in Rhyme_) to political and economic analysis (_Farmworkers and Agri-Business in California, 1947-60_).

Gabriel García Márquez (born 1928), a writer of novels and short stories, is one of the central figures in the so-called magical realism movement in Latin American literature. Born into poverty in Colombia, García Márquez began his career as a journalist. While acknowledging the influence on his work of Faulkner, Hemingway, and other American and English authors, he says that it was journalism that taught him that "the key is to tell it straight." García Márquez's work is characterized by magical realism, a combination of realism and fantasy. His best-known work is _One Hundred Years of Solitude_ (1967), an epic work that one critic said "should be required reading for the entire human race." In 1982 García Márquez was awarded the Nobel Prize in literature.

Nikki Giovanni (born 1943), christened Yolande Cornelia Giovanni, Jr., credits her warm and loving middle-class Tennessee family with giving her an emotionally secure childhood. While Giovanni was still in elementary school, her family relocated to a suburb of Cincinnati, Ohio. After high school, the self-confident seventeen-year-old enrolled in Fisk University. There, her independent streak caused conflict with school authorities, and she was asked to leave. Returning to Fisk several years later, Giovanni studied seriously, worked with the university's Writers' Workshop, and participated in the civil rights movement. She graduated in 1968. Between 1968 and 1970, she wrote prolifically about her African-American heritage and her own life, and published her first three books of poetry. She also taught at Rutgers University and gave birth to a son. As her reputation grew, Giovanni recorded readings of her poems against a background of gospel music and lectured in the United States and abroad. In addition to eleven volumes of poetry for adults, Giovanni has written several collections of poems for children.

Lorraine Hansberry (1930–1965) was the youngest daughter of a prosperous real estate broker. His children had to learn to assert their dignity through some hard and painful experiences. When Hansberry was still a child, her parents moved to a well-to-do, all-white Chicago neighborhood. Hansberry's memories of the time include "being spat at, cursed, and pummeled in the daily trek to and from school." Her family was finally thrown out of their home by a court order. Her father fought the order by bringing the case before the Supreme Court, which ruled in his favor. After Hansberry graduated from a Chicago public high school, she attended the University of Wisconsin, where she became interested in drama. In 1950 she moved to New York, where she studied African history, worked for *Freedom* magazine, and wrote. She married the song writer Robert Nemiroff in 1953. In 1959 her first play, *A Raisin in the Sun,* debuted on Broadway to great acclaim, and Hansberry became the first African-American playwright to win the New York Drama Critics' Best Play of the Year Award. She wrote several other plays before her early death from cancer at age thirty-four.

Eddy L. Harris is a young African-American journalist from St. Louis. In *Mississippi Solo,* his first book, he reveals much about himself and his observations of race relations in the United States.

Robert Hayden (1913–1980) was born in Detroit and attended the University of Michigan, where he twice won the Avery Hopwood Poetry Prize. He taught English first at the University of Michigan, then at Fisk University for twenty-two years, later returning to the University of Michigan. In 1940, his first collection of poems, *Heart Shapes in the Dust,* appeared, followed by several others, including *Figure of Time* (1955) and *A Ballad of Remembrance* (1962). Hayden once said that he was "driven" to write poetry, that he saw it as a way of "coming to grips with both inner and external realities." In 1976, he was appointed Poetry Consultant to the Library of Congress, the first African American to ever receive that distinction.

Le Ly Hayslip (born 1949) was the youngest of six children in a traditional Buddhist farming family in Vietnam. She was twelve when the Vietnam war turned her life into a nightmare of imprisonments, torture, and threats of execution. Her autobiographical work *When Heaven and Earth Changed Places* (1989) recounts how she survived the experience, both emotionally and physically. Hayslip now lives in Los Angeles and works for the East Meets West Foundation, a relief and world peace organization that she founded.

Jeanne Wakatsuki Houston (born 1934) and **James D. Houston** (born 1933) are Californians whose lives and writing have centered on their home state. They met as students at San Jose State College and married in 1957. In 1973 they published *Farewell to Manzanar,* the story of Jeanne's family's experiences at an internment camp for Japanese Americans during World War II. The Houstons also collaborated on the screenplay for an award-winning film based on the book. James D. Houston is a celebrated author in his own right. A 1982 nonfiction work, *Californians: Searching for the Golden State,* shows him to be a skilled chronicler of the lives of California residents. His novels *Continental Drift* and *Love Life* have also won praise. On her own, Jeanne Houston has written *Beyond Manzanar: Views of Asian American Womanhood* (1985).

Photo by Edward Weston; © 1981 Center for Creative Photography, Arizona Board of Regents

Langston Hughes (1902–1967) was born in Joplin, Missouri. His parents separated soon after his birth, and Hughes was raised alternately by his grandmother and mother. After graduating from high school, he joined his father in Mexico. His father paid for him to attend Columbia University, where Hughes began as an engineering student. Within a year, however, he rejected his father's plans for him to pursue a business career and left college to sign on as a seaman on a cargo ship bound for West Africa. By 1924 he was working in Paris nightclubs, absorbing the sounds of American jazz that permeated Parisian nightlife. Rejoining his mother in Washington, D.C., Hughes took a job as a hotel busboy. Although a number of his poems had already been published in the black periodicals *The Crisis* and *Opportunity,* it was not until Hughes slipped three of his poems to poet Vachel Lindsay, who was dining at the hotel's restaurant, that he received his first publicity break. Hughes went on to complete his college education and publish additional poetry, novels, and plays. Widely celebrated, he became known as the Poet Laureate of Harlem.

Zora Neale Hurston (1891?–1960) followed her mother's advice to "jump at de sun" and became the most accomplished African-American woman writer of her time. After her mother died when Hurston was nine, she was rejected by her father and his new wife. At sixteen she packed her only dress and became a wardrobe girl for a traveling theatrical troupe. Later she studied at Howard and Barnard Universities and did graduate work in anthropology at Columbia University. While she was active in the Harlem Renaissance Hurston decided to use anthropology to study African-American culture. She traveled widely collecting Southern and Caribbean folklore, which she published in *Mules and Men* (1935). Her best-known novel, *Their Eyes Were Watching God* (1937), is set in an all-black town, similar to Eatonville, Florida, where she was raised. In her later years, her poor health deterred her from writing. She was virtually forgotten by the literary community, and when she died, was buried in an unmarked grave. In recent decades, however, her work has received renewed interest, and her books have sold more copies than they did during her lifetime.

James Weldon Johnson (1871–1938) was a man of astonishing energy, a gifted writer and one of the most prominent black leaders of his time. Born into a middle-class family in Florida, he was a precocious child who read the books of Charles Dickens and Sir Walter Scott. After graduating from Atlanta University, Johnson taught school, toured New England with a vocal quartet, founded a daily newspaper, and became the first African American admitted to the Florida bar. Growing restless, he went to New York, where he became a successful Broadway songwriter. His song "Lift Every Voice and Sing" was adopted as the black national anthem. Johnson compiled several anthologies of poetry, the most famous of which is *God's Trombones* (1927). His introductions to these anthologies provide keen insights into African-American contributions to culture. In his later years, Johnson filled both administrative and artistic roles. While he was United States consul to Venezuela, for example, he wrote a novel. Later, he served as executive secretary of the National Association for the Advancement of Colored People and taught at Fisk University.

William Melvin Kelley (born 1937) is an award-winning author who writes about African Americans not as a cultural group but as separate and unique human beings. In this same spirit Kelley resents critics who try to group all African American writers into what he calls the "Negro literary ghetto." People who read black authors, says Kelley, immediately begin to search for profound comments on the relationships between black and white Americans. He does not want his work to be thought of as propaganda for a particular cause, he says, but rather as writing that will have continuing value and meaning. Kelley's articles and short stories have been widely published in magazines, anthologies, and textbooks. His novels include *A Different Drummer* and *Dunfords Travels Everywheres.*

Jamaica Kincaid (born 1949) was born and raised in St. John's, Antigua, in the West Indies. She emigrated to the United States at age seventeen and became a staff writer for the *New Yorker* in 1976. Antigua, however, stayed with her. Two books, *At the Bottom of the River* and *Annie John,* celebrate in poetic, tactile language the realities of life on the island and reveal Kincaid's bittersweet relationship with her homeland. In the nonfiction work *A Small Place,* feelings of anger rise to the surface as Kincaid protests the racism, government corruption, and poverty in Antigua. Reviewer Peggy Ellsberg called it "rage laced with lyricism." Kincaid's novel *Lucy* appeared in 1990 to considerable acclaim. She received the Morton Dauwen Zabel Award in 1983.

Martin Luther King, Jr. (1929–1968) was born in Atlanta, Georgia, the eldest son of a Baptist minister. When he was just fifteen, he entered Morehouse College, and he was ordained a minister shortly before he graduated in 1948. King then completed advanced studies at Crozer Theological Seminary and at Boston University, where he met Coretta Scott, whom he married in 1953. Two years later, while pastor of a church in Montgomery, Alabama, he helped organize a boycott to protest enforced racial segregation on public transportation. During the 381-day boycott, King was jailed, his house was bombed, and his life was threatened. His sacrifices ultimately paid off; in 1956 the Supreme Court outlawed the segregation of public transportation in Montgomery. Throughout his years in the civil rights movement, King advocated using nonviolent methods, such as sit-ins, marches, and voter registration drives, to confront discrimination. While serving a jail sentence for leading a march in Birmingham, Alabama, he wrote "Letter from Birmingham Jail," which is now considered a classic statement of the right of the oppressed to protest injustice. King wrote five books, including *Why We Can't Wait* (1964), and received the 1964 Nobel Peace Prize for his civil rights leadership. On April 4, 1968, while in Memphis, Tennessee, he was assassinated; more than one hundred thousand people later attended his funeral.

Julius Lester (born 1939) is "foremost among . . . black writers who produce their work from positions of historical strength" according to critic John A. Williams of the *New York Times Book Review.* Lester uses historical records and traditional folktales to create literary works that celebrate the heritage of African Americans. Because he believes that the history of minority groups has been neglected, he tries to give young readers what he calls "a usable past" that can influence their lives. This focus is especially evident in *To Be a Slave,* the 1969 Newbery Medal runner-up, in which he draws upon the narratives of ex-slaves to create a history of slavery. The son of a minister, Lester was born in St. Louis and educated at Fisk University. In addition to being a writer, he is a professional singer and musician and a university professor; he has also hosted live television and radio shows.

Barry Lopez (born 1945) spent the first ten years of his life in rural California, among horses, dogs, and pet pigeons. There, Lopez developed the affinity for animals that informs his later work. Although his family resettled in New York State, Lopez retained strong emotional ties to the West Coast, and when he was twenty-three, he moved back there with his wife. While studying at the University of Oregon, he wrote a book based on American Indian stories about Coyote, the traditional Native American trickster. In 1970 Lopez left the university to become a full-time writer. An article he wrote for *Smithsonian* magazine in 1974 grew into his critically acclaimed book *Of Wolves and Men* (1978). While researching the wolves, Lopez visited the Arctic, a region he feels pulls a person "up and out of oneself." Lopez made several more trips to the Arctic, where he gathered material for *Arctic Dreams: Imagination and Desire in a Northern Landscape* (1986). The book has won many awards, including a *New York Times Book Review* "Best Books" listing.

Paule Marshall (born 1929) makes good use of the lessons she describes in "From the Poets in the Kitchen." Lively expressions from her parents' native Barbados give the dialogue in Marshall's stories a unique richness. In her works, Marshall deals with issues of independence, emotional growth, and heritage as they relate to African-American women. In her novel *Brown Girl, Brownstones* (1959), which takes place in the Brooklyn neighborhood where the author grew up, a Barbadian girl's family is torn between island culture and American ways. In the award-winning *Praisesong for the Widow* (1983), a wealthy, unhappy American discovers her West Indian roots.

Mark Mathabane (born 1960) experienced overwhelming poverty, incessant hunger, inadequate education, and terrifying violence in his homeland of Alexandra, South Africa. Mathabane's determination to escape his situation is the subject of his autobiography, *Kaffir Boy: The True Story of a Black Youth's Coming of Age in Apartheid South Africa* (1986). He received an education because his mother, a washerwoman, stood in lines for a year to get the necessary papers. Helped by white tennis professionals, he got to the United States by winning a tennis scholarship. He now lives in the United States, where he works as a freelance writer and lectures on South Africa.

Claude McKay (1890–1948) was born and raised on the Caribbean island of Jamaica, the son of poor farm workers. When he was a teenager, his parents moved to Kingston, the capital of Jamaica, where the fresh sights and sounds moved McKay to start writing poetry. In 1912 his book *Songs of Jamaica* won a prestigious award, which enabled him to move to America. He studied agriculture at Tuskegee Institute and Kansas State College, but after a short while he decided to pursue a writing career and moved to Harlem. There his poems began to appear in small literary periodicals. In 1922 he published his most important collection, *Harlem Shadows.* The most militant of the Harlem Renaissance writers, McKay protested the injustices of black life in prose as well as poetry. Becoming interested in communism as a means to bring about social justice, he toured the Soviet Union in 1922. McKay then spent the next ten years living in France. By the mid-1930's, he was disillusioned with communism. He returned to the United States, converted to Catholicism in the 1940's, and spent the last years of his life teaching in parochial schools.

Toni Morrison (born 1931) is one of America's most acclaimed writers. Born in Loraine, Ohio, she graduated from Howard University and received an M.A. from Cornell, where she completed a thesis on the novels of William Faulkner and Virginia Woolf. Morrison's own novels—skillful, inventive, and experimental—draw upon African-American myths and rituals. *Song of Solomon* (1977), a Book-of-the-Month Club selection, won the National Book Critics Circle Award. *Beloved* (1987) has been a critical success and a popular triumph. According to Morrison, her writing shows readers "how to survive whole in a world where we are all of us, in some measure, victims of something."

Pablo Neruda (1904-1973) won the Nobel prize for literature in 1971 and is considered by many to be the greatest Latin American poet of his time. He published his first poems when he was only seventeen. In his early work, Neruda movingly explores his own feelings; his later poetry is filled with dreamlike, often violent, images and symbols with very personal meanings. In addition to writing poetry, Neruda was active in politics. He was a member of the Chilean foreign service, served in the Chilean Senate from 1945 to 1948, and was ambassador to France in the early 1970's.

Gloria Oden (born 1923) was a senior editor of math, science, and language textbooks before switching to a career of college teaching and poetry writing. Her work has appeared in numerous anthologies, and she has received two awards for creative writing.

Simon Ortiz (born 1941), an Acoma Pueblo Indian, was born in Albuquerque, New Mexico, and raised in the Acoma Pueblo community seventy miles west of that city. He attributes his love of words partially to his father, a carpenter who sang and talked to his son as he worked, and partially to his traditional heritage of song and storytelling. Ortiz attended Bureau of Indian Affairs elementary and high schools on the reservation. After graduation, he went on to study at the University of New Mexico and the University of Iowa. *Going for the Rain* (1976), his first collection of poetry, describes a journey from the Indian world through modern America and back again, a format he also used in his second book, *A Good Journey* (1977). *From Sand Creek: Rising in This Heart Which Is Our America* (1981), Ortiz's third book, is quite different, describing the pain and sadness of his stay in a Colorado Veterans Administration hospital. This powerful volume appeared in 1981 and won the Pushcart Prize the following year. Although he is best known as a poet, Ortiz has also written short stories and essays and has edited anthologies of Native American writing. He has taught at San Diego State University and at the University of New Mexico.

Américo Paredes (born 1915), the son of a Brownsville, Texas, rancher, is known as a scholar of the Mexican-American folk tradition. After serving in the infantry during World War II, Paredes attended the University of Texas, where he earned his bachelor's, master's, and doctoral degrees. Since 1954, he has been on the faculty of the university, where he is now a professor of English and anthropology and director of the school's Mexican-American studies program. Among his best-known works are *With His Pistol in His Hand: A Border Ballad and Its Hero* (1958), from which "The Legend of Gregorio Cortez" is taken, and *Folktales of Mexico* (1970). Paredes also has served as the editor of *The Journal of American Folklore* and has edited many works on cultural anthropology. For his achievement in preserving the Mexican-American folk tradition, Paredes has received several important awards, among them, the Order of the Aztec Eagle, Mexico's highest award to foreigners.

Alberto Alvaro Ríos (born 1952) was exposed to different cultures as a child. His parents were Mexican and British, and he grew up in Nogales, Arizona, near the Mexican border. Much of his writing reflects the experiences of his childhood. Ríos earned a master's degree in creative writing from the University of Arizona; his poetry and short stories have won many honors. *The Iguana Killer, Whispering to Fool the Wind,* and *Teodoro Luna's Two Kisses* are among the books he has published. He is currently a professor of English at Arizona State University.

Richard Rodriguez (born 1944), the son of Mexican immigrants, was born and raised in Sacramento, California. After an early struggle to learn English, Rodriguez became an ambitious student in Catholic grammar schools, where he strove hard to please his teachers. Rewarded with scholarships, he was able to attend Stanford and Columbia Universities. Soon afterward, he enrolled in the doctoral program in English at the University of California at Berkeley. Although his studies went very well, he became increasingly aware of his alienation from his Mexican heritage, describing himself as "haunted by how my education has made me different." He turned down several teaching positions at prestigious universities to devote himself to analyzing his past and eventually to write what he termed his intellectual autobiography, *Hunger of Memory* (1982). Rodriguez currently lives and writes in San Francisco.

Wendy Rose (born 1948), who is half Hopi Indian, writes and draws to erase prejudices toward Native Americans and to arouse a sense of justice about what has happened to them. She herself faced prejudice as a child: white children in her neighborhood teased her and were not allowed to play with her. "When you feel alone," Rose has advised, "just talk to yourself—on paper, with your voice, with your body through dancing, with colors." Her own creativity has been expressed in such books as *Hopi Roadrunner Dancing* and *The Half-Breed Chronicles,* both of which she illustrated herself. An anthropologist as well as a creative artist, Rose participates in many Native American organizations and is currently the coordinator of American Indian Studies at Fresno City College.

Leslie Marmon Silko (born 1948), raised in the Laguna Pueblo village in New Mexico, belongs to a family descended from three cultures—white, Mexican, and Laguna. Growing up, she often felt "on the fringes of all three." She now says "I don't apologize for this anymore. . . . My poetry, my storytelling, rise out of this source." Of the three cultures, the Native American was most influential. "I am of mixed-breed ancestry, but what I know is Laguna," Silko explains. After graduating from high school, she earned a bachelor's degree from the University of New Mexico. She originally planned to be an attorney and even began law school, but teaching and writing exerted a stronger pull. In 1969 she published her first story, "The Man to Send Rain Clouds." Eight years later her novel *Ceremony* (1977), whose main character is also of mixed heritage, brought her wide public recognition. In addition to fiction, Silko has written poetry—"Prayer to the Pacific" was her first published poem—and film scripts. She has taught at Navajo Community College in Arizona and at the University of New Mexico.

Gary Soto (born 1952) writes poetry that explores his childhood, his adolescence, and his ethnic identity. Although his grandparents were born in Mexico and he was raised in a home where Spanish was spoken, Soto himself was never formally taught Spanish. Rather, his family expected him to assimilate into mainstream American society. After graduating from high school in Fresno, California, in 1970, Soto entered Fresno City College as a geography major. While in college, he read Eugene Field's poem "Unwanted," in which he saw his own sense of alienation from society expressed. Deciding to become a poet, Soto transferred to California State University at Fresno to study writing with the poet Philip Levine. Soto graduated with high honors in 1974 and then earned a master's degree in creative writing from the University of California, Irvine. In 1977 he began to teach in the English and Chicano departments at the University of California, Berkeley. His many poetry collections include *Black Hair* (1985) and *Living Up the Street* (1985), the latter of which won an American Book Award.

Amy Tan (born 1952) was not always the proud Chinese American that she is now. She recalls dreaming when she was young of making her features look more Caucasian by having plastic surgery. It was not until she made her first trip to China in 1987 that Tan could truly accept both the Chinese and American cultures as her own. Though Tan won a writing contest at the age of eight, her identity as a writer was slow in coming. However, after successfully publishing some of her stories in magazines, Tan combined those stories with others to create a novel called *The Joy Luck Club,* which became a bestseller.

Jean Toomer (1894–1967) boasted of having black, Jewish, German, Indian, Welsh, French, and Dutch blood. In *Essentials* (1931), his collection of aphorisms, he wrote: "I am of no particular race. I am of the human race, a man at large in this human world, preparing a new race. I am of no specific region, I am of earth." Toomer was born in Washington, D.C., to parents who had migrated from a Georgia farm. In 1917 he arrived in New York to study at City College. During the next four years, he became a familiar figure on the New York literary scene, publishing poetry, prose, and criticism in small-circulation magazines. Four months as a school superintendent in rural Sparta, Georgia, brought him into contact with African-American folk culture. This encounter provided him with the raw material for *Cane* (1923), his best-known book. Frustrated by the limitations imposed by race in America, Toomer abandoned his literary career in the 1920's to seek a philosophy that would help him form a personal identity that transcended race. He became a follower of mystic George Gurdjieff and later moved to a Quaker pietist community.

© 1984 Layle Silbert

Luisa Valenzuela (born 1938) is one of the best-known writers of short stories and novels in Latin America. She was born in Argentina, and became a journalist in her teens, working for the magazine *Quince Abriles* and the Buenos Aires newspaper *La Mación*. In 1967 she published a book of thirteen short stories and a novel under the title *Los Heréticos*. Other fiction includes *The Lizard's Tail* (1983) and *Crime of the Other* (1989). Valenzuela's writing often contains humor and irony. An important theme in her work is the search for freedom, both political and personal. She once said that she writes to shake people up.

Alice Walker (born 1944) has come a long way from the small Georgia farm where she was raised. She has campaigned for welfare rights, helped in voter registration, and traveled to Kenya, Uganda, and the Soviet Union. She also has taught at Wellesley and Jackson State colleges and the University of Massachusetts. Her best-known novel is *The Color Purple,* which won the Pulitzer Prize and was made into a popular movie.

Margaret Walker (born 1915) won the Yale Younger Poets Award in 1942 for her first book of poetry, *For My People.* In 1966 she published *Jubliee,* a carefully researched novel of slavery and the Civil War. Besides being a writer, Walker has been a social worker, magazine editor, college English instructor, and mother to four children. In 1968 she was named director of the Institute for the Study of the History, Life, and Culture of Black Peoples.

Richard Wright (1908–1960), born in Mississippi, endured a childhood marked by gnawing hunger, physical beatings, and an intense internal struggle against the religious and racial restrictions imposed on him by family and culture. After his father abandoned the family in Memphis, Tennessee, when Wright was five, the boy was raised by his ailing mother and stern grandmother. Often left alone while his relatives worked, Wright was introduced to the violence of the ghetto streets at age six. He wrote later that it was only through books that he managed to stay alive, books that he obtained by borrowing a white man's library card. Escaping to Chicago at nineteen, Wright held a series of odd jobs until he joined the Depression-era Federal Writers' Project as a guidebook writer. He joined the Communist Party and remained a member from 1932 to 1942. Shortly after moving to New York to become editor of the Communist *Daily Worker*, Wright gained international fame for his novel *Native Son* (1940). His fiction and his autobiographies, *Black Boy* (1945) and *American Hunger* published posthumously in (1977), expose the brutal racism in American life. Wright settled in Paris in 1947, where he lived until his death.

Hisaye Yamamoto (born 1921), the daughter of Japanese immigrants, was born in Redondo Beach, California. Like many Japanese Americans, she was interned in a detention camp during World War II. While in camp, Yamamoto continued the writing career she had begun as a teenager. She wrote a column and news articles for the camp newspaper and published a serialized mystery. After the war she worked for three years for the African-American weekly newspaper the *Los Angeles Tribune* and then received a John Hay Whitney Foundation Opportunity Fellowship that allowed her to write fiction full time for a year (1950–1951). From 1953 to 1955, Yamamoto and her adopted son volunteered on a Catholic Worker rehabilitation farm on Staten Island. She then married Anthony DeSoto, returned to Los Angeles, and became mother to four more children. Although her output has been relatively small, Yamamoto's work has won critical acclaim. Four of her stories, including "Seventeen Syllables," have been included in Best American Short Story collections. Her stories, which always feature Japanese-American protagonists, often display sympathy for those on the fringes of American society.

Index of Essential Vocabulary

Index of Literary Terms

Index of Writing Modes and Formats

Narrative and imaginative writing
  ballad, 157
  booklet, 60
  comic strip, 20
  conversation, 118
  dialogue, 60, 208, 238, 393, 407
  diary entry, 20, 39, 221
  dramatic monologue, 187
  dramatic scene, 118, 126, 221, 273,
    385
  dramatic skit, 39, 208
  episode, 126, 285
  human interest story, 168, 273
  letter, 39, 50, 208, 238
  monologue, 85, 233, 285, 385
  narrative poem, 20
  note, 221
  notes, for story, 180, 273
  poem, 50, 85, 318
  rap song, 20
  scene, 221
  script, 143, 174, 233, 407
  sequel, 60, 273
  song lyrics, 30, 85
  story, 180, 208
  storyboard, 50, 157

Observation and description
  biographical sketch, 30, 157
  captions, 60, 110, 150, 248
  catalog, 248
  catalog copy, 280
  character sketch, 50, 157

descriptive essay, 248
eulogy, 20
eyewitness account, 273
introductory speech, 318
obituary, 20
pamphlet, 393
personality profiles, 393
poem, 157, 233
poster, 248
profile, 280
proposal, 297
TV commercial, 280
tribute, 168
word search puzzle, 407

Persuasion
  campaign poster, 157
  campaign speech, 157
  editorial, 150, 168, 256, 407
  grant proposal, 248
  handbill, 30
  introduction, 94
  letter, 385
  letter of complaint, 126
  letter of recommendation, 318
  memo, 50, 60
  nomination, 30
  persuasive speech, 248
  petition, 150
  press release, 60
  proposal, 20, 143, 407
  publicity slogans, 248
  recommendation, 50

sermon, 256, 407
slogans, 174
speech, 94

Reports (research)
  essay, 238
  expository essay, 233
  guidelines, 208
  informational footnotes, 60
  notes, for class presentation/report,
    85, 143
  notes, for panel discussion, 233
  oral presentation, 221
  report, 118
  summary, 208

Synthesis. See Informative (expository) writing: synthesis

Writing about literature
  annotations, 221, 238
  book review, 30
  evaluation, 126
  informal note, 280
  interpretative essay, 187
  letter, 187, 233, 273
  memo, 238, 318
  program notes, 143
  recommendation, 94, 126
  report card, 256, 318
  review, 150, 273, 297, 385
  story, 280

Index of Authors and Titles

Thunder's Mouth Press "Hiccups" by Léon Damas from *The Negritude Poets*, edited by Ellen Conroy Kennedy. Copyright © 1975 by Ellen Conroy Kennedy. Used by permission of the publisher, Thunder's Mouth Press.

University of Nebraska Press "High Horse's Courting" from *Black Elk Speaks* by John G. Neihardt. Copyright 1932, © 1959, 1972 by John G. Neihardt. Copyright © 1961 by the John G. Neihardt Trust. Reprinted by permission of the University of Nebraska Press.

University of Notre Dame Press Excerpt from *Barrio Boy* by Ernesto Galarza. Copyright © 1971 by the University of Notre Dame Press. Reprinted by permission of the University of Notre Dame Press.

University of Pittsburgh Press "Oranges" from *Black Hair* by Gary Soto. Copyright © 1985 by Gary Soto. Reprinted by permission of the University of Pittsburgh Press.

University of Southern California Press "My Mother Pieced Quilts" by Teresa Palomo Acosta from *Festival de Flor y Conte, An Anthology of Chicano Literature*. Reprinted by permission of El Centro Chicano and the University of Southern California Press.

The authors and editors have made every effort to trace the ownership of all copyrighted selections found in this book and to make full acknowledgment for their use.

Art Credits

Cover
Illustration by Ivan Chermayeff.

Author Photographs
AP/Wide World Photos, Inc., New York: Lucille Clifton 420, Lorraine Hansberry 423, William Melvin Kelley 425, Paule Marshall 426, Mark Mathabane 426, Richard Rodriguez 428; Bernard Charlon/Camera Press/Globe Photos, New York: James Baldwin 418; © Chicago Tribune Company, l987, all rights reserved: Gwendolyn Brooks 419; Nancy Crampton: Nikki Giovanni 423; Dahlgren/Camera Press/Globe Photos, New York: Pablo Neruda 427; © 1980 Michael Elderman: Wendy Rose 429; Karla Elling: Alberto Alvaro Ríos 428; Robert Foothorap: Amy Tan 429; Marlene Foster-Ortiz: Simon Ortiz 428; Globe Photos, New York: James Weldon Johnson 425, Richard Wright 431; The Granger Collection, New York: Countee Cullen 420; Handy's Photo Service, Jackson, Mississippi: Margaret Walker 430; Howard Ikemoto: Jeanne Wakatsuki Houston and James D. Houston 424; Nan Kene-Arthur/U.S. Photo Graphics, El Cajon, California: Le Ly Hayslip 424; Library of Congress: Frederick Douglass 421; M.L. Marinelli: Gary Soto 429; Lee Marmon: Leslie Marmon Silko 429; Jim Marshall: Alice Walker 430; Susan Meiselas/Magnum Photos, Inc., New York: Jorge Louis Borges 419; Moorland Spingarn Research Center, Howard University: Paul Laurence Dunbar 421; Frank Marshall Davis 421; Warren Morgan: Barry Lopez 426; National Portrait Gallery, Smithsonian Institution, Washington, D.C., Photograph by Edward Weston: Langston Hughes, 424; Reuters/Bettmann: Gabriel García Márquez 422; Gordon Robotham: Diana Chang 420; Schomburg Center for Research in Black Culture, The New York Public Library, Astor, Lenox & Tilden Foundations, New York: Léon Damas 421, Jamaica Kincaid 425; Smithsonian Institution, Photo No. 3303-C: Black Elk 419; Jean Toomer Papers, Yale Collection of American Literature, Beinecke Library: Jean Toomer 430; UPI/Bettmann, New York City: Maya Angelou 418, Martin Luther King, Jr. 425; Courtesy University of Notre Dame Press: Ernesto Galarza 422; University of Texas News & Information Service; photo by Larry Murphy: Américo Paredes 428; Carl van Vechten, Yale Collection of American Literature, Beinecke Library: Zora Neale Hurston 424, Claude McKay 427.

McDougal, Littell and Company has made every effort to locate the copyright holders for the images used in this book and to make full acknowledgment for their use.